FUNDAMENTALS OF FINANCIAL DERIVATIVES

FUNDAMENTALS OF FINANCIAL DERIVATIVES

Prafulla Kumar Swain
Professor, Faculty of Management,
Siksha "O" Anusandhan University,
BHUBANESWAR, ODISHA, INDIA.

First Edition : 2012
Edition : 2017
Edition : 2019

Published by : Mrs. Meena Pandey for **Himalaya Publishing House Pvt. Ltd.,**
"Ramdoot", Dr. Bhalerao Marg, Girgaon, **Mumbai - 400 004.**
Phone: 022-23860170/23863863, Fax: 022-23877178
E-mail: himpub@vsnl.com; Website: www.himpub.com

Branch Offices :

New Delhi : "Pooja Apartments", 4-B, Murari Lal Street, Ansari Road, Darya Ganj, New Delhi - 110 002. Phone: 011-23270392, 23278631; Fax: 011-23256286

Nagpur : Kundanlal Chandak Industrial Estate, Ghat Road, Nagpur - 440 018. Phone: 0712-2738731, 3296733; Telefax: 0712-2721216

Bengaluru : Plot No. 91-33, 2nd Main Road Seshadripuram, Behind Nataraja Theatre, Bengaluru-560020. Phone: 08041138821, 9379847017, 9379847005

Hyderabad : No. 3-4-184, Lingampally, Besides Raghavendra Swamy Matham, Kachiguda, Hyderabad - 500 027. Phone: 040-27560041, 27550139

Chennai : New-20, Old-59, Thirumalai Pillai Road, T. Nagar, Chennai - 600 017. Mobile: 9380460419

Pune : First Floor, "Laksha" Apartment, No. 527, Mehunpura, Shaniwarpeth (Near Prabhat Theatre), Pune - 411 030. Phone: 020-24496323/24496333; Mobile: 09370579333

Lucknow : House No. 731, Shekhupura Colony, Near B.D. Convent School, Aliganj, Lucknow - 226 022. Phone: 0522-4012353; Mobile: 09307501549

Ahmedabad : 114, "SHAIL", 1st Floor, Opp. Madhu Sudan House, C.G. Road, Navrang Pura, Ahmedabad - 380 009. Phone: 079-26560126; Mobile: 09377088847

Ernakulam : 39/176 (New No.: 60/251) 1st Floor, Karikkamuri Road, Ernakulam, Kochi – 682011. Phone: 0484-2378012, 2378016; Mobile: 09387122121

Bhubaneswar : 5 Station Square, Bhubaneswar - 751 001 (Odisha). Phone: 0674-2532129, Mobile: 09338746007

Kolkata : 108/4, Beliaghata Main Road, Near ID Hospital, Opp. SBI Bank, Kolkata - 700 010, Phone: 033-32449649, Mobile: 7439040301

DTP by : HPH, Editorial Office, Bhandup (Megha)

Printed at : M/s. Aditya Offset Process (I) Pvt. Ltd., Hyderabad. On behalf of HPH.

Preface

I always perceive to innovate new concepts, new theories and new models in the emerging areas of Financial Management. I find that, one such area is **Risk Management through Financial Derivatives**. This concept is new to me. But if there is a passion, there must be a success. Finally, I decide to write a textbook on this subject and handover this treatise in the hands of the millions of people in the global digital village.

Financial Derivatives are innovative instruments in the Financial Markets, both in the developed economies like USA, ENGLAND and emerging economies like INDIA, CHINA, JAPAN, KOREA, and INDONESIA etc. Basically, there are four categories of derivatives, i.e., Forwards, Futures, Options and Swaps. These derivatives are traded in two markets, i.e., Over the Counter (OTC) Markets and Exchange Trade Markets (ETM).

Banks, Financial Institutions, Mutual Funds, Corporations and Individual investors are the players in the derivative markets. They play in the derivative markets as Hedgers, Speculators and Arbitrageurs. Regulatory Authorities of a particular country promote and regulate derivative instruments and markets. In India, SEBI, RBI and Forward Market Commission (FMC) are the regulating authority for derivative markets and instruments. Besides Stock Exchanges, Commodity Exchanges and Clearing Houses are also facilitating the market operations particularly for Futures and Options.

This textbook **"FUNDAMENTALS OF FINANCIAL DERIVATIVES"** is written to inculcate the spirit of strategic use of all Participants, Finance Professionals, Academicians, Business Management students, Policymakers and Regulators of Financial derivatives markets in India as well as in other countries of the world.

Coverage and Structure

The entire text is divided into 14 Chapters. Chapter 1 lays down the conceptual framework on financial derivatives. Chapter 2 and 3 deal with derivative markets. Chapter 4 discusses Forward Contracts. Chapters 5, 6 and 7 deal with Futures derivatives. Chapters 8 to 13 deal with Option derivative. Chapter 14 highlights swap derivative.

Approach of this Book

The text is designed in a very well structured form incorporating the following features:

- Strategic Style
- Conceptual Framework
- Comprehensive Text
- Practical Utility
- International Outlook
- Self Study Approach

Who Should Use this Book?

This book is intended to provide wisdom to the following users of financial derivatives:

- Students of MBA, PGDBM, CA, ICWA, CS, M.Com., MFC, MFM and MBE etc.
- Teachers of Finance, Commerce, Economics and Management Studies.
- Executives of Banks, Financial Institutions, Stock Exchanges and Commodity Exchanges.
- Regulatory Authorities like SEBI and FMC in India.

- Financial Engineers, Financial Analyst, Risk Managers, Chartered Accountants, Cost and Management Accountants and Portfolio Managers.
- Facilitators in derivative trading, Brokers and all members of International Swap and Derivative Association.

Acknowledgements

I am grateful to Dr. Manoj Ranjan Nayak, President, Siksha O Anusandhan University, Bhubaneswar, Orissa for providing an environment conducive for learning, research and innovation without which this book would not have been possible.

I am especially grateful to Prof. (Dr.) Rajendra Prasad Mohanty, Honourable Vice Chancellor, Siksha O Anusandhan University for his noble guidance.

I am extremely indebted to my **"Gurus"** Prof. Nanda Kishore Puhan, Prof. Digambar Patri, Prof. Ayodhya Prasad Nayak and Prof. Rama Kanta Jena for their kind blessing to venture into this creative endeavour.

I express my sincere thanks to my friends Dr. R.K. Bal, Dr. B.N. Bal, Dr. Binshnupriya Mishra, Dr. Binayak Rath and Mr. Debaraj Biswal, CEO of Bhubaneswar Stock Exchange for their encouragement and valuable suggestion.

I am also thankful to my faculty colleagues Prof. Dr. Mayadhar Satpathy, Prof. Dr. Shakti Ranjan Mohapatra, Prof. Sanjeeb Pattnaik, Prof. Dr. Bibhuti Bhusan Pradhan, Mr. Ansuman Samal, Mrs. Sasmita Mohanty, Dr. Pinku Pal, Mr. Chinmaya Rout, Mr. Niranjan Swain, Prof. Shom Prasad Das.

Any textbook writer will tell you "that you cannot write a textbook of this scope without a substantial amount of help". For this, I express my thanks to my wife Smt. Krishna Swain. I also thank my daughters Dhupanwita and Nirlipta, son-in-law Rohitaswa and my lovely grandson Master Babul for their support during the preparation of this valuable manuscript.

Finally, I express my sincere gratitude to Mr. Niraj Pandey and Bijay Kumar Ojha of Himalaya Publishing House for their wholehearted support and encouragement to make this creative venture a great success.

"Jai Jagannath"

Prafulla Kumar Swain

3rd July, 2011
Rath Yatra

Detailed Contents

13. OPTIONS TRADING STRATEGIES 13.1 – 13.34

14. SWAPS 14.1 – 14.32

Introduction to Derivatives

Learning Objectives

After studying this chapter, you will be able to:

- Understand the concept and components of financial system
- Interpret what derivatives are
- Define a derivative in the language of finance
- Explain the features of derivatives
- Classify derivatives
- Explain various types of derivatives
- Understand the uses of derivatives
- Aware of the misconceptions and critiques

Chapter Outline

1.1 AN INTRODUCTION TO FINANCIAL DERIVATIVES

The new economic policy of liberalisation, privatisation and globalisation havė infused the operational growth of the following components of financial system in India:

- Financial Institutions
- Financial Markets
- Financial Instruments
- Financial Services

Financial institutions are the major players in the financial market. Financial markets facilitate buying and selling of financial claims, assets, services and securities. Money market and capital market are the two important segments of the financial market. Another segment in the financial market emerged in the form of DERIVATIVE MARKET. Financial claims, assets and securities dealt in financial market are known as financial instruments. The susceptible relationship among these four components are depicted below:

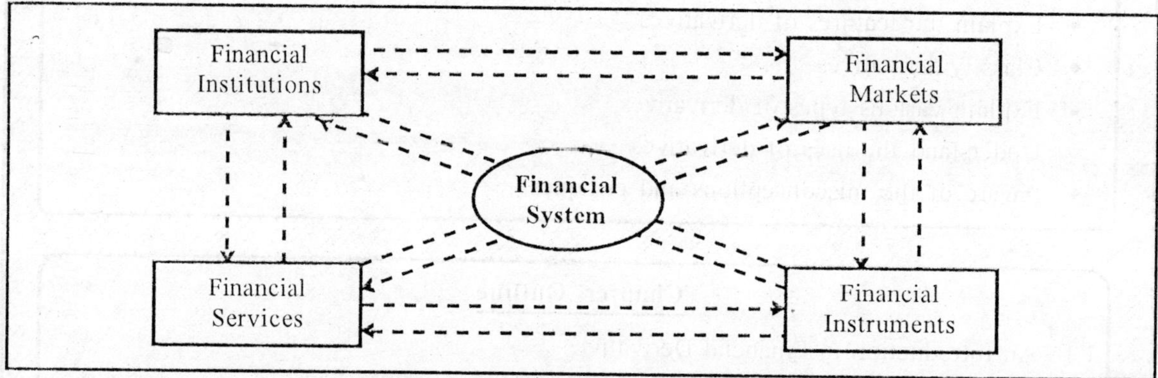

Fig. 1.1: The Financial System

As Indian financial market is developing gradually, the market participants, the investors and the regulatory authorities are looking at different ways on the following matters:

- Management of risk
- Generation of higher income
- Reduction of transaction cost
- Improvement of liquidity.

The types and the respective segments of financial market are shown in figure 1.2:

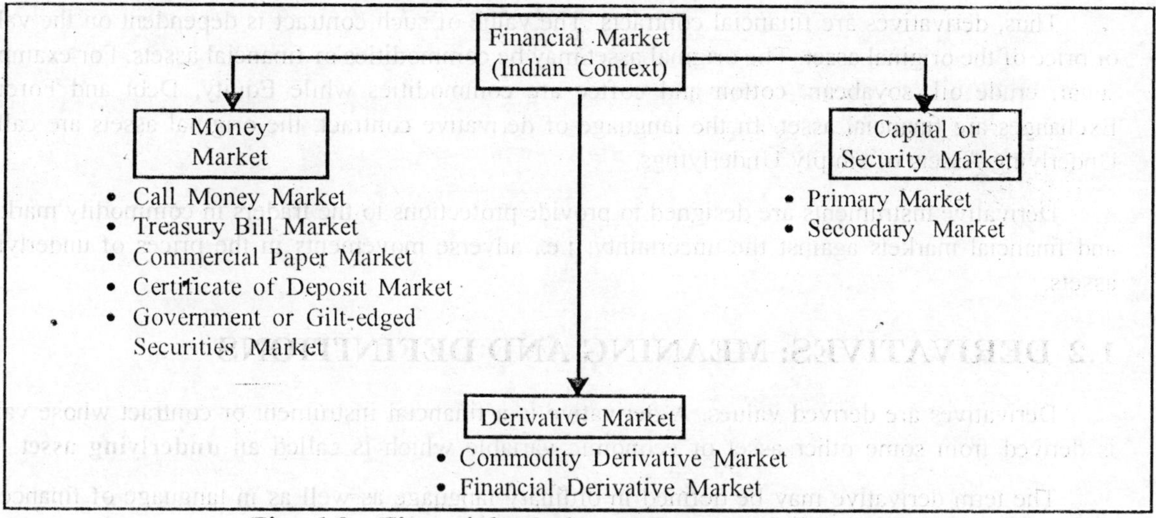

Fig. 1.2: Financial Market – Types and Segments

The evolution of derivatives and the commencement of trading in India are of recent origin.

The Odyssey of Indian derivative market has taken a momentum in 1997, since then, a number of derivatives on different underlyings have been introduced in the Indian derivative market. The common types of derivatives are Forward contracts, Futures contracts, Swaps and Options. Thus:

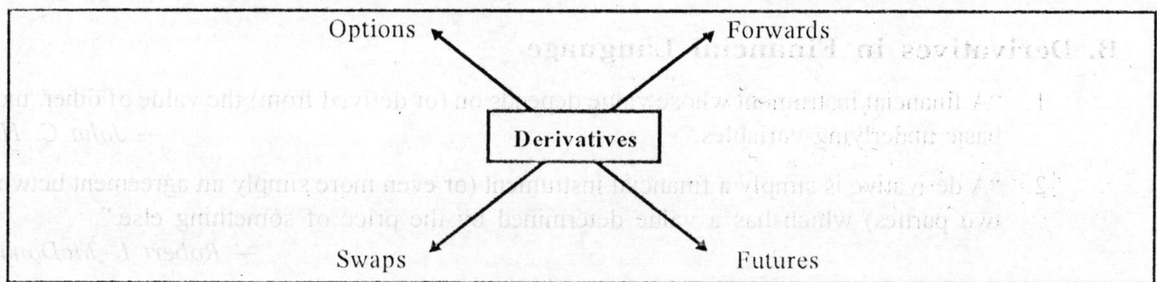

Fig. 1.3: Common Derivatives

The structural status of derivative market *vis-à-vis* Derivative Contracts is outlined below:

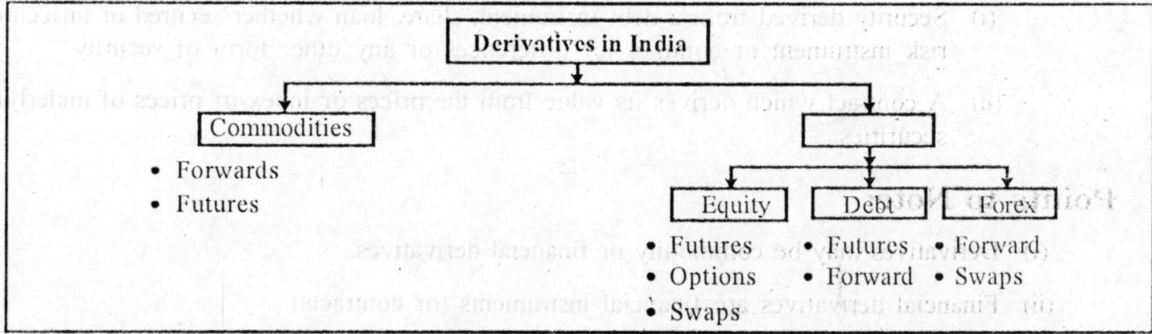

Fig. 1.4: Structural Concept of Derivatives

Thus, derivatives are financial contracts. The value of such contract is dependent on the value or price of the original asset. The original asset may be commodities or financial assets. For example, sugar, crude oil, soyabean, cotton and coffee are commodities while Equity, Debt and Foreign Exchanges are financial asset. In the language of derivative contract, the original assets are called Underlying Assets of simply Underlyings.

Derivative instruments are designed to provide protections to the traders in commodity markets and financial markets against the uncertainty, i.e., adverse movements in the prices of underlying assets.

1.2 DERIVATIVES: MEANING AND DEFINITIONS

Derivatives are derived values. A derivative is a financial instrument or contract whose value is derived from some other asset or economic variable which is called an **underlying asset**.

The term derivative may be defined in ordinary language as well as in language of finance in the following lines:

Definitions

A. Derivatives in Ordinary Language

"A substance that can be derived from another substance."

— *The Merriem Webster Dictionary*

B. Derivatives in Financial Language

1. "A financial instrument whose value depends on (or derived from) the value of other, more basic underlying variables." — *John C. Hull*
2. "A derivative is simply a financial instrument (or even more simply an agreement between two parties) which has a value determined by the price of something else." — *Robert L. McDonald*
3. The Securities Contracts (Regulations) Act, 1956, defines "derivatives" as under:

   "Derivative" include the following:

   (i) Security derived from a debt instrument, share, loan whether secured or unsecured, risk instrument or contract for differences or any other form of security.

   (ii) A contract which derives its value from the prices or index of prices of underlying securities.

Points to Note:

(i) Derivatives may be commodity or financial derivatives.

(ii) Financial derivatives are financial instruments (or contracts).

(iii) The value of the derivative depends on the value of the original asset.

(iv) The original asset (security or commodity or economic variable) from which the value of derivative instrument is derived is known as **Underlying Asset**.

(v) Derivatives are securities under the Securities Contracts (Regulation) Act and hence trading the derivatives is governed by the regulatory framework under this Act.

1.3 FEATURES OF FINANCIAL DERIVATIVES

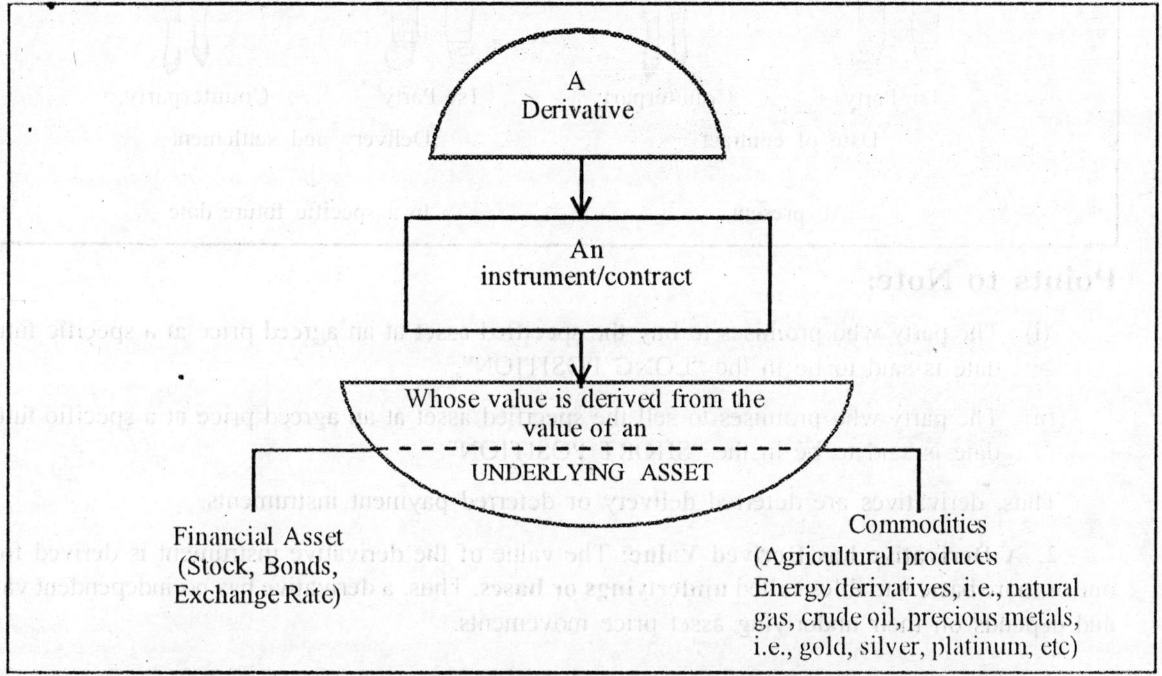

Fig. 1.5: The Concept of Derivative

Financial derivatives are the innovative risk management products and financial services. Essentially, it is a future contract which is made between two parties and its value is derived from the original financial asset which may be Equity, Bonds or Foreign Exchange etc. Depending upon the nature of financial transactions, a variety of derivative contracts (or instruments) are introduced. Such as Forward Contracts, Future Contracts, Options, Swaps etc. Each financial derivative has its own unique features. However, the general features of financial derivatives are as follows:

1. It is a Future Contract: A derivative contract is basically a future contract between two parties.

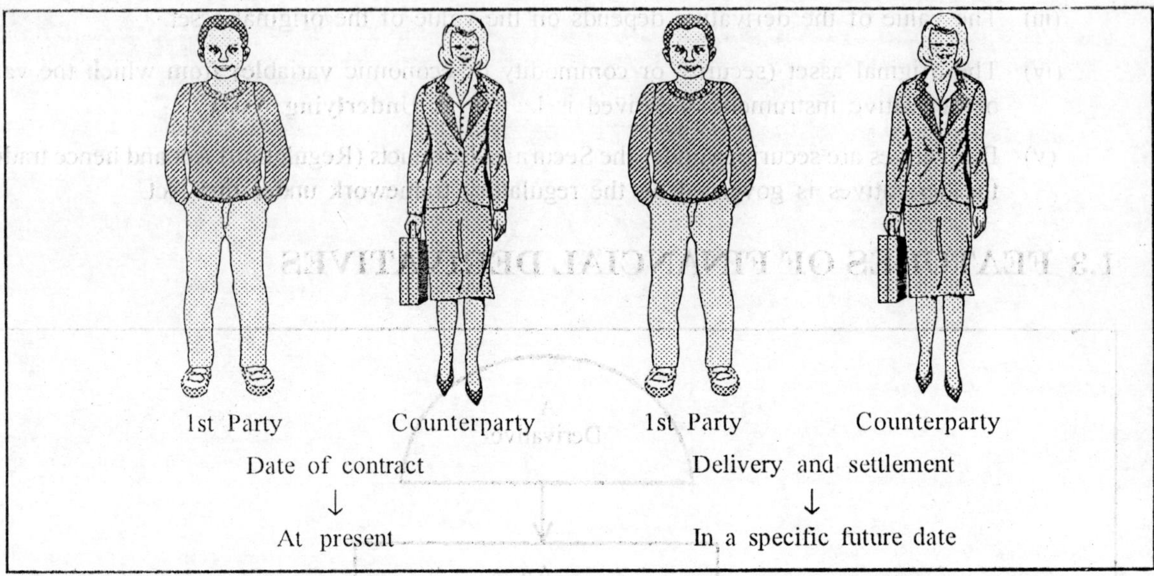

Points to Note:

(i) The party who promises to buy the specified asset at an agreed price at a specific future date is said to be in the "LONG POSITION".

(ii) The party who promises to sell the specified asset at an agreed price at a specific future date is said to be in the "SHORT POSITION".

Thus, derivatives are deferred delivery or deferred payment instruments.

2. A Derivative has Derived Value: The value of the derivative instrument is derived from one or more basic variables called **underlyings or bases**. Thus, a derivative has no independent value and depends on their underlying asset price movements.

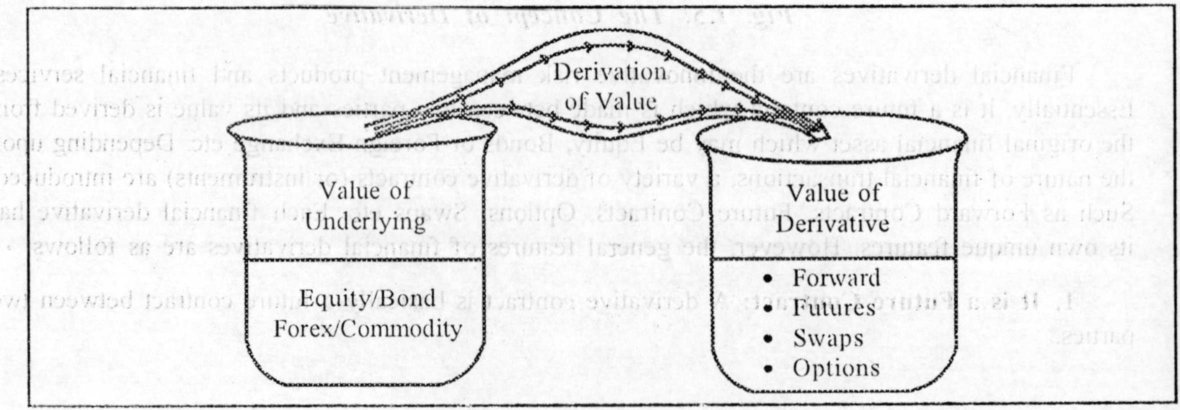

3. Specific Type of Derivatives Creates Specific Obligation of the Counterparty: Obligation (sell/buy/settle the payment) of the counterparty under the specific type of derivative is unique. Essentially, the nature of obligation would be different as per the type of the instrument of a derivative.

4. A Business Transaction through a Derivative may be Customised or Standardised: A **forward derivative** is a contract between two parties who mutually agree to transact (buy/sell) an underlying at a certain price at a certain date in future. Hence, it is a privately negotiated, customised, over-the-counter (OTC) traded derivative. But a "Futures" contract is nature of standardised and exchange traded derivative.

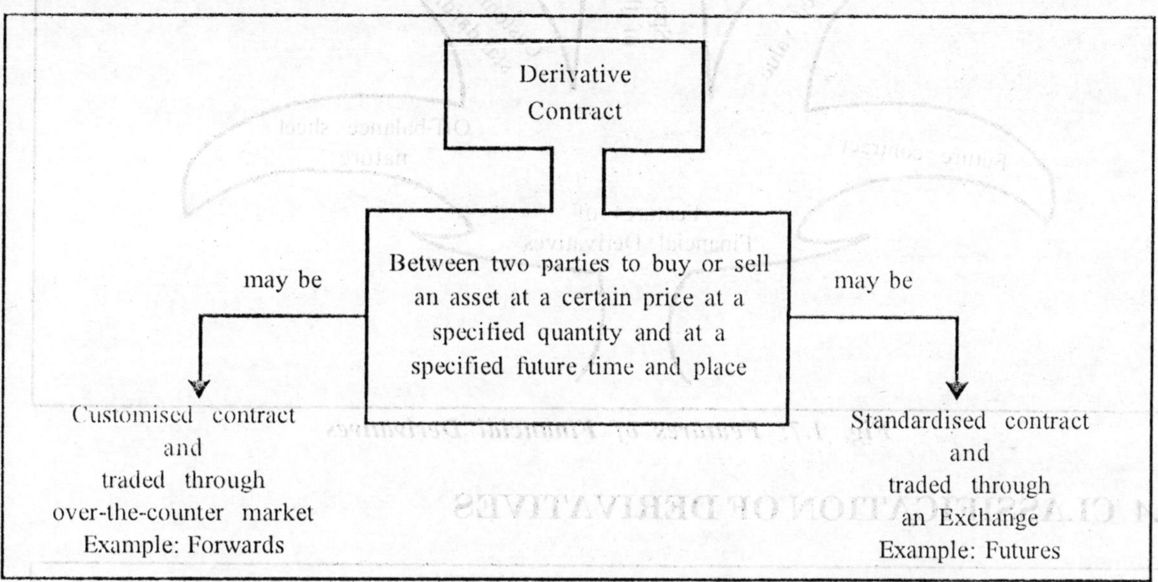

Fig. 1.6: Derivative Product: Customised or Standardised

5. The Trading Results through Financial Derivatives are Not Shown in the Financial Statements, i.e., Off-balance Sheet in nature: Particularly, in case of option, potential loss in underlyings and potential pay-off of derivatives are different. Due to this limitations, the trading results of options, will not be reflected in the financial statement, i.e., Balance Sheet. However, Accounting standards are now introduced to eliminate this limitation.

To sum up:

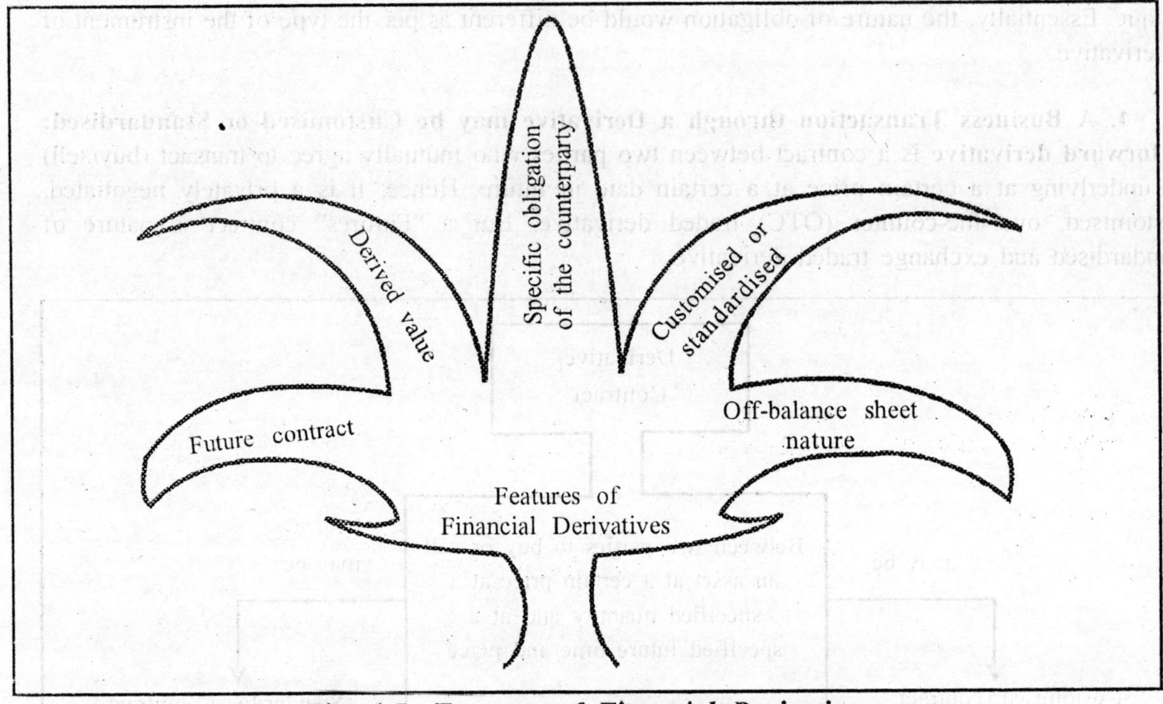

Fig. 1.7: Features of Financial Derivatives

1.4 CLASSIFICATION OF DERIVATIVES

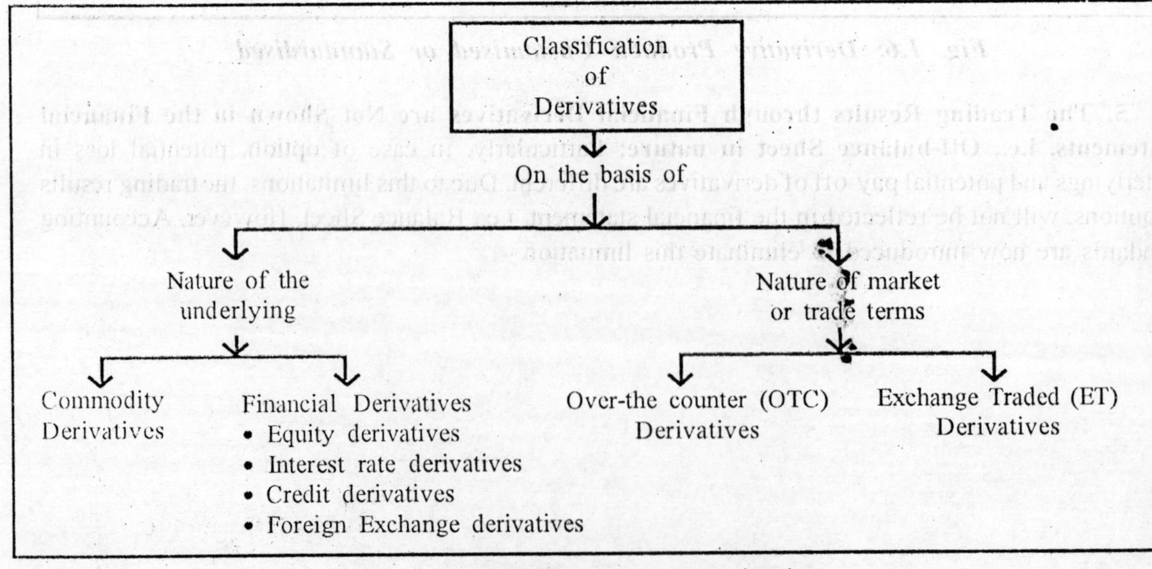

Fig. 1.8: Classification of Derivatives

1.5 TYPES OF DERIVATIVE CONTRACTS OR INSTRUMENTS

The popular derivative contracts are:

I. Forward contracts

II. Futures contracts

III. Option contracts

IV. Swaps

However, in the changing era of finance and technology, Complex and Hybrid or Exotic form of derivatives are introduced to manage the risk.

The details of their operations, trading mechanism and valuation methodologies will be discussed in the forthcoming respective chapters. However, a brief note on each type of derivative is given as follows:

I. Forward Contracts

These are simplest form4 of derivative contracts. A forward contract is an agreement between parties to buy/sell a specified quantity of an asset at a certain future date for a certain price. In other words, it is a simple customised contract between two parties to buy or sell an asset for a certain price at a certain time in future.

Mechanism: One of the parties to a forward contract assumes a *long position* and agrees to buy the underlying asset at a certain future date for a certain price. The other party to the contract assumes a *short position* and agrees to sell the asset on the same date for the same price. The price which is negotiated is known as delivery price. The contract terms like delivery price, delivery date and quantity, etc., are mutually agreed upon by the parties to the contract. No margins are generally payable by any one of the party to the other.

Features:

1. It is a Customised Contract: A forward contract is custom designed, and hence, it is unique in terms of contract size, maturity date, quality and quantity of asset, etc.

2. The Contract is Settled by Delivery: The contract is normally settled by the delivery of asset on the expiration date.

3. It is Exposed to Counterparty Risk: Forward contracts being bilateral contracts are exposed to counter party risk.

4. Cancellation or Reversion can be Made only through the Same Counterparty: If the party wishes to cancel the contract or any of its terms, it has necessarily to go to the same counterparty.

Example: On 1st October, Mr Hima enters into a forward contract with Mrs Laya and agrees to purchase 500 shares of 'T Ltd.' for a predetermined price of ₹ 130 three months forward. Here on the fixed future date, Mr Hima will get 500 shares and will pay the price, i.e., ₹ 65,000 and Mrs Laya will deliver the shares and will receive the money.

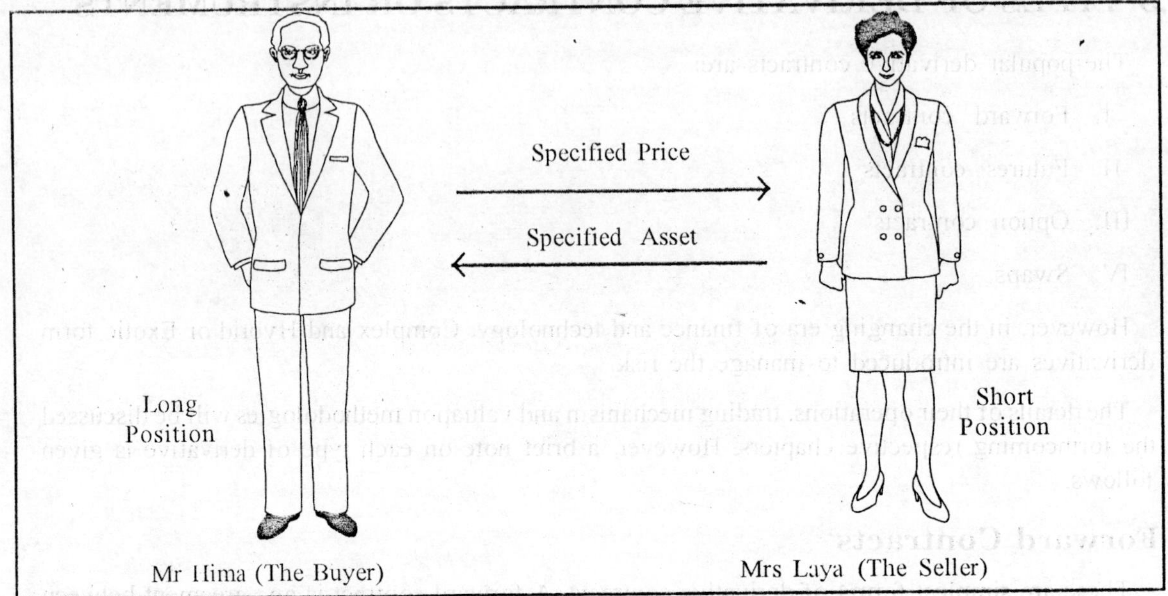

Fig. 1.9: The Forward Contract – Conceptual Framework

As per the terms of the contract, the settlement will be strictly on maturity date. The holder of the short position delivers the asset to the holder of the long position in return for a cash amount equivalent to delivery price.

Points to Note:

(i) Forward contracts are traded over the counter (OTC) and not dealt with on an exchange.

(ii) Forward contracts have certain flexibility and are self-regulatory.

(iii) Forward contracts afford **privacy** which is not found in exchange trading.

(iv) Lack of liquidity and counterparty default risks are the main drawbacks of a forward contract.

II. Futures Contracts

Futures contracts are special type of forward contracts. Many features of "Futures" are similar to Forward contracts. A **'futures contract'** differs from **a forward contract** in that the 'futures contract' is a standardised contract written by a clearing house that operates an exchange where the **underlyings** can be bought and sold. In a simple language, a futures contract is transacted through in exchange.

Features:

1. Standardised Specifications: A futures contract is characterised by standardised specifications, i.e., the underlying asset, quality of the asset, the month and date of delivery, etc.

2. Clearing House: It is associated with a clearing house to ensure smooth functioning of the market.

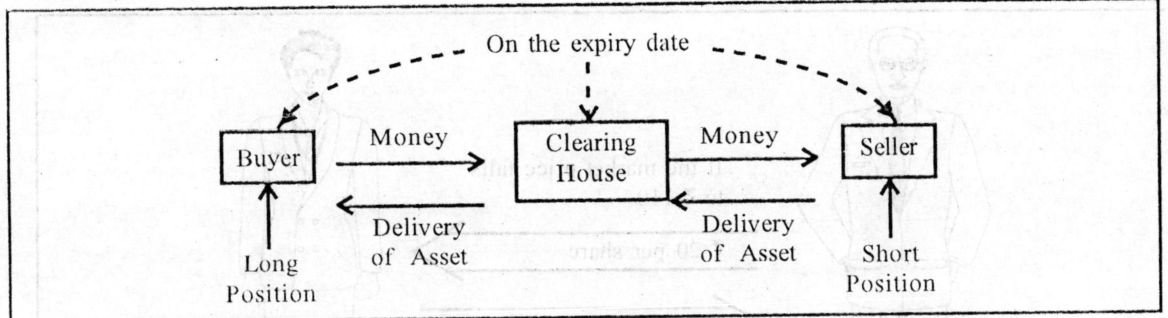

Fig. 1.10: Futures Contract and Its Relation with a Clearing House

3. Delivery through an Organised Exchange:

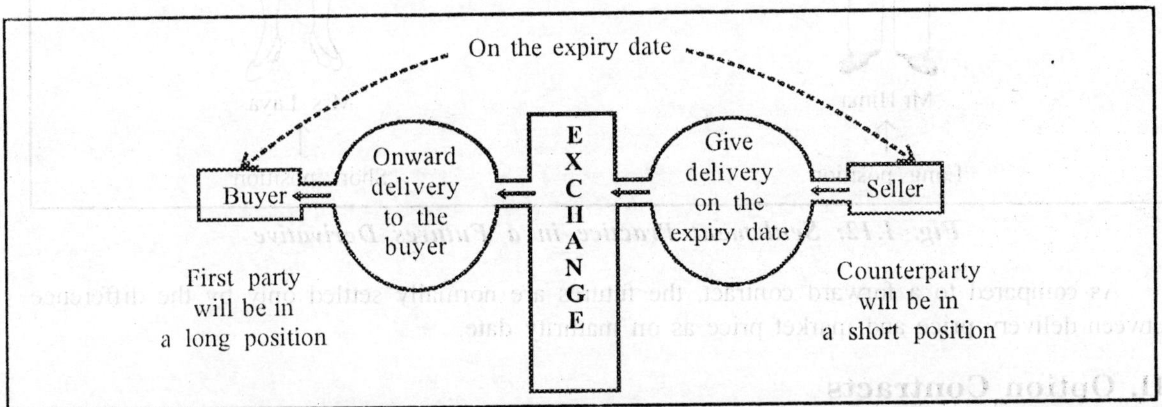

Fig. 1.11: Functional Status of an Associated Exchange in Futures Contract

4. Margin Requirements and Daily Settlement: The clearing house usually fixes the margin money to be deposited by the trader (through his broker). This margin money is treated as collateral security in order to minimise the risk of default by either party in the futures contract.

5. Existence of Regulatory Authority: All the futures contracts are regulated through exchanges (stock/commodity).

6. Settlement in Cash for Difference: A party in short (seller) or long (buyer) position has to settle in cash for the difference between the **agreed price** at which the contract was entered and the **cash price** at expiration date. This cash settlement is encouraged due to inconvenience or impossibility in delivery of underlying assets.

Example: On 1st January, Mr Hima enters into a Futures contract to buy 500 shares of 'T Ltd.' at an agreed price of ₹ 130 per share in March. If on maturity date (as determined by the Stock Exchange during the month of December), the price of the Equity share rises to ₹ 160/- per share, Mr Hima will receive ₹ 30 per share and otherwise if the price of share falls to ₹ 110, Mr Hima will pay ₹ 20 per share.

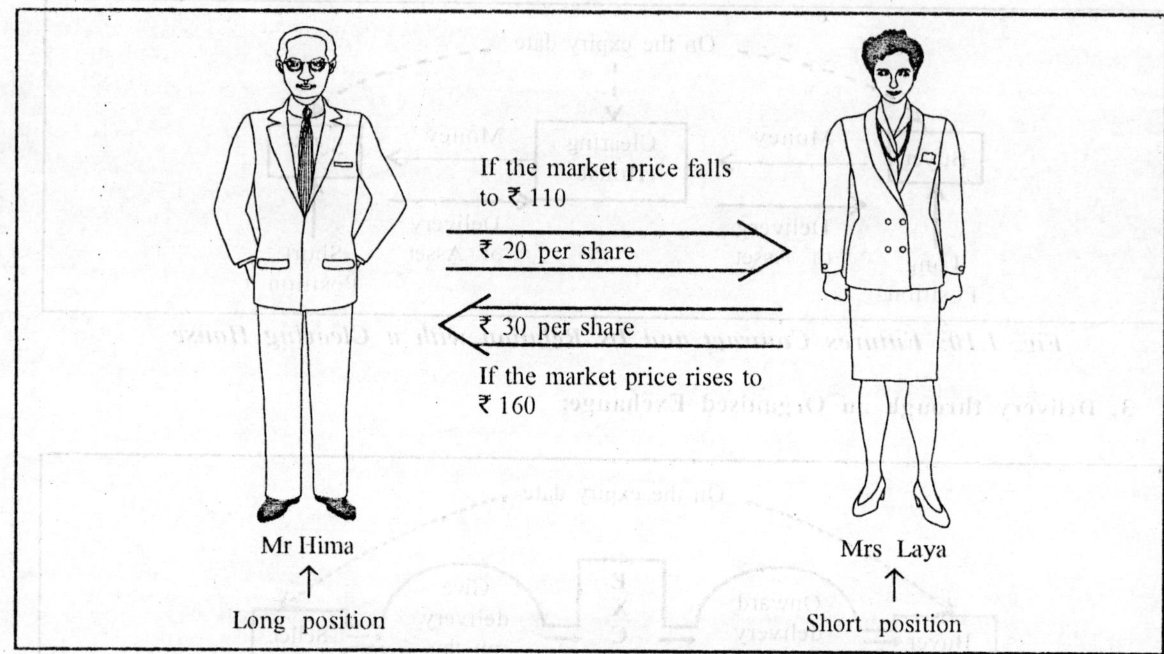

Fig. 1.12: Settlement Practice in a Futures Derivative

As compared to a forward contract, the futures are normally settled only by the difference between delivery price and market price as on maturity date.

III. Option Contracts

Literally, option means choice or an alternative for choice. In the derivative market also, this concept of option remains the same.

Definitions:

1. "An option is an instrument or contract which gives one party (the option holder) the right, but not the obligation, to perform a specified transaction with another party (the option issuer or option writer) according to specified terms".

2. "An option is an instrument or contract that gives the holder a right, without any obligation, to buy or sell specified quantity of the underlying assets at an agreed price on or before a specified future date".

From the above definitions, it is very clear that an *option* gives the holder of the option the right to transact without obligation. But in case of Forwards and Futures both parties have rights and obligations. Thus, an option holder is not under obligation to exercise the right. Another distinguishing feature is that, while it does not cost anything (except the margin requirements) to enter into a forward contract or a futures contract but in case of option contract, the writer (or seller) of the option contract charges an amount to the option holder (buyer) for granting the option right. The amount of consideration which is paid by the option holder (buyer) to the option writer (seller) for obtaining the option right in known as **Premium.**

Terminologies in Option Contract:

1. An Option: A derivative instrument which gives holder the right, without obligation, to trade (buy/sell) according to specified terms and conditions.

2. The Option Holder (or Buyer): The person who acquires the right to trade is known as the option holder or option buyer.

3. The Option Writer (or Seller): The person who grants the right to the option holders by receiving premium is known as option writer or seller.

4. Option Premium: The amount which is received by the option writer from the option holder for granting the right is known as option premium.

Note : The option 'premium' is synonymous with the option price.

5. Exercise Price or Strike Price: The price at which option can be exercised.

6. Underlying Assets: The assets such as shares, stocks, bonds, foreign currencies or commodities covered under the option agreement.

7. Expiration Data: The last date on which an option can be exercised is known as expiration date. It is also called exercise date or maturity date. On the expiration date, either the option is exercised or it expires automatically.

8. Modes of Exercise: There are three modes (styles) of option.

- **American Style of Option Exercise:** In this style, option is exercised on or prior to the expiration date. In other words, in American style, the option can be exercised at any time upto expiration date.
- **European Style of Option Exercise:** In this case, the option is exercised only on the expiration date.
- **Bermudan Style of Option Exercise:** A third form of exercise, which is occasionally used with over-the-counter (OTC) option is Bermudian exercise. In this style, option can be exercised on a few specific dates prior to expiration. As Bermuda is half way between America and Europe hence, this title is chosen. Thus,

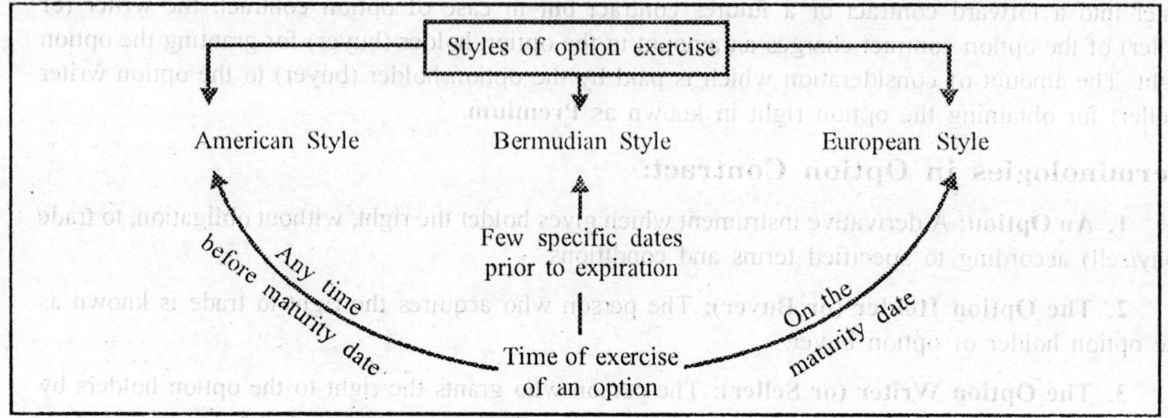

Fig. 1.13: Styles of Option Exercise

Notes: (i) The origin of the names **"American"** and **"European"** in this context are unknown. They are unrelated to practices common in any particular geographical region.

(ii) In an option contract, the specified price is called the **exercise price** or **strike price**, the specified date is called the **expiration date**, and the action to perform the buying or selling of the underlying asset according to the option contract is called **exercise**.

Types of Options: There are two types of options, i.e., Call option and Put option.

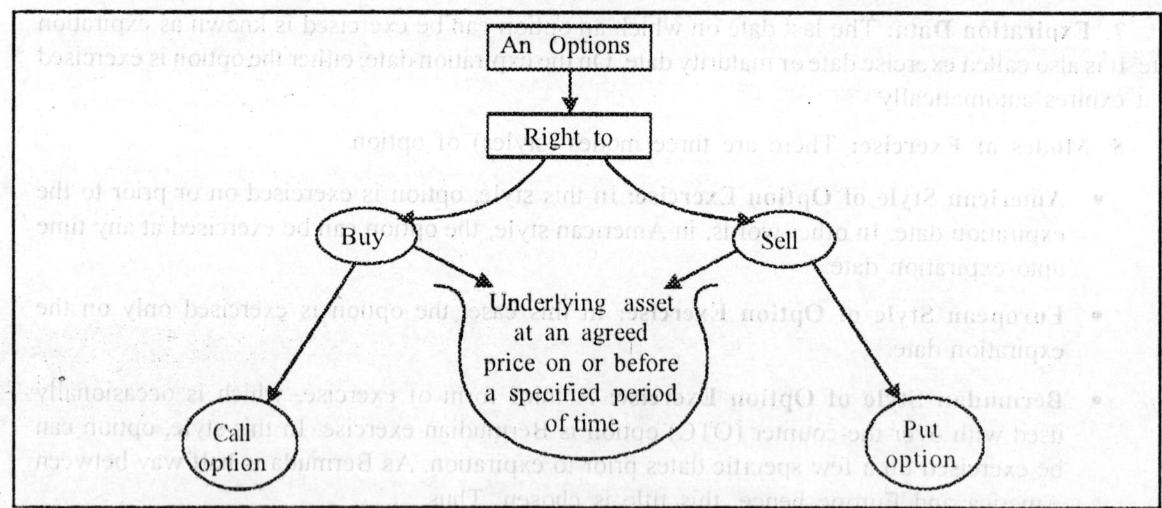

Fig. 1.14: Concept of an Option

Call Option: When an option gives that holder of the option the **right to buy** the underlying assets from the writer for a certain price on or before a certain future date, it is called a Call option.

Put Option: When an option gives the holder of the option the **right to sell** the underlying assets to the writer for a certain price on or before a certain future date, it is called a Put option.

IV. Swaps

Swap or swop means barter or exchange. A swap is a contract whereby parties agree to exchange obligations that each of them have under their respective contracts.

Definitions of Financial Swap

"A swap is an agreement between two parties to exchange sequence of cash flows over a period in the future".

"A swap is an agreement between counterparties to exchange future obligations of cash flows over a period of time".

From the above definitions, it is very clear that a swap is a private agreement between two counterparties. Hence, it is a typical form of Over-the-Counter (OTC) derivative. The swap agreement is primarily concerned with exchange of cash flows in future as per the predetermined formula along with other specified terms and conditions. In other words, the swap agreement stipulates the dates when the cash flows are to be paid and the way they are calculated. The amount of cash flow depends on future interest rates, exchange rates or other marked prices.

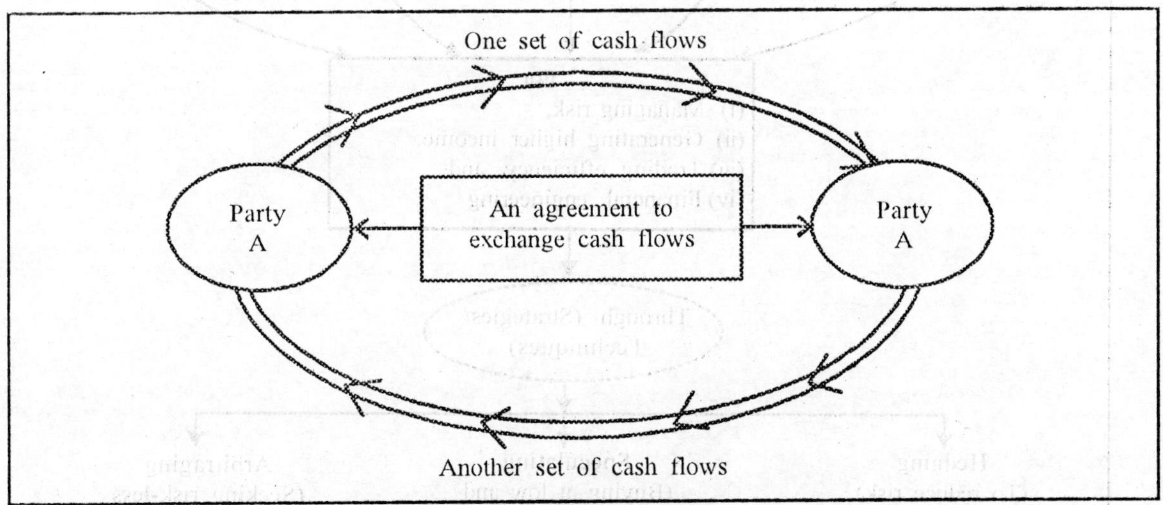

Fig. 1.15: A Generic Model of Swap

Types of Swaps: There are five basic types of swaps.

1. Interest rate swaps
2. Currency swaps
3. Equity swaps
4. Credit swaps
5. Commodity swaps

In the present world of finance, interest rate swaps account for the majority of bank's swap activity and the fixed-for-floating rate swap is the most common interest rate swap. In interest rate swap, one party agrees to make fixed-rate-interest payments in return for floating-rate-interest payments from the counterparty, with the interest rate payment calculations based on a hypothetical amount of principal called the Notional Amount. Notional Amount typically does not change hands and it is simply used to calculate payments.

In case of currency swaps, it involves exchange of currencies at specified exchange rates and to make a series of interest payments for the currency that is received at specified intervals.

1.6 USES OF DERIVATIVES

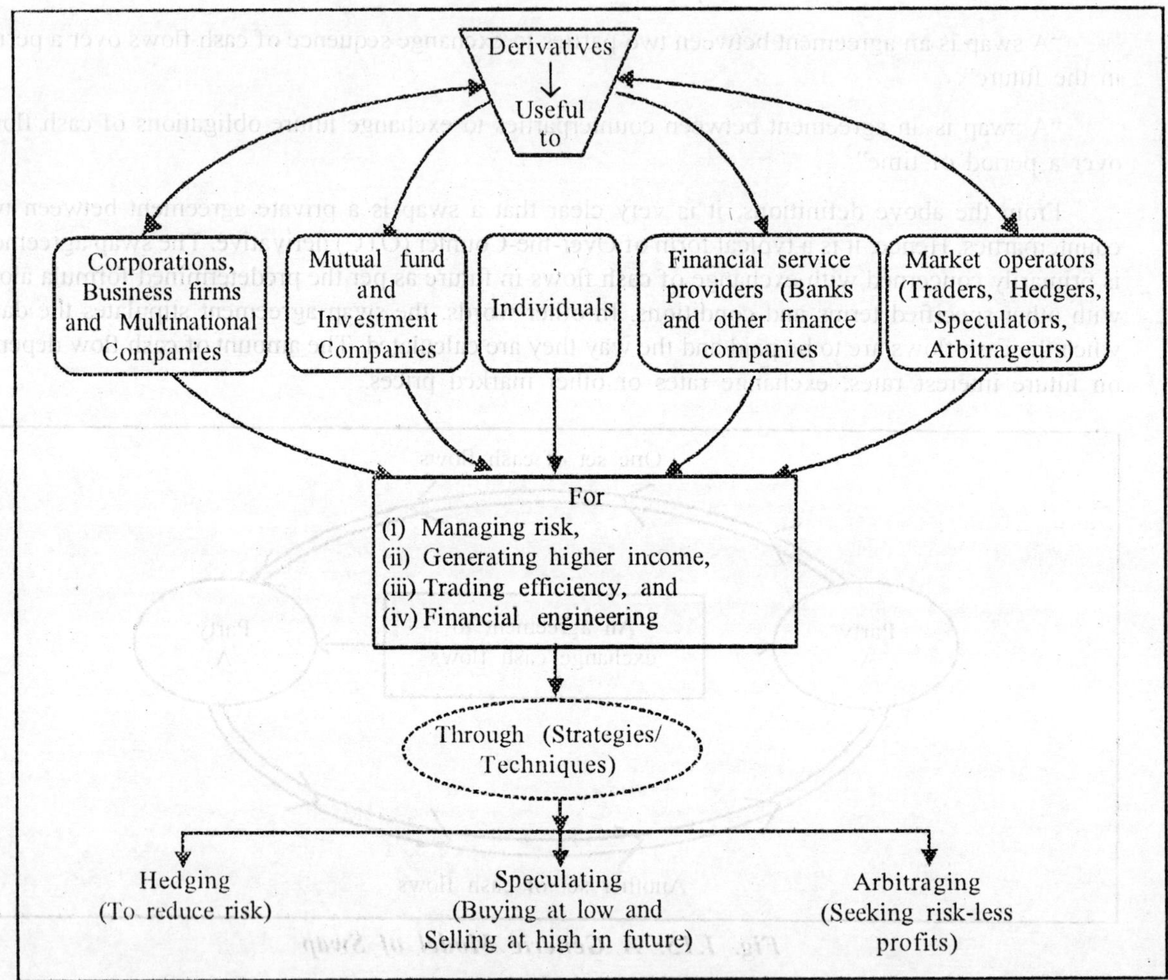

Fig. 1.16: Uses of Derivatives

Derivatives are useful tools for the corporations, business firms, multinationals, mutual funds, individuals banks and market operators (traders, hedgers, speculators, arbitrageurs) for managing risk, generating higher income and improving trading efficiency in commodity market, stock market, currency market and loan markets. Thus, Financial derivatives provide the following important services to the users.

1. Risk Management

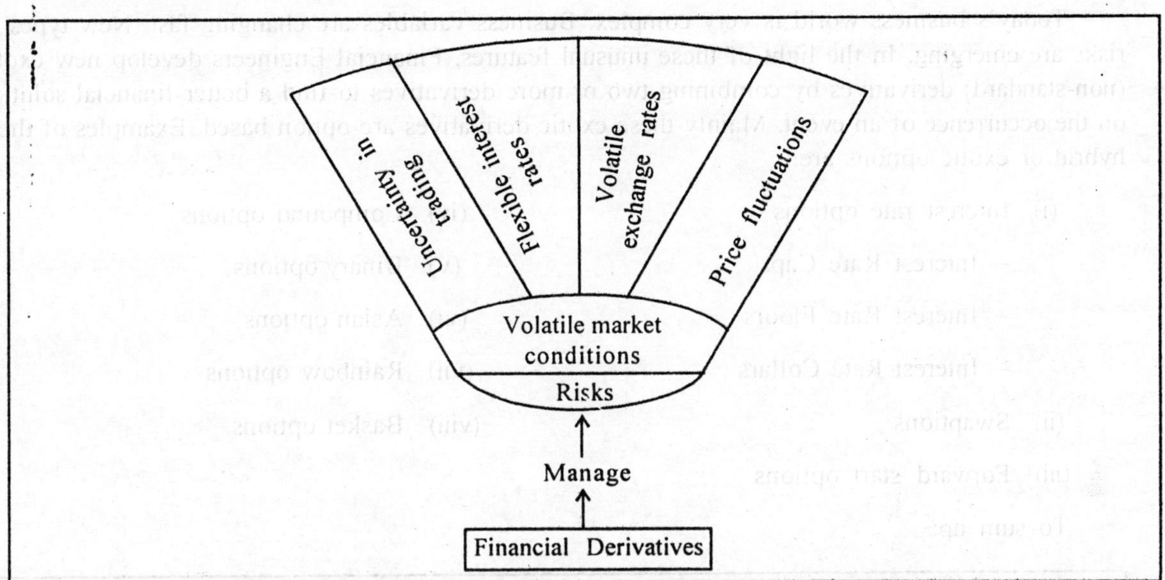

Fig. 1.17: Risk Management by Financial Derivatives

Risks are common and inherent in the financial markets and commodity markets like asset risk (stocks, bonds,......), interest rate risk, foreign exchange risk, commodity risk and so on. Financial derivatives provide a powerful tool for managing (limiting) risks that individuals and organisations face in the ordinary conduct of their business. For example, if underlying assets are stocks, bonds, foreign exchange rates and commodities etc., then the corresponding risk management instruments are stock futures (options), bond futures (options), currency futures (options) and commodity futures (options) etc., may be used to hedge the risk.

2. Income Generation

The most common use of derivative is to generate maximum income from trading or investment. Derivative strategy like **covered call option** is the best example. Further, trading with futures derivative requires margin money and trading with option derivative requires premium which are very low initial investment for a trader or an investor. Thus, derivative trading enhances liquidity position *vis-a-vis* reduces transaction cost, which generates maximum income.

3. Trading Efficiency

Derivative trading encourages large number of players in the market and thereby, increases trading volume in the country. This facilitates are disseminating of information relating to financial, commodity and derivative market. As a result, competitive trading is encouraged, price fluctuations can be smoothened out and market efficiency can be improved.

4. Financial Engineering

Today's business world is very complex. Business variables are changing fast. New types of risks are emerging. In the light of these unusual features, Financial Engineers develop new exotic (non-standard) derivatives by combining two or more derivatives to find a better financial solution on the occurrence of an event. Mainly these exotic derivatives are option based. Examples of these hybrid or exotic options are:

(i) Interest rate options
   - Interest Rate Caps
   - Interest Rate Floors
   - Interest Rate Collars

(ii) Swaptions

(iii) Forward start options

(iv) Compound options

(v) Binary options

(vi) Asian options

(vii) Rainbow options

(viii) Basket options

To sum up:

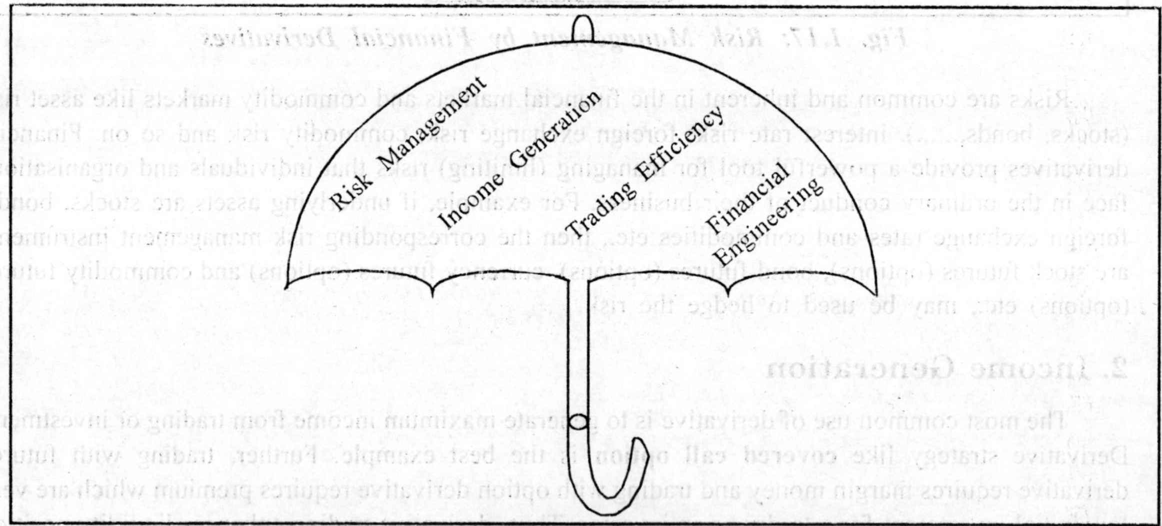

Fig. 1.18: Uses of Financial Derivatives

1.7 CRITIQUES OF DERIVATIVES

Derivatives are risk management tools. Among all the financial products, derivatives are gained a significant market worldwide. Successful risk management and financial engineering with derivatives require a thorough understanding of the principles that govern the pricing of the financial derivatives. Financial derivatives have changed the face of finance by creating new ways to understand, measure and manage financial risks. In the words of Mr Alan Greenpan, the Governor of Federal Reserve *"Although the benefits and costs of derivatives remain the subject of spirited debate the performance of the economy and the financial system in recent years suggest that those benefits have materially exceeded the cost"*. But some financial wizards have criticised the derivative and opine that derivatives have negative impact on the financial system *vis-a-vis* the economy of a country. Misuse of derivatives will result like boomerang and become the cause of the following negative outcomes:

1. Enhancement of Risk

Empirical studies on derivatives show that derivatives increase financial risk in many cases instead of hedging the same. Without a clearly defined risk management strategy, use of financial derivatives can be dangerous. It can threaten the accomplishment of a firm's long-term goal objectives.

2. Possible Large Losses

The use of derivatives can result in large losses because of the use of financial leverage or borrowing. Derivatives allow investors to earn large returns from small movements in the price of the underlying asset. However, investors could lose large amounts if the price of the underlying moves against them significantly.

Instances of massive losses in the derivative market due to misuse or abuse of derivatives:

(i) The loss of US $ 2 billion by Societe Generale in January, 2008, through misuse of futures contracts.

(ii) The loss of US $ 4 billion in the failed fund Amarnath Advisors, which was long natural gas in September, 2006, when the price moved downwards.

(iii) The loss US $ 6 billion in the failed fund Long-term Capital Management in 1998.

(iv) The loss of US $ 2 billion in equity derivatives in 1995, by Bearing Bank.

(v) The loss of US $ 3 billion in oil derivatives in 1993 and 1994 by Metallgesslschaft MG Refining and Marketing – A US subsidiary of a large German conglomerate.

3. Counterparty risk

Some derivatives, especially swaps expose investors to counterparty risk.

Example: Mr X wants to avail a fixed rate loan for his business from Bank of Maharashtra, Mumbai. But the Bank offers only at variable rates, i.e., MIBOR + 2%, Mr X swaps interest payment with another business man say Mr Y who wants a variable rate, synthetically creating a fixed rate for Mr Y. However if Mr Y goes bankrupt and is unable to pay its variable rate to the Bank, then Mr X will lose its fixed rate and will be paying a variable rate, i.e., (MIBOR + 2%) again. Further, if interest rates have increased, it is possible that Mr X may be adversely affected, because he may not be prepared to pay the higher variable rates.

Note: Different types of derivatives have different levels of counterparty risk.

4. Speculative and Gambling Motive

The term "derivative" is the fancy name for gambling. It is observed that the primary purpose of derivative is speculation and gambling. Speculation is an action characterised by willing to take risk with one's money by frequently buying and selling derivatives (futures, options) for the purpose of gaining from the frequent price changes. A speculator assumes the price risk, hoping to gain risky profits by holding certain positions (long or short). The use of *interest rate swap or currency swap* is an example of professional speculation. Today interest swap activity and the *fixed-for-floating rate swap* is the most common interest rate swap.

Note: Derivatives are purely speculative, highly leveraged instruments.

5. Large Notional Value and Cause of Instability of the Financial System

Derivatives typically have a large notional value. The dishonest practice of *rogue* traders leads to create micro and macro financial crisis in the financial market. As such, there is the danger that their use could result in losses that investors would be unable to compensate for. It leads to economic crisis.

The problem with derivatives is that they control an increasingly larger notional amount of assets and this may lead to distortions in the real capital and equities markets. The famed investor Warren Buffet pointed out that derivatives are *"financial weapons of mass destruction"*.

6. Displacement Effect in the Financial Market

Lack of awareness about the derivative tradings among the Indian financial institutions is a major reason for the reduction in the volume of derivative tradings. Besides the foreign financial institutions find the Indian derivative market too small and the size of the deals tiny. Due to this perception of the institutional players *vis-a-vis* the illiquidity nature of the derivative instruments, the financial market is not placed in a right position.

7. Leverage of an Economy's Debt

Derivatives massively leverage the debt in an economy. It creates such a situation where it will be very difficult to meet the debt obligations. This leads to curtailment of real economic activities, which can cause a recession or even depression. In view of Marriner S. Eccless, US Federal Reserve Chairman (November, 1934 to February, 1948), too high a level of debt was one of the primary causes of the 1920s-30s Great Depression.

8. Weak Regulatory Framework for Derivatives in India

Regulation is an effective substitute for sound risk management at the individual firm level. The regulatory framework in India is mostly consistent with the International Organisation of Securities Commission (IOSCO) principles. In India, it is based on the L.C. Gupta committee report on derivatives and J.R. Verma group reports on risk containment measures for the derivative products.

The L.C. Gupta committee report provided a perspective on division of regulatory responsibility between the Exchange and SEBI. It recommended that SEBI's role should be restricted to approving the rules, bye-laws and regulations of derivatives exchange and approval of proposed derivative contracts before commencement of trading. The emphasis should be on exchange level regulation while providing supervisory and advisory role to SEBI.

The J.R. Verma group suggested a methodology for risk containment measures for index futures market and for options on indices, stock options and single stock futures. The risk containment measures include calculation of margins, position limits, exposure limits and reporting and disclosure.

From the above discussion, it is very clear that scope and coverage of the regulatory framework for derivatives in India need to be improved. Thus, to regulate the derivative markets in India, the regulatory authority will have to be an extra burden.

To sum up, the criticisms on derivatives are outlined below:

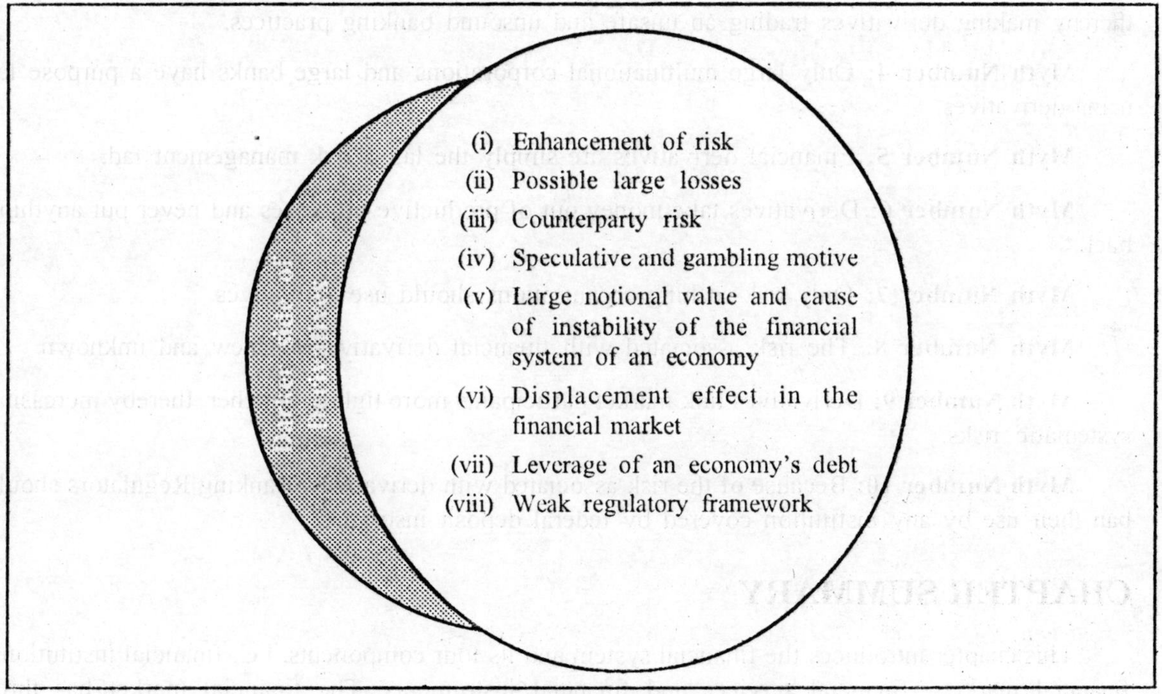

Fig. 1.19: Criticisms on Derivatives

1.8 MYTHS ABOUT DERIVATIVES

Thomas F. Siems is a senior economist and policy advisor at the Federal Reserve Bank of Dallas, has explored 10 myths, or common misconceptions about the financial derivatives.

Financial derivatives have changed the face of finance by creating new ways to understand, measure and manage financial risks. Ultimately, derivatives offer organisations the opportunity to break financial risks into smaller components and then to buy and sell those components to best meet specific risk management objectives. Moreover, under a market-oriented philosophy derivatives allow for the free trading of individual risk components, thereby improving market efficiency. Using financial derivatives should be considered a part of any business's risk management strategy to ensure that value enhancing opportunities can be persued.

As there is always an another side of the coin, derivatives also have a darker side. Some critics who oppose financial derivatives fear that these instruments can paralyse the world's financial market and force regulatory authorities to restore stability and prevent massive economic collapse. They believe that derivatives create risks that are uncontrollable. The 10 common myths about financial derivatives are explored below:

Myth Number 1: Derivatives are new, complex high-tech financial products created by stock market rocket scientists.

Myth Number 2: Derivatives are purely speculative, highly leveraged instruments.

Myth Number 3: The enormous size of the financial derivatives market dwarfs bank capital, thereby making derivatives trading an unsafe and unsound banking practices.

Myth Number 4: Only large multinational corporations and large banks have a purpose for using derivatives.

Myth Number 5: Financial derivatives are simply the latest risk management fad.

Myth Number 6: Derivatives take money out of productive processes and never put anything back.

Myth Number 7: Only risk-seeking organisations should use derivatives.

Myth Number 8: The risk associated with financial derivatives are new and unknown.

Myth Number 9: Derivatives link market participants more tightly together, thereby increasing systematic risks.

Myth Number 10: Because of the risk associated with derivatives, Banking Regulators should ban their use by any institution covered by federal deposit insurance.

CHAPTER SUMMARY

This chapter introduces the financial system and its four components, i.e., financial institutions, financial markets, financial services and financial instruments. The financial market has three segments, i.e., Money Market, Security Market and Derivative Market. Forwards, Futures, Options and Swaps are the types of derivatives in the derivative markets. Derivatives are instruments which derive their value from the underlying assets. The underlying assets may be commodity, stock, debt, stock index, interest rate and exchange rates etc.

The derivatives can be traded over-the-counter (OTC) or on the Exchange. Forwards are traded over-the-counter between the parties. These are agreements to buy or sell an underlying at a certain future time for a certain price. Futures are standardised contracts to buy or sell the underlying asset for a specified price at a certain future date and traded only in an organised exchange. An option is an instrument or contract which gives one party (the option holder) the right, but not obligation, to trade with another party (the option issuer or option writer) according to specified terms. There are two types of options, i.e., call option and put option. When an option gives the right to the holder to buy an underlying, it is called call option. Similarly, when an option gives the right to the holder to sell an underlying, then it is called a put option. A swap or swop means barter or exchange. In the language of finance, a swap is a derivative contract for the future exchange of cash flows between two parties according to specific formula. It is a customised contract in the form of OTC derivative. There are five generic types of swaps such as Interest Rate Swap, Equity Swap, Credit Default Swap, Currency Swap and Commodity Swap.

Financial derivatives have changed the face of finance by entering new ways to understand, measure and manage financial risks. Ultimately derivatives offer the organizations the opportunity to break financial risks into smaller components and then to buy or sell those components to best meet the specific risk management objectives. In the present highly uncertain business scenario, the importance of risk management is much higher then ever before. The emergence of derivative market is an ingenious feat of financial engineering that provides an effective and less costly solution to the problem of risk that is expressed in the price unpredictability at the underlying asset. Lastly, this chapter discusses various critiques and misconceptions of derivatives.

SUGGESTIONS FOR FURTHER READINGS

Chance D., *An Introduction to Derivatives*, 4th Edn., Oriando, FL Dryden Press, 1997.

John C. Hull, *Fundamentals of Futures and Options Markets*, 5th Edn., Pearson Education, 2009.

Gupta S.L., *Financial Derivatives, Theory, Concepts and Problems*, Seventh Printing, PHI Learning (P) Ltd., 2009.

Robert A. Strong, *Derivatives — An Introduction*, Thomson South Western, Third Indian Reprint, 2006.

Kolb Robert W., *Financial Derivatives*, John Wiley, New York, 2003.

EXERCISE

Quiz

State Whether the Following Statements are True or False.

(a) Financial derivatives are those assets whose value are determined by the value of some other assets, called underlyings.

(b) OTC traded derivatives expose the trading parties to operational risk, counterparty risk and legal risk.

(c) A futures contract is an agreement to buy or sell a particular asset between two parties in a specified future date at an agreed price through specified exchange.

(d) Forward contracts are traded on the over-the-counter (OTC) markets or by telephones and are self-regulatory.

(e) An option is the right, but not obligation, to buy or sell something at a stated date at a stated price.

(f) A 'call option' gives one the right to buy, where as a 'put option' gives one the right to sell.

(g) A swap can be defined as a barter or exchange.

(h) A swap is a contract between two or more parties to exchange stream of cash flows over a period of time in the future.

Ans: (a) True, (b) True, (c) True, (d) True, (e) True, (f) True, (g) True, (h) True.

QUESTIONS

A. Short Type Questions

1. What is a financial system ?
2. What are the components of a financial system ?
3. Define the term "Derivative".
4. Explain the following terms: (a) Forward contract (b) Futures (c) Option (d) Swaps
5. What do you mean by "underlyings" ?
6. What are the underlyings for: (a) Commodity derivatives (b) Financial derivatives
7. Explain the following concept in the language of financial derivative: (a) Long position (b) Short position
8. What do you mean by 'OTC' trading ?

B. Long Type Questions

1. Define the term "financial derivative". What are the features? Explain.
2. What are the different types of financial derivatives? Explain their features in brief.
3. What are the uses of financial derivatives? Discuss.
4. Compare between a Forward contract and Futures contract.
5. "Derivatives are considered as risk management tools by organisations and investors/individuals". Comment upon the statement.
6. Briefly discuss the various criticisms of derivatives.
7. What is a financial system? What are the four components? Discuss.
8. The value of a derivative instrument is derived from one or more basic variables called 'underlyings'. Comment upon this statement.
9. There are 10 myths or misconceptions about the financial derivatives. Discuss.
10. Briefly discuss the various derivative instruments traded in Indian financial and commodity markets.

Derivative Markets: History and Evolution

Learning Objectives

After studying this chapter, you will be able to:

- Know the history and evolution of derivatives markets
- Be familiar with different participants in the derivative markets
- Understand the factors contributing to the growth of financial derivatives
- Understand the functions of derivative markets

Chapter Outline

2.1 Introduction to Derivative Markets
2.2 History of Derivative Markets: A Global Perspective
2.3 Participants in the Derivative Markets
2.4 Factors Driving the Growth of Financial Derivatives
2.5 Functions of Derivative Markets
Chapter Summary
Suggestions for Further Readings
Exercises

2.1 INTRODUCTION TO DERIVATIVE MARKETS

Derivatives are old invention. It is evident from history that derivatives were known and used in ancient times probably as early as 2000 BC. Forward contracts are probably the first and oldest kind of derivatives. Historically, it is evident that Forward Tradings were developed in 12th century in England and France. In course of time, futures tradings were developed in the developed countries in 17th century. During the evolutionary stage, the derivative markets (Forwards and Futures Tradings) were limited to commodities only.

In the present world of finance, derivative markets are an integral part of capital market. The globalization effect expands the scope of this derivative segment globally. In India, it is marked that the derivative market is progressing in positive direction both in number of contracts as well as in volume of transaction since 2000.

2.2 HISTORY OF DERIVATIVE MARKETS : A GLOBAL PERSPECTIVE

Stage I: The concept of derivative was conceived and used in ancient ages probably in 2000 BC.

Stage II: The concept of Forward contracts were used during 12th century in England and France and restricted to agricultural produces, i.e., rice. Historically it is evident that the Forward contracts for rice were in practice in Japan during 17th century. It was known as **Cho-at-Mai** a kind of rice traded forward contract.

Stage III: First Futures Exchange was set up in 1730.

It is evident from history that the world's first organised Futures Exchange was set up in 1730, in Osaka, Japan. It was known as Dojima Rice Futures Market. The landlords in Japan were used to sell "RICE TICKETS". These rice tickets were bought or sold in the Dojima Rice Futures Exchange. These tickets were served as Future derivatives and represented the underlying as rice in warehouse or in the field.

This is the origin of first Future derivative in the world.

Stage IV: 19th Century Futures markets on commodity and agricultural produces.

(A) Global Futures Markets

- 1848 – Establishment of Chicago Board of Trade.
- 1872 – Butter and Cheese Exchange of New York was set up.
- 1877 – New York Mercantile Exchange (NYMEX) was set up.
- 1898 – (i) London Metal Exchange was set up.

  (ii) Chicago Mercantile Exchange (CME) was set up.

(B) Indian Futures Market

- 1875 – Bombay Cotton Trade Association Ltd., was set up. This is the first organised futures market in India.
- 1893 – Bombay Cotton Exchange Ltd., was set up.
- 1900 – Gujarati Vyapari Mandali was set up.

Stage V: 20th Century Derivative Market – The Emergence of Financial Derivatives.

During 19th century and even upto 1960, the futures markets were confined to commodities like soya, eggs, cheese, wheat and metals. In the early 1970s, it was witnessed that the financial markets were highly volatile and instable. All the commodities were exposed to various types of financial risks. As a result, **Financial Derivatives** emerged. The first financial derivatives were created only in 1970. By the end of 1990, it was found that financial derivatives accounted for 60% of derivative tradings and financial contracts. The first financial futures market was the International Monetary Market, set up in 1972, by the Chicago Mercantile Exchange. Similarly, London International Financial Futures Exchange was set up in 1982.

Stage VI: 21st Century Derivative Market – The Remarkable Growth Stage.

During 2001-2010, the global derivative markets have developed at an astonishing pace. The US has been dominating the futures contracts globally since 2000. The second player the futures market is witnessed was Europe.

2.3 PARTICIPANTS IN A DERIVATIVE MARKET

There are three main types of participants in the derivative markets. They are identified as Hedgers, Speculators, Arbitrageur, Day-traders/scalpers and Market makers.

1. Hedgers: They use futures and options derivatives to reduce or eliminate the risk associated with price of an asset in the market. Most producers and trading companies participate in the derivative market to shift or reduce the **price risks** in the underlying asset markets to secure anticipated profits.

Example: An Indian company will pay 1,00,000 USD to a US company in 90 days. Now the Indian company faces a currency exchange risk due to the uncertain ₹/USD exchange rates. If the USD goes up, it will burden the Indian company more for the payment, thus it will hurt the company's cash flows and profits. Suppose the current exchange rate is 46 ₹ = 1 USD and the USD may go up, the Indian company may consider the following hedging strategy:

Strategy I: Purchase a forward contract to buy 1,00,000 USD with 1 (one), 46,00,000 ₹ 90 days later and they lock the cost of the payment in Indian currency.

Strategy II: Purchase of *call option* to buy 1,00,000 USD with 1 (one), ₹ 46,00,000, 90 days later. The Indian company will pay a payment of ₹ 92,000 (assuming a 2% premium) for the option.

The following table shows the results of the above risk-avoiding strategies:

Currency exchange rate	90 days later rate ₹ USD	Hedging ₹	Forward contract hedge (₹)	Call option hedge (₹)
46 ₹ = 1 $	up ₹ 48 = 1 $	48,00000	46,00000	46,92,000
	down ₹ 45 = 1 $	45,00000	46,00000	45,92,000

From the above example it is very clear that if the Indian company adopts no hedging plan its payment will increase if the USD goes up, and thus, will hurt its total profits. If the Indian company signs a forward contract to lock the cost of the 90 days later payment, it can avoid a loss if USD goes up, but it will forgo the opportunity if the USD goes down. If the company buys a *call option*, it can prevent loss if the USD goes up and it can still gain if the USD goes down, but it must pay premium for the call option.

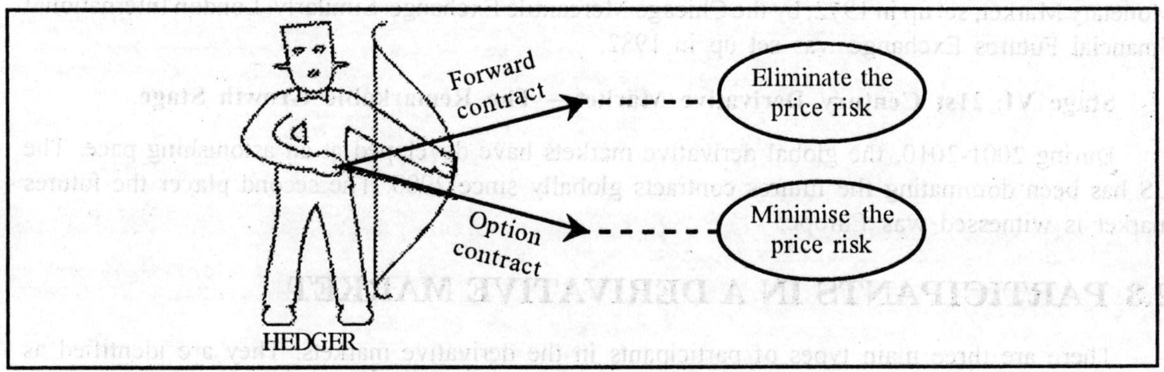

Fig. 2.1: The Strategy of An Hedger

Speculators

Speculators are risk-seeking traders or investors. They are willing to assume risk by taking future positions with the expectation to earn profits. They have specialised expertise in forecasting the future econcmic conditions. They can predict the directions of market's movements and accordingly take a position, i.e., long or short. Speculators only have a particular view about future price of a commodity, shares, stock index, interest rates or currency. They consider various factors like demand and supply, market positions, open interests, economic fundamentals, international events, etc., to make prediction. Thus,

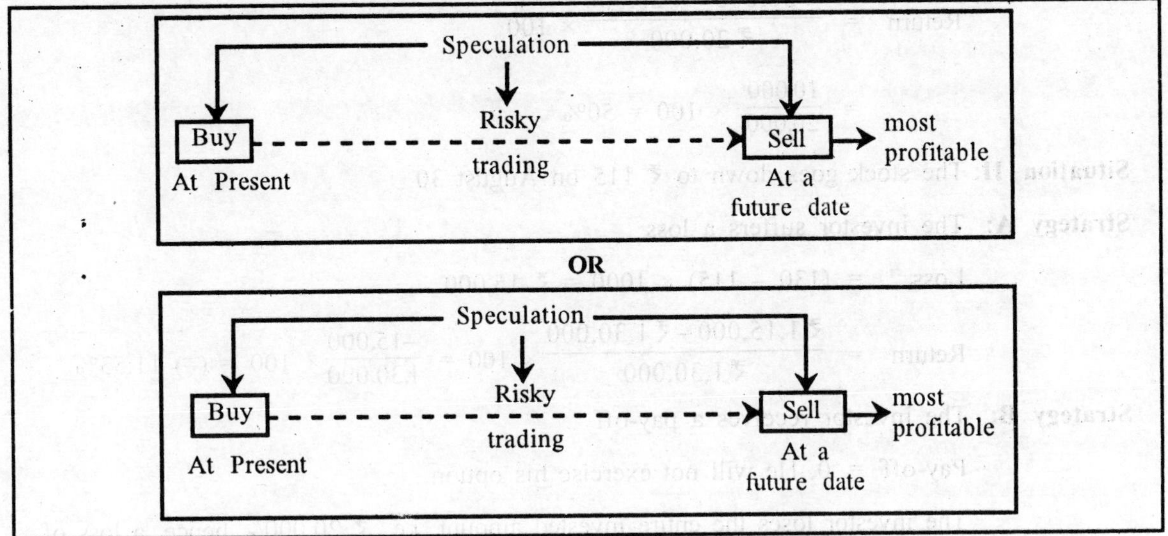

Fig. 2.2: The Strategy of a Speculator

Thus, a speculator assumes the price risk hoping to gain risky profits by holdings certain positions (long or short).

Speculators use futures and option contracts to get extra leverage in betting on future movements in the price of underlying assets. They can increase both the potential gains and potential losses by usage of derivatives in a speculative venture. Speculators are indispensable for the existence of hedging business. They take over the ;rice risks shifted from the hedgers. Hence, the speculators bear the major risks in the derivative market.

Example: Let the price of a certain shares is ₹ 130 per share on April 30. The price may go up in August 30. The investor may consider the following investing strategies.

A – The investor spends ₹ 1,30,000 in cash to buy 1000 shares on April 30.

B – The investor pays a premium of ₹ 20 per share (₹ 20,000 for 1000 shares) to buy a call option to purchase 1000 shares at the strike price of ₹ 130 per share on Aug 30.

Examine the following consequences:

Situation I: The share price goes up to ₹ 160 per share on August 30.

Strategy A: The investor sells the shares on August 30 to get ₹ 1,60,000 in cash.

$$\text{Return} = \frac{₹1,60,000 - ₹1,30,000}{₹1,30,000} \times 100 = 23\%$$

Strategy B: The investor exercises the option to receive pay-off

$$\text{Pay-off} = ₹\ 1,60,000 - ₹\ 1,30,000 = ₹\ 30,000$$

$$\text{Return} = \frac{₹\,30{,}000 - ₹\,20{,}000}{₹\,20{,}000} \times 100$$

$$= \frac{10{,}000}{20{,}000} \times 100 = 50\%$$

Situation II: The stock goes down to ₹ 115 on August 30.

Strategy A: The investor suffers a loss

$$\text{Loss} = (130 - 115) \times 1000 = ₹\,15{,}000$$

$$\text{Return} = \frac{₹\,1{,}15{,}000 - ₹\,1{,}30{,}000}{₹\,1{,}30{,}000} \times 100 = \frac{-15{,}000}{1{,}30{,}000} \times 100 = (-)\,11.53\%$$

Strategy B: The investor receives a pay-off

Pay-off = 0, He will not exercise his option.

The investor loses the entire invested amount, i.e., ₹ 20,000/-, hence, a loss of 100%.

Arbitrageur

Arbitrage is the simultaneous purchase and sale of the same underlying in two different markets with an objective to make profit from price discrepancies between the two markets.

Arbitrageur are third important group of participants in Futures, Forwards and Option derivative markets. They are in business to take advantage of a discrepancy between prices in two different markets. Their behaviour involves locking in a riskless profit by simultaneously entering into transactions in two or more markets. Arbitrage is not the same as speculation. Speculation is to seek profits promised by scientific forecasting of future prices, and thus **risky.** Arbitrage is to snatch profits originated in the reality of the price differences between markets and is therefore riskless.

An arbitrageur takes advantages of the price difference between markets. Hence, he gains riskless instant profit and such opportunity cannot last long. When an opportunity for arbitrage arises, the market price will soon reach a new balance due to this actions of the arbitraguers and then the opportunity will disappear.

Example: A stock is traded in both Mumbai Stock Exchange and Bhubaneswar Stock Exchange. The following quotes have been obtained on a particular day:

Mumbai Stock Exchange: ₹ 177 per share.

Bhubaneswar Stock Exchange: ₹ 170 per share

The Arbitrageur Strategy: Buy shares in Bhubaneswar Stock Exchange and sell shares in Mumbai Stock Exchange.

A Diagrammatic Presentation: The participants or traders in derivative markets may be exhibited in the following diagram:

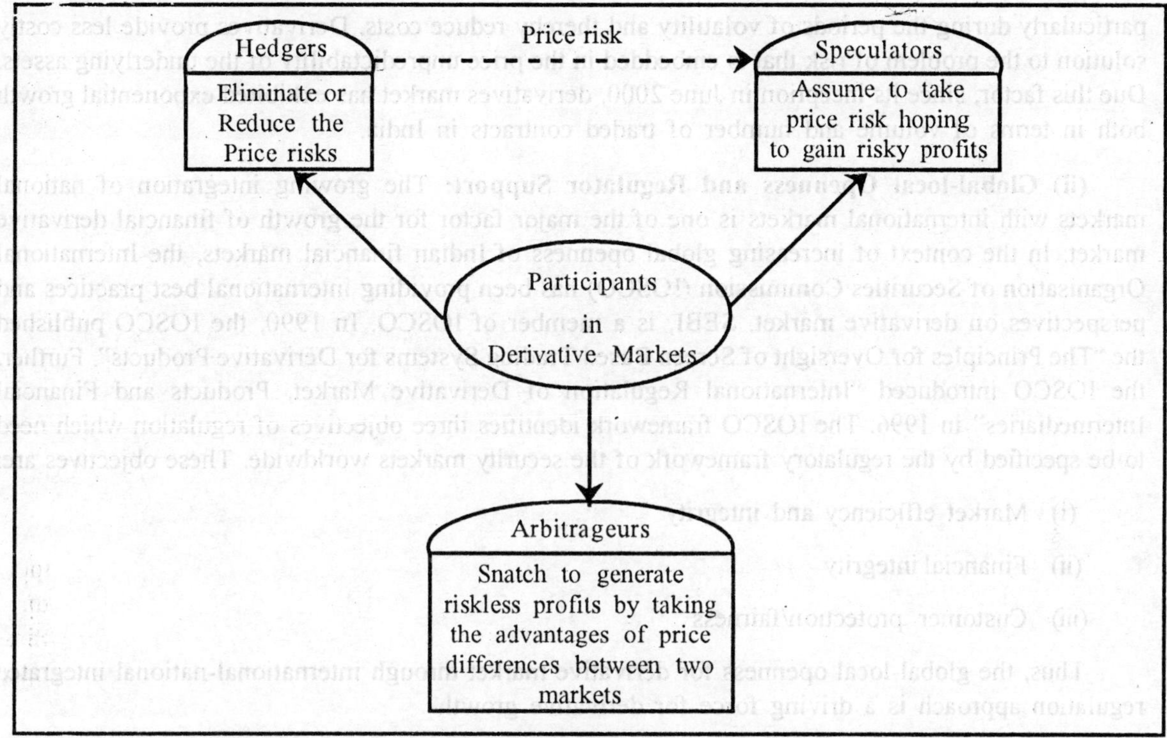

Fig. 2.3: The Participants/Traders in Derivative Markets

To sum up, there are three broad categories of participants – hedgers, speculators and arbitrageur trade in the derivative markets. Hedgers face risk associated with the price of an underlying asset. They use futures and options to reduce or eliminate risks. Speculators wish to bet on future movements in the price of an asset. Futures and options contract can give extra leverage, that is, they can increase both the potential gains and potential losses in a speculative venture. Arbitrageur are in business to take advantage of a discrepancy between prices in two different markets. The objective of arbitrage is simply to make profits without risk, but the complexity of arbitrage activity is such that it is reserved to particularly well informed and experienced professional traders, equipped with powerful calculations and data processing tools.

2.4 FACTORS DRIVING THE GROWTH OF FINANCIAL DERIVATIVES

Factors contributing to the growth of derivatives are ***Price volatility, Global-local openness and Regulatory support, Technological advancements, Development of more sophisticated risk management tools and Innovations in the derivative market.*** A brief discussion on the above factors are as follows:

(i) Price Volatility: In the present highly uncertain business scenario, the importance of risk management is much greater than ever before. Financial derivatives protect from possible adverse market movements and can be used to manage or offset exposures by hedging or shifting risks particularly during the periods of volatility and thereby reduce costs. Derivatives provide less costly solution to the problem of risk that is embedded in the price unpredictability of the underlying assets. Due this factor, since its inception in June 2000, derivatives market has exhibited exponential growth both in terms of volume and number of traded contracts in India.

(ii) Global-local Openness and Regulator Support: The growing integration of national markets with international markets is one of the major factor for the growth of financial derivative market. In the context of increasing global openness of Indian financial markets, the International Organisation of Securities Commission (IOSCO) has been providing international best practices and perspectives on derivative market. SEBI, is a member of IOSCO. In 1990, the IOSCO published the "The Principles for Oversight of Screen Based Trading Systems for Derivative Products". Further, the IOSCO introduced "International Regulation of Derivative Market, Products and Financial Intermediaries" in 1996. The IOSCO framework identifies three objectives of regulation which need to be specified by the regulatory framework of the security markets worldwide. These objectives are:

(i) Market efficiency and integrity

(ii) Financial integrity

(iii) Customer protection/fairness

Thus, the global-local openness for derivative market through international-national integrated regulation approach is a driving force for derivative growth.

An example: SEBI has given approval to National Stock Exchange (NSE) and United Stock Exchange (USE) for trading in currency options, a move that will provide an alternative to investors for hedging against currency fluctuations.

Source: Times of India, October 14, 2010.

3. Technological Advancements

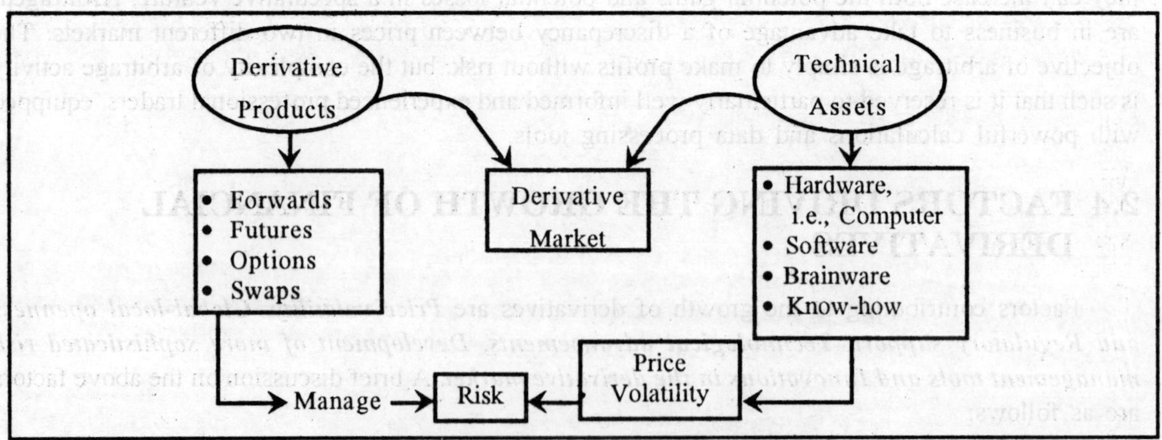

Fig. 2.4: Derivatives and Technology

The world is changing. As we move into the 21st century, the pace of change continues to increase. New technologies emerge and the dynamics of trade shifts. Flexibility and ability to quickly respond to change is the name of the game. The use of modern computers and software makes possible such flexibility. The emergence of Internet Technology has permitted the growth of mass customisation where a customer selects the features desired in a product online. The service provider develops the system capable of meeting the customer's demand. Advancement achieved in the computer and satellite technology has helped storage and rapid transmission of information. The volatility in prices is activated by the pressure of such technological advancement. Derivative instruments will help to manage the risks arising from price volatility.

4. Development of Sophisticated Risk Management Tools or Products

In certain derivative tradings, a typical type of risk or characteristic is emerged. To manage this, sophisticated tools will be developed. This "solution to derivative problems" adds further growth in derivative market.

Few example,

Typical Risks/Characteristics	Financial Derivatives
Foreign Exchange Risk (Forex) • Transaction exposure • Economic exposure • Translation exposure	Foreign Exchange Futures
Option to enter into a swap	Swaption
Pay-off based on average price of the underlying during the life of the option rather than just the value at maturity	Asian option

Thus, development of sophisticated risk management tools for typical risks provide the traders wider choice of risk management strategies.

5. Innovations in the Derivative Market

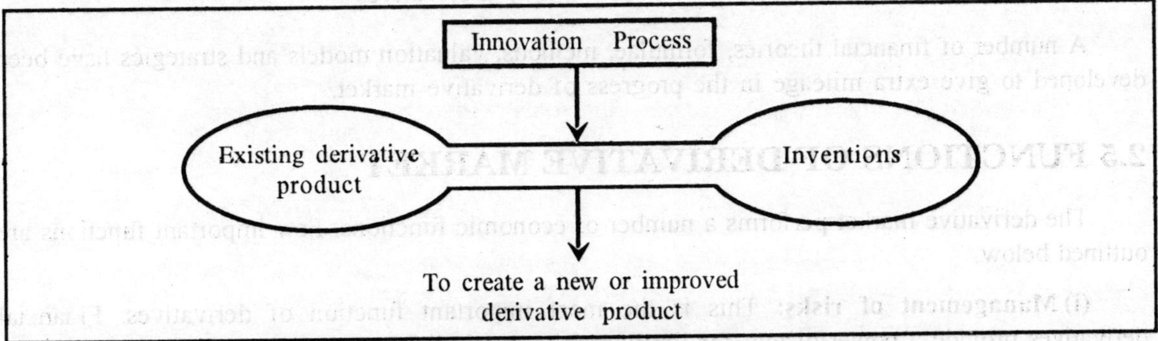

Fig. 2.5: Innovations in Derivative Market

Innovation is transformation of thoughts to new ideas, the application of these ideas to fulfill goals and therefore improve current business or create new business. In other words, implementing creative ideas to produce new and improved processes and products is innovation. Thus,

Innovation = Creativity + Productivity

= Idea + Action + Productivity

Note: When science (scientific discoveries) and technology (technological innovations) connect with market, they influence the economy of a nation.

Science and technology are linked through the discovery-invention-innovation-market sequence.

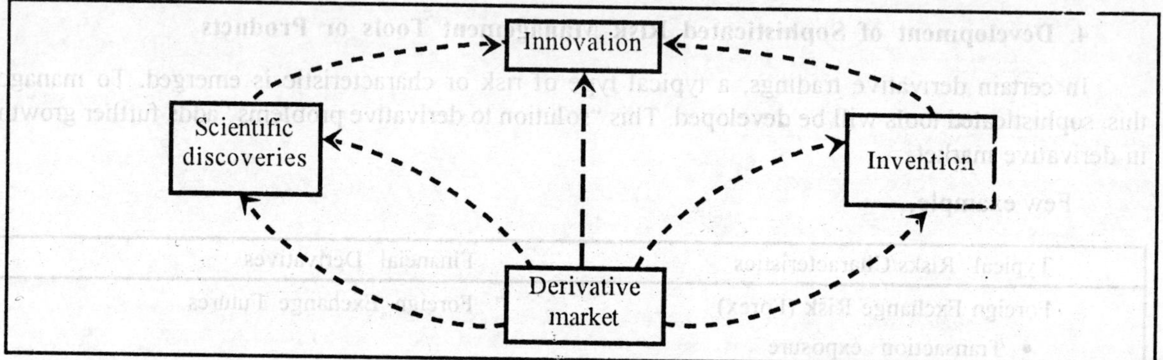

Fig. 2.6: Scientific Discovery — Invention — Innovation Process

The innovations in the derivative products are exhibited as follows:

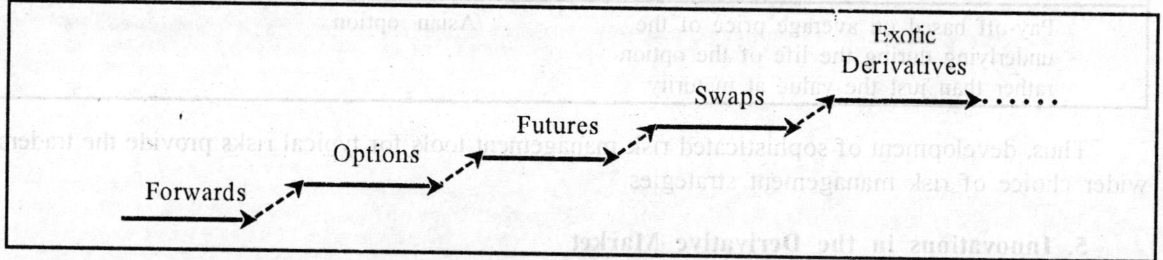

Fig. 2.7: Evolution of Derivatives

A number of financial theories, formulae, methods, valuation models and strategies have been developed to give extra mileage in the progress of derivative market.

2.5 FUNCTIONS OF DERIVATIVE MARKET

The derivative market performs a number of economic functions. Few important functions are outlined below.

(i) Management of risks: This is the most important function of derivatives. Financial derivatives provide a powerful tool for limiting risks that individuals and organisations face in the ordinary conduct of their business. Different kinds of risks faced by participants are: (a) credit risk, (b) market risk, (c) liquid risk, (d) legal risk and (e) operational risk. Thus,

Derivatives → Powerful tools to manage	→ Credit risk → Market risk (Price variability risk) → Liquidity risk → Legal risk → Operational risk

Derivatives offer protection from possible adverse market movements and can be used to manage or offset exposures by hedging or shifting risks particularly during period of volatility thereby reducing costs.

(ii) Efficiency in Trading (Market Efficiency): Derivatives bring efficiency in the market and make the market a full complete due to the following reasons:

(a) Low transaction costs

(b) Minimisation of risks

(c) Clear reflection of the market perception. Derivatives help to discover both future and current prices of underlying assets.

(d) Protection to investors from financial risks.

(e) Facilitating the trading activities under controlled/regulated form.

(iii) Price Discovery: In an organised derivatives market prices reflect the perception of market participants about the future. This leads the prices of underlying to the perceived future level. As a result, the prices of derivatives converge with the prices of the underlying at the expiration of derivative contract. Thus, derivatives help in discovery of future as well as current prices of underlyings.

(iv) Price Stabilisation Function: Derivatives provide a significant tool or mechanism through which all the investors or the participants can judge the movement of prices and protects themselves from financial risk. Indirectly derivatives stabilise the price movements through a participative controlled mechanism.

(v) Catalyst for New Entrepreneurial Activity: Derivatives offer new business and employment opportunities across the globe. At present, there are so many active people working in the stock markets as agents, traders, advisors and many more with distinctive responsibilities. The attractive gains through low investment instills a drive within educated people to earn more and start their own business.

To sum up, the economic functions of derivative products as well as derivative markets are enumerated as follows:

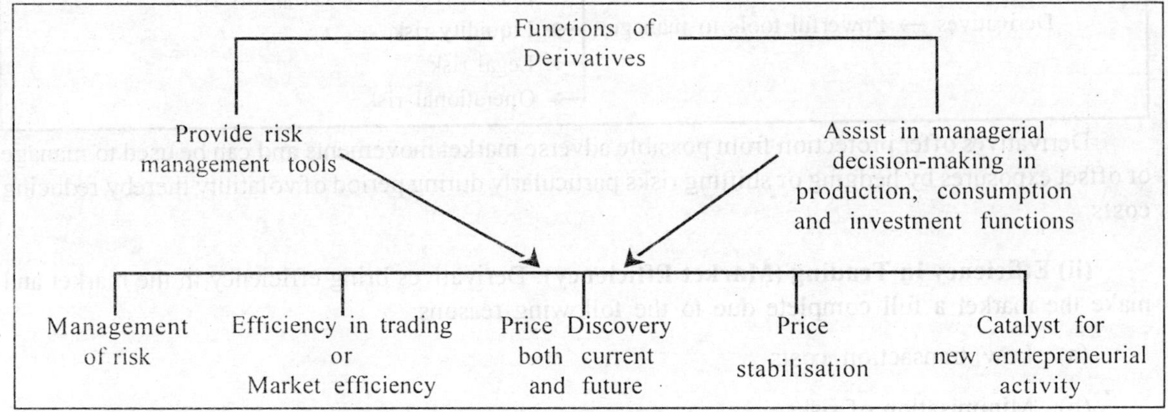

Fig. 2.8: Economic Functions of Derivatives

CHAPTER SUMMARY

This chapter highlights the evolution and growth of derivative markets in the globe since 2000 BC. On research study it is found that there are five stages in the evolution and growth of derivatives till 21st century. In India, the emergence and growth of financial derivative market is relatively a recent phenomenon. Since its inception in 2000, the derivative market has shown rapid growth both in terms of volume and number of traded contracts.

There are three broad categories of participants in the derivative markets. They are Hedgers, Speculators and Arbitraguers. However, the Day-traders/Scalpers and Market Makers are participating in certain events. **Hedgers** use futures and options to hedge (reduce or eliminate) the price risk. **Speculators** enters into the market purely for making profits by buying and selling the derivatives. The speculators wish to bet on future movements in the price of an asset and make profit. **Arbitraguers** make risk free profits by simultaneously buying and selling similar instruments in different markets.

A **Market Maker** is a trader who competes with a number of participants by quoting both and offer price simultaneously with a motive to ensure that the public will receive a market-determined price for their trades. A Day-trader is a person who opens security positions or futures contracts and closes them on the same day.

Over the last three decades, the global derivatives market has seen a phenomenal growth. A large variety of derivative contracts have been launched at exchanges across the world. The important factors driving the growth of financial derivatives are:

1. Increased volatility in the underlyings (assets) in financial markets.
2. Increased integration of national financial markets with the international financial markets.

3. Technological advancement, improvement in communication facilities and sharp declining in their costs.

4. Development of more sophisticated risk management tools, providing a wider choice of risk management strategies.

5. Innovations in the derivative markets.

At the end of this chapter, the key economic functions of derivatives have been explained. The important economic functions are:

- Management
- Efficiency in trading
- Price discovery
- Price stabilisation in the market
- Catalyst for new entrepreneurial activity

SUGGESTIONS FOR FURTHER READINGS

1. Hull, John C., *Fundamentals of Futures and Options Markets,* Prentice-Hall of India, New Delhi, 2006.
2. Gupta S.L., *Financial Derivatives, Theory Concepts and Problems.*
3. *Derivatives and Financial Innovations* – Stock Exchange Mumbai (2004).
4. Gordon & Natarajan, *Financial Markets and Services,* Himalaya Publishing House, Mumbai.
5. Websites:

   http://business.mapsofindia.com

   http://www.moneytank.in

   http://www.fmc.gov.in

EXERCISES

Quiz

1. Select the Correct Answer from the Alternatives.

(a) At present, derivatives market is an integral segment of ____ market.

(i) National (ii) US (iii) Commodity (iv) Financial

(b) ____is not a participant in the derivative market.

(i) Arbitraguer (ii) Speculator (iii) Hedger (iv) Insurer

(c) Prices of in an organised derivatives market reflect the —— of market participants.
(i) personality (ii) behaviour (iii) quality (iv) perception

(d) In the absence of an organised derivatives market, ______ trade in the underlying cash market.
(i) Bank (ii) Hedger (iii) Arbitraguer (iv) Speculator

Ans: (a) Financial, (b) Insurer, (c) Perception, (d) Speculator

2. State Whether the Following Statements are True or False.

(a) Participants in forward/futures markets are hedgers, speculators, day-traders/scalpers, market makers and arbitraguers.

(b) Hedger is a user of the market, who enters into futures contract to manage the risk of adverse price fluctuations in respect of his existing or future asset.

(c) Arbitrage refers to the simultaneous purchase and sale in two markets so that the selling price is higher than the buying price by more than the transaction cost, so that the arbitraguer makes riskless profit.

(d) A trader, who trades or takes position without having exposure in the physical market, with the sole intention of earning profit is a speculator.

(e) A Day-trader is a speculator who takes position in futures or options contracts and liquidate them prior to the close of the same trading day.

(f) A Market Maker (MM) is a trader, who simultaneously quotes both bid and offer price for a same commodity.

Ans: (a) True, (b) True, (c) True, (d) True, (e) True, (f) True.

A. Short Type Questions

1. What do you mean by derivative market?
2. When and where was the first futures exchange set up in the world?
3. Why is 20th century derivative market the age of emergence of financial derivatives?
4. Explain the following concepts in the language of derivatives:

   (a) Hedging (b) Speculating (c) Arbitraging
5. Who are the participants in derivative markets? Name them.
6. Write short notes:

   (a) Price volatility

   (b) Global-local openness

   (c) Technology support to derivatives

   (d) Risk management tools

   (e) Innovations in derivatives
7. Explain the following concepts with reference to economic functions of derivatives.

   (a) Management of risk

   (b) Market efficiency through derivatives

(c) Price stabilization through derivatives

(d) Price discovery

8. Why derivatives market is a catalyst for new entrepreneurial activity ?

B. Long Type Questions

1. Briefly discuss the history of derivative markets.
2. Bring out the historical development of financial derivatives.
3. Compare and contrast between hedging, speculation and arbitrage.
4. There are three major participants in derivative markets. They are Hedgers, Speculators and Arbitraguers. Explain their functions with suitable examples.
5. Briefly discuss the factors contributing to the growth of financial derivatives.
6. What are the economic functions of derivative markets? Discuss.

Financial Derivative Markets in India

Learning Objectives

After studying this chapter, you will be able to:

- Know the evolution of derivative markets in India
- Know the derivative exchanges in India
- Aware of derivative markets, tradings and regulatory authorities
- Know the growth of financial derivatives in India

Chapter Outline

3.1 Introduction

3.2 Evolution of Derivative Markets in India

3.3 Derivative Exchanges in India

3.4 Categories of Derivatives Trading and Regulatory Authorities in India

3.5 Derivative Markets in India – The Structural Look

3.6 Growth of "Exchange–Traded" Derivatives Market in India

- 3.6.1 Financial Derivatives
- 3.6.2 Growth of Financial Derivatives Market: The Statistical Analysis
- 3.6.3 Growth of Exchange Traded Commodity Derivative Markets in India: The Statistical Analysis

Chapter Summary

Suggestions for Further Readings

Exercises

3.1 INTRODUCTION

Derivatives market is a segment of financial market. Derivatives have gained a significant position among all the financial products. Innovated derivatives have revolutionised the landscape of financial industry worldwide. One cannot think of the existence of financial market without the derivative instruments.

The derivative market can be divided into two parts, i.e., Exchange Traded Derivatives Market and Over the Counter (OTC) traded derivatives market. Further, derivatives may be commodity derivatives or financial derivatives. Thus, the derivative market whether belonging to commodities or financial have become today, an integral part of the financial system of a country.

In India, the emergence of financial derivatives is relatively a recent phenomenon. But commodity derivatives have a fairly long history in India. Due to the wave of globalisation and liberalisation, the derivative markets in India have been growing rapidly since 2001.

3.2 EVOLUTION OF DERIVATIVES MARKET IN INDIA

Derivatives markets in India were originated in last part of 19th century. Since then, the following sequential development have been noticed:

I. Stage 1: Pre-independent era of commodity derivatives market.

(i) 1875 Bombay Cotton Trade Association Ltd., was set up. It was an organised market.

(ii) 1893 Bombay Cotton Exchange Ltd., was set up.

(iii) 1900 Gujarati Vyapari Mandali was established.

(iv) 1919 Calcutta Hessian Exchange Ltd., was formed.

II. Stage 2: Post-independent era of commodity derivatives market.

(i) 1952 Forward Contracts (Regulation) Act was passed and enacted.

(ii) 1953 Forward Market Commission under Ministry of Consumer Affairs, Food and Public Distribution was set up to regulate the future derivative contracts in India.

(iii) 1956 Securities Contract and Regulation Act (SCRA) was enacted to prevent desirable speculations in securities.

(iv) 1969 Ban in trading in derivatives by SCRA.

(v) 1980 Reintroduction of futures tradings as per the recommendation of Khusro Committee.

(vi) 1983 Government of India amended the bye-laws and regulations of stock exchanges of Bombay, Calcutta and Ahmedabad and allowed to continue carry forward trading in specified shares with carry forward facility.

(vii) 1992 SEBI was set up and SEBI Act was enacted.

(viii) 1993 Ban on carry forward transactions by SEBI. Transactions should be on delivery basis. Tradings in futures and forwards should be permitted in separate market.

III. Stage 3: Evolution of legal framework for derivative trading through recommendations of various committees during 1994-1998.

Sr. No.	Year	Name of the Committee	Recommendations
1	1994	Kabra Committee	Futures trading in a commodities
2	1995	G.S. Patel Committee	Revise carry forward system
3	1996	L.C. Gupta Committee (by SEBI)	Development of regulatory framework for derivative tradings
4	1997	Verma Committee	Introduction of cross-currency (forex) derivatives
5	1998	Verma Committee	Risk containment measures for derivative tradings

Finally, in 1999, The Securities Laws (Amendment) Bill was passed by the Parliament permitting a legal framework for derivatives trading in India in December 1999.

IV. Stage 4: Revolutionized era of derivative market through innovative instruments during 1999-2003, vis-a-vis, through redefined regulatory framework.

(i) 1999 RBI permitted Forward Rate Agreements (FRAs) and swaps.

(ii) Trading in Index futures began on BSE and NSE.

Note: The Central Government lifted a three decade old prohibition on forward trading in securities on 1st March, 2000. Simultaneously in order to promote an orderly development of the market, the Government issued another notification on 1st March, 2000, delineating the area of responsibility between RBI and SEBI.

(iii) 2001 Trading options derivatives on index and stocks began on BSE and NSE.

(iv) 2002 Trading on single stock futures began on BSE and NSE.

(v) 2003 (a) Introduction of Interest Rate Futures (IRF) on NSE.

(b) Introduction of rupee of options.

(c) Permission for futures tradings on almost all commodities. But options on commodities still prohibited.

(c) Commencement of National Commodities and Derivatives Exchange of India (NCDEX) and Multi Commodity Exchange (MCE).

Thus, derivatives trading commenced in India in 2000, with the introduction of Index Futures at BSE and subsequently on NSE. Since then, derivatives market in India has witnessed tremendous growth in terms of trading value and number of traded contracts. At present, the following type of derivatives are permitted for trading in the Indian market.

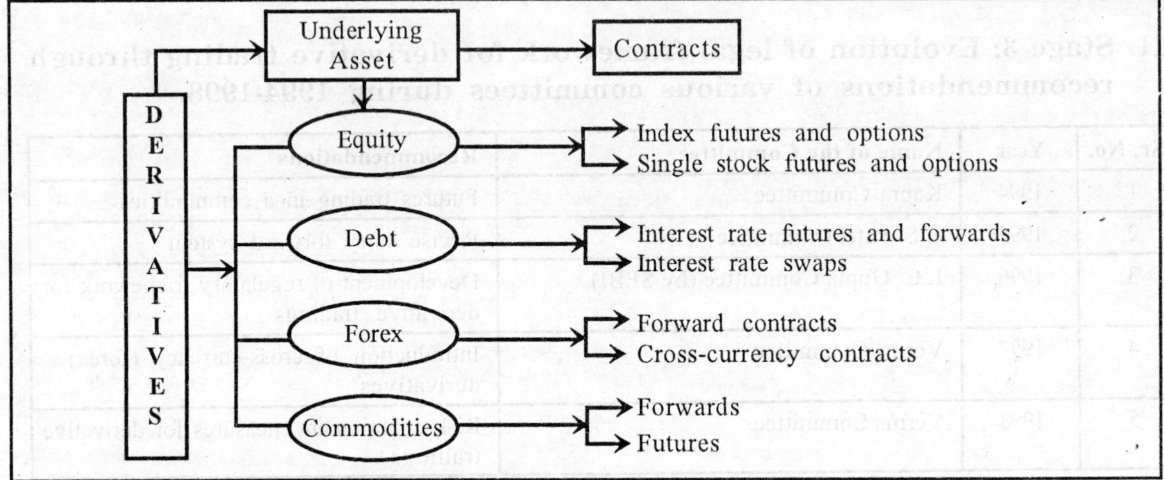

Fig. 3.1: Derivatives Contracts Permitted by SEBI and RBI for Trading in India

3.3 DERIVATIVE EXCHANGES IN INDIA

There are two sorts of derivative markets in India. These are:

(i) Over The Counter (OTC) markets

(ii) Exchange Traded markets

SEBI and RBI are regulatory authority to permit the following stock exchanges for Equity, Debt and Forex related derivatives.

(i) National Stock Exchange

(ii) Bombay Stock Exchange

(iii) United Stock Exchange

(iv) MCX-SX

It may be noted that Forward Markets Commission (FMC) headquartered at Mumbai, is the regulatory authority under the Ministry of Consumer Affairs, Food and Public Distribution, Govt. of India. It is a statutory body set up in 1953, under the Forward Contracts (Regulation) Act 1952. It grants recognition to an association for commodity derivative trading.

Till the end of October, 2010, the following exchanges are recognised derivative (commodity) exchanges in India.

1. National Commodity and Derivative Exchange Ltd. (NCDEX), Mumbai.

2. Multi Commodity Exchanges of India Ltd. (MCX), Mumbai.

3. National Multi Commodity Exchanges India Ltd. Ahmedabad.
4. Indian Commodity Exchange Ltd., Gurgaon.
5. Ace Derivatives and Commodities Exchange Ltd., Ahmedabad.
6. Bikaner Commodity Exchange Ltd., Bikaner.
7. Bombay Commodity Exchange Ltd., Vashi.
8. Chamber of Commerce, Hapur.
9. Central India Commodity Exchange Ltd., Gwalior.
10. Cotton Association of India Ltd., Mumbai.
11. East India Jute and Hessian Exchange Ltd., Kolkata.
12. First Commodity Exchange of India Ltd., Kochi.
13. Haryana Commodities Ltd., Sirsa.
14. India Pepper and Spice Trade Association, Kochi.
15. Meerut Agro Commodities Exchange Ltd., Meerut.
16. National Board of Trade, Indore.
17. Rajkote Commodity Exchange Ltd., Rajkote.
18. Rajdhani Oils and Oilseeds Exchange Ltd., Delhi.
19. Surendranagar Cotton, Oil and Oilseeds Association Ltd., Surendranagar.
20. Spices and Oilseeds Exchange Ltd., Songli.
21. Vijay Beopar Chamber Ltd., Mirzaffarnagar.

3.4 CATEGORIES OF DERIVATIVES TRADING AND REGULATORY AUTHORITIES IN INDIA

There are six categories of derivatives traded in India. These are regulated by the appropriated regulatory authorities in India. A brief outline of these derivatives are as follows:

1. Commodity Futures:

Derivative Contract	Underlying Asset	Regulatory Authority
Commodity Futures	Coffee, oil seeds oil, gold, silver pepper, cotton, jute	Forward Market Commission

Note: There are 22 commodity exchanges recognised by FMC.

2. **Index Futures:** It is future contract on a stock index or other index.

Derivative Contract	Underlying Asset	Regulatory Authority
Single Index Futures	Sensex Index, NIFTY Index	SEBI

3. Forward Rate Agreement

Derivative Contract	Underlying Asset	Regulatory Authority
FRA/Interest Rate Swap (IRS)	Short-term security or national principal	RBI

4. Stock Option

Derivative Product	Underlying Assets	Regulatory Authority
Stock options (Option on individual shares of common stock)	Individual shares	SEBI through NSE & BSE

Note: These stock options are American style. All the shares/securities for derivative tradings are stipulated by SEBI.

5. Stock Futures on Individual Securities

Derivative Products	Underlying Assets	Regulatory Authority
Futures on Individual Security	Stocks	SEBI through NSE and BSE

6. Interest Rate Futures

Derivative Contract	Underlying Assets	Regulatory Authority
Interest Rate Futures	91-days T-Bills 19 Years Bonds 10 Years Zero Coupon Bonds	RBI

3.5 DERIVATIVE MARKETS IN INDIA — THE STRUCTURAL LOOK

A derivative contract (Vayada Kabala) is an enforceable agreement. This agreement may be a standardised contract or a customised contract.

The following diagrams exhibit the structural look of the above concept:

(A) Structural Diagram – 1

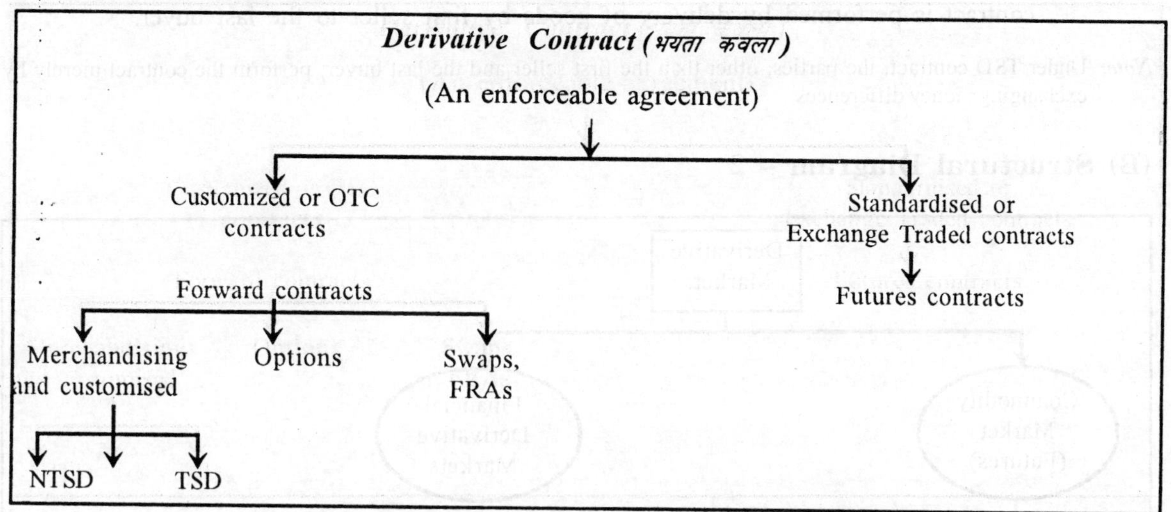

Fig. 3.1: Structure of Derivative Contracts in India

The various derivative contracts as exhibited above are explained below:

1. **Customised Contracts:** All the OTC contracts are customised contracts. Forward contracts (other than futures) are customised.
2. **Standardised Contracts:** Future contracts are standardised. In other words, the parties to the contracts do not decide the terms of future contracts, but they merely accept terms of contracts standardised by the Exchange.
3. **Forward Contract:** A forward contract is a legally enforceable agreement for delivery of the underlying assets on a specific date in future at a price agreed on the date of contract. Under Forward Contracts (Regulation) Act, 1952, all the contracts for delivery of goods, which are settled by payment of money difference or where delivery and payment is made after a period of 11 days are forward contracts.
4. **Futures Contract:** Futures contract is specific type of Forward contract. These are exchange traded contracts to sell or buy standardised financial instruments or physical commodities for delivery on a specified future date on agreed price. As the terms of the contracts are standardised, these are generally not used for merchandising purposes. These contracts are generally for protecting against risk of adverse price fluctuations.
5. **Non-transferable Specific Delivery (NTSD) Contract:** It is an enforceable bilateral agreement under which the terms of contract are customised and the performance of the contract is by giving specific delivery of goods. Cannot be transferred by transferring delivery order, railway receipt, bill of lading, warehouse receipts or any other documents of titles of underlyings or goods.

6. **Transferable Specific Delivery (TSD) Contract:** It is an enforceable customised agreement where the rights and liabilities under the delivery order, railway receipt, bill of lading, warehouse receipts or any other documents of title to the goods are transferable. The contract is performed by delivery of goods by first seller to the last buyer.

Note: Under TSD contract, the parties, other than the first seller and the last buyer, perform the contract merely by exchanging money differences.

(B) Structural Diagram – 2

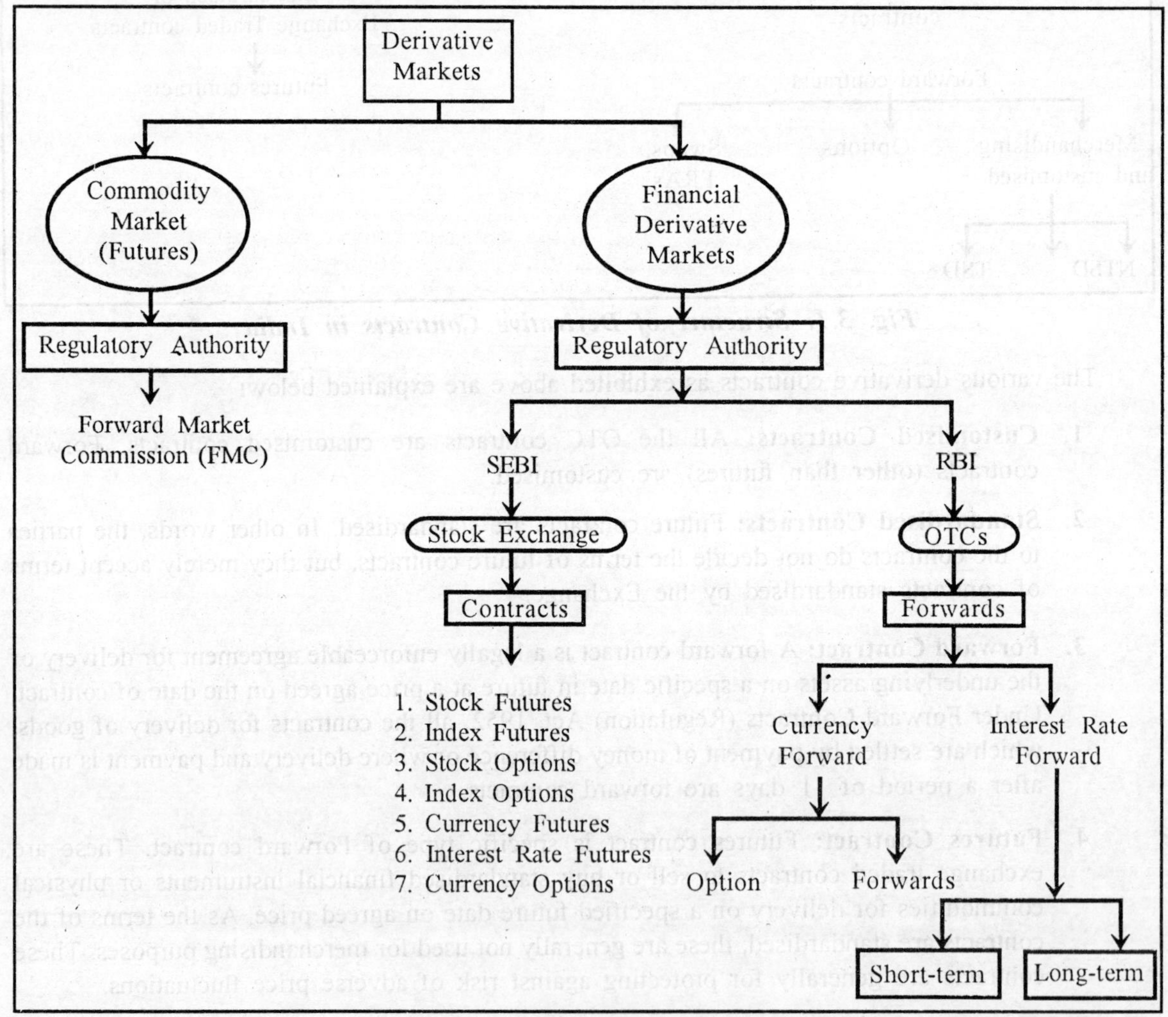

Fig. 3.2: Structure of Regulatory Authorities for Derivatives Markets in India

3.6 GROWTH OF "EXCHANGE-TRADED" DERIVATIVES MARKET IN INDIA

India is one of the most successful developing countries in terms of a vibrant market for exchange-traded derivatives. The exchange-traded derivatives market in India has witnessed tremendous growth in terms of trading value and number of trading contracts since 2000.

The growth trend is outlined below:

3.6.1 Financial Derivatives

Financial derivatives such as Index Futures, Index Options, Stock Futures and Stock Options, etc., commenced in Indian Market in 2000, at BSE and NSE.

(i) Derivatives Products Traded in Derivatives Segments of Bombay Stock Exchange: They launched trading in Sensex based **Index Futures** contract for the first time in India on 9th June 2000. It was followed by trading in **Index Options** on 1st June 2001. Subsequently, **Stock Options** (31 stocks) on 9th July 2001 and **Single Stock Futures** (31 stock) on 9th November 2002. Further Bombay Stock Exchange launched Weekly Options a unique product unparalleled worldwide in the derivatives markets in India on 13th September 2004. It permitted trading in the stocks of the following four leading companies:

(i) Satyam, (ii) Reliance Industries Ltd., (iii) State Bank of India, and (iv) Tata Steel.

BSE also launched Chhota (Mini) SENSEX on 1st January 2008. With a small or 'Mini' market lot of 5, it allows for comparatively lower capital outlay, lower trading costs, more precise hedging and flexible trading. It is a step to encourage and enable small investors to mitigate risk and easy access to India's most popular index 'SENSEX' through Futures and Options. Further development was made by BSE when Currency Futures were introduced on 1st October, 2008 to enable participants to hedge their currency risks through trading on the US Dollars-Rupee Futures platform.

The following table exhibits the introduction and date of commencement of various Futures and Options in Bombay Stock Exchange during the period of 2000 to 2008.

Table 3.1: Derivatives Products Introduced in BSE

Sr. No.	Derivative Product	Underlyings	Date of Introduction in BSE
1	Index Futures	SENSEX	9th June, 2000
2	Index Options	SENSEX	1st June, 2001
3	Stock Option	31 Stocks	9th July, 2001
4	Stock Futures	31 Stocks	9th Nov, 2002
5	Weekly Options	Satyam, RIL, SBI TISCO Stocks	13th Sept, 2004
6	Chotta (Mini)	SENSEX (lot of 5)	1st January, 2008
7	Currency Futures	US Dollar-Rupee	1st October, 2008

(ii) Derivatives Products Traded in Derivatives Segment of National Stock Exchange (NSE): On 12th June 2000, National Stock Exchange started trading in Index Futures. This financial derivative Index Future is based on the popular underlying S & P CNX Index. NSE introduced Index Options on 4th June 2001. Futures on individual securities started on 9th November 2001.

The futures contracts are available on 233 securities stipulated by SEBI. Trading in options on individual securities commenced from 2nd July 2001. The options contracts are American style.

Trading in Interest Rate Futures was introduced on 24th June 2003 but it was closed subsequently due to pricing problems. The NSE has introduced Mini Index Futures and Options with a minimum contract size of ₹ 1 lakh. Further NSE introduced the trading of Currency Futures on US Dollar-Rupee in the Indian derivative market.

The following table exhibits the introduction and date of commencement of various new Futures and Options in National Stock Exchange during the period from 2000 to 2008:

Table 3.2: Derivatives Products Introduced in NSE

Sr. No.	Derivatives Products Traded with Underlying Asset	Date of Introduction
1	Index Futures – S & P CNX Nifty	June 12, 2000
2	Index Options – S & P CNX Nifty	June 4, 2001
3	Stock Option on 233 Stocks	July 2, 2001
4	Stock Futures on 233 Stocks	November 9, 2001
5	Interest Rate Futures – T-Bills and 10 Years Bond	June 23, 2003
6	CNX IT Futures & Options	August 29, 2003
7	Bank Nifty Futures & Options	June 13, 2005
8	CNX Nifty Junior Futures & Options	June 1, 2007
9	CNX 100 Futures & Options	June 1 2007
10	Nifty Midcap 50 Futures & Options	October 5, 2007
11	Mini Index Futures & Options – S & P CNX Nifty Index	January 1, 2008
12	Long Term Option contracts on S & P CND Nifty Index	March 3, 2008
13	Currency Futures on US Dollar-Rupee	August 29, 2008
14	S & P CNX Defty Futures & Options	December 10, 2008

3.6.2 Growth of Financial Derivatives Market: The Statistical Analysis

In India, Equity Derivatives Market has registered an "explosive growth" and is expected further growth in future. Since 2000, Financial Derivatives Market in India has shown a remarkable growth both in terms of volumes and number of traded contracts.

The trading results and growth trend of derivatives in NSE and BSE during the period for 2000 to 2008, are furnished below:

Table 3.3: NSE Derivatives Segment Turnover (₹ Cr.)

Year	Index Futures	Stock Futures	Index Options	Stock Options	Interest Rate Futures	Total	Average Daily Turnover
2008-09	2583617.92	2558863,55	2358916.90	149498.40	0.00	7650896.80	46938.02
2007-08	3820667.27	7548563.23	1362110.88	359136.55	0.00	13090477.75	52153.30
2006-07	2539574	3830967	791906	193795	0	7356242	29543
2005-06	1513755	2791697	338469	180253	0	4824174	19220
2004-05	772147	1484056	121943	168836	0	2546982	10107
2003-04	554446	1305939	52816	217207	202	2130610	8388
2002-03	43952	286533	9246	100131	–	439862	1752
2001-02	21483	51515	3765	25163	–	101926	410
2000-01	2365	–	–	–	–	2365	11

Source: Complied from NSE Website

Table 3.4: Number of Contract Traded at NSE Derivatives Segment

Year	Index Futures	Stock Futures	Index Options	Stock Options	Interest Rate Futures	Total
2008-09	136476747	149159997	116790708	7826231	0	410253682
2007-08	156598579	203587952	55366038	9460631	0	425013200
2006-07	81487424	104955401	25157438	5283310	0	216883573
2005-06	58537886	80905493	12935116	5240776	0	157619271
2004-05	21635449	47043066	3293558	5045112	0	77017185
2003-04	17191668	32368842	1732414	5583071	10781	56886776
2002-03	2126763	10676843	442241	3523062	–	16768909
2001-02	1025588	1957856	175900	1037529	–	4196873
2000-01	90580	–	–	–	–	90580

Source: Complied from NSE Website

Table 3.5: BSE Derivatives Segment Turnover

Year	Index Futures	Stock Futures	Index Options		Stock Options		Total
			Call	Put	Call	Put	
2007-08	234660	7609	31	8	0	0	242309
2006-07	55491	3515	0	0	0	0	59006
2005-06	5	1	3	0	0	0	9
2004-05	13600	213	1471	827	2	0	16112

2003-04	6572	5171	0	0	174	157	12452
2002-03	1811	644	1	0	21	0	2478
2001-02	1276	452	39	45	79	35	1922
2000-01	1673	–	–	–	–	–	1673

Source: Complied from BSE Website and Various Issues of SEBI Bulletins

Table 3.6: Number of Contract Traded at BSE Derivatives Segment

Year	Index Futures	Stock Futures	Index Options		Stock Options		Total
			Call	Put	Call	Put	
2007-08	7157078	295117	951	210	9	6	7453371
2006-07	1638779	142433	2	2	0	1	1545169
2005-06	89	12	100	0	2	0	03
2004-05	449630	6725	48065	27210	72	17	531719
2003-04	246443	128193	1	0	4391	3230	382258
2002-03	111324	25842	41	2	783	19	138037
2001-02	79552	17951	1139	1276	3605	1500	105527
2000-01	77743	–	–	–	–	–	77743

Source: Complied from BSE Website and SEBI Bulletin

The growth and development of financial derivatives markets are encouraging. It is observed that the equity derivatives markets on the NSE and BSE have been restricted to only four products namely Index Futures Stock Futures, Index Options and Stock Options upto December 2008. Further these derivatives are also limited to certain selected stocks only. Recently as per the recommendation of SEBI, newly innovated derivatives are added to contribute extra mileage in the derivative growth.

3.6.3 Growth of Exchange Traded Commodity Derivatives Market in India: The Statistical Analysis

It is found that the Exchange Traded Commodity derivatives have realised its full potential in terms of growth and trading during the period from 2002-03 to 2008-09. The following growth results are marked:

Table 3.7: Commodity Derivatives in India

Year	Volume of Derivative Trading (in lakh tonnes)	Value of Derivative Trading (in ₹ crores)
2002-03	314.46	66530.74
2003-04	492.99	129363.68
2004-05	1942.10	571759.56
2005-06	6788.71	2155122.02

2006-07	6129.29	3676926.67
2007-08	5573.41	4065989.47
2008-09	3810.90	3316206.92

Source: Forward Market Commission Reports

CHAPTER SUMMARY

This chapter highlights the financial derivative markets in India. The evolution and growth of derivatives markets in India witnessed in four stages till 2011. The stage I, was the pre-independent era of commodity derivatives markets. During this era, only few commodity exchanges were formed till 1919. The second stage was the post-independent era of commodity derivatives. During this era, Forward Contract (Regulation) Act was passed in 1952. Only few developments were witnessed till the SEBI Act was passed in 1992. The stage three was the era of evolution of legal framework for derivatives through recommendations of various committees during 1994-1998, like Kabra Committee, G.S. Patel Committee, L.C. Gupta Committee, Verma Committee, etc. Finally in 1999, The Securities Law (Amendment) Bill was passed by the Parliament permitting a legal framework for derivatives tradings in India in December, 1999. The stage four is the revolutionised era of derivative market through innovative instruments since 2000. Till 2011, four stock exchanges and twenty-one commodity exchanges were associated legally for derivative tradings. The derivative instruments like Commodity Futures, Index Futures, Forward Rate Agreements, Stock Option, Stock Futures on Individual Securities, Interest Rate Futures were permitted to trade. The Forward market commission have clearly defined the terms and conditions of various derivative contracts like OTC, Exchange traded, NTSD, TSD, FRAs, Swaps and Futures for creating a better platform for the derivative players. The regulatory framework of derivative markets has exhibited in structural diagrammatic form for easy understanding.

At the end of the chapter, the growth of exchange traded of financial derivatives as well as commodity derivatives in India have been presented in a systematic manner along with statistical achievements.

SUGGESTIONS FOR FURTHER READINGS

1. Susan, Thomas, *Derivatives Markets in India*, Tata McGraw-Hill, New Delhi, 2003.
2. Somanathan, T.V., *Derivatives*, Tata McGraw-Hill, New Delhi, 2005.

EXERCISES

Quiz

1. Select Whether the Following Statements are True or False.

(a) Forward Markets Commission regulates the trading of the commodities futures.

(b) Index futures based on Sensex and NIFTY index are traded under the supervision of SEBI.

(c) NTSD contract stands for Non-transferable Specific Delivery contract.

(d) NSE/BSE derivatives trading was started in June 2001.

(e) The two types of derivative tradings are exchange traded derivatives and over-the-counter traded derivatives.

(f) FRA is a derivative contract by which counterparties lock-in a forward interest note.

(g) The first exchange traded financial derivative in India commenced with the trading of index futures.

(h) Interest Rate Futures is not an example of a derivative on security derivative.

(i) Hedgers, Speculators and Arbitrageurs are the participants in the derivative markets.

(j) Nifty includes the 50 most liquid stocks that trades on NSE.

Ans: (a) True, (b) True, (c) True, (d) True, (e) True, (f) True, (h) True, (i) True, (j) True.

A. Short Type Questions

1. What are the two important parts of derivative markets in India?
2. Differentiate between Exchange Traded derivatives and Over-the-Counter derivatives.
3. What are the instruments traded in derivative market?
4. What are the recommendations of various committees during 1994-1998, on derivatives tradings in India?
5. Give a list of stock exchanges which are recognised for derivative tradings in India.
6. What is NTSD?
7. What do you mean by TSD?
8. What is customised contract?
9. What is standardised contract?
10. Write a short note on:

    (a) Forward Market Commission

    (b) Derivative Regulatory Authority in India

B. Long Type Questions

1. Discuss the evolution and growth of derivative markets in India.
2. The evolution and growth of derivatives markets passed through four stages till 2011. Discuss.
3. Briefly discuss the evolution of legal framework of derivatives trading through recommendations of various committees during 1994-98.
4. Write an essay on "Growth of Exchange Traded Derivatives Markets" in India.

FORWARD CONTRACT

Learning Objectives

After studying this chapter, you will be able to:

- Understand the meaning and concept of forward contracts
- Know the features of forward contracts and their advantages and disadvantages
- Understand the Forward Trading Mechanism
- Calculate the pay-off from the forward contracts
- Be familiar with valuation and pricing methodologies of Forward Derivatives
- Know the hedging with Forward
- Understand the offsetting the Forward Position (long or short) before maturity

Chapter Outline

4.1 INTRODUCTION

In finance, a **forward contract** or simply a **forward** is a non-standardised contract between two parties to buy or sell an underlying asset at a specified future time at a price agreed today. There are five types of forward contracts in Indian derivatives market. These are as follows:

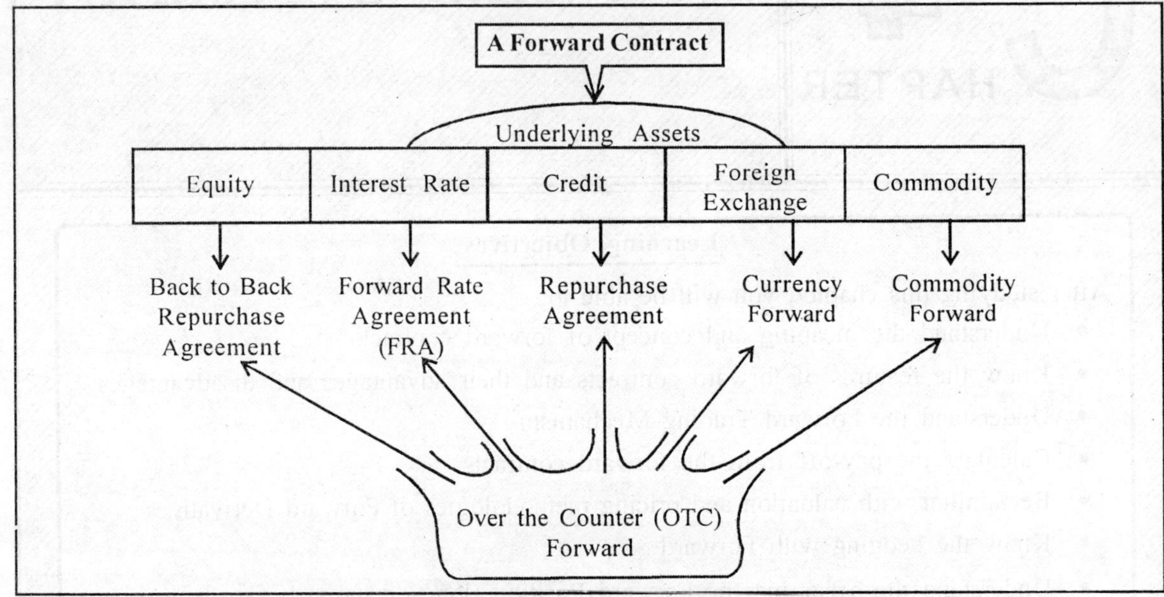

Fig. 4.1: The Forward Market Concept in India

Normally, a forward contract is traded in the Over the Counter (OTC) market.

4.2 FORWARD CONTRACTS – MEANING

A forward contract is a legally enforceable agreement between two parties to buy or sell an asset on a specific date in the future at a price agreed on the date of contract. Essentially, it is a financial contract obligating the buyer to buy and the seller to sell a given asset at a predetermined price and the date in the future. A forward contract is traded in over the counter. Accordingly the terms of the deal can be customised to fit the needs of both the buyer and the seller.

One of the parties to a forward contract assumes a **long position** (buyer) and agrees to buy the underlying asset at a certain future date for a certain price. The other party to the contract known as seller who assumes a **short position** and agrees to sell the asset on the same date for the same price.

4.3 FEATURES OF A FORWARD CONTRACT

1. It is an Enforceable Agreement: A forward contract is an agreement between two parties to buy or sell an asset. All the terms relating to quantity of assets, quality of asset, price at which such asset will be delivered and the date of delivery etc. are mutually agreed upon at the time of making the contract. A forward contract is governed under the provisions of the Forward Contracts (Regulation) Act 1952.

2. Obligations: A forward contract is a financial contract which obligates the seller to sell and also the buyer to buy a given asset at a predetermined price and the date in future.

3. Customised Contracts: Forward contracts are customised. In other words, the terms of forward contracts are individually agreed between two counterparties. These contracts are also commonly known as OTC contracts.

4. Performance of a Forward Contract: A Forward contract can be performed on the expiry date by settlement. Such settlement may be by actual delivery of assets or payment of differential prices in cash without delivery of assets.

4.4 DIFFERENCES BETWEEN FORWARD CONTRACT AND SPOT CONTRACT

A Forward contract is a non-standardised contract between two parties to buy or sell an asset at a specified future date at a price agreed today. This is in contrast to a spot contract, which is an agreement to buy or sell an asset today.

The differences between a Forward contract and a Spot contract are enumerated as follows:

Points of Difference	Forward Contract	Spot Contract
Timing of payment	Payment is deferred till the expiry of the contract	Immediately as it is a spot trading.
Timing of delivery	Delivery is deferred till the expiry of the contract. In other words, the buyer has paid the forward price on delivery date only.	Immediately as it is a spot trading
Credit risk	Credit risk prevails in a forward contract.	No credit risk as delivery and payment take place simultaneously.

Thus, a forward contract differs from a spot contract in three points, i.e., timing of payment, timing of delivery and the counterparty's performance or credit risk.

Diagrammatically

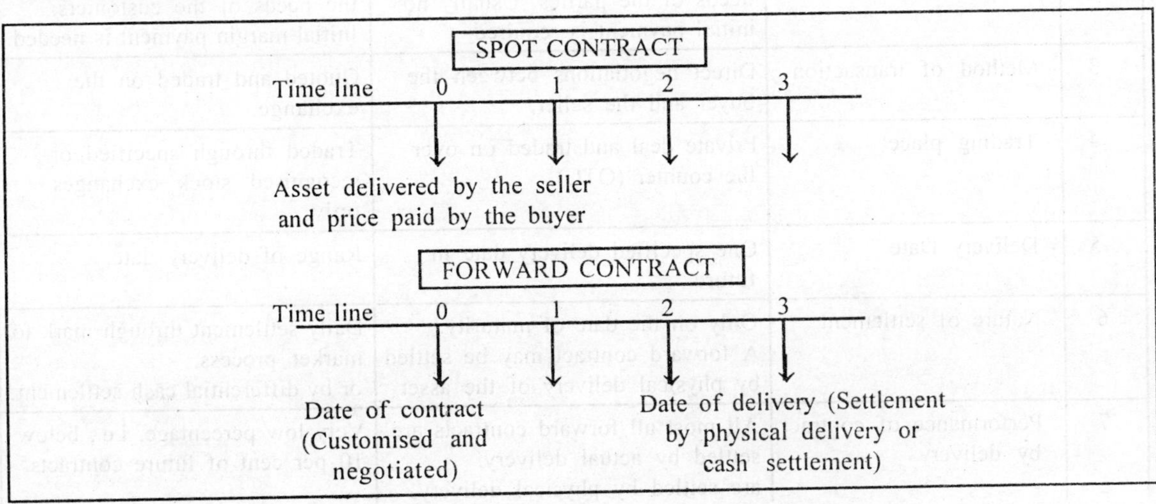

It may be noted that a forward contract helps to mitigate the **Price risk**, i.e., the asset price will change between the date of contract and date of delivery, but the counterparties still to bear the performance risk or the credit risk when the contract matures. This type of risk is not a feature of a spot contract.

4.5 DISTINCTION BETWEEN FORWARD CONTRACTS AND FUTURE CONTRACTS

A **Forward contract** is a private contract between a buyer and a seller. In this contract, the buyer agrees to buy and the seller agrees to sell a decided quantity of products or security, at a price which is mentioned in the contract. The forward contract differs from other contracts in a way that the delivery and payment of the underlying asset does not take place immediately, but in the specified future date. To avoid any kind of problems in future, before signing a forward contract, as a seller or even as a buyer, make sure that all terms and conditions are clear to them. There should not be any confusions regarding delivery terms, locations, quality of the agreed products, credit terms, payment terms, etc. After making sure that there is absolutely no confusion, then sign the contract.

A **Futures contract** is a special type of forward contract. It is a standardised contract, traded on a Futures Exchange, to buy or sell a certain underlying instrument at a certain date in the future, at a specified price. Thus, a futures contract is a publicly traded contract, i.e., they are traded on recognised exchanges under the specified rulers and guidelines of the exchange. The concept behind futures contract and forward contracts are same. However, they differ in the following points:

Sl. No.	Points of Distinction	Forward Contract	Futures Contract
1.	What is it? (concept)	A forward contract is an agreement between two parties to buy or sell an asset (which can be of any kind) at a certain future date for a certain price agreed upon now.	A futures contract is a standardised contract, traded on a future exchange, to buy or sell a certain underlying instrument at a specified price, at a certain future date.
2	Structure	The contract is customised to the needs of the parties. Usually no initial payment is required.	This contract is standardised to the needs of the customers. Initial margin payment is needed.
3	Method of transaction	Direct negotiations between the buyer and the seller.	Quoted and traded on the exchange.
4	Trading place	Private deal and traded on over the counter (OTC).	Traded through specified or recognised stock exchanges only.
5	Delivery Date	One specified delivery date in future.	Range of delivery date.
6	Nature of settlement	Only on the date of maturity. A forward contract may be settled by physical delivery of the asset	Daily settlement through mark to market process. or by differential cash settlement.
7	Performance of contract by delivery	All most all forward contracts are settled by actual delivery.	Very low percentage, i.e., below 10 per cent of future contracts are settled by physical delivery.

8	Probability of premature closure	No.	Fair chance.
9	Guarantee	Contracting parties.	Clearing House.
10	Size of the contract	Depends on how big the transaction and what are the requirements of the transaction.	The size of the contract is standardised through Future Exchange.
11	Risk	There is a chance of non-performance risk as well as credit default risk.	No such chance occurs in a future contract as it is an Exchange traded deal.
12	Quantum of counterparty risk	High counterparty risk.	Low counterparty risk.

4.6 HOW DO FORWARD CONTRACTS WORK?

A forward contract methodology involves the following two sequential steps:

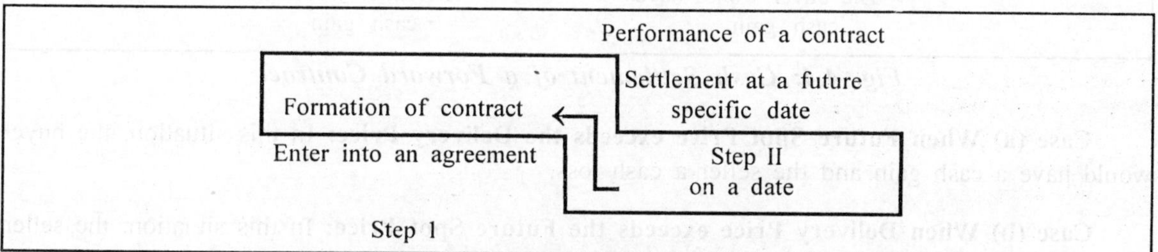

Fig. 4.2: The Steps in Forward Contract

Step I:

In a forward contract, the buyer and the seller enter into an agreement on a particular date, i.e., agreement date. They agree upon a price, quantity and date in the future in which the contract will be performed. Since it is a trade over the counter (OTC), so the terms of the agreement can be customised to the needs of both the buyer and seller.

Step II: Performance of a Forward Contract

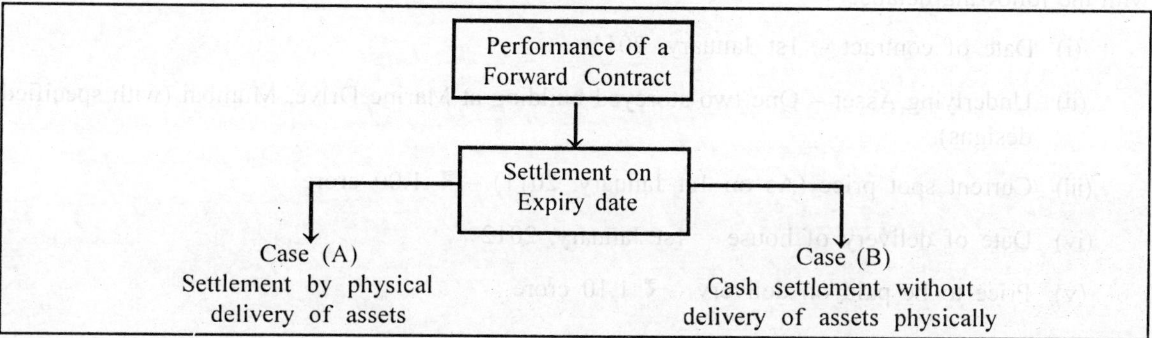

Fig. 4.3: Performance of a Forward Contract

Performance of a future contract entails settlement by both the parties on the date of its expiry. There are two ways the settlement can be made:

(a) Settlement by Physical Delivery of Assets: On the delivery date, the buyer pays the seller the agreed upon price and receives the agreed upon quantity of the asset.

(b) Cash Settlement for Different Prices without Physical Delivery of Goods: Cash settlement is an alternative way of discharging a forward contract without physical delivery of the goods. In this method, there may be the following two alternative situations on the date of expiry.

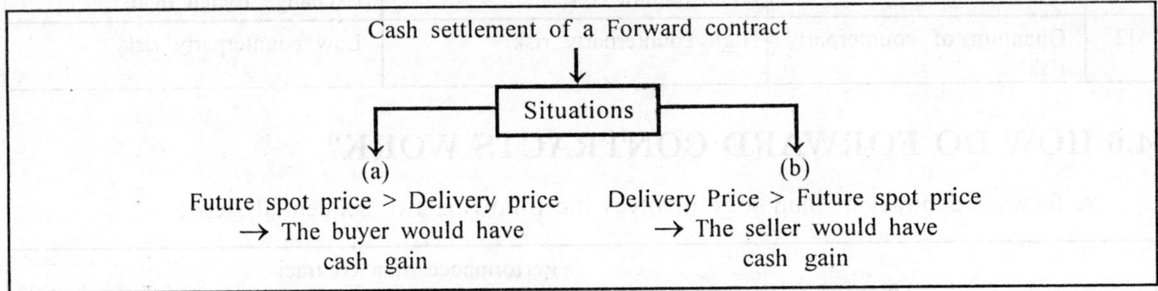

Fig. 4.4: Cash Settlement of a Forward Contract

Case (a) When Future Spot Price exceeds the Delivery Price: In this situation, the buyer would have a cash gain and the seller a cash loss.

Case (b) When Delivery Price exceeds the Future Spot Price: In this situation, the seller has a cash gain and a buyer has a cash loss.

Notes : **(i)** The market price or spot price of an asset on the expiry date is known as **Future Spot price**.

(ii) In cash settled forward contracts, both the parties agree to simply pay the profits or loss on the assets, rather than physically exchanging the assets.

(iii) A forward contract of cash settled nature is a **"Zero-sum-game"**, i.e., the cash profit of one party is equal to the cash loss of the counterparty.

Example 1

Mrs Uma wants to purchase a house from Mr Shankar. Both have entered into a forward contract with the following details:

(i) Date of contract – 1st January, 2011

(ii) Underlying Asset – One two-storeyed building at Marine Drive, Mumbai (with specified designs).

(iii) Current spot price (As on 1st January, 2011) – ₹ 1.00 crore

(iv) Date of delivery of house – 1st January, 2012

(v) Price to be paid on delivery – ₹ 1.10 crore

Solution:

Suppose that the future market valuation of Shankar's house as on 1st January, 2012 is ₹ 1.30 crores. But Shankar is obliged to sell the house to Mrs Uma for only ₹ 1.10 crore as agreed upon. Thus, Mrs Uma would have a profit of ₹ 0.20 crores which is a potential loss to Mr Shankar.

In case Mrs Uma is not interested to take delivery of the house physically from Mr Shankar on 1st January 2012, then she may claim the differential price as cash settlement. Accordingly, Mr Shankar will pay ₹ 0.20 crore to Uma towards final settlement of this future contracts.

Why Forward Price (Delivery Price) of ₹ 1.10 crore is agreed upon between Mrs Uma (the buyer) and Mr Shankar (the seller) on the first day of contract, i.e., on 1st January, 2011?

Here, on 1st January 2011, the delivery price which will be paid or received after one year, i.e., on 1st January, 2012 is determined. In this case, the spot price as on 1st January 2011 is ₹ 1.00 crore and the delivery price as on 1st January, 2012 is ₹ 1.10 crore. The logic is that the underlying asset 'House' is an Investment Asset. If we assume the rate of interest is 10% p.a., then the terminal value of investment of ₹ 1.00 crore will be ₹ 1.10 crore at the end of one year at 10% compound interest. In this methodology, the delivery price is fixed and worthwhile as the opportunity cost has been recovered.

Example 2

A Forward contract is formed between Mr X and Mr Y. The details of this agreement are as follows.

(i) Position of the counterparties:

Mr X is the buyer (Long position)
Mr Y is the seller (Short position)

(ii) Date of contract: 1st April, 2011

(iii) Nature of transaction: Delivery of 5000 kg Basmati Rice

(iv) Date of Delivery: 31st July, 2011

(v) Prices

(a) Current spot price: ₹ 80/- per kg

(b) Delivery price as on 31st July, 2011: ₹ 90/- per kg

Calculate the amount of gains or losses of Mr X and Mr Y if –

(a) The market price as on 31st July, 2011 is ₹ 100/- per kg.

(b) The market price as on 21st July, 2011 is ₹ 85/- per kg.

Solution:

(a) If the market price is increased to ₹ 100/- per kg, then Mr X will be the gainer of ₹ 10/- (₹ 100 – ₹ 90) per kg and Mr Y will be the looser of ₹ 10/- per kg. The pay-off of both the parties:

Mr X : 5000 kg @ ₹ 10/- per kg = ₹ 50,000/- profit.

Mr Y : 5000 kg @ ₹ 10/- per kg = ₹ 50,000/- loss.

(b) If the market price as on 31st July is decreased to ₹ 85/- per kg, then profit or loss of the buyer and seller would be as follows:

Loss to Mr X (the buyer) = 5000 kg @ ₹ 5/- per kg = ₹ 25,000/-

Profit to Mr Y (the seller) = 5000 kg @ ₹ 5/- per kg = ₹ 25,000/-

Thus, the profit or loss pay off is symmetrical in both the cases. This can be shown in the following figure.

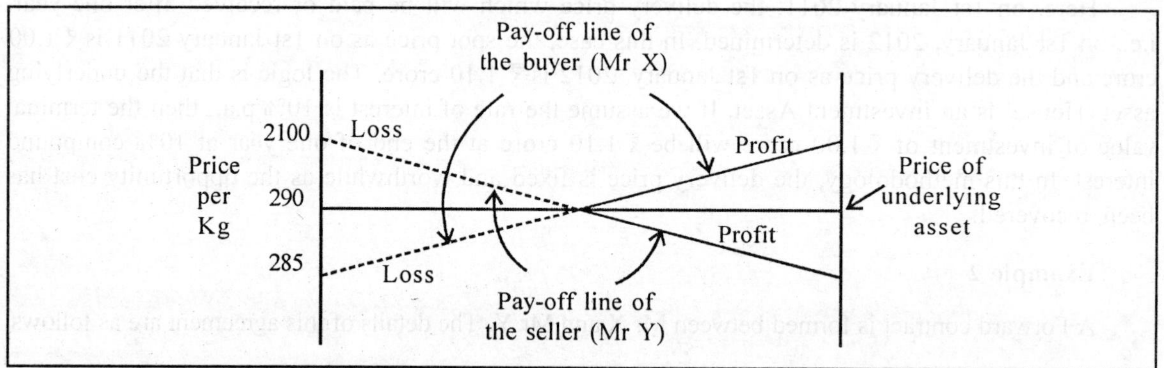

Fig. 4.5: Positions of Parties in a Forward Contract

The buyer always expects the price should move upward whereas the seller has the reverse expectation in a forward agreement.

To sum up:

Forward buyer's gain = Spot Price on Delivery Date – Delivery (or Contract) Price

= Forward Seller's loss

Forward seller's gain = Delivery Price – Spot Price on Delivery Date

= Forward Buyer's loss

4.7 CLASSIFICATION OF FORWARD CONTRACTS

A forward contract creates an obligation for the buyer to buy and simultaneously for the seller to sell a given asset at the terms agreed upon today. These are traded over the counter. The terms of deal can be customised to fit the needs of both the buyer and seller.

The **Futures** and **Options** are the extensions of forward contracts in the following equation forms:

Future contract = Forward contract + Exchange traded + Stringent financial regulation.

Option contract = Forward contract + Right without obligation.

It may be noted that the growth of future markets and option market followed the growth of forward market. Ordinarily, Forward contracts are classified into the following categories:

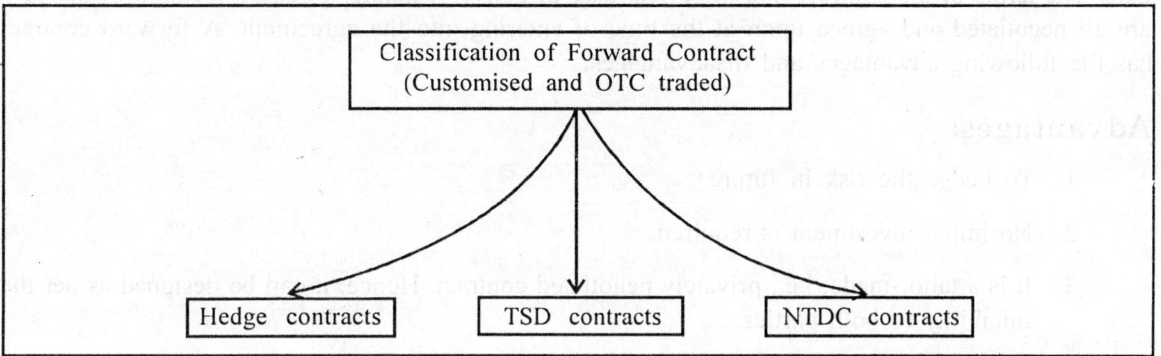

A brief discussion of the above stated categories of Forward contracts are as follows:

1. Hedge Contracts: It is based on the features of **free transferability** and **non-specification** of any particular lot, consignment or variety of assets.

2. TSD Contracts: In this transferable specific delivery (TSD) forward contract, the right or liabilities under the delivery order, railway receipt, bill of lading, warehouse receipts or any other title to the goods are transferable. The performance of contract is completed by delivery of goods by first seller to the last buyer. The parties, other than the first seller and the last buyer, perform the contract merely by exchanging money differences. Hence, a Transferable Delivery Contract (TDC) is an enforceable customised agreement.

3. NTDC Contracts: A Non-transferable Delivery Contract (NTDC) is an enforceable bilateral agreement. It has the special characteristics:

(i) The terms of contract are customised.

(ii) The performance of contract is by giving specific delivery of goods.

(iii) The rights or liabilities cannot be transferred by transferring delivery order, railway receipt, bill of lading, warehouse receipt or any other documents of title to the goods.

It may be noted that as per the provisions of Forward Contracts Regulation Act, 1952, certain goods are regulated or even prohibited for forward contract tradings. But the Government of India have freed NTDC contracts from such regulation or prohibition by issue of notification No. 369(E) dated 1.4.2003.

4.8 ADVANTAGES AND DISADVANTAGES OF FORWARD CONTRACTS

A forward contract is the simplest form of derivative instrument. In this contract, there are two parties, one party promises to buy and other party agrees to sell the underlying asset in a future date. The terms of the contract like the price, date of delivery, quality of asset, location of delivery are all negotiated and agreed upon at the time of entering into the agreement. A forward contract has the following advantages and disadvantages.

Advantages:

1. To hedge the risk in future.
2. No initial investment is required.
3. It is a tailor-made, i.e., privately negotiated contract. Hence, it can be designed as per the suitability to both parties.
4. In certain forward contracts, the facility of TSD, i.e., transferable specific delivery can be enjoyed by the parties.

Even the Government of India have freed the restriction of NTDC contracts, *w.e.f.,* 1st April, 2003.

Disadvantages:

Through a forward contract is a simple form of derivative, yet it suffers from the following limitations:

1. High Risk: There is every possibility of non-performance risk as well as credit default risk in a forward contract. The overall risk is very high as it is a private negotiated contract.

2. Difficult to Get a Counterparty as per the Choice: As a forward contract is a private deal, so to get a right counterparty is a problem in a forward contract.

3. Chances of Cancellation: As forward contracts do not allow the arbitrageurs to derive any gain, so there is every possibility of cancellation of a forward contract.

4. It Encourages the Traders for Reverse Forward Contract: In general, banks or traders may square up their long/short positions by entering into a reverse position, i.e., short/long. It is a typical problem as the parties normally plan to increase bid-ask spread to avoid loss due to price movements.

To sum up, the advantages and disadvantages of forward contracts are depicted as follows:

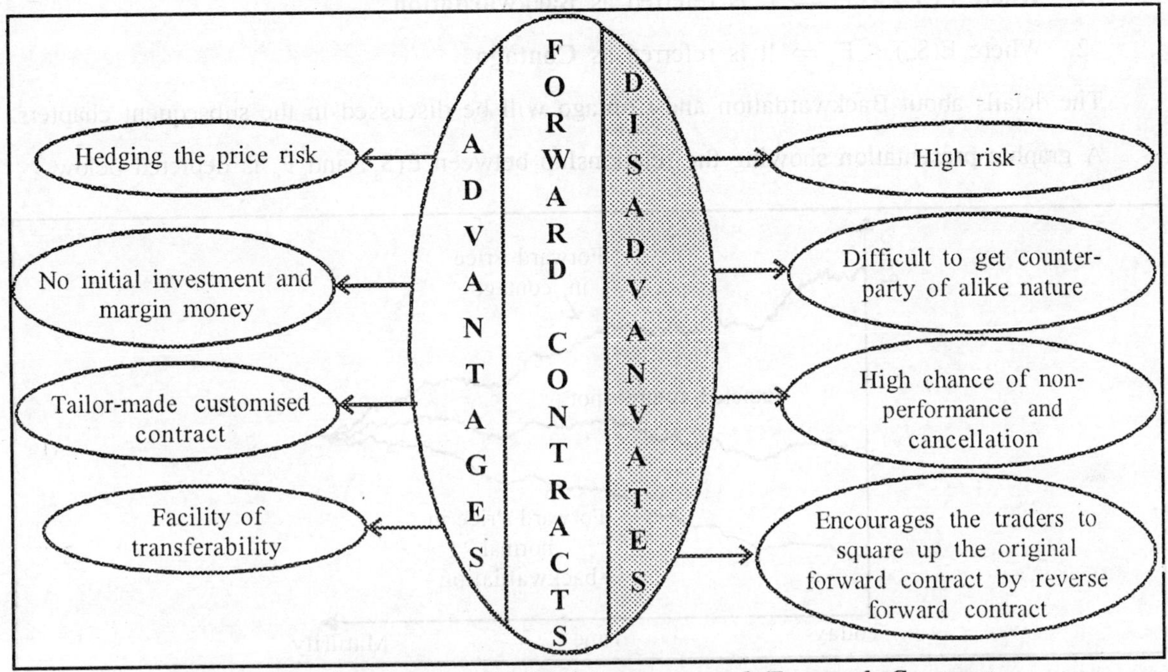

Fig. 4.6: Advantages and Disadvantages of Forward Contracts

4.9 RELATIONSHIP BETWEEN THE FORWARD PRICE (F_0) AND THE EXPECTED FUTURE SPOT PRICE (S_T)

It has been discussed in the earlier section that the Forward Price for a particular forward contract at a particular point of time is the *delivery price* that would apply if both counterparties were entered into such contract at that time. Further, the spot price of the underlying asset on the expiry or delivery date is the market price or future spot price.

Now the question is, can we able to predict the expected future spot price $E(S_T)$ with the help of current forward price (F_0). There are number of different hypotheses which try to explain the relationship between the current forward price (F_0) and the expected future spot price $E(S_T)$.

In the forward market, the main players are the hedgers and speculators. The hedgers are interested to reduce risk and collectively hold a net short position. While, the speculators are interested in making money and hold a net long position.

Thus, if speculators are holding a net long position, it must be the case that the $E(S_T)$ is greater than the (F_0). In other words, the expected pay-off to the speculator at maturity.

$[E(S_T)] - [k]$, where k is the delivery price at maturity

Note: At the time of formation of a forward contract, there is no difference between the delivery price (k) and forward price (F_0).

Market situations: On comparison between $E(S_T)$ and (F_0), we may get the following situation:

1. Where $E(S_T) > F_0 \Rightarrow$ It is referred as **Backwardation**
2. Where $E(S_T) < F_0 \Rightarrow$ It is referred as **Contago**

The details about Backwardation and Contago will be discussed in the subsequent chapters.

A graphic presentation showing the relationship between $E(S_T)$ and F_0 is depicted below.

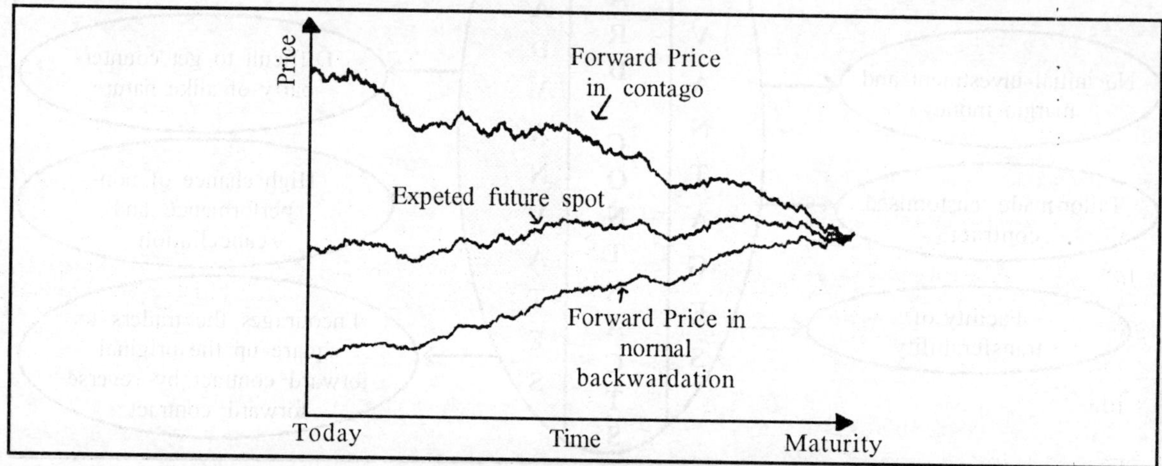

Fig. 4.7: Relationship between Forward Price and Expected Future Spot Price

4.10 DETERMINATION OF FORWARD PRICES

A forward contract is an agreement between two parties in which one party agrees to buy or sell an asset at a fixed time in the future for a particular price that they agree upon today. It is actually a private contract between the buyer and the seller. Essentially, the buyer agrees to buy and the seller agrees to sell a decided quantity of products or security (assets), at a **Price** which is mentioned in the contract. This forward contract differs from other contracts in a way that the delivery and payment does not take place immediately, but in the specified future date which is mentioned in the agreement. On the delivery date, the buyer pays the seller the agreed upon price and receives the agreed upon quantity. This price agreed upon which is specified in a forward contract is called **delivery price**. This price must be "fair", i.e., it must be determined in such a way that the value of the contract to both parties is zero. This concept is based on the principle of **"no arbitrage"**.

To understand the pricing methodology, one has to get clear concept on the following pricing terminologies.

1. **Spot Price:** Price of the underlying asset for immediate delivery. It is known to both buyer and seller.

2. **Future Spot Price:** The spot price at maturity of the contract. It is not known to buyer or seller at the time of contract. Thus, it is the market price that will prevail on the date of maturity.

3. **Delivery Price:** The price which is agreed upon to be paid by the buyer to the seller at the maturity of the forward contract is called **delivery price**. It is the forward contract price.

   Features of Delivery Price:

   (i) Delivery Price is predetermined. It is determined at the first day of the contract. Hence, it is called forward contract price.

   (ii) It is a negotiated price. Both buyer and seller agree this price mutually for transaction in a future date.

   (iii) It is paid by the buyer to the seller on delivery date, i.e., date of maturity.

4. **The Forward Price:** In general, "Delivery Price" is the Forward Price on maturity of the forward contract.

• In special, the forward price at a particular time is the delivery price if the contracts were entered into at that time. Let A and B entered into a Forward contract. The date of delivery is 31st March, 2011. The dates of contract and respectively delivery prices are as follows:

Date of Contract (For Same Asset)	Forward Price on 31st March, 2011
1st January, 2011	25,00,000
15th January, 2011	24,98,000
31st January, 2011	24,96,000

The question now is how to determine a fair (no arbitrage) delivery price that both parties can agree upon. To determine the most fair delivery price, the following three factors must be judiciously considered:

1. Nature of the underlying asset
2. Generation of income during contract period
3. Cost of holding the underlying assets during contract period

Consider the following figure:

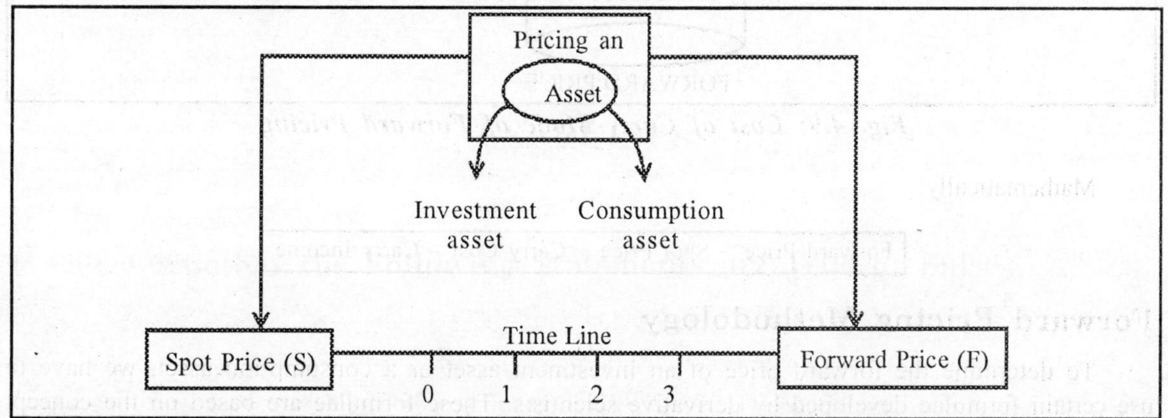

Fig. 4.8: Conceptual Relationship between Spot Price and Forward Price of an Asset

Forward price of an asset is based on the principle of spot-forward parity. This principle provides the link between the spot and forward price of the underlying asset. The overall effect can be described as **cost of carry**. There are three components of cost of carry effect. These components are as follows:

1. Nature of Underlying Asset: The asset may be:

(a) An Investment asset, i.e., an asset held primarily for investment purpose such as gold, financial securities like stocks, shares, bonds etc.

(b) A consumption asset, i.e., an asset held primarily for consumption like oil, soyabeans and foodgrains, etc.

2. Generation of Income: Some known income may be generated by the asset during period of holding, i.e., from the date of contract to the date of delivery. It is called **carry return**.

3. Cost of Holding: Whether the assets are investment assets or consumption assets, certain costs are to be incurred to make them ready for delivery. These costs are warehousing costs, storage costs, insurance of underlying assets, costs, transportation costs and maintenance costs etc. These costs are commonly regarded as carry costs. The following figure makes the point clear:

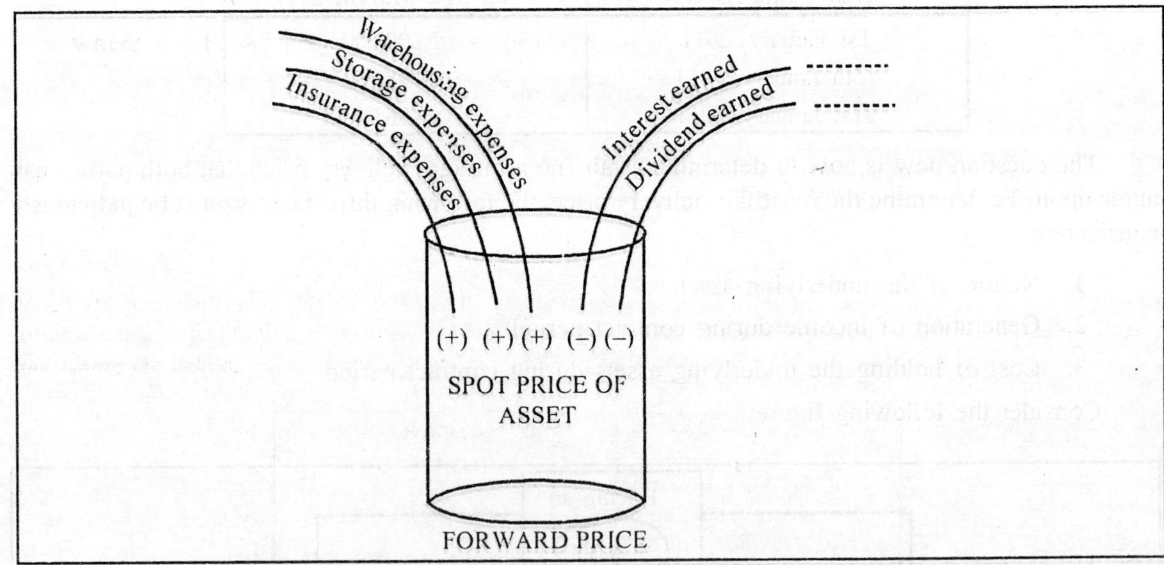

Fig. 4.9: Cost of Carry Mode of Forward Pricing

Mathematically,

Forward Price = Spot Price + Carry Cost – Carry Income

Forward Pricing Methodology

To determine the forward price of an investment asset or a consumption asset, we have to use certain formulae developed by derivative scientists. These formulae are based on the concept of continuous compounding which is discussed below:

Continuous Compounding

Interest on any sum (principal) may be compounded annually, semi-annually, quarterly, weekly or even daily. When interest is compounded daily, it is called continuous compounding. In case of continuous compounding, the future value and present value will be calculated by using the formula.

$$FV = P\,e^{rT} \text{ or } P = FV\,e^{-rT}$$

Where FV = Future value

P = Present value

r = Rate of interest p.a.

T = Time (no. of years)

e = 2.71828

Example: An amount of ₹ 50,000 is invested for 1 year at 12% annual interest. Calculate the terminal value of the investment at the end of the year, assuming continuous compounding of interest.

Solution: FV $= \rho e^{rT}$

$= 50{,}000\ e^{(0.12 \times 1)}$

$= 50{,}000 \times 2\ 71828^{0.12}$

$= 50{,}000 \times 1.1275$

$= 56{,}379$

The forward pricing methodology is based on certain assumptions which are mentioned below:

Assumptions for Forward Pricing

1. There are no transaction costs.
2. The market is perfect and frictionless. Information flows is instantaneous and available freely to each participant.
3. There are large number of participants in the derivative market.
4. Borrowing and lending are available at the equal rate of risk-free interest.
5. Arbitrage opportunities, i.e., "buy at low and sell at high" through simultaneous transaction, are also available to traders.

Foundations of Forward Pricing Formulae

The following elements are necessary to develop the formula for determining the price of a forward contract:

(i) Spot or current price of the underlying asset on the date of contract.

(ii) Contract period.

(iii) Risk-free rate of interest per annum.

(iv) Time to maturity.

(v) e = constant = 2.7183

Now we will discuss the formulae of forward prices of different types of assets.

(I) Forward Price for Investment Asset

In case of an investment asset, there may be three following cases:

(a) Investment assets generate no income

(b) Investment assets generate a known cash income

(c) Investment assets generate a known dividend

Case (a): Forward Price for an asset that provides no income

In this case, Forward Price will be determined with the help of spot price of the underlying.

Formula:

$$F_0 = S_0\, e^{rT}$$

where F_0 = Forward Price of an asset today

S_0 = Spot or Current Price of the underlying asset

e = Constant = 2.7183

r = Risk-free rate of return per annum compounded continuously

T = Time to maturity

Note : The intuition behind this result is that the trader (buyer) wants to own the asset at time T, there should be no difference in a perfect capital market between ***buying the asset today and holding it*** and ***buying the forward contract and taking the delivery***. Thus, both approaches must cost the same in present value terms. Thus,

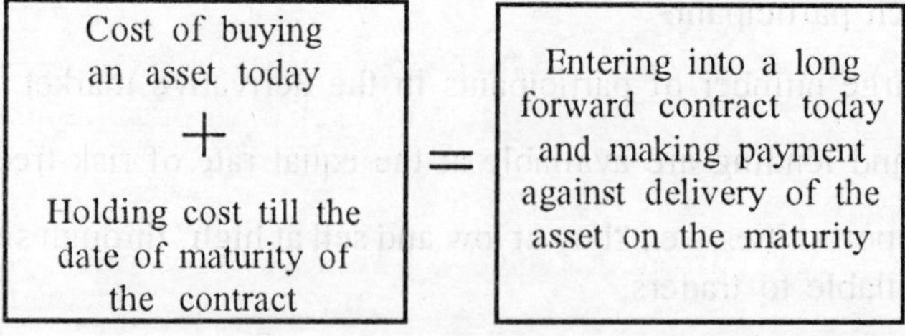

Example 1:

Calculate forward price from the following information:

The current price of the asset (S_0) = ₹ 5,00,000

Risk-free rate of return (r) = 5% p.a.

Time to expiration (T) = 6 months

Solution:

$F_0 = S_0 e^{rT}$

Here S_0 = Spot Price of the asset = ₹ 5,00,000

r = Risk-free rate of return per annum = 5% = 0.05

T = Time to expiration = 6 months = years

= 0.5 years

Therefore, $F_0 = S_0 e^{rT}$

$= 5{,}00{,}000\ (2.7183)^{0.05 \times 0.5}$

= ₹ 5,12,650

Arbitrageur's Investment Strategy: After calculating F_0 by using the formula $S_0 e^{rT}$, the arbitrageur (the trader) may compare with the contracted forward price (delivery price). The contracted forward price may be higher or lower than the calculated forward price. According to the situation, an arbitrageur will apply the following strategy:

Let F_1 = Contracted Forward Price higher than Calculated Forward Price (F_0) and F_2 = Contracted Forward Price lower than Calculated Forward Price (F_0),

Strategy I: When $F_1 > F_0$

(When quoted forward price is higher than computed forward price)

The arbitrageur can buy the asset and will go for **short forward** contract on the asset.

Strategy II: When $F_2 < F_0$

(When quoted forward price is less than the computed forward price)

The arbitrageur would sell the asset and enter a **long forward** contract on that asset.

Example 2:

Taking the data from example 1, we have

F_0 = ₹ 5,12,650

Let F_1 = ₹ 5,20,000 and F_2 = ₹ 5,10,000

Strategy I: When $F_1 > F_0$, the strategy will be as follows:

1. Borrow ₹ 5,00,000 at 5% interest.
2. Buy the asset at current price for ₹ 5,00,000.
3. Enter into short forward to sell the asset for ₹ 5,20,000 in 6 months time.
4. After 6 months, sell the asset at ₹ 5,20,000 and repay the bank loan for ₹ 5,12,650, i.e., 5,00,000 + interest 12,650.
5. Earn the pay-off of ₹ 5,20,000 – ₹ 5,12,650 = ₹ 7,350.

Thus, the trader will have a risk-free profit of ₹ 7,350 using this strategy.

Strategy II: When $F_2 < F_0$

Here, F_2 = ₹ 5,10,000, F_0 = ₹ 5,12,650

The strategy will be as follows:

1. Sell the asset for ₹ 5,00,000.
2. Deposit ₹ 5,00,000 in the bank @ 5% interest p.a.
3. Enter into a forward to buy the asset for the delivery price ₹ 5,10,000.
4. After 6 months, he will receive ₹ 5,12,650, i.e., ₹ 5,00,000 + interest ₹ 12,650 from bank and buy the asset for the delivery price ₹ 5,10,000.
5. Earn the pay-off of ₹ 5,12,650 – ₹ 5,10,000 = ₹ 2,650

Thus, the trader will have a risk-free profit of ₹ 2,650 using this strategy.

Notes : 1. If the Forward Price is F_1 or F_2 whereas $F_1 > F_0$ or $F_2 < F_0$, the arbitrageur will take advantage and earn profit. Hence F_1 and F_2 cannot be fair price because these prices yield arbitrage opportunities.

2. In case of F_0, i.e., $S\,e^{rT}$, there is no chance of arbitrage opportunity. Hence, F_0 will be considered as fair or arbitrage free forward price.

Case (b): Forward Price for an asset that provides a known cash income

In this case, Forward Price (F_0) will be determined with the help of spot price (S_0) of the underlying and the know Income (I).

Formula:

$$F_0 = (S_0 - I)\,e^{rT}$$

where F_0	=	Forward Price of an asset today
S_0	=	Spot or Current Price of the underlying asset
I	=	Present Value of Known Income
r	=	Risk-free rate of return per annum compounded continuously
T	=	Time to maturity
e	=	Constant = 2.7183

Example 3

Calculate Forward Price from the following data:

(i) A forward contract is entered into to purchase a coupon (interest) bearing bond.

(ii) Current or Spot Price of Bond = ₹ 10,000

(iii) Date of Forward Contract = 1st January, 2011.

Date of Maturity = 31st December, 2011.

(iv) Coupon (interest) payments:

On 30.6.2011 (after six months) = ₹ 500

On 31.12.2011 (after one year) = ₹ 500

(v) Risk-free interest rates (continuously compounded)

- 10% p.a. for six months
- 12% p.a. for one year

Solution:

Forward Price will be calculated by using the following formula:

$$F_0 = (S_0 - I)\, e^{rT}$$

Here S_0 = Spot Price = ₹ 10,000

I = Present values of coupon payments = $500\, e^{-0.10 \times 0.5} + 500\, e^{-0.12 \times 1}$

$= 500 \times 0.9512 + 500 \times 0.8860$

$= 475.60 + 443.00 = 918.60$

Now $F_0 = (S_0 - I)\, e^{rT}$

$= (10{,}000 - 918.60)\, e^{0.12 \times 1}$

$= 9081.40 \times$

$= 9081.40 \times 1.2407$

= ₹ 11,267/-

Conclusion:

Here F_0 = Fair Price of Forward Contract = ₹ 11,267/-

If Forward Price is higher or lower than this F_0, then the arbitrageur will take the advantages and will apply Strategy I or Strategy II as discussed in the previous case and will have a gain.

Case (c): Forward Price of an asset that provides known dividend yield (When the Asset pays continues income)

Yield means income expressed as percentage of the value of the asset throughout the life. In this case, known yield means a constant rate of income which is generated by the asset throughout the life of the forward contract.

Examples of Assets giving known yield : Treasury Bills, Equity shares.

The forward price for an asset that provides a known income is calculated by the following formula :

$$F_0 = S_0\ e^{(r-q)T}$$

where F_0 = Forward Price of asset today

S_0 = Spot Price of the underlying asset at present

r = Risk-free rate of interest per annum continuously compounded

T = Time remained upto delivery date in the contract

q = The average yield per annum (income expressed as % p.a.) with continuous compounding, on the asset during the remaining life of a forward contract.

Example 4

Calculate Forward Price of the asset from the following data:

(i) Spot price of the underlying asset = ₹ 50,000

(ii) Risk-free interest p.a. = 10%

(iii) Yield per annum = 4%

(iv) Time to expiry = 6 months

Solution:

$$F_0 = S_0\ e^{(r-q)\ T}$$

Here S_0 = ₹ 50,000

$r = 10\% = 0.10$

$q = 4\% = 0.04$

$$T = \frac{6}{12} = 0.50$$

Putting these values in the above formula, we get,

$$F_0 = 50{,}000\ e^{(0.10-0.04)\times 0.5}$$

$$= 50{,}000\ e^{0.06\times 0.5} = 50{,}000\ e^{0.03}$$

$$= 50{,}000 \times 1.0305 = 51{,}525$$

Arbitrage Strategy

Strategy I: If $F > S_0\ e^{rT}$, then the arbitrageur can buy the asset and will go for the short forward contract on the asset.

Strategy II: If $F < S_0 e^{rT}$, then the arbitrageur can sell the asset and go for the long forward contract on the asset.

Here F represents the negotiated forward price.

II. Pricing of Consumption Assets of a Forward Contract

Consumption assets are typically raw material commodities which are used as a source of energy or in a production process.

Examples: crude oil, coal, iron ore.

The users of these commodities may feel that there is a benefit from physically holding the asset in inventory as opposed to holding a forward contract on the asset. These benefits of holding these inventories are:

(i) Avoid temporary short rates

(ii) Keep production process to continue

These benefits are referred to as **"Convenience yield"**.

Taking the above factors into consideration, the price of the consumption asset of a forward contract will be calculated as follows:

Formula:

$$F_0 = (S_0 + U)e^{(r - y)T}$$

where, F_0 = Forward price at present

S_0 = Spot price of the asset at present

U = Storage cost

r = Risk-free interest

y = Convenience yield

T = Time to maturity

Points to Note:

1. The convenience yield provides a benefit to the holder of the asset but not holder of the forward. So, it can be modelled as a type of dividend yield.
2. Convenience yield is a non-cash item and reflects the probability of future availability of commodities in the market.
3. If users have low inventories of the commodity, this implies a greater chance of shortage, which means a higher convenience yield. The opposite is true when high inventories exist.

4.11 VALUE OF A FORWARD CONTRACT

There is a fundamental difference between the forward price and the value of a forward contract. In the previous section, we have discussed the basic methodologies for determining the prices of the various assets under forward contracts. Essentially this forward price (F_0) is fair and free from arbitrage. So, it is equally acceptable to the buyer and the seller. At this price (F_0), the value of the forward contract is zero at its inception. But at later stage, the price of the underlying asset will change as new information comes to the derivative market.

In such situation, the current value of a forward will be calculated as follows:

Step 1: Find out the current forward price by using the formula:

$$F_{new} = S\ e^{rT}$$

Step 2: Find the difference between the original or old forward price say $F_{(old)}$ and current forward price $F_{(new)}$.

Step 3: Find the present value of the Step 2, i.e., ($F_{new} - F_{old}$) by using the following formula.

$$\text{PV of } \{F_{old} - F_{new}\} = |\ F_{old} - F_{new}\ |\ e^{-rT}$$

Step 4: The result is the current value of a Forward contract.

Mathematically,

$$\boxed{\text{Current value of a Forward} = (F_{old} - F_{new})e^{-rT}}$$

A party to a forward contract may follow the following principles after knowing the value of the forward:

Principle I. At the inception when the forward contract is first written, the value of the forward must be zero. In case of variation, the results will be as under:

(i) If the forward contact has positive value at the inception, no party will sell forward.

(ii) If the forward contact has negative value at the inception, no party will buy forward.

Principle II. After some period of time, the forward contract has a non-zero value because the price of the underlying asset will change as new information available in the market. As a matter of fact this change leads the existing forward contract to be some an asset or liability to one of the counterparties. The results in this situation will be as under:

(i) If the forward prices rise, the benefit will go to the buyer.
(ii) If the forward prices decline, the benefit will go to the seller.

The above principles can be explained through the following example:

Example 5

(i) Counterparties : Mr. Ajaya (Long position), the buyer.

Mr. Bijaya (Short position), the seller.

(ii) Date of contract : 1st January, 2011

(iii) Underlying asset : 1 kg gold

(iv) Spot price on 1.1.2011 : ₹17,30,000

(v) Risk-free interest : 10% p.a

(vi) Contract period : 6 months

Delivery Date : 30th June, 2011

(vii) Delivery Price : ₹ 18,00,000

Additional information as on 1st April, 2011

(viii) Spot price as on 1st April, 2011 : ₹ 17,60,000

(ix) Interest rate as on 1.04.2011 : 12%

Now we calculate forward price as on 1.4.2011

$$\text{Forward Price (F)} = S\ e^{rT}$$

$$= 17{,}60{,}000 \times 1.0305$$

$$= 18{,}13{,}680$$

Here, the old contract, which is having a residual maturity at 3 months, will be valuable to this buyer, as it will enable him to buy at ₹ 18,00,000 because the new forward contract price ₹ 18,13,680 is higher.

Here, the original delivery price (F_{new}) = ₹ 18,13,680

The difference between these two prices

$= |F_{old} - F_{new}|$ = ₹ 13,680

This difference will be paid for the underlying on 30.6.2011. But as on 1.04.2011, it will be equal to its present value.

The present value of this differential amount is the value of the forward as on 1.04.2011 which will be calculated as follows:

$$\text{PV of Forward Contract} = (F_{old} - F_{new})e^{-rT}$$

Where, F_{old} = Original forward price = 18,00,000

F_{new} = New forward price = 18,13,680

r = Risk-free interest = 12%

T = Time to expiration = 3 months

Now, putting these values, we get,

$(13,680)e^{-0.12\times0.25}$ = 13680 × 0.9704

= ₹ 13275.

Result: As on 1.4.2011, Mr. Ajaya the buyer will be loser for ₹ 13,275 and Mr. Bijaya, the seller will be gainer for the same.

SOLVED PROBLEMS

Problem 1. Mr A and B entered into a forward contract as per the following details:

Date of contract	: 1st April
Buyer (Long position)	: Mr. A
Seller (Short position)	: Mr. B
Asset	: 1 kg gold
Date of Maturity	: 30th September
Delivery price	: ₹ 18,00,000
Future spot price as on 30th September	: ₹ 18,40,000

Calculate the profit or loss of Mr. A and Mr. B.

Solution:

Here Mr A will be in profit position while Mr. B will be loser on 30th September. Profit to Mr. A = Future spot price – Delivery Price = ₹ 18,40,000 – ₹ 18,00,000 = ₹ 40,000

Loss to Mr B = ₹ 18,00,000 – ₹ 18,00,000 = ₹ 40,000

Problem 2. Calculate forward price from the following information:

The current price of the asset = ₹ 5,00,000

Risk-free rate of return = 7.5% p.a. (A/360)

Time to expiration = 75 days

Solution:

Forward price will be calculated by the following formula:

$$F_0 = S_0 e^{rT}$$

Here F_0 = Forward price

S_0 = Spot price of the asset = ₹ 5,00,000

r = Risk-free rate of return p.a. = 7.5% = 0.075

T = Time to expiration = 75 days = $\frac{75}{360}$ = 0.21

F_0 = $5,00,000 \times e^{0.075 \times 0.21}$

= $5,00,000 \times e^{0.01575}$

= ₹ 5,07,873

Problem 3. A forward contract is entered into to purchase a coupon (interest) bearing bond. Calculate the forward price of such bond from the following data:

Current spot price of the bond = ₹ 20,000

Date of forward contract = 1st October, 2011.

Date of maturity = 30th September, 2012

Coupon (interest) payments:

On 31st March, 2012

(after six monthly) = ₹ 1000

On 30th September, 2012

(after one year) = ₹ 1000

Risk-free interest rates

(Continuously compounded)

– 10% p.a for six months

– 12% p.a. for one year.

Solution:

Forward Price will calculated by using the formula:

$F_0 = (S_0 - I)e^{rt}$

Here, S_0 = Spot Price = ₹ 20,000

I = Present value of coupon interest

= $1000\ e^{-0.10 \times 0.5} + 1000e^{-0.12 \times 1.00}$

= $1000 \times 0.9512 + 1000 \times 0.8860$

= 951.20 + 886.00

= 1837.20

Now, $F_0 = (20000 - 1837.20)e^{rT}$

$= 1862.80 \times e^{0.12 \times 1}$

$= 18162.8 \times 1.2407$

$=$ ₹ 22534.58

Problem 4. Calculate the forward price from the following data:

(i) A forward contract is entered into to purchase a coupon (interest) bearing bond.

(ii) Current price of the Bond ₹ 10,000

(iii) Coupon rate = 8% p.a.

(iv) Interest is payable semi-annually.

(v) Interest is payable after 3 months and 9 months respectively from the date of entering into the forward contract.

(vi) The maturity period of the forward contract is 10 months.

(vii) Risk-free interest = 6% p.a.

(viii) Spot price of the bond is ₹ 9,500.

Solution:

Here asset is a Bond.

Type of asset: Generating known cash income

In this case, forward price will be determined by the following formula:

$F_0 = (S_0 - I)\, e^{rT}$

Here, $S_0 = 9{,}500$

$I =$ Present value of cash income from investment

$T =$ Time to maturity = 10 month = 10/12

$r =$ Risk-free interest = 6% = 0.06

Now $I = 400\, e^{-(0.06 \times 0.25)} + 400\, e^{-(0.06 \times 0.75)}$

$= 394 + 382.40 = 776.4$

$F_0 = (S_0 - I)\, e^{rT}$

$= (9500 - 776.1)$

$= 8723.60 \times 2.71828\, e^{\left(0.006 + \frac{10}{12}\right)}$

$= 8723.60 \times 1.05127$

$=$ ₹ 9170.86

Problem 5. From the following information, find the value of a forward contract.

Date of contract = 1st January, 2012

Forward Price as on 1st January 2012, with expiry date 30th June 2012 = ₹ 50,000

Forward Price as on 1st April with expiry date 30th June 2012 = ₹ 64,000

Rate of interest = 5% p.a.

Solution:

Current value of Forward $= |F_{old} - F_{new}|\, e^{-rT}$

Here $F_{old} = 50{,}000,\ F_{new} = 64{,}000$

$r = \frac{0.5}{100} = 0.5,\ T = \quad = 0.25$

Forward value $= |\,50{,}000 - 64{,}000\,|\ e^{-0.05 \times 0.25}$

$= 14{,}000 \times 0.98614$

$=$ ₹ 13,806

CHAPTER SUMMARY

This chapter explained the concept of forward derivative along with its features lucidly. A forward contract is a legally enforceable agreement between two parties to trade (buy or sell) an underlying asset on a specific date in future at a price agreed upon. It is purely a customised contract and traded over-the-counter. The five important features of a forward contract are enforceable agreement between two parties, obligations of the parties, customised contract, over-the-counter (OTC) deal and performance by settlement.

A **forward contract** differs from a **spot contract** in three points, i.e., timing of payments, timing of delivery and risk. Similarly, it differs from a **future contract**. A future contract is a special type of forward contract. It is a standardised contract, traded on a future exchange.

This chapter further explained the working modes of a forward contract. There are two steps in a forward deal, i.e., formation of a forward contract and performance of such contract by the parties on maturity.

A forward contract is the foundation of futures and options. The relationship can be understood by the following equations.

(i) Forward contract + Exchange Traded + Stringent regulation = Futures contract.

(ii) Forward contract + Right without obligation = Option contract.

There are three types of forward contracts. These are Hedge contracts, TSD contracts and NTDC contracts. TDS represents transferable specific delivery while NTDC represents non-transferable delivery contract.

A party can enjoy the various benefits of a forward contracts like hedging price risk, no need to invest any money at the time of entering into a forward contract and no need to deposit any margin money. The most important advantage is that it is a customised and designed as per the suitability of the parties. However, the disadvantages are high risk, difficult to arrange a suitable counterparty, high chance of non-performance of contract and cancellation. It encourages the investors/traders to square up the original forward contract by reverse forward contract.

This chapter lucidly explained the pricing methodologies of two kinds of underlyings i.e., investment assets and consumption assets. The formulae for determining the forward prices are:

I. Investment Assets

Case (a): An Asset that provides no income

$$F_0 = S_0 e^{rT}$$

where F_0 = Forward

S_0 = Spot price of the underlying as on the date of agreement

r = Risk-free rate of return p.a. compounded continuously

T = Time to maturity

Case (b): An asset that provides a known cash income

$$F_0 = (S_0 - I)e^{rT}$$

Here I = Present value of known income

Case (c): An asset that provides known dividend yield

$$F_0 = S_0 e^{(r-q)r}$$

Here q = The average yield per annum (income expressed as % p.a.) with continuous compounding on the underlying during the remaining life of a forward contract.

II. Pricing of consumption asset like crude oil, iron ore etc.

$$F_0 = (S_0 - U)e^{(r-y)T}$$

Here U = Storage cost of an asset

y = Convenience yield

At the end, this chapter explained the concept of value of a forward and how to determine it.

Formula:

Current value of a forward= $(F_{old} - F_{new}) e^{-rT}$

Here F_{old} = Forward price on a previous date, i.e., date of contract

F_{new} = Forward price on the subsequent date

e^{-rT} = Present value

SUGGESTIONS FOR FURTHER READINGS

1. P. Vijaya Bhaskar, *Derivative Simplified* – Response Book, Sage Publications Pvt. Ltd., New Delhi.
2. John C. Hull, *Fundamentals of Futures and Options Markets*, Pearson Education Ltd., New Delhi, Second Indian Reprint 2004.
3. Varma, Jayanth Ram, *Derivatives and Risk Management*, Third Reprint 2010, Tata McGraw-Hill.

EXERCISES

Quiz

1. Select Whether the Following Statements are True or False.

(a) A forward contract is a standardised contract.

(b) A forward is traded over-the-counter.

(c) Long position means the position like a buyer.

(d) The market price or spot price of an asset on the expiry date is known future spot price.

(e) TSD means Transferable Specific Delivery.

(f) The forward contract price is known as delivery price.

(g) Buy at low and sell at high through simultaneous transactions are considered as arbitrage opportunity.

(h) Forward price = Spot Price + Carry cost – Carry income.

(i) Forward price for an asset which provides no income is calculated by the following formula:

$$F_0 = S_0 e^{rT}$$

where F_0 = Forward price of an asset today

S_0 = Spot price of the underlying asset

r = Risk-free rate of return compounded continuously

T = Time to maturity.

(j) The forward price and value of a forward contract is one and same.

Ans: (a) False, (b) True, (c) True, (d) True, (e) True, (f) True, (h) True, (i) True, (j) True.

A. Short Type Questions

1. Define a forward contract.
2. What are the features of a forward contract?
3. What are the two steps in a forward contract deal?
4. What do you mean by forward price?
5. What do you mean by value of a forward contract?
6. How a forward contract differs from a spot contract?
7. What do you mean by customised contract?
8. What is credit risk in a forward contract?
9. What are the two methods of performance of a forward contract?
10. What is OTC?

B. Long Type Questions

1. Define a forward contract. Discuss its features with suitable examples.
2. (a) Distinguish between a spot contract and a forward contract.
   (b) Distinguish between a forward contract and a futures contract.
3. How do forward contracts work? Discuss.
4. What is a forward contract? What are the various types forward contracts? Explain.
5. Briefly discuss the advantages and disadvantages of forward contracts.
6. Explain the following with suitable examples:
   (a) Spot Price (b) Future Spot Price (c) Delivery Price
   (d) Forward Price (e) Continuous Compounding
7. How to determine the price for the following investment assets:
   (a) Investment asset which generates no income.
   (b) Investment asset which generates a known cash income.
   (c) Investment asset which generates a known dividend.
8. What do you mean by "Value of a forward contract"? How to determine the value of a forward contract? Explain.

PRACTICAL PROBLEMS

1. An amount of ₹ 70,000 is invested for 2 years at 10% p.a. Calculate the terminal value of the investment at the end of the 2nd year, assuming continuous compounding of interest.
2. Calculate forward price from the following information:
   The current price of the asset (S_0) = ₹ 10,00,000
   Risk-free rate of return (r) = 6% p.a.
   Time to expiration (T) = 1 year.
3. Calculate forward price from the following data.
   Underlying = Coupon (interest) bearing bond
   Face value = ₹ 20,000
   Date of maturity = 31st March 2012
   Coupon interest payments:
   on 30th September 2011 = ₹ 1000
   on 31st March 2012 = ₹ 1000
   Risk-free interest rates (continuously compounded)
   – 8% p.a. for six months
   – 10% p.a. for one year.
4. From the following information find the value of a forward contract:
   Date of contract – 1st April 2011
   Date of maturity – 31st December 2011
   Forward Price as on 1st April 2011 with expiry date 31st December 2011 = ₹ 20,000
   Forward Price as on 1st July 2011, with expiry date 31st December 2011 = ₹ 25,600
   Rate of interest = 6% p.a.

Futures: The Basics

Learning Objectives

After studying this chapter, you will be able to:

- Understand the concept of financial futures derivatives/contracts.
- Define a futures contract.
- Know the various features of a futures contract.
- Compare a futures derivative with forward derivative.
- Know about the various types of futures like stock index futures, interest rate futures, foreign currency futures, bond index futures and commodity futures.
- Familiar with futures trading mechanism.

Chapter Outline

5.1 INTRODUCTION

Futures contracts are exchange traded contracts to sell or buy standardised financial instruments or physical commodities. Today, most common assets which are traded in the futures market are commodities, agricultural products, equities, stock index and so on. It is observed that the Commodity Futures market has witnessed a remarkable growth in India since 2003. During 2003, National Commodity and Derivatives Exchange Ltd., Mumbai (NCDEX) and Multi Commodity Exchange of India Ltd., Mumbai (MCX) were commenced. The three national level multi exchanges, i.e., NCDEX, NCX and National Multi Commodity Exchanges of India Ltd., Ahmedabad become operational during this period and Futures trading started in a large number of agricultural and industrial commodities. During 2002-2003, the exchange traded transactions value was ₹ 66,531 crores which raised to ₹ 40,65,989 crores in 2007-08. The market has grown over 61 times in 2007-08. Now all futures exchanges are facilitating online screen-based trading using a networked computer system. Despite this phenomenal growth and online facility, the economic rationale and functioning of the future market are not clearly understood by many stockholders. In this chapter, we will focus on methodology of designing a Futures Contract and Mechanism of Futures market trading.

5.2 FUTURES DERIVATIVE/CONTRACT: MEANING AND DEFINITION

A futures contract is an agreement between two parties to buy or sell a particular asset on a specified future date. These are traded on recognised exchanges like NCDEX, MCX, NSE and BSE etc. The terms and conditions of a futures contract like contract size (quantity/amount of the asset), price and price limits, delivery terms (delivery place and time) and position of a trader (long or short) are standardised by the exchanges where they trade. Thus, *futures* is an exchange-traded derivative that is similar to a forward.

Definition:

1. *"Futures are exchange traded contracts to sell or buy financial instruments or physical commodities for future delivery at an agreed price."*

   – *Website of Bombay Stock Exchange (BSE)*

2. *"Futures contracts are organised/standardised contracts, which are traded on the exchanges.*

   – *www.derivativesindia.com*

Note: Futures contracts are commonly known as **futures**.

5.3 FEATURES OF FUTURES CONTRACTS

The **Futures** have the following salient features:

1. Exchange Traded

Futures contracts are organised/standardised contracts, which are always traded on the exchanges. In brief:

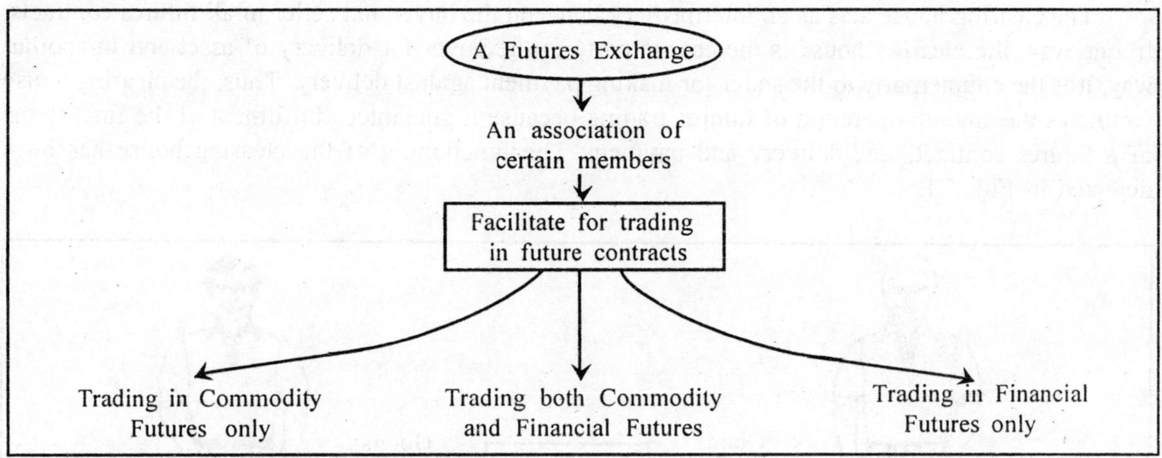

2. Standardised Specifications

Futures contracts are exchange traded contracts to sale or buy financial assets or commodities. All the terms and conditions of these contracts such as quantity of the asset, quality of the asset, the delivery date, the place of delivery, the process of delivery, the price and settlement are standardised (finalised as per the norms and practices) by the Exchange. Once these specifications are standardised by the Exchange, all the parties must have to abide by these specifications and perform the futures contract accordingly. Thus,

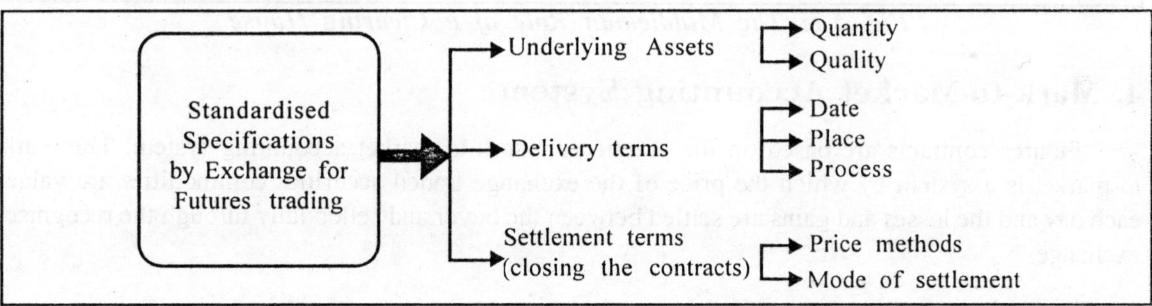

Indeed, Futures are Forwards whose terms have been STANDARDISED so that they can be traded in a public marketplace.

3. Performance of the Contract through an Associated Clearing House of the Futures Exchange

Each Futures Exchange has an Associated Clearing House. The seller has to deliver the asset to the clearing house and the clearing house deliver the same to the buyer. Similarly, the buyer has to make payment to the clearing house and the clearing house has to pay to the seller.

The clearing house acts as an intermediary between the buyer and seller in all futures contracts. In one way, the clearing house is the counterparty to the buyer for delivery of asset and in another way, it is the counterparty to the seller for making payment against delivery. Thus, the clearing house facilitates the smooth operation of futures trading because it guarantees fulfilment of the final terms of a futures contract, i.e., delivery and payment. The functioning of the clearing house has been depicted in Fig. 5.1.

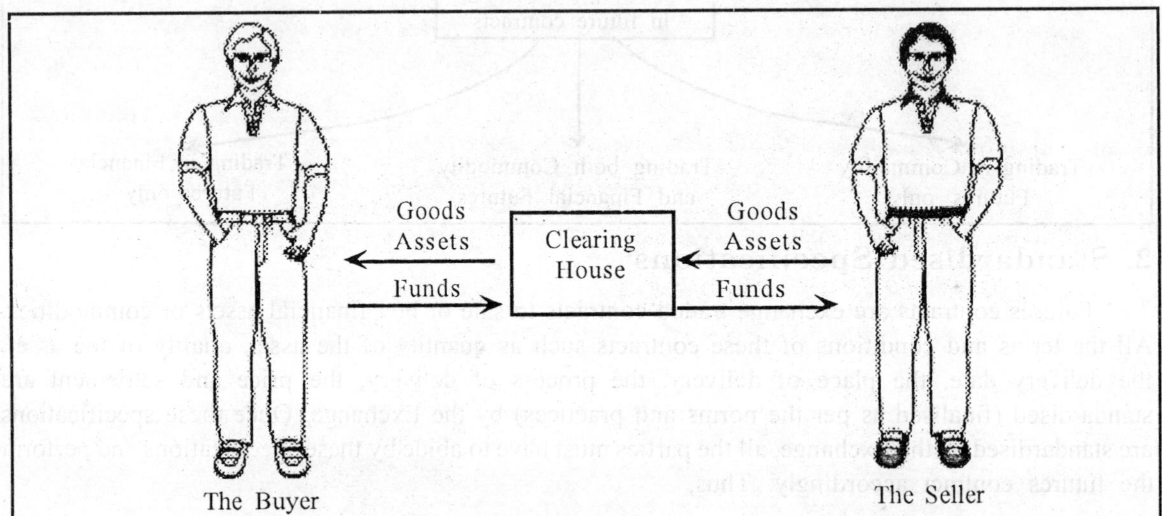

Fig. 5.1: The Middleman Role of a Clearing House

4. Mark-to-Market Accounting System

Futures contracts are based on the practice of mark-to-market accounting system. The mark-to-market is a system by which the price of the exchange traded securities/commodities are valued each day and the losses and gains are settled between the buyer and seller daily through the recognised exchange.

Example:

Date		Price fixed by exchange
1st Day	₹ 18,000	—
2nd Day	₹ 17,500	The buyer has to pay ₹ 500 to the exchange and the exchange will pay ₹ 500 to the seller.
3rd Day	₹ 17,400	The buyer has to pay ₹ 100 to the exchange and the exchange will pay ₹ 100 to the seller.
4th Day	₹ 18,300	The seller will pay ₹ 900/- to the exchange and the exchange will pay ₹ 900 to the buyer.

5. Margin Money

A clearing house collects margin money from the participants of a futures contract. It acts as an intermediary in a future contracts and performs the obligations of both buyers and sellers. Thus, a clearing house undertakes the following two types of default risks:

(i) **In Case of Buyer's Default:** The clearing house has to buy the commodities/securities from the seller and pay the money.

(ii) **In Case of Seller's Default:** The clearing house has to buy the commodities from the open market, give delivery to the buyer and collect the money from him.

In both the cases, the clearing house bears the performance risk as well as credit risk. In order to minimise or eliminate such risks, the clearing house prescribes a margin money system for trading in future contracts. There are different margins payable by the participants in future contracts. These are:

(i) Initial/Ordinary margin

(ii) Market-to-marked (MTM or M2M) margin

(iii) Special margin/Variation margin/Daily margin

(iv) Volatility margin

(v) Delivery margin

The maintenance of the margin accounts will be discussed in the subsequent sections.

6. Basis

Another special feature of a Futures derivative is "Basis". It is normally calculated as CASH PRICE minus the FUTURES PRICE of an asset.

Mathematically,

$$\text{Basis} = \text{Cash Price} - \text{Future Price}$$

It can be either positive or negative. A positive number indicates a futures discount (Backwardation) and a negative number indicates a futures premium (Contago). Basis may change its sign several times during the life of the contract. It turns to zero at maturity of the futures, i.e., both cash and future prices converge at maturity.

It is shown in the following figure:

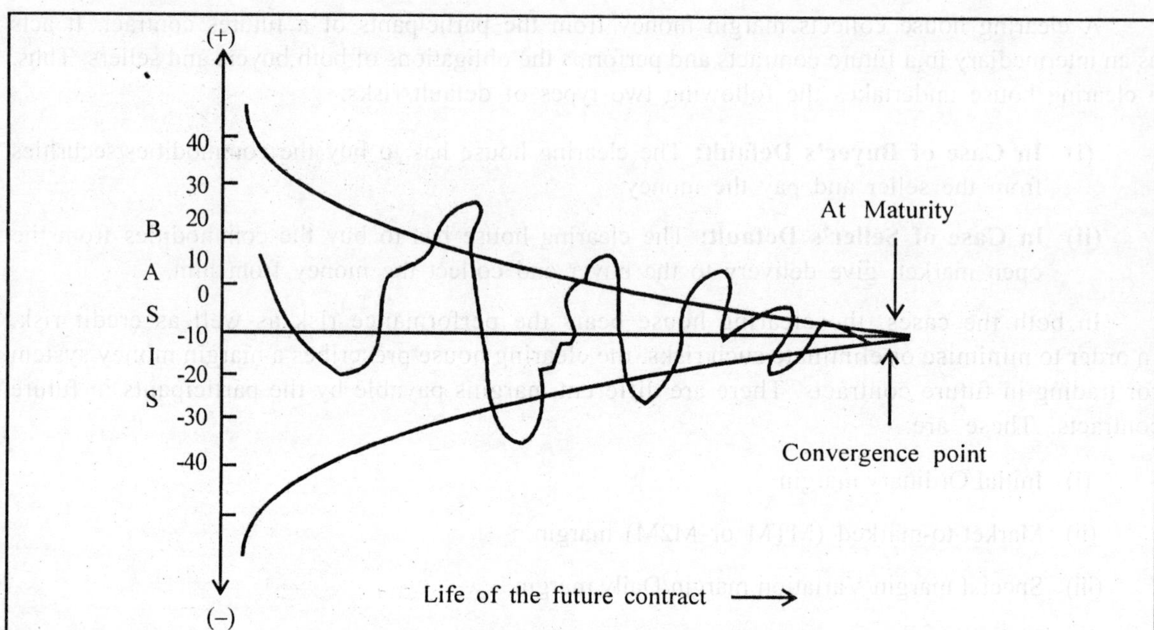

Fig. 5.2: The Basis for Future Contract

Points to Note:

1. Contago: It is a situation where futures contract price is higher than the cash price (spot price).
2. Backwardation: It is a situation where the spot price is higher than the futures price.
3. The basis will narrow down when futures contract approaches to maturity and becomes zero at maturity because at expiration the futures price and the spot price must be the same.

7. Delivery

A futures contract is an exchange traded forward contract. As a principle, at maturity the seller delivers the underlyings and the buyer makes the payment. But the high degree of standardisation of future contract (but not future contracts by the exchanges create risk for delivery). Because the cash market positions of many traders may differ from the standardised specifications of the future contract in terms of quality, location and timing. This results as follows:

(i) 95 per cent of futures contracts are closed out before maturity.

(ii) Only 5 per cent futures contracts are performed by delivery and payment at maturity.

8. Settlement

A Futures contract can be settled by any one of the following methods:

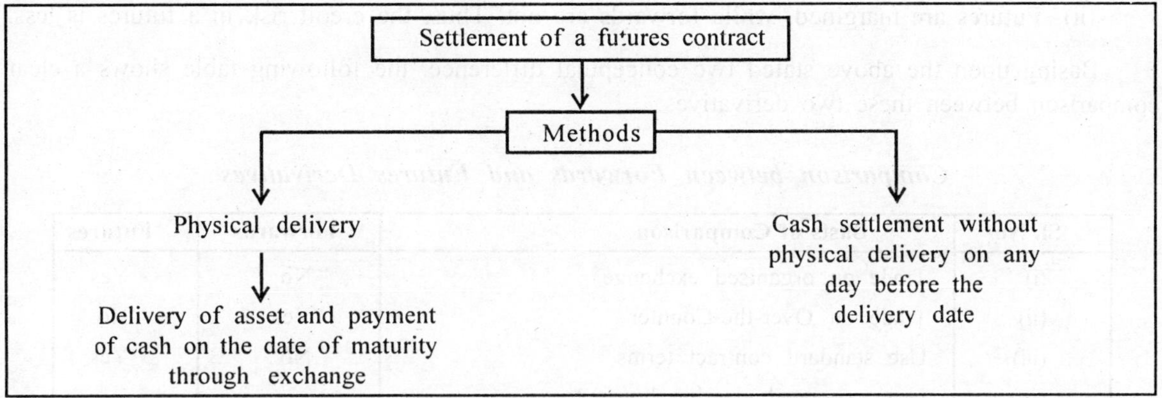

Fig. 5.2.1: Settlement of a Futures Contract

To sum up:

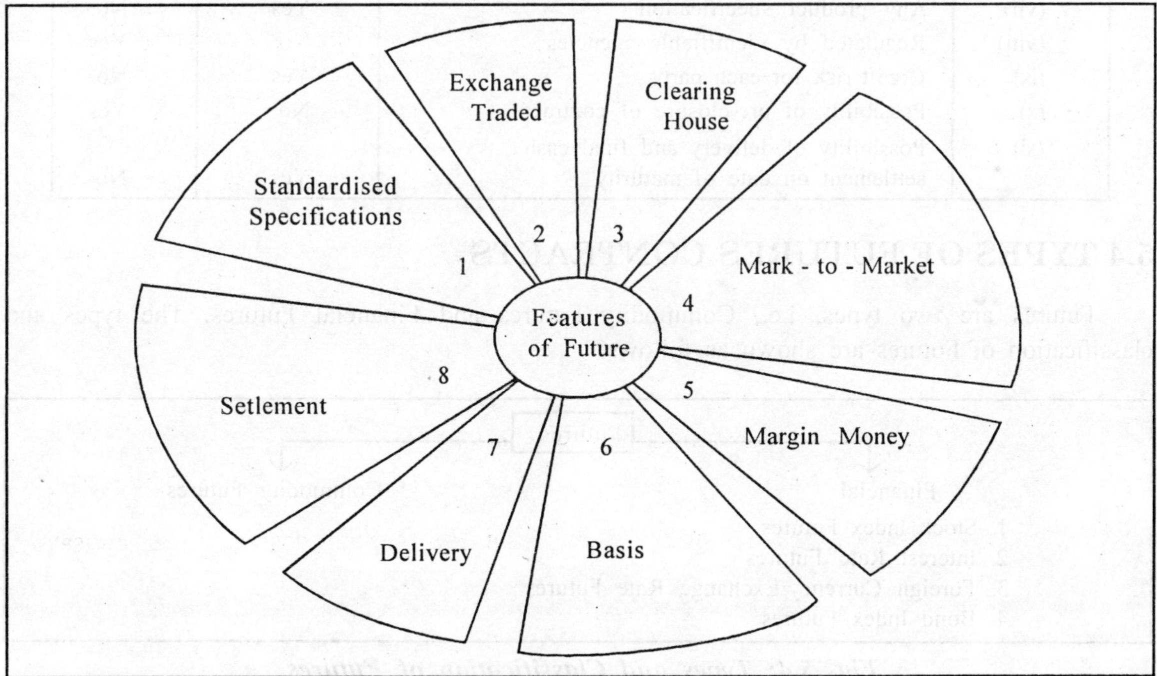

Fig. 5.3: Features of Futures

5.3.1 Comparison between Futures and Forwards

Futures and Forwards are both are similar with respect to deliver of an asset on a future date at a predetermined price. However, they differ mainly in two aspects:

(i) Futures are exchange traded while forwards are traded over-the-counter. Thus, futures are standardised and face an exchange, while forwards are customised and face a non-exchange counterparty.

(ii) Futures are margined, while forwards are not. Thus, the credit risk in a futures is less.

Basing upon the above stated two conceptual difference, the following table shows a clear comparison between these two derivatives:

Comparison between Forwards and Futures Derivatives

Sl. No.	Basis of Comparison	Forwards	Futures
(i)	Trade on organised exchange	No	Yes
(ii)	Trade on Over-the-Counter	Yes	No
(iii)	Use standard contract terms	No	Yes
(iv)	Use associated clearing house to guarantee contract fulfilment	No	Yes
(v)	Require margin payments and daily settlement	No	Yes
(vi)	Contract size – Any quality	Yes	No
(vii)	Any product specification	Yes	No
(viii)	Regulated by identifiable agencies	No	Yes
(ix)	Credit risk for each party	Yes	No
(x)	Possibility of pre-closure of contract	No	Yes
(xi)	Possibility of delivery and final cash settlement on date of maturity	Yes	No

5.4 TYPES OF FUTURES CONTRACTS

Futures are two types, i.e., Commodity Futures and Financial Futures. The types and classification of Futures are shown as follows:

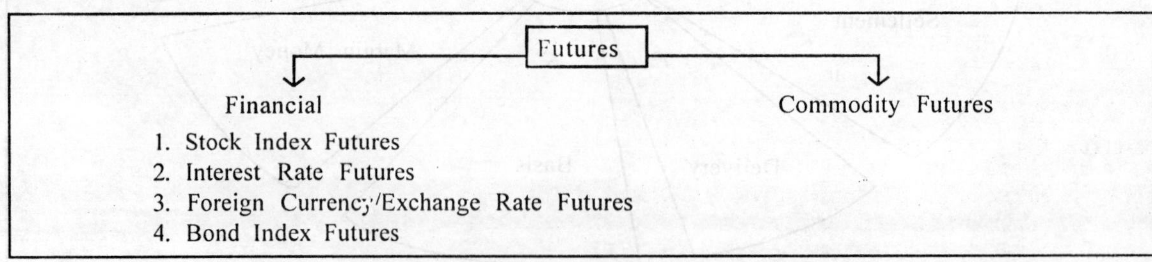

Fig. 5.4: Types and Classification of Futures

1. Stock Index Futures (SIF)

In India, popular stock indices are Sensex and Nifty. Special type of stock indices are also constructed in India like BSE.PSU (Bombay Stock Exchange Public Sector Undertakings) index and

CNX IT sector index. Essentially, a stock index is used to measure the change of direction and magnitude of the general stock market.

Stock Index Futures is an index derivative that derives its value from an underlying stock index like **Nifty** or **Sensex**. An investor can use SIF to hedge price risk of stocks in the stock market. Thus SIF is treated as shielding tool.

Examples of Stock Index Futures:

(a) In India

1. BSE Sensitive Index
2. S&P CNX NIFTY

(b) In other countries

S&P 100, S&P 500 in USA, Nikkei 225 in Japan, FTSE 100 in UK, DAX in Germany and CAC 40 in France.

2. Interest Rate Futures (IRF)

An Interest Rate Futures (IRF) is a financial derivative which is written on fixed income securities or instruments. It is designed to help borrowers and lenders to hedge interest risk. Interest Rate Futures are classified into two broad categories: (a) Short-term interest rate futures, and (b) Long-term interest rate futures. Thus,

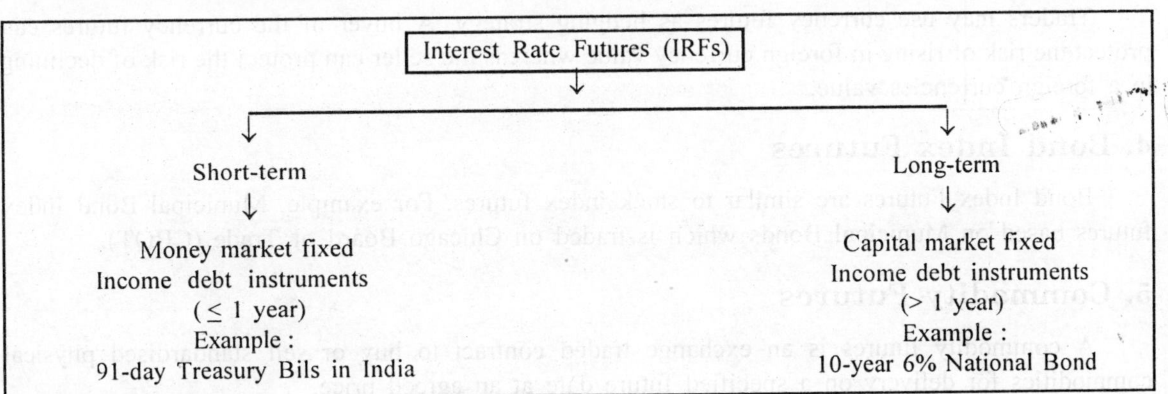

Points to Note:

(i) Short-or long-term fixed interest (income) bearing securities or instruments are underlying for the IRFs.

(ii) In India, only cash settlement is permitted and no physical delivery of securities take place in the interest rate segment.

3. Foreign Currency/Exchange Rate Futures

A Foreign Currency Futures is a contract to exchange one currency for another currency at a specified exchange rate on a future date.

Currency Futures were first traded in CME (The Chicago Mercantile Exchange) in 1972. In India, trading in futures was launched on August 29, 2008. To facilitate the operational framework, the RBI has prescribed the policies while SEBI handle, the trading, settlement and execution aspect.

Foreign currency exchange is a *relative price* exchange rate. It may be quoted as direct or indirect. A direct quote gives the home currency price of a certain amount of foreign currency. In case of indirect quoting, the value of one unit of home currency is presented in terms of foreign currency.

Example:

Direct Rate	Indirect Rate
₹ 45 = 1 $	₹ 1 = 0.2222 $

When a client deals with a futures contract, he has to operate through the commission agent. The commission agent may be a bank or Financial Institution. The client has to deposit the margin money with the clearing house. Daily settlement starts and continues till final settlement on maturity. In the majority of futures contracts, delivery of currencies is not made but is offset by a reversing deal. The client gets only the difference between the two deals.

To sum up, the currency futures are standardised in terms of quantity, size, delivery and margin. These are mark-to-market (MTM) in which at the end of the trading session all the outstanding contracts are repriced at the settlement price of that session.

Traders may use currency futures as hedging strategy. A buyer of the currency futures can protect the risk of rising in foreign currency value whereas the seller can protect the risk of declining in a foreign currencies value.

4. Bond Index Futures

Bond Index Futures are similar to stock index futures. For example, Municipal Bond Index futures based on Municipal Bonds which is traded on Chicago Board of Trade (CBOT).

5. Commodity Futures

A commodity futures is an exchange traded contract to buy or sell standardised physical commodities for delivery on a specified future date at an agreed price.

At present, there are 22 registered/recognised commodity exchanges in India. Further, under section 15 of Forward Contracts Regulation Act, 1952, there are 105 commodities in the regulated list. These listed commodities will be traded only between, within, or through members of recognised exchanges. The commodities other than those listed under section 15 are conventionally referred as **'Free'** commodities. Forward trading in these commodities can be organised by any exchange/ association after obtaining a Certificate of Registration from Forward Markets Commission.

Points to Note:

1. Under the Forward Contracts (Regulation) Act, 1952, futures trading in commodities notified U/S 15 of the Act can be conducted only on the Exchanges which are granted

recognition by the Central Government (Department of Consumer Affairs, Ministry of Consumer Affairs, Food and Public Distribution).

2. A certificate of Registration is required to conduct futures tradings on any other commodities other than the 105 listed commodities.

To sum up,

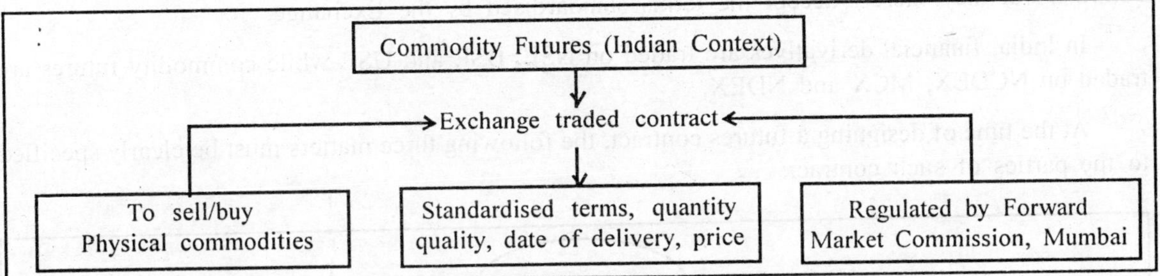

Fig. 5.5: Conceptual Framework of Commodity Futures

5.5 FUTURES MARKET TRADING MECHANISM

Futures contracts are traded on an organised exchange and the contract terms are standardised by that exchange. The trading process of futures contracts are based on the following elements:

I. Futures Contract Design

II. Futures Market Operational Guidelines

III. Derivatives Trading Regulations

IV. Futures Contract Delivery cum Settlement Procedure

The conceptual framework of futures trading process is portrayed as:

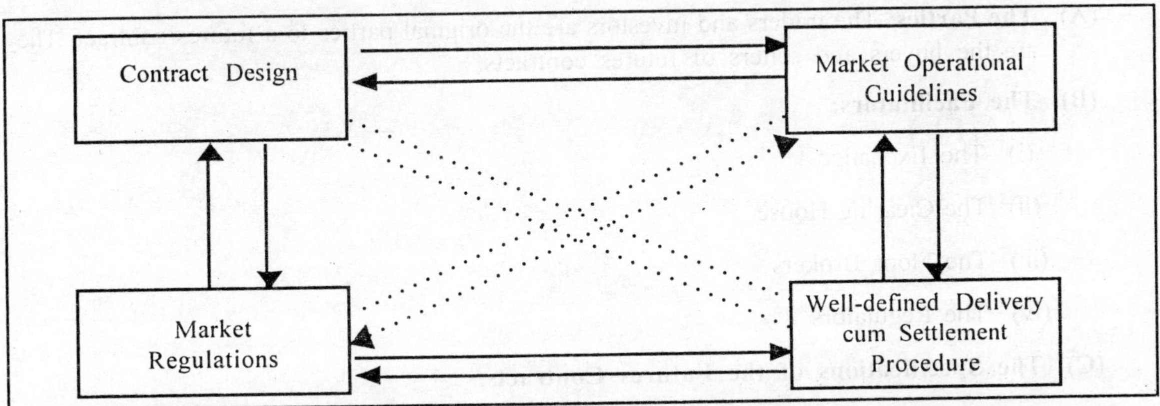

Fig. 5.6: Conceptual Framework of Futures Trading Process

To understand the futures trading process, we now discuss these four elements in detail.

5.5.1 Futures Contract Design

Futures are exchange traded contracts. The terms of the contracts are standardised by the exchanges. The most important principle for designing a future contract is to take into account the systems and practices being followed in the cash market. While designing a future contract, care should be taken that contract designed is fair to both buyer and seller and there would be adequate supply of the deliverable asset. The parties to a futures contract do not decide the terms of futures contract, but they merely accept the terms standardised by the Exchange.

In India, financial derivatives are traded on NSE, BSE and USE while commodity futures are traded on NCDEX, MCX and NDEX.

At the time of designing a futures contract, the following three matters must be clearly specified to the parties of such contract:

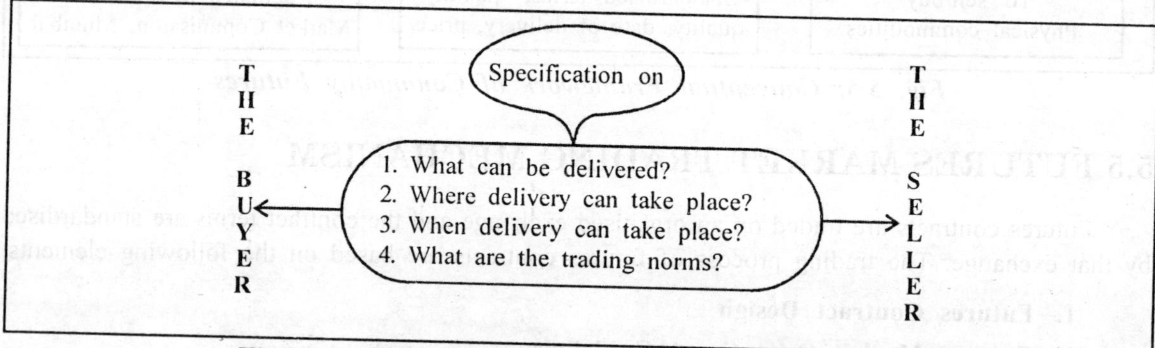

Fig. 5.7: The Matters in a Futures Contract Design

Foundations of Futures Contract Design

A well-designed futures contract is based on the following foundation:

(A) The Parties: The traders and investors are the original parties to a futures contract. They are the buyers and sellers of futures contracts.

(B) The Facilitators:

(i) The Exchange

(ii) The Clearing House

(iii) The Floor Brokers

(iv) The Regulators

(C) The Specifications of the Futures Contracts:

(i) The Asset

(ii) The Contract Size

– Lot Size

– Tick Size

(iii) Contract cycle

(iv) The margin money

(v) Delivery terms

– Month

– Place

(D) Closing/Settlement of a Futures Contract

A futures contract is designed to solve the problems that exist in forward contract. A well-designed futures contract can be structured as follows:

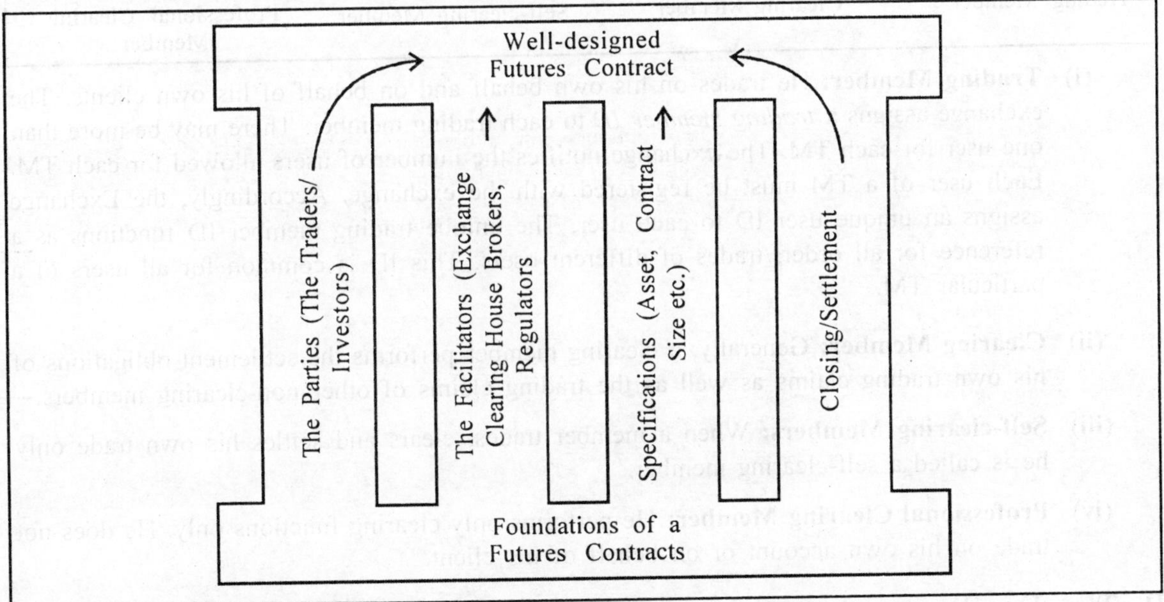

Fig. 5.8: Well-designed Futures Contract

Now we discuss these foundations in brief:

A. The Parties of Futures Contracts

The original parties of the futures derivatives (contracts) are the buyers and sellers. They are the real traders or investors of the deal.

An exchange provides a physical marketplace for futures transaction. This place is known as *The Floor*. A member of the exchange can participate in the futures trading in such floor. When the actual trader (buyer/seller) is not a member of an exchange, he has to contact an authorised broker (a member) who can trade on the floor on his behalf. Then only a futures contract can be registered in a particular exchange through the broker member. In case the trader is a member of an exchange, he is eligible to trade in the floor of an exchange directly.

In financial futures trading in India, all Resident Indians, Non-resident Indians, Foreign Institutional Investors and Mutual Funds are eligible to participate. But only the members are eligible to coordinate the trading activities for financial futures. SEBI has classified these members into four categories according to their nature of obligations. These are:

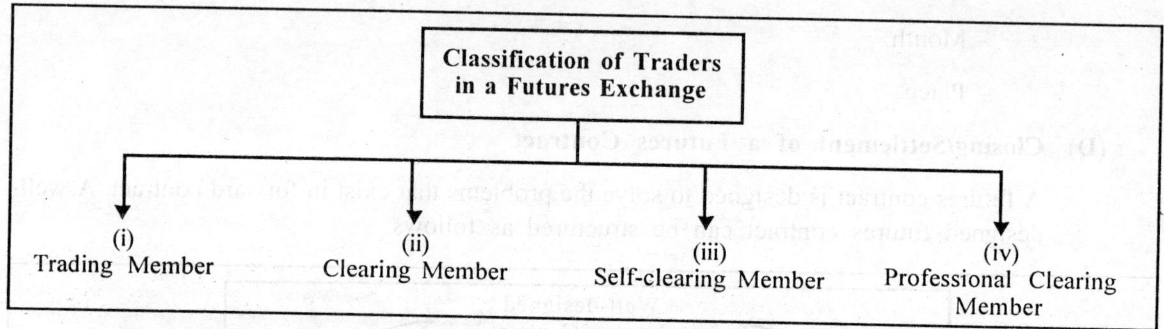

(i) Trading Member: He trades on his own behalf and on behalf of his own clients. The exchange assigns a *trading member ID* to each trading member. There may be more than one user for each TM. The exchange notifies the number of users allowed for each TM. Each user of a TM must be registered with the exchange. Accordingly, the Exchange assigns an unique user ID to each user. The unique trading member ID functions as a reference for all orders/trades of different users. This ID is common for all users of a particular TM.

(ii) Clearing Member: Generally, a clearing member performs the settlement obligations of his own trading claims as well as the trading claims of other non-clearing members.

(iii) Self-clearing Members: When a member trades, clears and settles his own trade only he is called a self-clearing member.

(iv) Professional Clearing Member: He performs only clearing functions only. He does not trade on his own account or on behalf of his client.

B. The Facilitators of Futures Trading

The facilitators support the original traders for smooth functioning of futures deal. These facilitators are:

(i) The Exchange

(ii) The Clearing House

(iii) The Brokers

(iv) The Regulators

The functions and the supporting roles of these facilitators have been discussed here as under.

(i) The Exchange

The Facilitators of a Futures Contract

An Exchange itself does not trade but acts like a facilitator. In India, there are two categories of futures exchanges, i.e., Commodity Futures Exchanges and Financial Futures Exchanges.

Commodity Futures Exchanges: At present, the Government of India has granted permanent recognition to three national level multi-commodity exchanges namely, (i) Multi-commodity Exchange of India (MCX), Mumbai, (ii) National Commodity and Derivatives Exchange Limited (NCDEX), Mumbai and (iii) National Multi-commodity Exchange of India Limited (NMCE), Ahmedabad to facilitate commodity futures derivatives.

Eligibility Criteria of Commodities to be Suitable for Futures Trading:

All the commodities are not suitable for futures trading. For a commodity to be suitable for futures trading, it must possess the following characteristics:

1. The commodity should have a suitable demand and supply conditions, i.e., volume and marketable surplus should be large.
2. Prices should be volatile to necessitate hedging through futures trading. In this commitment face a price risk. As a result, there should be a demand for hedging facilities.
3. The commodity should be free from substantial control from Government regulations (or other bodies) imposing restrictions on supply, distribution and prices.
4. The commodity should be homogeneous or alternatively it must be possible to specify a standard grade and to measure deviations from that grade. This condition is essential for the futures exchange to deal in standardised contracts.
5. The commodity should be storable. In the absence of this condition, arbitrage would not be possible and there would be no relationship between the spot and futures market.

Source : www.fmc.gov.in

Online Trading System Facility: These National Commodity Exchanges facilitate online trading activities in all commodities, to which Section 15 of Forward Contracts (Regulation) Act, 1952 is applicable. For other commodities neither listed U/S 17 nor defined U/S 15 of the said Act, will be traded subject to the approval of the Forward Markets Commission, Government of India.

Financial Futures Exchanges: Securities and Exchange Board of India has permitted the following stock exchanges to facilitate the futures trading in India:

1. Bombay Stock Exchange
2. National Stock Exchange
3. United Stock Exchange.

These exchanges will determine the stocks, bonds and indices on which futures contracts would be introduced. The parameters of such determination of stocks, bonds and indices are based on the criteria laid down by SEBI. These eligibility criteria is as follows:

Eligibility Criteria for Underlyings (Stocks/Indices)

1. The stocks should figure in the top 500 stocks in terms of average daily market capitalisation and average daily traded value in the previous six months on a rolling basis.
2. The medium quarter sigma order size over the last six months should not be less than ₹ 1.00 lakh.
3. The market-wide position limit in the stock should not be less than ₹ 50 crore.
4. The futures contracts on an index can be issued only if 80% of the index constituents are individually eligible for derivative trading.

Online Trading System Facility: It is interesting to know that trading of derivative contracts on NSE, BSE and USE are facilitated through an order-driven automated online system. For example, the following forms of computerised platforms are adopted by these exchanges :

- **NEAT – F&O Trading System** – National Exchange for Automated Trading – Futures and Options.
- **DTSS** – Derivative Trading and Settlement System.

How the order-driven automated online system works?

We now exhibit this operating system through a flow chart.

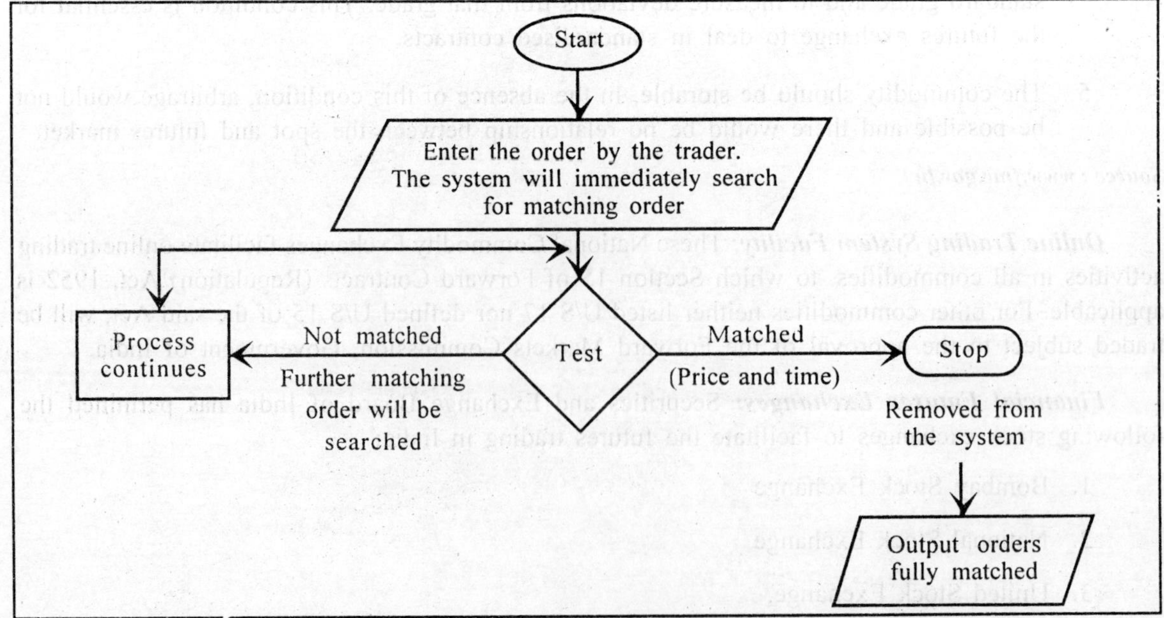

Fig. 5.9: Flow Chart on Automated Online Futures Trading System

Types of Futures Contract Orders

A *Futures order* originates with the customer, and is simply a set of instructions for the executing broker. A customer (trader) uses futures order to instruct his broker exactly what to trade (buy or sell), when to trade and at what price. Thus, a futures order refers to a set of instructions given to a broker by a customer requesting that the broker will take certain actions in the futures market on behalf of the customer. Correct placement of an order saves time and assures that the customer is doing what he is intending to do in the futures trading.

There are many types of orders, each being used during different occasions. All orders are assumed to be day orders, meaning that they automatically expire at the end of the trading day if not filled or executed, unless it is specified that the order is **"Open"** or **Good Till Cancelled (GTC)**. A GTC order remains a working order ***Session after Session*** until it is filled or cancelled by the customer who gives the order.

A standard format of futures order may be designed as follows:

Futures Order Form

Order No : ....

Date : ....

1. Name of the Customer : ....

2. Account Number : ....

3. Name of the Futures Exchange : ....

4. Particulars of the Commodity : ....

- **Name :**
- **Specification :** ....
- **Quantity :**
- **Delivery Details :** ....

5. Futures Contract Month and Year : ....

6. Order Valid Session: ....

7. Specifications : ....

(Type of Orders) : ....

To

The Broker .... **Futures Exchange**

Signature of the Customer : ....

Date :

The most common type of orders are:

1. The Market Order
2. The Limit Order
3. The Stop Order
4. The MIT (Market-if-Touched) Order
5. The Stop-limit Order
6. The Market on Open (MOO) Order
7. The Market on Close (MOC) Order
8. The Spread Order
9. The Fill or Kill Order
10. The Good Till Cancelled (GTC) Order

Now we will discuss the features of these orders in brief:

1. The Market Order

A market order instructs the executing broker to buy or sell futures contracts immediately at the market price, ***the best possible price*** for immediate execution. In other words, a market order is executed at the best possible price as soon as the order reaches the floor broker on the trading floor.

The market order is the most frequently used order when the greatest priority of the customer is for immediate execution. Thus, in this case, the customer is less concerned about the price s/he will receive, and more concerned with the speed of execution. Market orders are easiest way to enter or exist a market since the customer receives immediate execution and must pay or receive whatever price is necessary for immediate execution.

Example: A customer who wants to sell 10th May cotton futures immediately would instruct his broker with a **Market Order** to sell 10th May cotton at the best possible price in the market.

Difficulties in Executing a Market Order:

In certain cases, a market order may not result in immediate execution. Some futures contract markets have ***Price limits*** outside of which no trade can be executed. Consider the following cases:

Case (a): If prices rise and reach the upper limit, one may be unable to get execution of a market order to buy since sellers may be waiting for prices to go even higher.

Case (b): If prices fall to the lower price limit, one may be unable to get execution of a market order to sell since buyers may be waiting for prices to fall even further.

In these two cases, the trader must wait until the price limits are expanded.

Case (c): A market order may not result in immediate execution during times when trading is very thin or illiquid. In such situation, there is no available counterparty to the futures trade and the market order consequently goes unfilled.

As explained above, a market order is used to enter a new position or to exit an existing position. So, this order may be:

(i) **Market On Open (MOO):** As the name implies, this order will be executed on the market open within the opening range. This trade is used to enter a new trade, or exist an open trade.

(ii) **Market On Close (MOC):** As the name implies, this order will be executed on the market close. The fill price will be within the closing range which may in some markets be substantially different from the settlement price. This trade is used to enter a new trade or exist an open trade.

2. The Limit Order

A limit order is like a market order with one exception that price takes the highest priority. A limit order may be *limit buy order* or *limit sell order*.

(a) Limit Buy Order: For limit buy orders, the customer includes a special instruction along with the type and quality of futures contracts to purchase, a maximum price to pay for the contracts. A customer will use a *limit buy order* if he desires to buy the future contract, but wants to pay no more than a specified price, since the customer would have otherwise entered a market order.

Example: September Gold is trading at ₹ 18,800 per 100 grams. A customer who enters a limit order to buy 10th September contracts at ₹ 18,500 per 100 grams. A limit order to buy is only executed if the market price declines to the limit price, i.e., ₹ 18,500.

Result: Limit orders are assumed to be day orders, meaning that if prices have not declined to the specified limit by the end of the day, then the order is left unfilled and cancelled.

(b) Limit Sell Order: For limit sell orders, the customer includes, along with the type and quantity of futures contracts to sell, a minimum price to sell, a minimum price to receive for the contracts. A customer will use a limit sell order if he desires to sell the futures contract, but wants to receive at least some specified price – the limit price. This price is always above the prevailing market price, since the customer would have otherwise entered a market order.

Example: September Gold is trading at ₹ 18,800 per 100 grams. A customer who enters a *limit order* to sell 10th September contracts at ₹ 19,000 per 100 grams is willing to sell gold futures only at a price ₹ 19,000 per 100 grams or higher. A limit order to sell is only executed if the market price rises to the limit price.

Thus, limit orders are placed at a specific price or at a better price. It is very clear that the trader will accept a better price than the price on the futures order if the floor broker can execute the futures order at the better price.

3. The Stop Order

A Stop Order is an order to buy or sell an existing futures position at the market but only after the specific stop price has been reached.

It is similar to Market Order. According to the nature of this order, the customer intends to buy or sell at best available price, however, this order is processed only when the market reaches a specific price.

Example: The market price is ₹18,900 per 100 grams gold. If the customer place a *buy order* with a price ₹ 18,700 per 100 grams gold. Then this stop order is converted to a regular market when the market price reaches ₹ 18,600.

Note: A stop order is activated only when the market trades at the stop price or passes the price.

Further, a *stop order*, like a *limit order*, is only executed once a specific price is reached to a particular level, but the motivation for the transaction is different. Whereas the *limit order* is typically used to enter into a futures position at a specific price, a stop order is usually used to exist or close a futures position at a specific price.

Stop orders are most often used to close a position that is losing money, and are hence, regarded as a useful *risk management tool.*

A stop order to buy has a price that is **above** the market price and would be used by a customer having a **short futures position**. If the prices rise so that loss accrues on the customer's short position, the stop loss provides a limit to the loss as soon as prices rise to the stop price, the order is executed as a market order.

A stop order to sell has a price that is **below** the market price and would be used by a customer having a **long futures position**. If prices fall so that loss accrues on the customer's long position, the stop loss provides a limit to the loss as soon as prices fall to the stop price, the order is executed, thereby, closing out the initial long position.

Diagramatically,

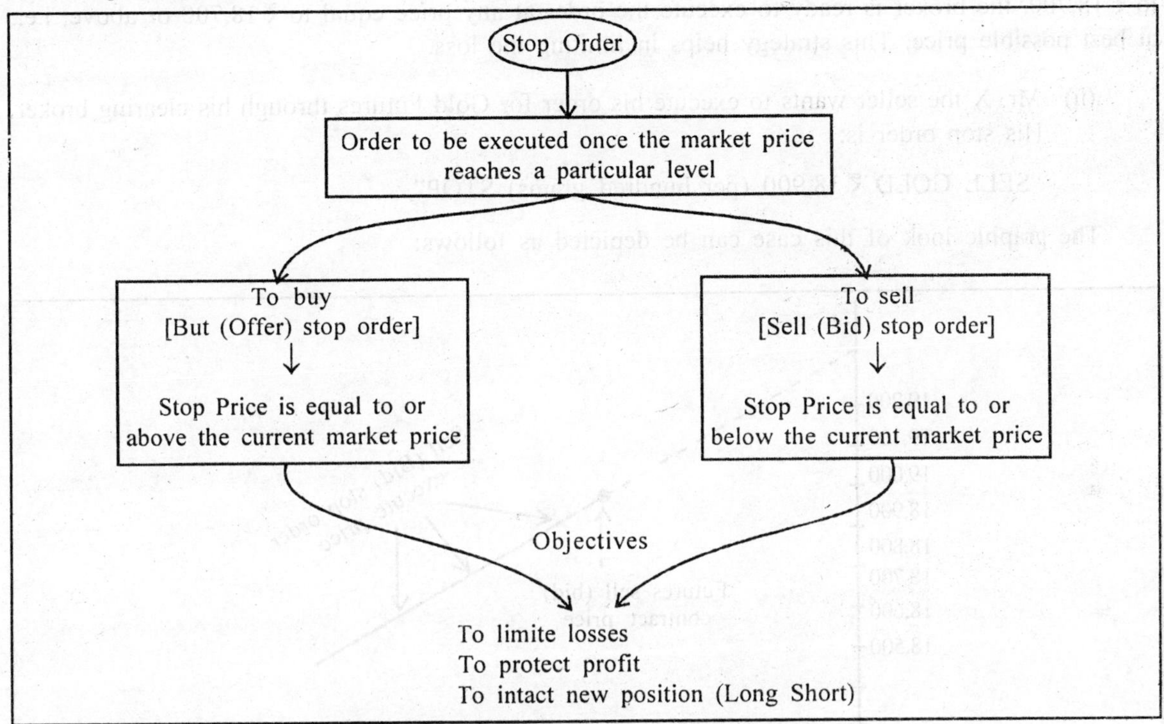

Fig. 5.9: The Concept of Stop Order

Consider the following two cases:

(i) Mr. X, the buyer wants to execute his order for Gold Futures through his broker. His stop order is:

"BUY GOLD ₹ 18,700 per hundred grams STOP"

The graphic look of this case can be depicted as follows:

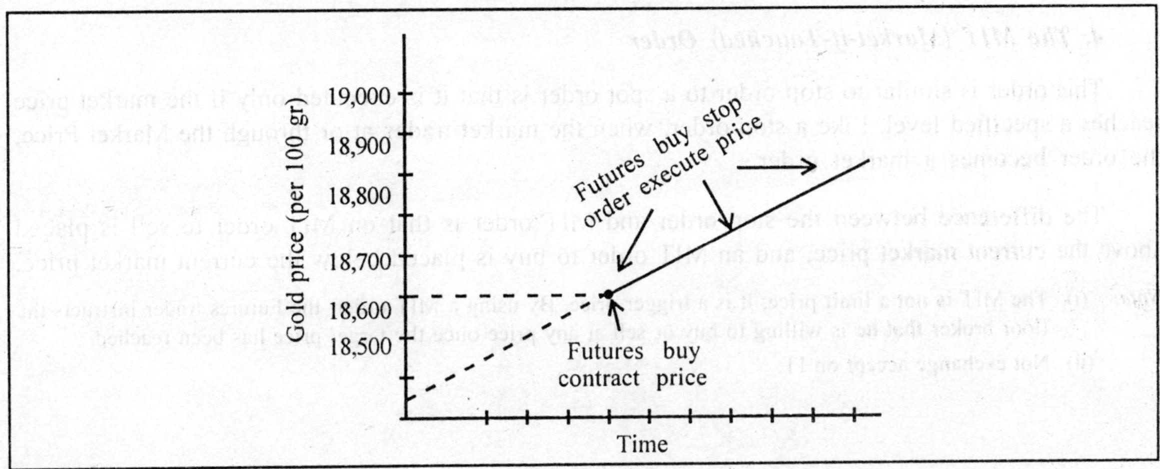

In this case, the futures contract price is fixed ₹ 18,700. When the market price is reached to ₹ 18,700, the broker is ready to execute the order at any price equal to ₹ 18,700 or above, i.e., at best possible price. This strategy helps in limiting the loss.

(ii) Mr. X the seller wants to execute his order for Gold Futures through his clearing broker. His stop order is:

"SELL GOLD ₹ 18,900 (per hundred grams) STOP"

The graphic look of this case can be depicted as follows:

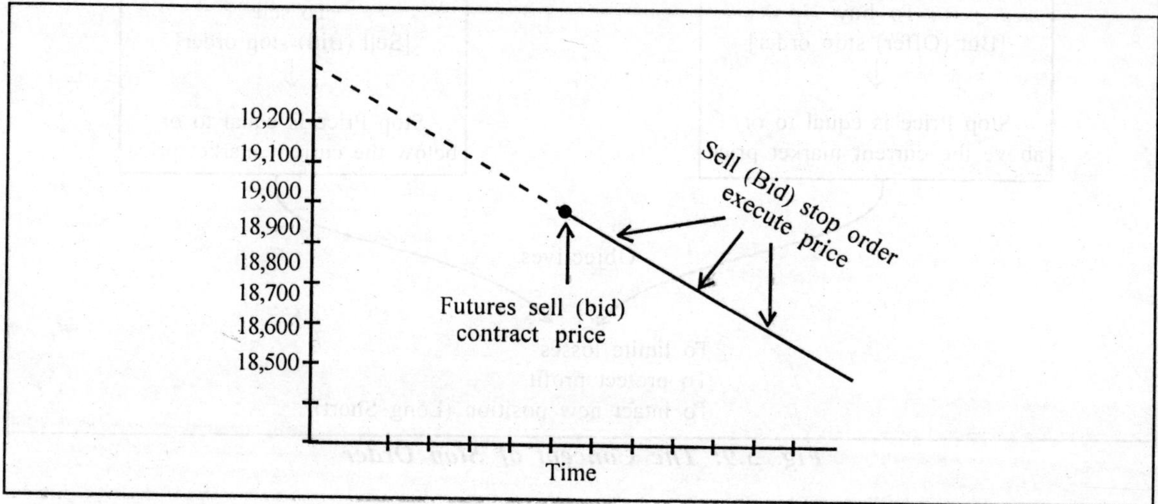

In this case, the futures contract price is fixed ₹ 18,900. When the market price is reached to ₹ 18,900, the broker is ready to execute the order at any price equal to ₹ 18,900 or below, i.e., at best possible price. This strategy helps in limiting the loss.

Note: Stop orders do not guarantee that the loss on a futures position will be confined to the stop price. Prices may continue to move adversely as the stop order is being executed resulting in larger loss than anticipated. This should be taken into account when using stop orders as a risk management tool.

4. The MIT (Market-if-Touched) Order

This order is similar to stop order to a spot order is that it is executed only if the market price reaches a specified level. Like a stop order, when the market trades at or through the Market Price, the order becomes a market order.

The difference between the stop order and MIT order is that on MIT order to sell is placed above the current market price, and an MIT order to buy is placed below the current market price.

Note: (i) The MIT is not a limit price, it is a trigger price. By using a MIT order, the Futures trader instructs the floor broker that he is willing to buy or sell at any price once the target price has been reached.

(ii) Not exchange accept on IT.

5. Stop-limit Order

It is a combination of a stop order and a limit order. In a stop-limit order, two prices are specified. The second part of the order specifies a limit price.

Thus, a stop-limit order is used in similar way as a regular stop order is used in similar way as a regular stop order except that the execution of the transaction is restricted to the limit price or better.

Example: "Buy 1 July 2011 ₹ 18,800 stop-limit."

"Sell 1 July 2011 ₹ 18,700 stop-limit."

Note: (i) The stop price may or may not equal to the limit price. If a trader does not give a limit price, the stop price and the limit price are meant to be identical.

(ii) A floor broker may not able to execute a stop-limit order in a fast market because of the restrictions placed on the execution price.

6. Market on Open (MOO) Order

It is a market order with a condition that the trader (customer) wishes to execute his/her order during the opening range of trading at the best possible price obtainable within the opening range. Not all exchanges recognise this type of order.

7. Market on Close (MOC) Order

It is a market order with a condition that the order will be filled during final seconds of trading at whatever the price is available.

Note : A floor broker reserves the right to refuse an MOC order upto fifteen minutes before the close depending upon the market condition.

8. Spread Order

A spread order directs the broker to buy and sell simultaneously two different futures contracts, either at the market or at a **specified spread premium.**

In other words, the trader wishes to take simultaneous long and short position with a view to earn profit via the price differential or 'spread' between two prices.

A spread can be established between different months of the same commodity, between related commodity or between the same or related commodities traded on two different exchanges.

9. Fill or Kill (FOK) Order

In this order, the trader instructs to the floor broker to execute the order immediately otherwise it will be cancelled. A Fill or Kill Order can either be filled in whole, or his part. In case of a part is fullfilled, then the outstanding balance of the futures order must be cancelled.

10. Good Till Cancelled (GTC) Order

GTC order is an open order. It is used in conjuction with a limit or stop order. This GTC order will remain valid until the trader cancels the order, or it is filled, or contract expires.

If an order is not designated Good Till Cancelled, it is a Day Order and will expire at the end of the current trading session unless filled or cancelled prior to the close.

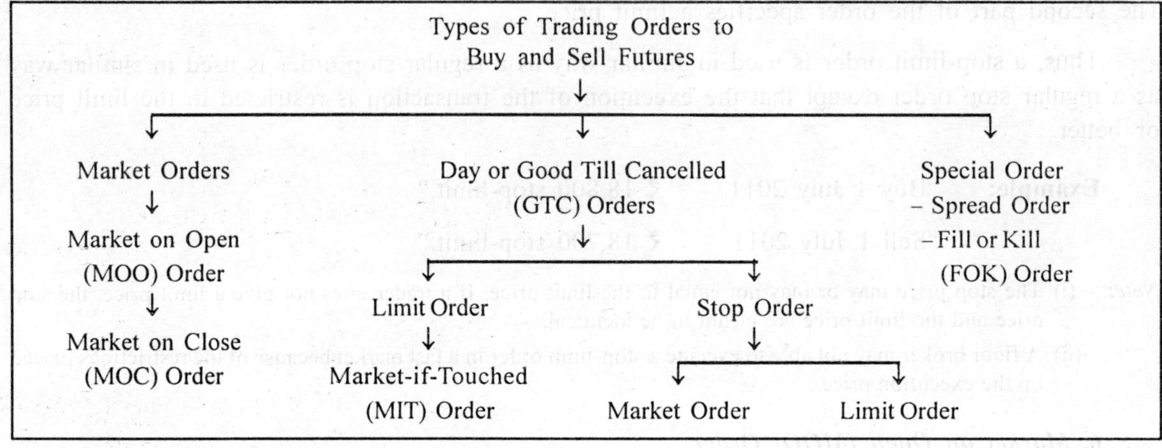

(ii) The Clearing House

Every futures exchange has a clearing house associated with it which clears all the transactions of that exchange. A clearing house is a financial institution that provides clearing and settlement services for financial and commodity derivatives and securities transactions.

The Constitution and Status of a Clearing House: A clearing house may be formed as a separate body corporate or it may be a part of the futures exchange. It carries the obligation to clear all the transactions of the affiliating or constituent futures exchange. For example, National Securities Clearing Corporation Limited (NSCCL) acts as the clearing house of National Stock Exchange (NSE).

A clearing house acts a an intermediary between two traders (Clearing Members) with an obligation to reduce the risk of one of such clearing member when the counterparty fails to honour the trade obligation. It has a number of members who are only allowed to trade. Sometimes, brokers or commission merchants who are not clearing house members, they may channel their trade transactions through a clearing member.

Functions of a Clearing House:

An associated clearing house is an integral part of derivative exchange. It performs the following important functions.

It Acts as a Legal Counterparty to the Buyer as well as Seller: First, the buyers and sellers agree to price, quantity, quality, expiration month and the underlying asset etc. as per the specification of the exchange. The moment the deal is concluded, the clearing house act as a third parties to all futures contracts – as a buyer to every clearing member seller and a seller to every clearing member buyer. In other words, the clearing house assumes the obligation to buy the seller's contract and to sell it the buyer. As a result, the original parties to the trade will have to deal only with the clearing house. Because the clearing house is the trade to both parties, they don't have to worry about performance of the contract. Furthermore, the clearing house allows each trader to close out his position independently of the other.

A conceptual framework of the futures trading through the clearing house has been shown in the following figure.

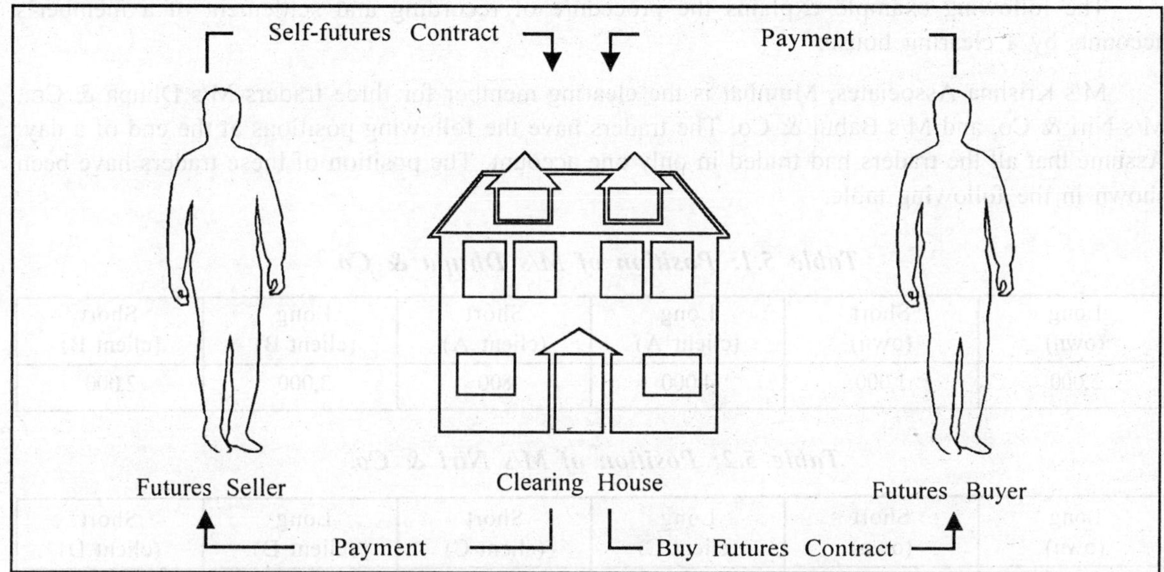

Fig. 5.10: Operational Framework of a Clearing House

It may be noted that in case of cash market, the intermediary (middlemen) will never become the legal counterparty to the transactions, but in case of futures derivative, the clearing house plays a distinct role as a legal counterparty to both buyer and seller.

2. It Records and Settles the day-to-day Trading Results: At the beginning, a clearing member enters his futures order. He should clearly specify whether the transaction is his own or his client. Accordingly, the clearing house records all transactions and works out the open positions of all the trading members. Thus:

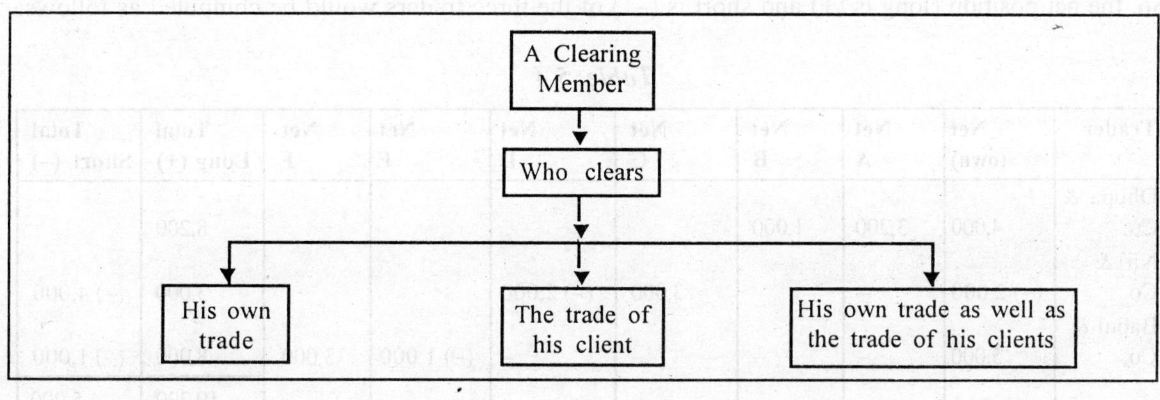

It may be noted that, all the transactions take place through the clearing house have to be settled through a clearing member only. For each clearing member, the clearing house computes daily net gain or loss and transfer funds from the account in loss to the account in gain. If we add all gains and losses of all the long and short futures of a day, the total will be always zero.

The following example explains the procedure of recording and settlement of a member's accounts by a clearing house:

M/s Krishna Associates, Mumbai is the clearing member for three traders M/s Dhupa & Co., M/s Niri & Co. and M/s Babul & Co. The traders have the following positions at the end of a day. Assume that all the traders had traded in only one account. The position of these traders have been shown in the following table.

Table 5.1: Position of M/s Dhupa & Co.

Long (own)	Short (own)	Long (client A)	Short (client A)	Long (client B)	Short (client B)
5,000	1,000	4,000	800	3,000	2,000

Table 5.2: Position of M/s Niri & Co.

Long (own)	Short (own)	Long (client C)	Short (client C)	Long (client D)	Short (client D)
3,000	5,000	6,000	3,000	5,000	7,000

Table 5.3: Position of M/s Babul & Co.

Long (own)	Short (own)	Long (client E)	Short (client E)	Long (client F)	Short (client F)
8,000	3,000	6,000	7,000	5,000	2,000

Solution:

The result of both long and short positions of an individual trader can be adjusted through netting. So, the net position (long is (+) and short is (–1) of the three traders would be computed as follows:

Table 5.4

Trader	Net (own)	Net A	Net B	Net C	Net D	Net E	Net F	Total Long (+)	Total Short (–)
Dhupa & Co.	4,000	3,200	1,000					8,200	
Niri & Co.	(–) 2,000	–	–	3,000	(–) 2,000			3,000	(–) 4,000
Babul & Co.	5,000	–	–	–	–	(–) 1,000	3,000	8,000	(–) 1,000
								19,200	5,000

The final position of M/s Krishna Associates, clearing member of their own, and on behalf of other 3 traders would be:

Trader	Total Long Position	Total Short Position	Grant Net
Dhupa & Co	8,2000	0	(+)8,2000
Niri & Co	3,000	(–)4,000	(–)1,000
Babul & Co	8,000	(–)1,000	(+)7,000
Total	**19,200**	**(–)5,000**	**(+)14,200**

Thus, exchange members provide daily reports of future trades to the clearing house. The clearing house monitors all the transactions taken place daily. Basing upon the recorded trade deals, the clearing house calculates the net position of all members.

3. It Gives Guarantee to the Performance of Futures Contracts: A clearing house acts as a legal counterparty to both buyers and sellers of futures contracts. It regulates, monitors and protects the clearing members. It gives guarantee to the performance of all future contracts. As netting is permissible, so a clearing house normally adopts the facility of clearing on a net basis.

(iii) The Floor Broker

A floor broker is a person who executes futures transactions on the **trading floor** on behalf of clients of a firm (member of an exchange), in contrast with a floor trader who makes deals on his or her own behalf.

Floor brokers take the responsibility for executing the orders to trade futures contracts that are accepted by the clients. These stock market professionals can work for client firms of all sizes, and they may specialise in a particular type of commodity, or work more generally in a stock exchange.

Functions of a Floor (Pit) Broker: A floor borker is also known as a **pit broker**. He receives order from his client firm and execute the order on the floor. His objective is to get the best deal, whether he involves in buying or selling for the clients. Once the order is completed, it is recorded and the client is informed that the deal has been successfully completed. One of the advantage of working as a floor broker is that one is not exposed directly to risks of market volatility when a deal goes badly.

A floor broker should be capable to deal with a wide range of personalities, and to deal with a fast paced work environment. He should possess some more basic skills like his ability to clearly project his voice in the floor so that he can be heard over the din of the trading floor, and the aggressiveness to make a good trade and confirm it.

Every exchange has slightly different conventions and rules which floor brokers must become familiar with. It conducts specialised training programmes for the floor brokers to update their skills.

(iv) The Regulators of Futures Contracts and Market

To regulate the futures derivatives each nation has set up the statutory regulators. In India, the following regulatory system is in practice:

- **For Commodity Futures:** Forward Contracts (Regulation) Act, 1952 was passed in India. It is implemented by Forward Market Commission under Ministry of Consumer Affairs, Food and Public Distribution, Government of India.
- **For Financial Futures:** The Securities Contract and Regulation Act (1952) was passed. It is implemented by SEBI since 1992 (the year of set-up).

C. The Specifications of the Futures Contracts

A futures (commodity/financial) exchange provides and maintains a physical marketplace, i.e., trading platforms, enforces financial and ethical standards and promotes the business interests of members by standardising the following elements:

(i) The Underlying Asset

(ii) The Contract size
- Lot size
- Tick size

(iii) Contract cycle

(iv) The Margin money

(v) The Delivery terms
- Month
- Day
- Place

As each futures contract has standard set of specifications, now we discuss these elements in brief as under:

(i) The Underlying Asset

What does the futures contract represent? It is a commodity, i.e., foodgrains, metals, oils, gas and so on in commodity futures market, while it is a stock index, interest rate, foreign currency and so on.

Each asset must be well-defined and unambiguous with respect to its quality and grade.

Examples:

(a) Stock Index Futures (SIF) is an index derivative which draws its value from an underlying stock index. In India, for example, the exchange must specify whether the stock index of a futures contract would be:

- BSE Sensex
- S&PCNX Nifty

(b) A 3 months T-Bill as underlying for a T-Bill futures contract in National Stock Exchange.

(ii) The Contract Size

The term **'contract size'** refers to the deliverable quantity of underlying commodities of a futures, forward or option contract. Each contract will have well-defined contract size. It is the minimum number of units in which a trading can take place.

Definitions: We may define the concept "contract size" in the following words:

(i) "The size or amount of an underlying asset to be delivered".

(ii) "Quantity of the underlying asset that is to be traded at the time of contract settles".

Examples:

1. In America, the Chicago Board of Trades main wheat contract (corn futures) is for 5,000 bushels (approximately 135 tonnes). Similarly this CBT also has a wheat mini contract for 1,000 bushels (approximately 27 tonnes).

2. In India, the corn futures contract specified by National Commodity and Derivative Exchange Limited (NCDEX) and the Multi Commodity Exchange (MCX) is for 10 tonnes.

3. **Equity Index Futures:** In this case, the contract size is specified by the index multiplier or contract multiplier.

   — **Contract Multiplier:** Contract multiplier is the minimum number of the underlying, i.e., stock or index that a participant has to trade while taking position in the derivative segment. It may be noted that for index futures, it is the price per index point. For example, the contract multiplier for Sensex futures is ₹ 50. It means each sensex point is worth ₹ 50.

   — **Contract Lot Size:** It means number of underlying securities in one contract. For example, if the contract multiplier for SENSEX is 15, then the Rupee notional value of a sensex future contract would be 15 times the contract value.

   The following table gives a few example of the notional value:

Contracted price of futures (₹)	Notional value in ₹ (based on Market Lot of 15) (₹)
19,500	2,92,500
19,600	2,94,000
19,750	2,96,250
19,900	2,98,500

   It may be mentioned here that the market lot may be changed by the Exchange in consultation with NSE as per the guidelines of SEBI.

   — **Tick Size:** This means that the minimum price fluctuation in the value of a contract the tick size is presently "0.05" or 5 paise. In rupee terms, this translates to a minimum price fluctuation of ₹ 0.75 for a single transaction of SENSEX Futures contract (Tick size × contract multiplier = 0.05 × ₹ 15).

(iii) Contract Cycle

It is the period over which a contract trades.

Example: The NSE specifies the contract cycle for its Indexed Futures. These contracts have one-month, two months and three months expiry cycles which expiry on the last Thursday of the month. Thus, a January expiration contract expires on the last Thursday of January and a February expiration contract expires on the last Thursday of February.

A new futures contract having a 3 months expiry will be introduced for trading on the Friday following the last Thursday.

(iv) The Margin Money

A futures exchange provides a platform for buyers and sellers to transact business. An exchange designs a future contract for trading on its platform. In ordinary trade, for every buyer there is a seller and if buyer does pay, the seller at risk. But a future exchange guarantees the performance of the contract registered with it. Each Exchange has associated clearing house which clears all the registered contracts. Although puyers and sellers enter into buy/sell transactions, teachnically the seller sells to the clearing house and the buyer buys from the clearing house. In other words, the exchange interposes itself between the buyer and seller. The exchange thus becomes a seller to each buyer and buyer to each seller. Essentially, the exchange becomes the counterparty to every contract. Because buyers and sellers transact through the exchange, so it is the responsibility of the exchange to ensure performance of the contract and also to provide a financially secure environment for its participants.

To minimise the risk of default by the participants (both buyers and sellers) and to safeguard the integrity of the market, the exchange collects security deposit or performance bonds from the customers and members. These security deposit or performance bond is known as **MARGIN MONEY**.

Objectives of Margining System

1. To Safeguard the Integrity of the Futures Market: An exchange provides a platform for buyers and sellers to trade and simultaneously also provides a financially secure environment for its participants. A small movement in prices of underlying could result big gains or big losses to the traders which is very risky. In such situation, a counterparty may be in default. To safeguard the integrity of the market, margining system for derivatives becomes an important mechanism for smooth functioning of the futures market.

2. To Ensure the Performance of the Futures Contract: A holder of a financial derivative has to deposit a collaterial in the form of cash or securities (which is called margin) to cover some or all of the credit risk of his counterparty. In USA, this margin was formerly known as performance bond. As the exchange becomes the counterparty to every contract, so make sure of performance of contract as well for its own interest, it imposes margin money on clearing members or traders. Futures margin represents a commitment by the futures traders that the financial obligations of the futures contract will be met.

Types of Margins

A Futures exchange imposes different types of margins. The amount of margin varies from contracts to contracts. These are:

1. Initial or Ordinary margin
2. Mark-to-Market margin
3. Exposure margin
4. Maintenance margin

These above stated margins are explained below:

1. Initial or Ordinary Margin: Initial margin is the amount to be deposited by the market participants in their margin account with the clearing house before they can place buy or sell order of a future contract. **In other words, the amount of security money that must be deposited in the MARGIN ACCOUNT at the time a futures contract is first entered into is knownas INITIAL MARGIN**. Since it is deposited by the market participants to establish their futures position (long/short) initially, so it is ordinarily called INITIAL MARGIN.

How is Initial Margin Computed?

To compute the initial margin the following approach, use of software and methodology are to be used globally.

(a) *Approach:* **Portfolio Based Approach:** Initial margin is computed on the basis of a portfolio (a collection of futures positions) based approach.

(b) *Software:* The initial margin calculation is carried out using a software called SPAN®. SPAN® means Standard Portfolio Analysis of Risk.

Points to Note:

(i) This SPAN® software has been developed by Chicago Mercantile Exchange (CME).

(ii) It is extensively used by leading stock exchanges of the world.

Margining System in India: National Securities Clearing Corporation Ltd. (NSCCL) uses the SPAN® system, a portfolio based margining system, for the purpose of calculating initial margin. It is computed separately for the following three levels:

- For Clearing Members (CMs)
- For Trading Members (TMs)
- For Clients (Traders)

(c) *Methodology to Compute Initial Margin:* In India, NSCCL has developed a comprehensive risk containment mechanism for the futures derivative segment as follows:

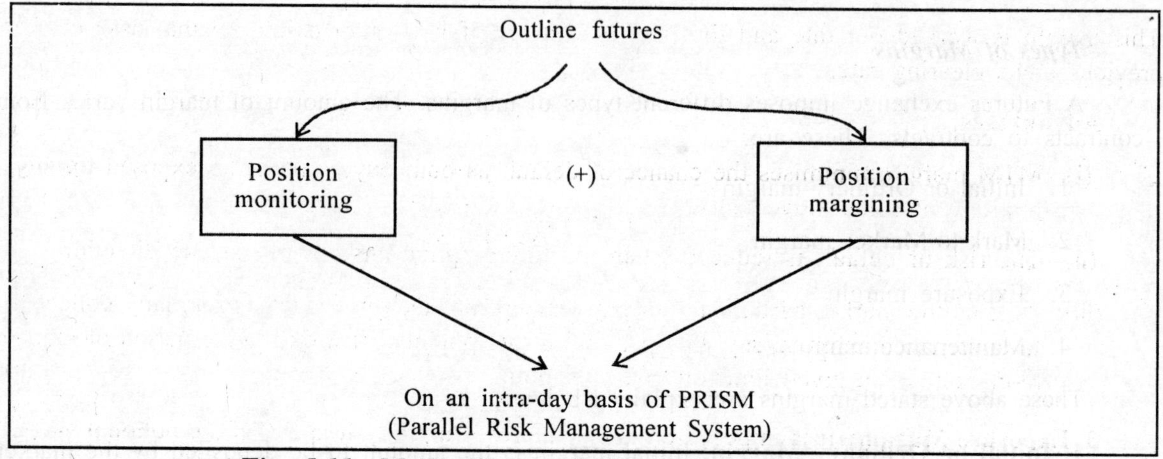

Fig. 5.11: Methodology of Computing Initial Margin

The SPAN® software is used to assess the the specific set of market conditions, i.e., risk containment. It is called Risk Scenario. The assessment of risk containment incorporates the following two elements:

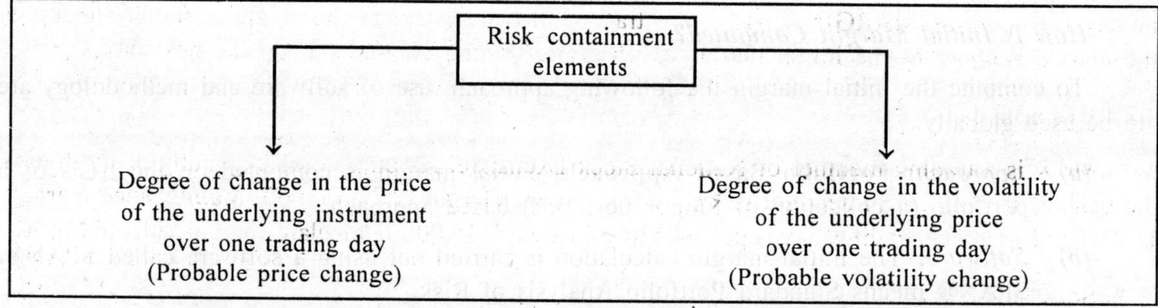

Fig. 5.12: Risk Containment Elements of a Future Contract

Points to Note:

(i) Higher the volatility, higher would be the margin.

(ii) The exchange has the right to increase or decrease the amount of initial margin depending upon the risk containment elements.

(iii) The initial margin amount must be maintained throughout the time their position is open and refundable at delivery, expiry or closing out of the contract.

2. Mark-to-Market Margin: An Exchange imposes mark-to-market margin to protect its interest. The exchange clears all the transactions at the closing price of the day, profits and losses are either paid in or paid out. Mark-to-market margin is payable based on the closing price at the end of each trading day. It will be paid by the buyer if the price declines and by the seller if price rises. Thus, at the end of each trading day, the margin account is adjusted to reflect the trader's gainn or loss depending upon the future closing price. This is known as mark-to-market margin.

This margin is worked out rate and the rate of contract (if it is entered into on that day) or the previous day's clearing rate.

Advantages:

(i) MTM margin minimises the chance of default as both buyer and seller exposed to only one day of price movements.

(ii) The risk of default is reduced when the futures price moves only in one direction.

(iii) It helps the market participants to pay less upfront margin, which is normally collected to cover the maximum, say 99.9 per cent of the potential risk during the period of mark-to-market, for a given limit on open position.

3. Exposure Margin: It is imposed on Index futures. Currently it is 3% of the notional value.

4. Maintenance Margin: Maintenance margin is the minimum amount that the trader must have in his account. Generally, it is lower than the initial margin and approximately 75 per cent of the initial margin. It represents the minimum level in margin account of a trader. The moment the balance in the margin account falls below the maintenance margin level the trader will receive a call (demand notice) to pay the short fall amount. Hence, the demand for deposit of shortfall amount of margin money is known as MARGIN CALL. The trader must then deposit the adequate money to bring the margin account to the initial margin level before trading commences on the next day.

Example 1

Mr X is a trading member of National Stock Exchange. As on date of beginning of the trade, the balance in his margin account is ₹ 1,10,000. Initial margin is ₹ 1,00,000. Maintenance margin is ₹ 75,000. On the trading day, open position loss is ₹ 45,000. Calculate margin call of Mr X.

Solution:

Actual balance = ₹ 1,10,000

Initial margin = ₹ 1,00,000

Position loss = ₹ 45,000

Balance in Margin Account = ₹ 1,10,000 – ₹ 45,000 = ₹ 65,000

Margin call = Initial amount – Present balance = ₹ 1,00,000 – ₹ 65,000 = ₹ 35,000

Thus, the trader will make a call (Margin call) to replenish the margin account to ₹ 1,00,000, the level of initial margin by depositing a sum of ₹ 35,000.

Note: The difference of initial margin and the balance in the margin account, i.e., ₹ 35,000 here is known as Variation margin.

Example 2

Mr X is a trading member of National Stock Exchange. On a particular trade day, the position of his margin accounts are as follows:

Account Balance ₹ 1,10,000

Initial Margin ₹ 1,00,000

Maintenance Margin ₹ 75,000

Open position loss ₹ 45,000

If Mr X closes his trade or offset his position, calculate the amount to be refunded by NSE to Mr X.

Solution:

The amount to be refunded is ₹ 1,10,000 – ₹ 45,000 = ₹ 65,000

Accounting of Margin Money – A Practical Approach

Initial margins are collected from the clients by the Clearing Members (CMs) and Trading Members (TMs). The collection of margins at client level in the derivative markets is essential as derivatives are leveraged products and non-collection of margins at the client level would provide zero cost leverage.

In the derivative markets, all money paid by the client towards margins is kept in trust with the Clearing House/Clearing Corporation and in the event of default of the Trading or Clearing Member the amount paid by the client towards margins are segregated and not utilised towards dues of the defaulting member.

As a matter of practice, clearing members are required to report on a daily basis details in respect of such margin amounts due and collected from their trading members/clients.

Similarly, trading members are also required to report on daily basis details of the amount due and collected from their clients.

The reporting of the collection of the margins by the clients is done electronically through the system at the end of each trading day. The reporting of collection of client level margins plays an important role not only in ensuring that members collect margin from clients but it also provides the clearing corporation with a record of the quantum of funds it has to keep in trust for the clients.

V. Delivery Norms

The exchange must specify the timing and place of delivery of underlying.

- **Delivery Month:** The exchange must specify the delivery month. The delivery months vary from contracts to contracts. Thus, delivery month is the specified month within which a futures contract matures.

- **Delivery Date:** The seller has to give a delivery notice showing his intention to make delivery against outstanding short open futures positions on a particular date. Accordingly, the exchange informs the buyer for taking the underlying physically.

- **Place of Delivery:** Most of the contracts in agricultural commodities traded at the Exchanges are "Compulsory Delivery Contracts", i.e., all the outstanding position on the maturity of the contract has to compulsory result in deliveries. In such situation, an exchange specifies the place of delivery which is convenient to both the parties.

D. Closing/Settlement of a Futures Contract

Generally, all future contracts are cash settled, i.e., through exchange of cash. For example, the underlying for index futures of the NIFTY INDEX cannot be delivered. These contracts, therefore, have to be settled in cash. Futures on individual securities can be delivered as in the spot market. Here, the terminal value of the individual securities is deemed to be equal to the price seen on the spot market. This is used to determine cash transfers from the counterparties of the futures contract. This cash transfer is treated as settlement.

5.5.2 Futures Market Operational Guidelines

For smooth functioning futures market, guidelines in the following are essential:

(a) Trading system

(b) Trader's workstation

(c) Market instruments

(d) Eligibility criteria of instruments for derivatives tradings

(a) Guidelines on Futures Trading System: NSE has developed the futures and options trading system, called NEAT – F&O trading system. It provides a fully automated screen-based trading for Index futures and stock futures on a nation-wide basis. It also provides an online monitoring and surveillance mechanism. This NEAT – F&O system extends all kinds of support for an **order-driven** futures market and provides complete transparency of trading operations.

(b) Guidelines on Access to the "Trader's Workstation": In the era of advance information technology, all most all exchanges display all information through various windows on the trader's workstation screen.

The common windows are:

- Inquiry window
- Market watch window
- Order/trade window
- System message window

(c) Guidelines on Market Instruments: Only selective futures trading instruments are permitted by an exchange. In India the following financial future instruments are permitted:

- Index based futures
- Individual stock futures.

Example:

Futures Exchange	Futures Instruments	Contract Cycle
National Stock Exchange	Nifty, CNS IT, Bank Nifty Junior CNX 100 Nifty	One month, Two month, Three month Midcap 50, Mini Nifty 50

An exchange issues guidelines in each instrument for smooth trading.

(d) Guidelines on Eligibility Criteria of Instruments for Derivative Tradings:

- **Commodity Futures:** Futures trading can be conducted on any commodity subject to the approval/recognition of the Government of India. At present, 105 commodities are in the regulated list. These 105 number of commodities have been notified U/S 15 of the Forward Contracts (Regulation) Act. Forward trading in these commodities can be conducted only between, with or through members of recognised associations.

- **Free Commodities:** Any other commodity which is not in the list of 105 is referred as free commodity. Forward trading in these commodities can be organised by any association after obtaining a Certificate of Registration for FMC.

  Thus, an exchange issues guidelines for futures trading only for those eligible commodities.

- **Financial Futures:** Guidelines for trading of stock futures and index futures enable the participants for efficient trading. The criteria for stocks and index eligibility for trading in Indian futures markets are briefed as follows:

Eligibility Criteria for Individual Stock

- The individual stock is chosen from amongst the top 500 stocks. The basis of selection are average daily market capitalisation and average daily traded value in previous six months on a rolling basis.

- The stock's median quarter-sigma order size over last six months should not be less than ₹ 5 lakh.

- The market-wide position limit in the stock should not be less than ₹ 100 crore.

Eligibility Criteria of Indices

A Stock Index derivative contract will be introduced by an Exchange, if the stocks contributing to 80% weightage of the index are individually eligible for derivative trading.

This eligible criteria is applied every month, if the index fails to meet the eligibility criteria for three months consecutively, then no fresh month contract would be issued on that index.

5.5.3 Regulations for Derivatives Trading

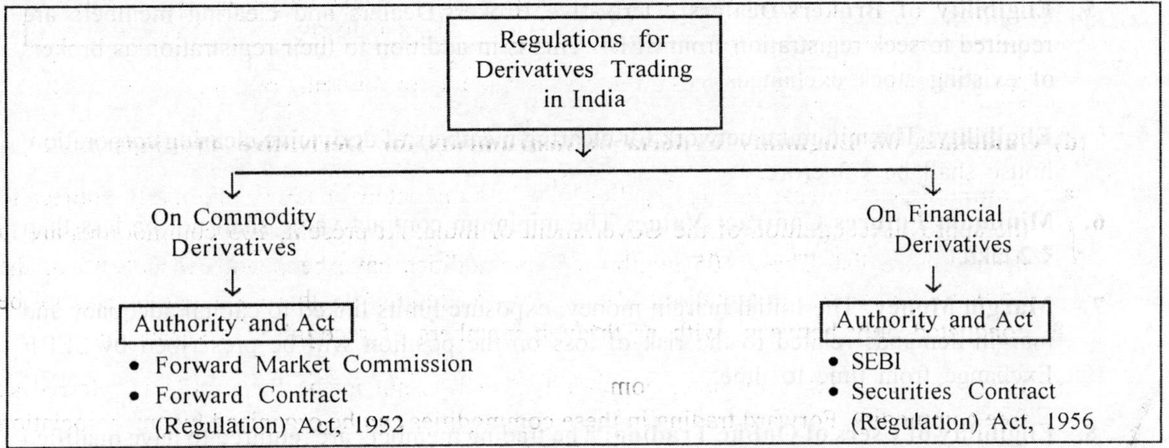

Regulations for Commodity Derivatives: Forward Market Commission is a regulatory body for commodity futures trade in India. This was set up under Forward Contracts (Regulation) Act of 1952. It is responsible for regulating and promoting Futures/Forward trade in commodities. The FMC has the following functions:

(a) FMC advises Central Government in respect of grant of recognition or withdrawal of recognition of any association.

(b) It keeps forward market under observation.

(c) It collects and publishes information relating to trading conditions and submit to Government periodical reports.

(d) It recommends for improving the organisation and working of Forward/futures markets.

(e) It inspects books of accounts and other documents of recognised/registered associations.

Regulations for Securities Derivatives

SEBI set up a 24 member committee under the chairmanship of Dr. L.C. Gupta to develop the appropriate regulatory framework for derivatives trading in India. Accordingly, Stock Index Futures was introduced for derivative trading in India in 1998. The provisions in the SC(R) Act and the regulatory framework developed thereunder govern trading in securities are as follows:

1. **Eligibility criteria for an Exchange:** An exchange is eligible for derivative trading if it fulfills the criteria as prescribed in L.C. Gupta Committee. Then SEBI grants recognition under Section 4 of the SC(R) Act, 1956. It has the separate governing council.

2. **Membership:** The exchange should have minimum 50 members. The trading/clearing members shall be limited to maximum of 40% of the total members.

3. **Eligibility Criteria of Members:** The members of the derivative segment would need to fulfill the eligibility conditions as laid down by the L.C. Gupta Committee.
4. **Eligibility of Clearing Corporations:** The clearing and settlement of derivatives trades would be through SEBI approved clearing corporation/house.
5. **Eligibility of Brokers/Dealers:** Derivative Brokers/Dealers and clearing members are required to seek registration from SEBI. This is in addition to their registration as brokers of existing stock exchanges.

   Eligibility: The minimum network for clearing members of derivative clearing corporation/ house shall be ₹ 3 crore.
6. **Minimum Futures Contract Value:** The minimum contract value shall not be less than ₹ 2 lakh.
7. **Margin Money:** The Initial margin money, exposure limits linked to capital adequacy and margin demands related to the risk of loss on the position will be prescribed by SEBI/ Exchange from time to time.
8. **Eligibility of Users of Online Trading:** The trading members are required to have qualified approved user and salesperson who have passed a certificate approved by SEBI.

5.5.4 Futures Contract Delivery and Settlement Procedure

There are four modes to close the futures position. These are:

(a) Physical Delivery

(b) Cash Settlement

(c) Offsetting

(d) Exchange of Futures for Physicals

Now we discuss the each settlement procedure with suitable example.

(a) Settlement by Physical Delivery

Steps:

- The party in short position has to send a notice to the exchange regarding the date, the place and specified underlying to be delivered.
- The exchange has to select a party with an outstanding long position to accept delivery.
- Then, the long position party will take delivery and the short position party will make delivery.
- After that, the clearing house will notify and record such transaction and proceed to settle the account. The exchange imposes certain costs on the trader like storage cost, insurance cost, shipping cost and brokerage fees.

(b) Cash Settlement

All futures contracts are cash settled, i.e., through exchange of cash. For example, the underlying for Index Futures cannot be delivered. These index future contracts, therefore, have to be settled in cash. Futures on individual securities can be delivered as in the spot market.

Points to Note:

(i) As per the recent rule, stock futures will be cash settled.

(ii) The settlement amount for clearing members is netted across all their trading members/ clients with respect to their obligations on mark-to-market settlement. Thus, cash settlement futures contracts are settled at the spot price.

In practice, there are two types of settlement for futures. There are Daily MTM settlement and Final settlement.

1. Daily Mark-to-Market (MTM) Settlement: All future contracts for each members are daily settled on the basis of mark-to-market settlement price. The profits/losses are computed as the difference between:

1. The trade price and the day's settlement price for contracts executed during the day but not squared up.
2. For brought forward contracts: The previous day's settlement price and the current day's settlement price.
3. The buy price and the sell price for contracts executed during the day and squared up.

Example:

Clearing members – Mr X

Exchange – NSE

Underlying – Stock

Position 1:

Brought forward futures – 100

Settlement price on 15th October, 2011 – ₹ 100

Settlement price on 16th October, 2011 – ₹ 110

Position 2:

Contracts executed on 16th October, 2011

Bought 300 @ ₹ 100

Sold 200 @ ₹ 108

Settlement price ₹ 108

Position 3:

Open position 100 shares

Settlement price ₹ 110

Solutions

For brought forward contract, the margin changed is the difference between the previous day's settlement price of ₹ 100 and today's settlement price ₹ 110. Hence, on account of the position brought forward, the MTM shows a profit of ₹ 1,000.

For contracts executed during the day, i.e., 16th October, 2011, the difference between the buy price and sell price determines MTM. In this example, 300 units are bought @, 100 and 200 units sold @ 108 during the day. Hence the MTM for the position closed during the day shows a profit of ₹ 1,600.

Finally, the open position of contracts traded during the day, i.e., 16th October, 2011, is margined at the day's settlement price and the profit of ₹ 1,000 credited to the MTM account. So, the MTM account shows a total profit of ₹ 3,600 on 16th October, 2011.

The above stated MTM calculations are shown in the following table.

	Trade details	**Units bought and sold**	**Settlement price**	**MTM (₹)**
(i)	Brought forward from 15th Oct, 2011	100 @ ₹ 100	110	1,000
(ii)	Traded during 16th Oct, 2011			
	Bought	300 @ ₹ 100		
	Sold	200 @ ₹ 108	108	1,600
(iii)	Open position (not squared up)	100 @ ₹ 100	110	1,000
	Total			**3,600**

2. Final Settlement: On the expiry day of the futures contracts, after the close of trading hours, the clearing corporation/house marks all positions of a CM to the final settlement price and the resulting profit/loss is settled in cash. Final settlement loss/profit amount is debited/credited to the relevant CM's clearing bank account on the day following expiry day of the contract.

(b) Offsetting or Reverse Trade

A futures contract can be closed by an offsetting future transaction or via a reverse trade. In this case, the initial buyer (long) liquidates his position by selling (short) an identical futures (same commodity and same delivery terms).

Example

Original futures contract (As on 1st January, 2012)	Offsetting futures contract (As on 31st January 2012)
Initial Buyer : Mr X (Long position)	Final buyer : Mr Y (Long position)
Initial Seller : Mr Y (Short position)	Final Seller : Mr X (Short position)
Contract : A standardised futures	Contract : Same standardised futures
Date of contract : 1st January 2012	Date of contract : 31st January, 2012
Date of expiry : 31st January 2012	Date of expiry : 31st March, 2012

After executing offset deals, there are to be reported to the clearing house. Then only their trade obligations will be extinguished on the books of the broker and clearing house. Thus, a clearing house plays a vital role in facilitating settlement by offset trading. Offsetting entails only the usual brokerage cost.

(d) Exchange of Futures for Physicals (EFP)

In this method, the original terms and conditions are changed between the counterparties with due permission from the exchange and settled accordingly. For example, physical delivery may take place prior to contract maturity.

CHAPTER SUMMARY

Future contracts are exchange traded contracts between two parties to trade (buy/sell) standardised financial instruments or physical commodities. The terms of the contract such as quality, quantity, delivery time, delivery place and settlement procedure are standardised by an Exchange.

This chapter discussed the various characteristics of futures contract. These features are:

(i) Exchange traded, (ii) Standardised terms, (iii) Performance of the contract through an associated clearing house, (iv) Mark-to-market (MTM) Accounting system, (v) Margining system, (vi) Basis, i.e., cash price minus Futures Price, (vii) Delivery and settlement procedure.

Further, a clear comparison is made between a forward contract and futures contract. Various types of financial futures such as Stock Index Futures, Interest Rate Futures, Foreign Currency Futures and Bond Index Futures have been discussed.

This chapter lucidly explained the futures market trading mechanism by highlighting the four basic foundations as follows:

(i) Future Contract Design

(ii) Futures Market Operational Guidelines

(iii) Regulations for Derivative Tradings

(iv) Futures Contract Delivery cum Settlement Procedure

Under future contract design, the various aspects like the parties, the facilitators, the specifications of futures contracts and closing of a future contracts have been systematically discussed.

Under futures market operational guidelines, the various aspects like futures trading system, use of trader's workstation, market instruments and eligibility criteria of instruments for derivatives tradings have been discussed in the light of practical exposure.

Lastly, this chapter focussed on futures contract delivery and settlement procedure. Basically there are four methods to close and settle a futures contract. These are physical delivery, cash settlement, offsetting and exchange of futures for physicals.

SUGGESTIONS FOR FURTHER READINGS

1. Hull, John C., *Fundamentals of Futures and Options Markets*, Pearson Education, New Delhi, 2004.

Websites:

www.nseindia.com > NSCCL > Notifications VaR Margins Rates

BSCE : www.bseindia.com > equity > vor/EL Margin.

www.mysensex.com/futures trading.

EXERCISES

Quiz

1. State Whether the Following Sentences are True/False.

(a) Futures contracts are exchange traded contracts to sell or buy standardised financial instruments.

(b) In futures the seller directly make delivery of the goods to the buyer ignoring the clearing house.

(c) Mark-to-market system facilitates settlement of profit/loss daily.

(d) The concept basis in futures derivative is the cash price + futures price.

(e) If futures price is higher than cash price, it is called Contago.

(f) Stock Index Futures (SIF) is an index derivative which draws its value from the underlying stock.

(g) Contract lot size means number of underlying securities in one contract.

(h) Margin money is collected from the clearing house by the Exchange.

(i) The amount of security money that must be deposited in the margin account at the time a futures contract is first entered into is known as initial margin.

(j) Forward Market Commission regulates financial futures derivate market.

Ans: (a) True, (b) False, (c) True, (d) False, (e) True, (f) False, (g) True, (h) False, (i) True, (j) False.

A. Short Type Questions

1. Define the term "futures".
2. What the the basis in futures derivative?
3. What are the different types of futures?

4. What do you mean by futures contract design?
5. Who are the members in a future exchange?
6. What is a market order?
7. What is a limit order?
8. What is stop order?
9. What is MIT?
10. What is fill or kill order?
11. What are the functions of a clearing house?
12. What do you mean by margin money?
13. What are the different types of margin money imposed by an exchange?
14. SPAN is a portfolio based margining system.
15. Margining on the NSE's derivatives market is done using PRISM system.
16. What is Initial Margin money?
17. What is mark-to market-margin?
18. What is maintenance margin?
19. What is trading system?
20. What do you mean by free commodities?
21. What is off-setting?
22. What is Exchange for Futures for Physicals?

B. Long Type Questions

1. Define the concept "Futures contract". Discuss its features.
2. Compare a futures contract with a forward contract.
3. What is a futures contract? Discuss various types of futures contracts.
4. What are the foundations of a futures contract design? Discuss.
5. Discuss the role of various facilitators in futures market.
6. What is a futures order? Discuss various types of futures orders?
7. Briefly discuss the functions of a clearing house in a futures market.
8. An exchange in a future market standardises the various terms of a futures contract. Discuss with suitable example.
9. What is margin money? Why it is collected? What are the different forms of margin money?
10. Discuss the closing or settlement procedure of a futures contract.
11. Briefly discuss the futures market trading mechanism in India.

THEORIES OF FUTURES PRICES

Learning Objectives

After studying this chapter, you will be able to:

- Understand the concept of futures pricing
- Know how to read futures price quotations
- Understand the basis of futures pricing
- Know the spreads in futures tradings
- Know about the various theories of futures pricing
- Understand the fundamental characteristics of futures prices

Chapter Outline

6.1 AN INTRODUCTION TO FUTURES PRICES

A Futures contract is a standardised agreement to buy or sell an asset on a future date at a price predetermined on the date of contract. The price at which two participants agree to transact as on the settlement date is known as **Futures price.**

All financial futures are standardised in four specifications:

- Asset being exchanged.
- Settlement dates
- Face value of the contact
- Price quotations

A futures trading involves the following basic steps:

1. **Agree to Trade:** It creates long and short positions.
2. **Margin Requirements:** It requires initial margins and maintenance margins.
3. **Offsetting Contracts:** The majority of futures contracts are offset before maturity, because it is costly to take delivery.

The day on which the futures contract is signed, the contract should be designed in a such a method that the value to both the parties is zero. Therefore, none of the buyer or seller will have to pay to the other party for the contract.

On futures trading, only out-of-the pocket payment is margin. Both the buyer and the seller, however, will have to deposit into a margin account which is used to guarantee the fulfilment of the contract. The Exchange collects initial margin and mark-to-market margins depending upon the various factors of a futures contract. An exchange practices daily settlement of any gains and losses on the futures contract to minimise the risk of default at its maturity. Thus, the margining system is designed to make Futures Market accessible to all market participants like speculators, arbitrageurs, traders, investors or hedgers.

The day on which a futures contract is made between two counterparties, no payments are required for the contract, as well as for the underlying assets until the settlement of the contract.

Now, the problem is to determine the futures price which will be acceptable to both buyer and seller. The price of future contract is based on the following factors:

- The nature of the underlying
- The market behaviour
- The risk involved in performance
- The spot price of the underlying.

In this chapter, we will discuss the various approaches for determining futures prices after explaining the basic fundamentals like BASIS and SPREAD.

6.2 HOW TO READ FUTURES PRICE QUOTES?

Future prices are reported daily in major newspapers such as **The Wall Street Journal.** The newpaper quotes contain futures price, volume, etc., from the previous trading session. Contracts are grouped into like commodities such as food and fibre, metals and petroleum, livestock and meat and financial futures.

EXAMPLE: A standardised format containing details about futures price quote of CME (Chicago Mercantile Exchange) is furnished below.

Commodity Futures Quotes at Chicago Mercantile Exchange

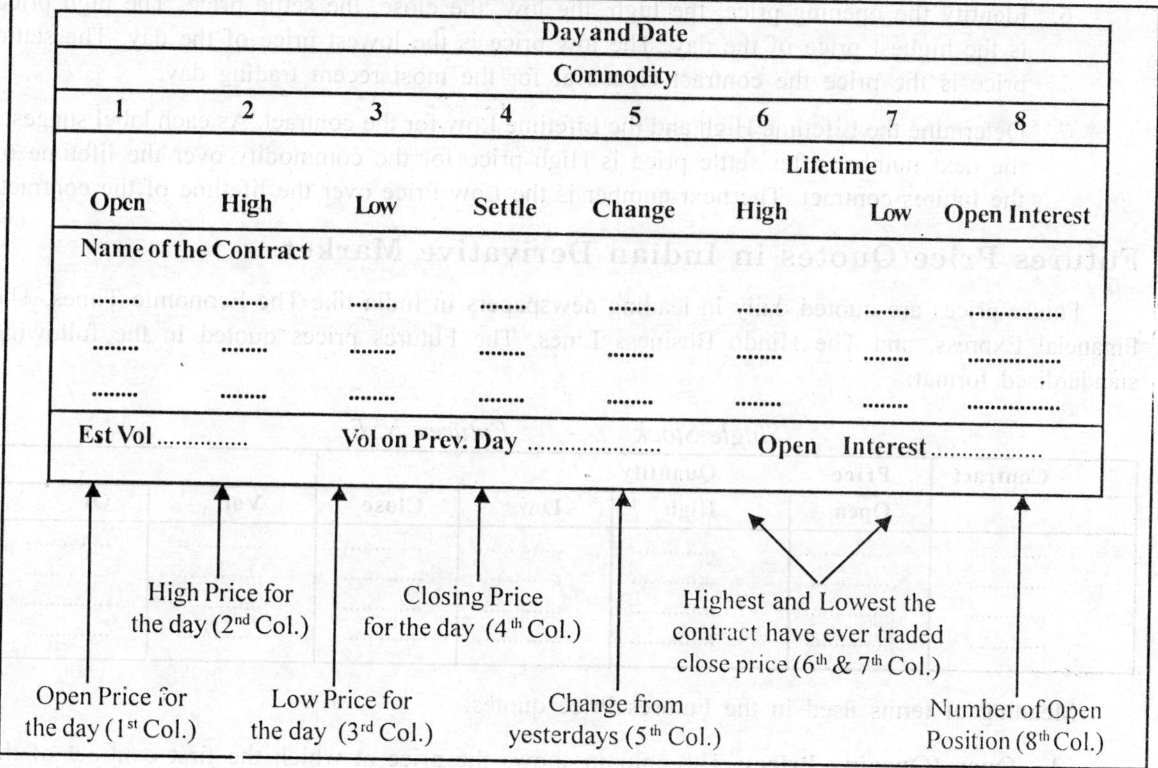

Points to Note:

At the bottom of each contract, heading (under the quotes for the particular commodity) is another line that provides the following detail information:

- The estimated volume of the contracts trading on a particular day.
- The volume traded in the previous session.
- Total open interest for all contracts in this particular commodity.
- The net change in open interest, i.e., change in open positions from yesterday's trading.

A futures market participant may follow the following instructions for understanding how to read futures prices:

1. Obtain a financial/business newspaper, i.e., The Economic Times or The Hindu Business Line. The Financial Express (India) or The Wall Street Journal (American).
2. Turn to Section entitled "Derivatives".
3. Determine the exchange on which the contract is traded.
4. Determine the futures contract size (total value of the contract)
5. Determine the contract maturity or delivery month (the day contract expires). This is listed underneath the contract detail. Contract is due to settle. The current month will be listed first, followed by the next month.
6. Identify the opening price, the high, the low, the close, the settle price. The high price is the highest price of the day. The low price is the lowest price of the day. The settle price is the price the contract closed at for the most recent trading day.
7. Determine the Lifetime High and the Lifetime Low for the contract. As each label suggests the next number after settle price is High price for the commodity over the lifetime of the futures contract. The next number is the Low Price over the lifetime of the contract.

Futures Price Quotes in Indian Derivative Market

Future prices are quoted daily in leading newspapers in India like The Economic Times, The Financial Express, and The Hindu Business Lines. The Futures prices quoted in the following standardised format:

Single-Stock — Futures NSE

Contract	Price	Quantity				
	Open	High	Low	Close	Vol	OI
....	....	....	....	....	....	....
....	....	....	....	....	....	....
....	....	....	....	....	....	....
....	....	....	....	....	....	....

Meaning of terms used in the Futures Price quotes:

1. **Open (Opening Price):** The column shows the price at which the first contract of the day was traded. It is the price for the day's first trade during the designated time period.
2. **High (Highest Price):** The highest price of the contract recorded during the day.
3. **Lowest (Lowest Price):** The lowest price of the contract recorded during the day.
4. **Close (Closing Price):** The close column refers to the settlement price which is recorded at the last minutes of trading of a day. It is the Last Traded Price (LTP).
5. **Settle (Settlement Price):** The settlement price is same as closing price except that it offers as average of the last few minutes of trading. This settlement price is used to compute the mark-to-market margins.

6. **Change (Price Change):** This column shows the change in the settlement price. In other words, the change in previous day's settlement price and today's settlement price is recorded in this change column. This change is settlement price may be either positive or negative.
7. **Lifetime High and Low:** This column refers to the highest and the lowest futures prices during the entire lifetime of the futures contract. It is customary to show high and low price of his futures contract during the lifetime of the contract. But in reality, many futures have a life only a few months.
8. **Volume:** Volume refers to the total number of contracts that are traded on a given day. It may be noted that the total number of contracts bought will be equal to the total number of contracts sold. Thus, volume on any given day will be equal to the number of contracts bought or number of contracts sold.

Points to Note:

Under quantity column there are two sub columns. One is Volume and other one is Interest. The "Volume" represents the efficiency of futures trading over a period of time, may be a day or week or month.

9. **Open Interest (OI):** It refers to total number of futures contract outstanding at the close of the previous day's trading.

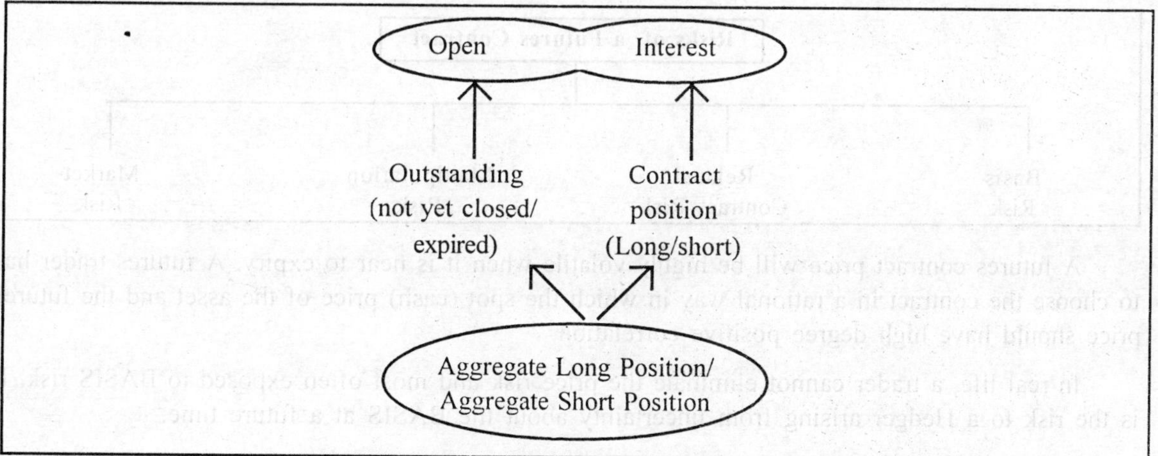

Fig. 6.1: The Concept of Open Interest

The following examples make the understanding of Open Interest (Open/Outstanding futures contracts) very clear:

Example 1. On October 01, 2011, the Open Interest for Nifty October futures is reported as ₹ 10,75,50,000. It means that there are 2,15,100 contracts yet to be traded (10,50,50,000 divided by market lot, which is 500 for Nifty).

Example 2. On October 01, 2011 Mr *X* buys a Nifty Futures contract from Mr. *Y* at the beginning of trading. He sells this futures contract to Mr. *Z* on the same day at 3 p.m.

In this case, the volume of contracts will be two but the open interest will be zero since neither *X* nor *Y* have one open position.

6.3 BASIC CONCEPTS IN FUTURES PRICING

Some basic concepts which are commonly used is futures pricing. These are:

1. Basis
2. Convergence
3. Repo Rate
4. Arbitrage
5. Spreads

We now discuss these concepts with suitable examples.

6.3.1 The Basis

Understanding the concept "BASIS" is a key to hedging. A futures contract is associated with four types of risks. These are:

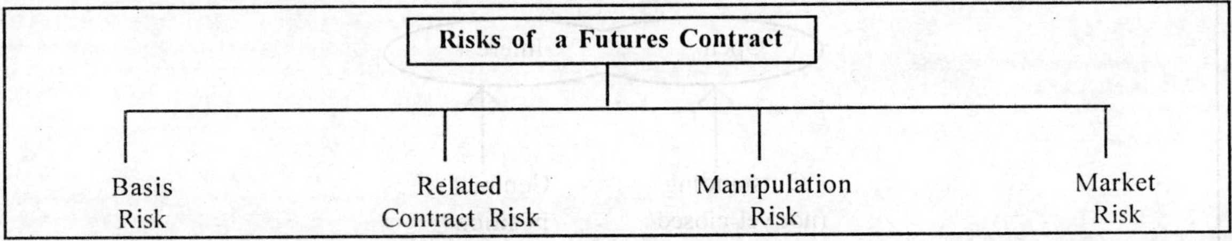

A futures contract price will be highly volatile when it is near to expiry. A futures trader has to choose the contract in a rational way in which the spot (cash) price of the asset and the futures price should have high degree positive correlation.

In real life, a trader cannot eliminate the price risk and most often exposed to BASIS risk. It is the risk to a Hedger arising from uncertainty about the BASIS at a future time.

The term BASIS in a futures contract is the difference between the current cash (spot) price of an underlying asset and the future price of the same asset. In a very simple language, the difference between the spot (cash) price and the futures price of an asset is called BASIS.

Mathematically,

$$\text{Basis} = \text{Futures Price} - \text{Spot or Cash Price}$$

OR

> Basis= $F_{0,t} - S_0$
> Where,
> $F_{0,t}$ = Current Futures price for delivery of the asset at time t
> S_0 = Current cash (spot) price of the asset

For example, if the cash price of a commodity is ₹ 21,000 and October futures on the same asset is priced at ₹ 21,600, then as per the definition: Basis = ₹ 21,600 – ₹ 21,000 = ₹ 600

6.3.2 Convergence

The concept of "convergence" is based on the behaviour of the basis over time. Consider the following behaviour of basis:

(i) On Maturity the Basis is Zero.

When the futures contract matures, the futures price and the spot price must be same. That is BASIS must be equal to zero, except for minor discepanies due to transportation and other transactions cost.

(ii) The Basis Decreases Gradually and Approaches to Zero at Expiration.

The day on which the futures agreement is signed by the parties, the basis is high. As time to expiration approaches to delivery date, the futures price will change to approach (converge) the spot price.

The above stated two characteristics are depicted as follows:

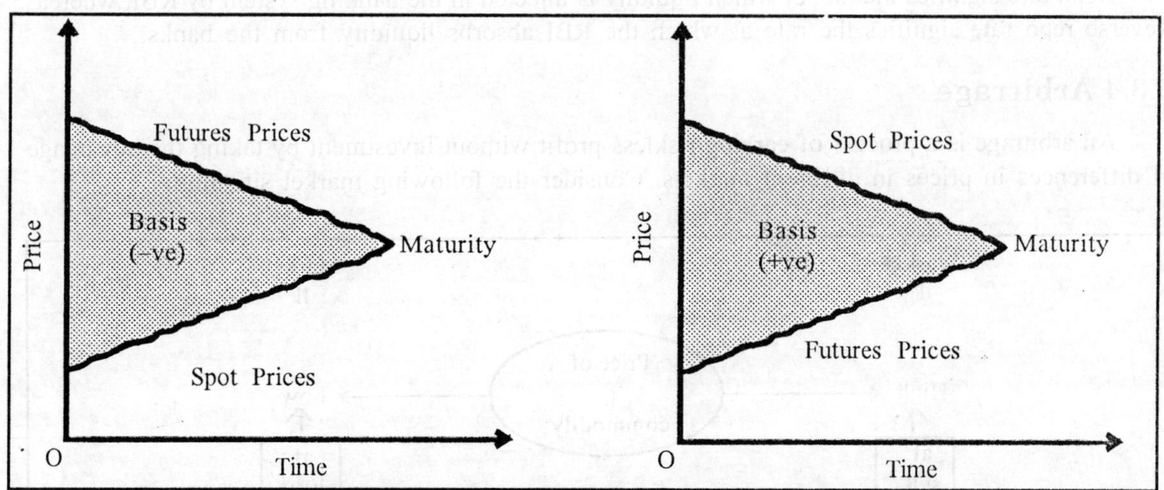

Fig. 6.2: The Concept of Convergence

Interpretation: Consider the situation (i) above when the futures price is above the spot price. When the futures price is above the spot price, a trader will *short a futures contract,* buy an asset and make delivery. It is a clear case of arbitrage opportunity. Due to this arbitrage practice, the futures price will tend to decrease and the spot price will tend to increase. Similarly, when spot price is above the futures price, a trader will long a futures contract and sell an asset. It leads to an arbitrage opportunity. Due to this arbitrage process, the spot price will tend to fall and the futures price will tend to increase. This process of change will continue till the date of expiration when the both prices will converage.

6.3.3 Repo Rate (Repurchase Rate)

A repo or repurchase agreement is an instrument of money market. Usually Reserve Bank of India and Commercial Banks involve in repo transaction but not restricted to these two. Nowadays, individual traders, banks, financial institutions also participate in repurchase agreement.

Repo is a collateralised lending. The commercial banks borrow money from RBI through issue of bonds with an agreement to repurchase the same at a predetermined rate and date. The RBI changes some interest rate on the cash borrowed by the banks. The rate is usually less than the interest rate on bonds as the borrowing is collataral. This interest rate is REPO RATE.

Borrower of funds is called as seller of repo and lender of funds is called as buyers of repo. When the term of the loan is for one day, it is known as overnight repo and if it is more than one day it is called a term repo.

Thus, Repo (Repurchase) rate is the rate at which RBI lends short-term money to the banks. When the repo rate increases borrowing from RBI becomes more expensive.

Reverse Repo rate is the rate at which banks park their short-term excess liquidity with RBI.

Point to Note:

Repo rate signifies the rate at which liquidity is injected in the banking system by RBI, whereas Reverse repo rate signifies the rate at which the RBI absorbs liquidity from the banks.

6.3.4 Arbitrage

An arbitrage is a process of earning riskless profit without investment by taking the advantage of differences in prices in different markets. Consider the following market situation:

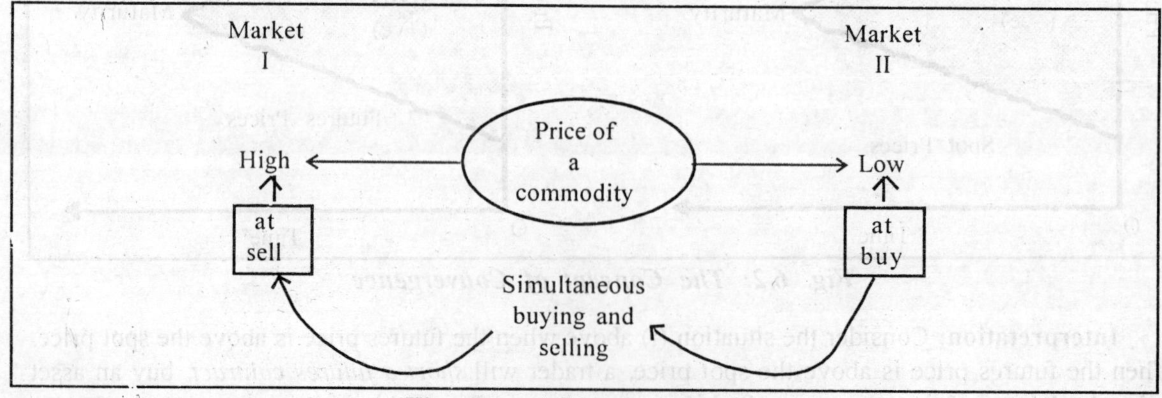

Fig. 6.3: Arbitrage Process

6.3.5 The Spread

Sometimes futures contracts can be made on the same commodity for two different maturity dates. The term "Spread" is defined as the difference in price between two futures contracts on the same commodity for different maturity dates.

Mathematically,

$$\text{Spread} = F_{0,(t+k)} - F_{0,t}$$

Where,

$F_{0,t}$ = The current futures price for the delivery of the underlying at time t.

$F_{0,(t+k)}$ = The current futures price for delivery of the underlying at time t + k.

For example, if t = 3 months, then t + k may be 6 months.

Notes: (*i*) Spread relationship is very important for speculation.

(*ii*) The word "Spread" is commonly known as "calender spread" because it is the difference in price between two futures contracts that have the same underlying commodity, but two different settlement dates.

6.4 THEORIES (APPROACHES OR MODELS) OF FUTURES PRICES

How to calculate fair price of a futures contract? The fair price would be determined in such a way that there would be no opportunities for making arbitrage profit.

The futures price is determined by the following main factors:

(i) The market price of the underlying asset.

(ii) The money market rate.

(iii) Expected dividend/income that arises on the underlying asset during the life of the futures.

(iv) Supply and demand of the assets.

There are the four important models for determining futures prices. These are:

1. Cost of Carry Model
   - In perfect market
   - In imperfect market
2. Expectation Model
3. Normal Backwardation Model
4. Capital Asset Pricing Model

We shall now discuss these model in a very simple way.

6.4.1 Cost-of-Carry Model

The common way to value a futures contract is by using the Cost-of-Carry Model. According to this model, futures prices depend upon two elements.

— The current spot (cash) price of a commodity.

— The cost of carrying or storing the underlying commodity from the present to the delivery date of the futures contract.

It is very clear that there are two determinants for futures prices, i.e., the spot price and the carrying costs.

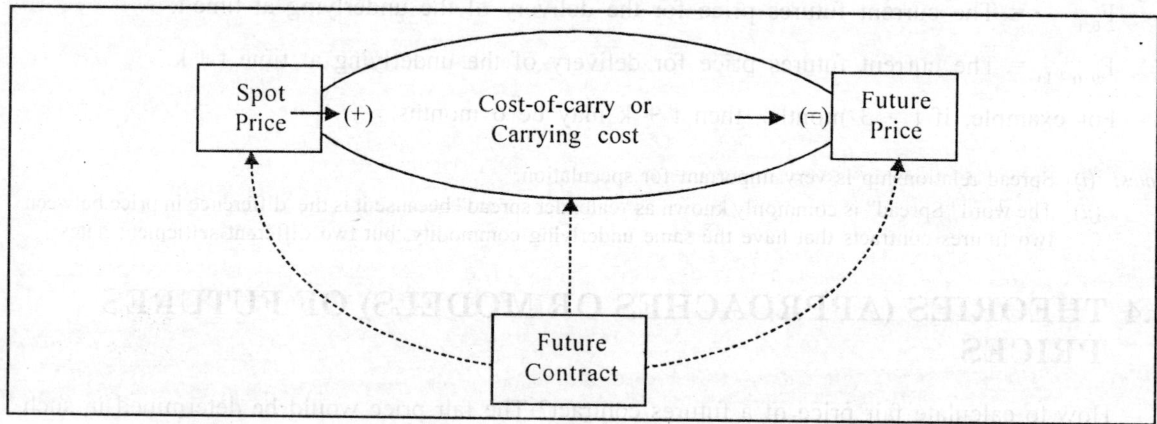

Fig. 6.4: Relationship between Spot Price and Futures Price

It is seen above that the interrelationship between spot price and futures price is developed by the carrying costs.

Cost-of-Carry: There are several components of carrying cost. We may classify all carrying costs of an underlying of a futures contracts into four categories. These are as follows:

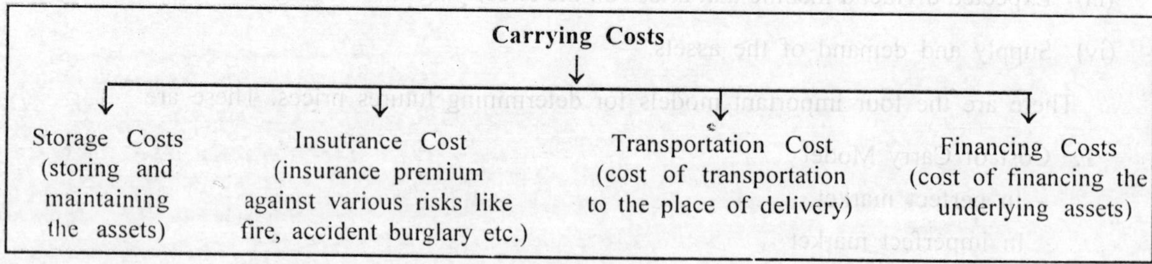

Further, the carrying cost may be gross carrying costs or net carrying costs.

- **Gross Carrying Costs** = Storage costs + Insurance costs + Transportation costs + Cost of financing.
- **Net Carrying Costs** = Gross carrying costs − Convenience yield.

Convenience yield is the benefits that arise from ownership of an asset during the life of the futures contract.

We shall now discuss the cost-of-carry model in perfect market and imperfect market separately.

Cost-of-Carry Model in Perfect Market:

The cost-of-carry model is based on the following assumptions:

1. There are no transaction costs for carrying out trades.
2. There are no restrictions in short selling, in borrowing and lending etc.
3. Investors can borrow and lend.
4. There is no credit risk. Hence, no margin is required.

The Cost-of-Carry model can be expressed as:

$$\boxed{F_{0,t} = S_0(1 + C_{0,t})}$$

Where,

$F_{0,t}$ = The current futures price for delivery of the product at time t

S_0 = The current spot price

$C_{0,t}$ = Cost of carry expressed as a percentage of the spot price

Illustration 1

Determine the futures price from the following data:

Spot price of the commodity – ₹ 1,00,000

Storage costs = 5% p.a

Insurance costs = 3% p.a

Transportation cost = 5% (fixed)

Financing cost = 10% p.a.

Carry period = Time to expiration = 6 months

Use cost-of-carry model.

Solution:

$$\boxed{F_{0,t} = S_0(1 + C_{0,t})}$$

Where

$F_{0,t}$ = Futures price to be determined

S_0 = Current spot price = ₹ 1,00000

$C_{(0,t)}$ = Cost of carry from today until time t

$$= \frac{1}{2}(\text{Storage cost} + \text{Insurance cost} + \text{Financing cost}) + \text{Transportation cost}$$

$$= \frac{1}{2}(5 + 3 + 10) + 5$$

$$= 9 + 5 = 14\% = 0.14$$

$$\text{Now } F_{0,t} = 1{,}00{,}000\ (1 + 0.14)$$

$$= ₹\ 1{,}14{,}000$$

Points to Note:

(i) If contracted futures price is greater than the calculated futures price, arbitrage will take place. Such arbitrage is known as ***Cash-and carry-arbitrage.***

(ii) If negotiated (contracted) futures price is less than the calculated futures price, arbitrage will take place. Such arbitrage is known as ***reverse cash and carry arbitrage.***

Cash-and-Carry Arbitrage

When contracted futures price is higher than the computed futures price, cash-and-carry arbitrage occurs. In such situation, a market participant borrows money, buys the goods today for cash, sells futures contract, carries the goods to the expiration of the futures contract. On expiration, he delivers the commodity against a futures contract and pays off the loan. The profit of such strategy is cash-and-carry arbitrage profit.

Thus,

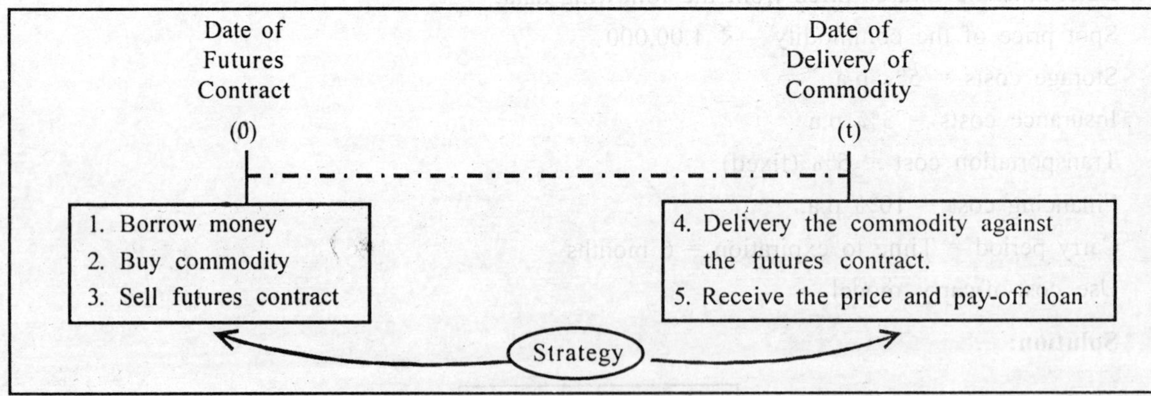

Fig. 6.5: Cost-of-Carry Arbitrage Process

Illustration 2

Calculate cash-and-carry arbitrage profit from the following data of a futures contract:

Spot Price = ₹ 1,00000

Cost-of-carry = 14% of spot price for the carry period

Contracted Futures Price = ₹ 1,20,000

Solution:

Futures Prices = Spot Price + Cost-of-carry
= 1,00,000 + 14% of 1,00,000
= ₹ 1,14,000

Contracted Futures Price = ₹ 1,20,000

Cash and Carry Arbitrage profit = ₹ 1,20000 – ₹ 1,14,000
= ₹ 6,000.

Reverse Cash-and-Carry Arbitrage

When contracted futures prices is lower than the computed futures price, the reverse cash-and-carry arbitrage occurs. In such situation, a market participant sells the commodity today for cash. Then he purchases a futures contract which will be used to honour the short sale commitment. Further, he lends the sale proceeds of the commodity upto the date of expiration of futures contract. On the expiration date, he accepts delivery against the futures contract and settles the payment. The profit of such strategy is reverse cash-and-carry arbitrage profit.

The following architectural concept makes the process clear:

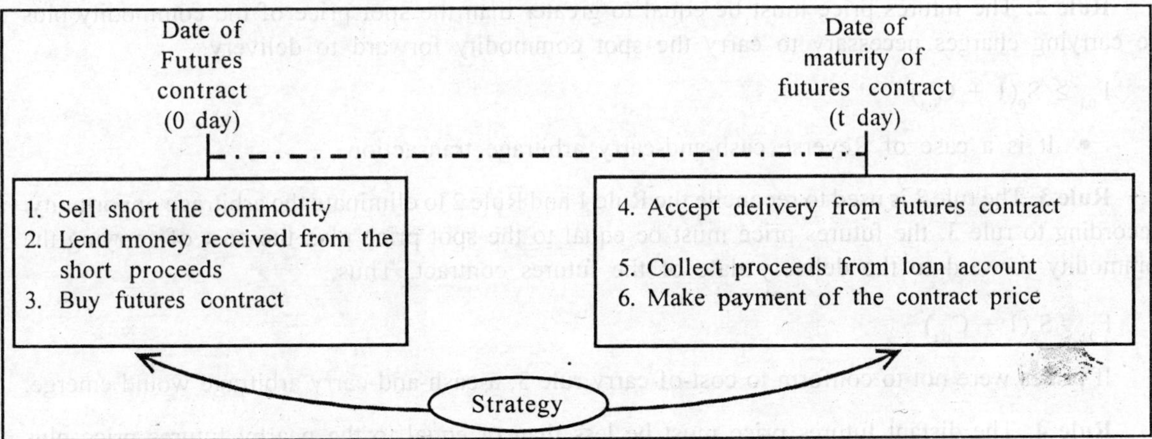

Fig. 6.6: Reverse Cash-and-Carry Arbitrage

Comparison between Cash-and-Carry and Reverse Cash-and-Carry Arbitrage Strategies

From the above discussion, now we make comparison between cash-and-carry arbitrage strategy and Reverse cash-and-carry arbitrage strategy.

Comparison between Cash-and-Carry Arbitrage Strategy and Reverse Cash-and-Carry Arbitrage Strategy

Point of Comparison	Cash-and-Carry Strategy	Reverse Cash-and-Carry Strategy
Fund Management	Borrow funds equal to spot price	Lend funds out of sale proceeds
Transaction	Buy asset and store	Sell asset and lend the sale proceed
Futures contract	Sell Futures	Buy futures
Delivery	Delivery against futures	Accept delivery set at expiration

Rules of Cost-of-Carry

Rule 1. The futures price must be less than or equal to the spot price of the commodity plus the carrying charges necessary to carry the spot commodity forward to delivery.

Thus,

$$F_{0,t} \leq S_0(1 + C_{0,t})$$

- It is a case of cash-and-carry arbitrage transaction.

Rule 2. The futures price must be equal to greater than the spot price of the commodity plus the carrying charges necessary to carry the spot commodity forward to delivery.

$$F_{0,t} \geq S_0(1 + C_{0,t})$$

- It is a case of Reverse cash-and-carry arbitrage transaction.

Rule 3. The rule 3 is used to reconcile the Rule 1 and Rule 2 to eliminate the arbitrage opportunity. According to rule 3, the futures price must be equal to the spot price plus the cost of carrying the commodity forward to the delivery date of the futures contract. Thus,

$$F_{0,t} = S_0(1 + C_{0,t})$$

If prices were not to conform to cost-of-carry rule 3, a cash-and-carry arbitrage would emerge.

Rule 4. The distant futures price must be less than or equal to the nearby futures price plus the cost of carrying the commodity from the nearby delivery date to the distant delivery date,

$$F_{0,d} \leq F_{0,n}(1 + C_{n,d})$$

Where $d > n$

$F_{0,d}$ = The futures price at $t = 0$ for the distant delivery contract maturing $t = d$

$F_{0,n}$ = The futures price at $t = 0$ for the nearby delivery contract maturing at $t = n$

$C_{n,d}$ = Cost of carry from $t = n$ to $t = d$

Points to Note:

If prices were not conform to cost-of-carry rule 4, a cash-and-carry arbitrage would emerge.

Rule 5. The nearby futures price ($F_{0,n}$) plus the cost of carrying the commodity from the nearby delivery date to the distant delivery date ($C_{n,d}$) cannot exceed the distant future price. Thus,

$$F_{0,n}(1 + C_{n,d}) \leq F_{0,d}$$

If prices were not conform to cost-of-carry rule 5, a reverse cash-and-carry arbitrage would emerge.

Cost-of-Carry Model in Imperfect Market

The assumptions of cost-of-carry model in perfect market have no practical implication. There are five important imperfections noticed in the market. These are as follows:

1. Transaction costs.
2. Unequal borrowing and lending rates.
3. Restrictions on short selling.
4. Sell-buy profit (Bid-ask spread).
5. Limitations to storage.

Models: With transaction cost.

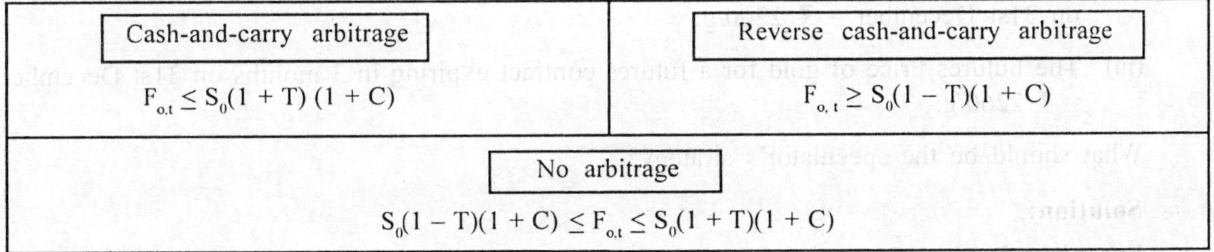

Point to Note:

Like transaction costs, other variables like unequal borrowing and lending rates, restrictions on short selling and limitations to storage, etc., may be taken in similar way and Futures pricing models can be developed.

6.4.2 The Expectation Model

The Expectation model of futures pricing is based on the perception of the market participants. All the market participants know the nature of the commodity, demand and supply positions, the behaviour of the market and the price pattern. They have to forecast, the *expected futures spot price* by using certain quantitative techniques.

The expectation model of futures pricing states that the *current future price* must be equal to the *expected futures spot price.*

Model

$F_{0,t} = E_0(S_t)$

Where

$F_{0,t}$ = Futures Price at t = 0

E_0 = Expectation at t = 0

S_t = Spot price at t

$E_0(S_t)$ = Expectation at t = 0 of the spot price to prevail at time t.

Results:

(i) If the above model $F_{0,t} = E_0(S_t)$ is considered as correct, then a speculator cannot expect any profit or loss from a position in the futures market. Then

Expected Profit = $E_0(S_t) - F_{0,t} = 0$

(ii) If $F_{0,t} \neq E_0(S_t)$, speculative opportunities emerge and speculators would exploit the opportunities and ultimately there would be parity between these prices. The above results can be explained through an example.

Illustration 3:

(i) Spot price of gold as on 1st October = ₹ 2100/g.

(ii) The expected future spot price of gold for a future contract expiring in 3 months, i.e., on 31st December = ₹ 2200/g.

(iii) The Futures Price of gold for a futures contract expiring in 3 months on 31st December = ₹ 2260/g.

What should be the speculator's strategy?

Solution:

Speculator's Strategy:

(i) Sell gold futures contract at ₹ 2260/g.

(ii) On 31st December, he will buy in the spot market at ₹ 2200/g (the spot price expected to prevail at that time).

(iii) He will deliver the gold against the gold futures contract and collect ₹ 2260/g.

(iv) Earn a profit of ₹ 60/g.

Illustration 4:

Spot price of gold as on 1st October ₹ 2100/g.

Expected future spot price of gold for a future contract expiring 3 months, i.e., on 31st December = ₹ 2200/g.

The futures price of gold for a futures contract expiring in 3 months ending on 31st December = ₹ 2170/g.

What should be the speculator's strategy?

Solution:

Speculator's strategy:

(i) Buy futures at ₹ 2170/g.

(ii) On 31st December, take delivery of gold under futures contract.

(iii) Sell gold immediately in the spot market at ₹ 2200/g.

(iv) Earn profit ₹ 30/g.

Points to Note:

1. Condition for speculative profit:

(i) If speculative profit > transaction cost

(ii) If speculative profit > risk (expected loss)

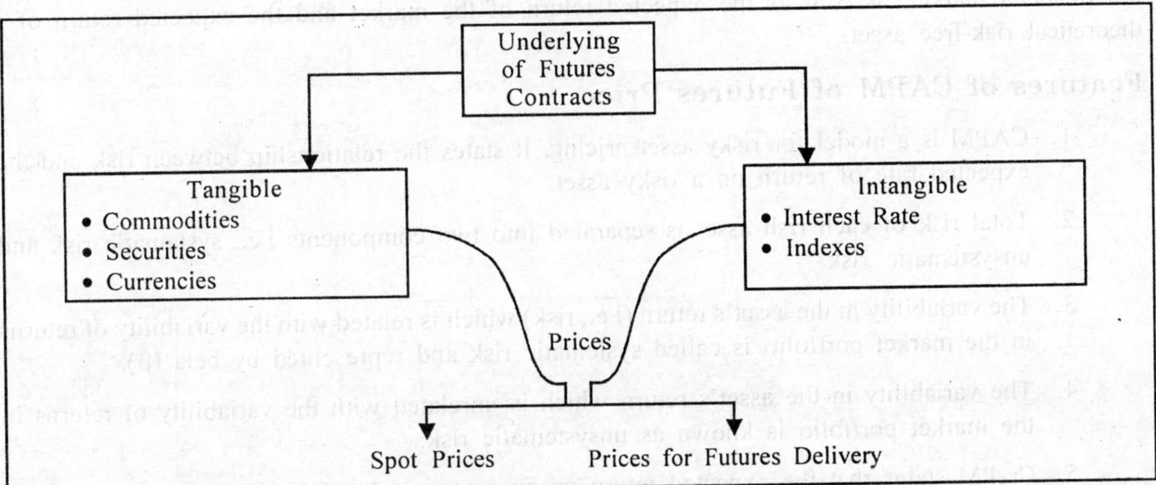

6.4.3 Normal Backwardation Model

Where the price of an underlying asset of a futures contract is higher than the spot price, or where a distant future delivery price is higher than a nearer future delivery is known as "CONTAGO".

Where the price of an underlying asset of a futures contract for future delivery is lower than the spot price, or where a distant future delivery price is lower than a nearer future delivery, is known as BACKWARDATION.

Thus,

$F > S \rightarrow$ Contago $\rightarrow$ Negative Basis

$F < S \rightarrow$ Backwardation $\rightarrow$ Positive Basis

Where,

F = Futures Price

S = Spot Price

The concept NORMAL BACKWARDATION means a market where futures prices are below expected future spot prices.

Model : **F = E + rp**

Where F = Future Price

E = Expected price at that date

rp = Risk premium

6.4.4 Capital Asset Pricing Model (CAPM)

This CAPM describes the relationship between risk and expected return and that is used in the pricing of risky securities. This model takes into account the assets sensitivity to non-diversifiable risk (also known as systematic risk or market risk), often represented by the quantity beta (β) in the financial market, as well as the expected return of the market and the expected return of a theoretical risk-free asset.

Features of CAPM of Futures Price

1. CAPM is a model for risky asset pricing. It states the relationship between risk and the expected rate of return on a risky asset.
2. Total risk of each rish asset is separated into two components i.e., systematic risk and unsystematic risk.
3. The variability in the asset's return (i.e., risk) which is related with the variability of returns in the market portfolio is called systematic risk and represented by beta (β).
4. The variability in the asset's return which is unrelated with the variability of returns in the market portfolio is known as unsystematic risk.
5. CAPM states that the expected return on an asset is related to systematic risk and not to its total risk.

Assumptions of CAPM

1. Perfectly competitive market.
2. No tax and no transaction cost.
3. Investors are risk-averse. They prefer highest expected returns for a given level of risk. They will take the risk only if they are compensated for the risk.
4. Investors have homogeneous expectations about the expected return and risks of securities.
5. All investors have same holding aperiod.
6. Risk-free rate at which all investors can lend and borrow.

Methodology of CAPM

The-risk averse investors expect higher return than the risk-free return. The Capital Market Line (CML) defines this relationship by the following equation.

$$E(R_P) = R_j + \left\{\frac{E(R_m)-R_j}{\sigma_m}\right\}\sigma_P$$

Where, $E(R_P)$ = Expected portfolio return

R_j = Risk-free return

$E(R_m)$ = Expected return on market portfolio

σ_m = Standard deviation of the market portfolio

σ_P = Standard deviation of the portfolio

As mentioned above, beta (β) represents the systematic risk. It can not be minimised. A beta of 1.0 indicates average level of risk. A beta more than 1.0 signifies that the security's return more than that of the market portfolio. However, a zero beta means no risk.

Expected Return on Security:

The following model is used to measure the expected return on a security:

$$E(R_j) = R_j + (R_m - R_j)\,\beta_i$$

Where, $E(R_j)$ = Expected return on security

R_j = Risk-free rate

R_m = The Market Return

β_j = The measure of the security's systematic risk

$$= \frac{\sigma_j}{\sigma_m} \text{cov}_{jm}$$

Points to Note:

(i) The above stated equation represented by a line in a graph is known as security market line (SML).

(ii) The beta (β) is ratio of the covariance of return of a security j and the market portfolio m (the numerator), to the variance of return of the market portfolio (the denominator).

Mathematically,

$$B_j = \frac{\text{Cov}_{jm}}{\text{Var}_m} = \frac{\sigma_j \sigma_j r_{jm}}{\sigma_m^2} = \frac{\sigma_j}{\sigma_m} = \sigma_{lm}$$

Where σ_j = Standard deviation of security price

σ_m = Standard deviation of market portfolio

r_{jm} = Correlation of j and m.

(iii) $r_{jm} = \frac{Cov_{jm}}{\sigma_j \sigma_m}$

$\Rightarrow Cov_{jm} = \sigma_j \sigma_m \sigma_{jm}$

Conclusion:

This beta (B) is the key decision factor in futures pricing. The market participant may use the beta factor as follows:

Degree of B	Long Future	Short Future
If $\beta > 1$	The futures price should rise over time.	The futures price should fall over time.
If $\beta = 0$	The futures price should not change.	The futures price should not change.
If $\beta < 1$	The future price should fall over time.	The futures price should rise over time.

CHAPTER SUMMARY

Many finance professionals have been continuing their attempts for determining the futures prices of an asset underlying the futures contract. Till 2011, only four approaches came to light. These are:

- Cost-of-carry approach
- Expectation approach
- Normal Backwardation approach
- The Capital Asset Pricing model.

Before discussing these approaches (models), this chapter explained the basic awareness to read the futures price quotes. The various terms which are normally used in futures quotes like Open price, High price, Low price, settle/close price change, Lifetime High, Lifetime low, Open Interest (OI), etc have been explained in lucid manner.

Further, to understand the methodology of various approaches of futures prices, one should be familiar of certain basic concepts like BASIS, CONVERGENCE, REPO RATE, ARBITRAGE and SPREADS. These fundamental concepts have been explained before the pricing models.

The common way to value a futures contract is **COST-OF-CARRY MODEL**. According to this model, futures price is equal to the spot price plus cost of carry cost of carry represents carrying cost which includes storage cost, insurance cost, transportation cost and financing cost.

"The cost-of-carry model can be used in two market conditions, i.e., perfect market condition and imperfect market condition. The summary of cost-of-carry model is put as follows:

Cost-of-Carry Model

Perfect Market	Imperfect Market
Assumptions:	*Assumptions:*
• No transaction cost • No restriction on short selling. • No restriction in borrowing and lending. • Same rate of interest for borrowing and lending. • No credit risk, no margin. *Formula:* $F_{o,t} = S_0 (1 + C_{ot})$	• Transaction cost • Restriction on short selling. • Restrictions on borrowing and lending. • Unequal borrowing and lending rates. • Credit risk and requirement of margin. *Formula:* $S_0(1 - T)(1 + C) \le F_{o,t} \le S_0(1 + T)(1 + C)$

The second approach to pricing a futures contract is **Expectation Model.** According to this model, the current futures price must be equal to the expected future spot price. The difference between expected future price and initial futures price is the expected futures profit.

Mathematically,

$$F_{o,t} = E_0(S_t)$$

Where $F_{o,t}$ = Future price at t_0

$E_0(S_t)^*$ = Expectation at t = 0 of the spot price to prevail at time t.

But in real life situation $F_{o,t} = E_0(S_t)$. In such situation speculators take advantages to earn profit provided that the transaction cost and risk is less than such speculative profit.

Besides, there are two other models can be used for determining the futures price in the context of risk aversion. These are the Normal Backwardation Model and Capital Asset Pricing Model. The Backwardation is a market situation in which the futures price is less than the cash or spot price and thereby resulting in positive basis. In reverse case, i.e., if the basis is negative it is a contago market. Thus,

Basis	Market
Positive	Backwardation
Negative	Contago

The last method is CAPM which is used for pricing of risky securities. According to this model:

Expected return on each pure asset = Current spot price – Expected future spot price.

"If you expect too much, you will be frustrated. If you don't want to be frustrated don't expect. Live without expectations and there will be no frustration."

SOLVED PROBLEMS

Problem 1. Determine the futures price from the following data.

Spot Price = ₹ 17,00000

Cost-of-Carry = 12% p.a.

Carry period = 6 months

Use cost-of-carry model.

Solution:

$$F_{0,t} = S_0 (1 + C_{0t})$$

Where, $F_{0,t}$ = Spot Price = ₹ 17,00000

$$C_{0,t} = \text{Carrying cost p.a} \times \frac{6}{12}$$

$$= 12 \times \frac{6}{12} = 0.06$$

$$F_{0,t} = 17,00,000\ (1 + .06)$$

= ₹ 18,02,000

Problem 2. Calculate the profit or loss from the following transactions.

Spot Price = ₹ 21,00,000

Interest rate = 8% per annum

Storage cost = 4% of commodity per annum

Transportation cost = Nil

Use cost-of-carry model.

Solution:

Transaction Strategy	Cash Flow (₹)
(a) Borrow ₹ 21,00,000 for six months	+ 21,00,000
(b) Buy commodity	(–) 21,00,000
(c) Sell a futures contract for 23,50,000 for delivery	Nil
(d) Net cash flow as on the date of contract	Nill
(e) Delivery the commodity against futures contract	23,00,000
Repay the loan including the interest	(–) 21,84,000
Cost of carry	(–) 42,000
(f) Net Profit/loss	74,000

Problem 3. From the following data compute beta of a security?

σ_j = 10%, σ_m = 8%, Cov_{jm} = +.65

Solution:

$$\beta_j = \frac{\sigma_j \sigma_m}{\sigma_m^2} = \frac{10 \times 8 \times 65}{8^2} = \frac{52}{64} = 0.8125$$

Problem 4. Calculate the expected rate of return for an underlying asset from the following information:

R_j = 12%; R_m = 16%; β = 1.25

Solution:

The expected return of the underlying asset will be:

$$E(R_j) = R_j + (R_m - R_j)\,\beta_j$$

$$= 12\% + (16\% - 12\%)\ 1.25$$

$$= 12\% + 5\% = 17\%$$

SUGGESTIONS FOR FURTHER READINGS

1. Boz, Jamil and Chacko, George, *Financial Derivatives: Pricing Application and Mathematics*, Cambridge University Press, New York, 2003.
2. Epps, T.W., *Pricing Derivatives Securities, World Scientific,* River Edge, New Jersey, 2000.

EXERCISES

Quiz

1. State whether these are True or False.

(a) As on the date of a futures contract, no exchange of cash flow is made between two parties.

(b) In a derivative quote, the 'open' column shows the price at which the first contract of the date was traded.

(c) The LTP refers last traded price.

(d) The total number of futures contracts outstanding at the close of the previous day's trading is known as open interest.

(e) The difference between the spot price and futures price of an asset under a futures contract is known as basis.

(f) On maturity of a futures contract, the basis is zero.

(g) If the futures price is greater than the spot price, the basis is negative and *vice versa.*

(h) The difference in price between two futures contracts on the same commodity for different maturity dates is known as spread.

(i) Spot price plus cost-of-carry is futures price.

(j) Storage cost, insurance cost, transportation cost and financing costs are four elements of carrying cost.

(k) If Futures price exceeds spot price, it is called contago.

(l) If Futures price is less than spot price, it is called backwardation.

Ans: (a) True, (b) True, (c) True, (d) True, (e) True, (f) True,
(h) True, (i) True, (j) True, (k) True, (l) True.

A. Short Type Questions

1. What are the steps in futures trading?
2. What is open interest?
3. What is settlement price?
4. What are the risks associated in a futures contract?
5. What is basis?
6. What do you mean by convergence?
7. What is Repo rate?
9. Define the concept "Spread".
10. What is the formula of cost-of-carry model?
11. What are the approaches of futures pricing?
12. What is Contago?
13. What is Backwardation?
14. What is cash-and-carry arbitrage?
15. What is reverse cash-and-carry arbitrage?
16. Give the mathematical model of Expectation approach of futures pricing.
17. In which asset CAPM is used for futures pricing?

B. Long Type Questions

1. How to read futures price quotes? Explain the various terms used is such quotes.
2. Briefly discuss the following concepts used is pricing methodology of futures contracts.
   (a) Basis (b) convergence (c) Repo Rate (d) Arbitrage (e) Spread
3. What are the various approach to pricing of futures contracts? Discuss.
4. Discuss the cost-of-carry model of futures pricing.
5. Briefly discuss the six rules of cost-of-carry model of futures pricing.
6. Briefly discuss the following risk aversion method of futures pricing:
   (a) The Normal Backwardation Method (b) The CAPM
7. Briefly explain the following arbitrage strategy of cost-of-carry model:
   (a) Cash-and-carry arbitrage (b) Reverse cash-and-carry arbitrage.

PRACTICAL PROBLEMS

1. Current futures price for delivery of the asset after 4 months = ₹ 10,500

   Current cash (spot) price of the asset = ₹ 10,3000

   The rate of return = 12% p.a.

   Calculate Basis.

2. The current futures price for the delivery of the underlying asset after 3 months = $F_{0,3}$ = ₹ 16,000

   The current futures price for delivery of the underlying after 6 months.

   $F_{0,6}$ = ₹ 16,600.

   Find Spread.

3. Determine the futures price from the following data:

   Spot price of the commodity = ₹ 90,000

   Storage cost = 6% p.a. of spot price

   Insurance cost = 4% p.a. of spot price

   Transportation cost = 3% (fixed)

   Financing cost = 12% p.a.

   Carry period = 6 months

   Use cost-of-carry model.

4. Calculate cash-and-carry arbitrage profit from the following data of a futures contract:

   Spot price = ₹ 70,000

   Cost-of-carry = 12% of spot price for the carry period

   Contracted future price = ₹ 90,000.

5. Calculate the expected rate of return for an underlying asset from the following information.

   R_j = 10%; R_m = 12%, B = 1.75.

HEDGING STRATEGY USING FUTURES

Learning Objectives

After studying this chapter, you will be able to:

- Know the concept of hedging
- Understand the basics of long and short hedges
- Understand the concept of basis and basis risk
- Formulate a hedging strategy by understanding the objective, environmental/situational analysis and optimal hedge ratio
- Calculate hedge ratio
- Know how to implement hedging strategy
- Evaluate and control hedging strategy
- Familiar with MAE model

Chapter Outline

7.1 INTRODUCTION

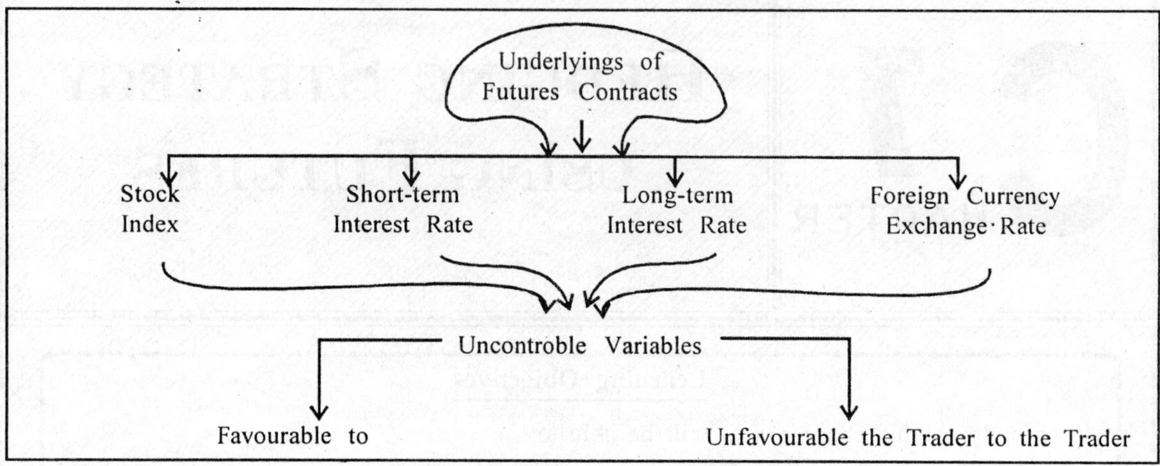

The unfavourable change in the price of an underlying of a futures contract is backed by "Risk and Uncertainty" and uncontrollable in nature. In other words, this adverse price movements in an asset is treated as price risk or market risk. This price risk cannot be eliminated but can be reduced. Hedging strategy is used to reduce or manage such price risks.

Futures can be used as an effective risk management tool. Hedging strategy using futures can secure protection against a potentially adverse outcomes

7.2 HEDGING: MEANING AND DEFINITIONS

Hedging is a method of reducing risk of loss caused by price fluctuations.

Example: A commodity trader may purchase and sell equal quantities of the same or very similar commodities in two different markets, at approximately the same time, with the expectation that a future change in price in one market will be offset by an appropriate change in the price in another market. This act of managing price risk is an example of hedging.

Thus, traders use this hedging strategy when they are unsure of where the market will go.

Definitions

The concept "hedging" has been defined as follows:

1. The practice by which a business or investor limits risk by taking position that tend to offset each other. — *Dictionary of Cultural Literacy: Economics*
2. A concept that involves offsetting a risk position. — *Barron's Law Dictionary*
3. Hedging is a strategy to reduce risk by taking opposite of what one already has.
4. Hedging is about protecting one's market position from an unanticipated or unwanted price fluctuations in the market.

5. Hedging is a method used by the traders to reduce loss due to market fluctuations.
6. A perfect hedge is a no-risk-no-gain precaution against futures price risk.
7. Hedging means taking a position in a futures market opposite to a position held in the cash market to minimise the risk of financial losses from an unfavourable changes in price.

Thus, hedging means designing a trading method to reduce price risk. To do in practice, a trader has to take a position in the futures market which is opposite to the spot market, with the objective of reducing or limiting risks associated with price changes.

7.3 HEDGING: A TWO STEP PROCESS

A hedge is a position in a derivative market that reduces the exposure to a market risk from a futures purchase or sale of an underlying asset.

A hedging process undergoes in two steps:

(I) Determination of profits which are affected by change in asset price, security price, interest rate or exchange rate.

(II) Entering into a futures position with the opposite exposure with an objective to reduce the risk.

Points to Notes:

1. If the exposure is such that the trader gains when the price of the asset increases and loses when the price of the asset decreases, a **short hedge** is appropriate.
2. If the exposure is such that the trader gains when the price of the asset decreases and loses when the price of the asset increases, a **long hedge** is appropriate.

Example: Mr. X wants to enter into an agreement with Mr. Y to supply 20 metric tons of a particular commodity. The specifications are as follows:

Date of contract : 1st October, 2011

Date of supply : 1st December, 2011

Spot price as on 1st October 2011 = ₹ 5100 per quintal.

Mr. X plans to buy the commodity for delivery to Mr. Y on 31st December. Now Mr. X is exposed to the risk of rising prices between 1st October and 31st December.

To hedge this price risk, Mr. X buys on 1st October and December contract of 20 metric tons at ₹ 5250 per quintal from the exchange.

The commodity spot price rises to ₹ 5550 per quintal during December. Let us assume the Futures price on 31st December is ₹ 5800 per quintal.

Hedging Strategy:

On 1st October, Mr. X has to buy the commodity from the spot market at a price of ₹ 5500 per quintal where Mr. X pays ₹ 400 per quintal more. However, since the future price has risen by ₹ 550 per quintal, i.e., (5800 – 5250), he makes a profit by squaring off his futures position, i.e., he sells one lot 20 metric tonnes. Thus, Mr. X effectively offsets his loss in the spot market by making a gain in the futures market. The net purchase price of commodity may be worked out as follows:

Spot price as an 1st October	₹ 5500 p.q.
Less: Gain through futures contract	₹ 550 p.q.
Net purchase price	₹ 4950 p.q.

Further, the net gain per quintal is ₹ 5100 minus ₹ 4950, i.e., ₹ 150 per quintal.

7.4 CLASSIFICATION OF HEDGING STRATEGIES

There are two ways an hedger can apply his strategy. These are:

(i) A Long (Buying) Futures Hedge

(ii) A Short (Selling) Futures Hedge.

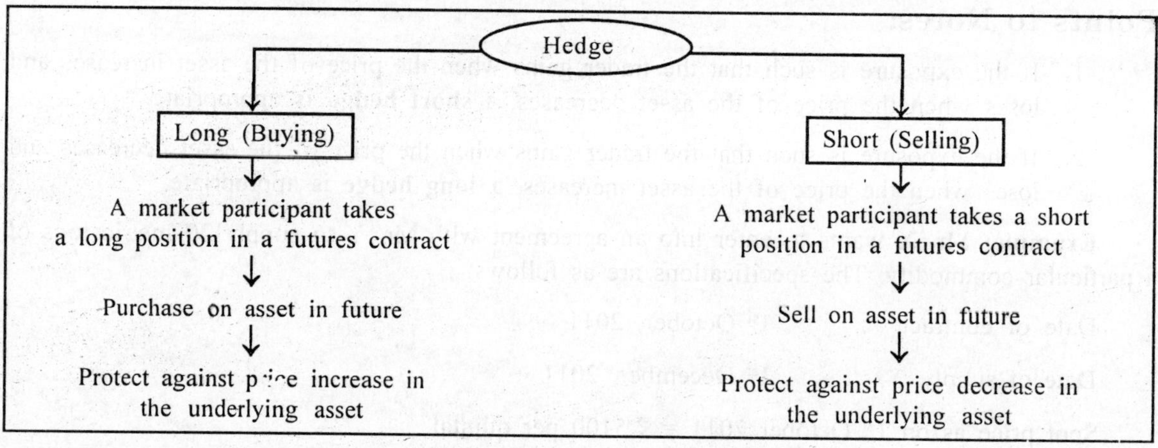

Suitability:

- A long futures hedge is suitable when a market participant has to purchase an asset in the future and wants to lock in the price now.
- A short futures hedge is suitable when a market participant has to sell an asset in the future and wants to lock in the price now.

7.5 BASIS RISK AND HEDGING

Basis: The concept and value.

Basis is the difference between the spot price and futures price of an underlying asset.

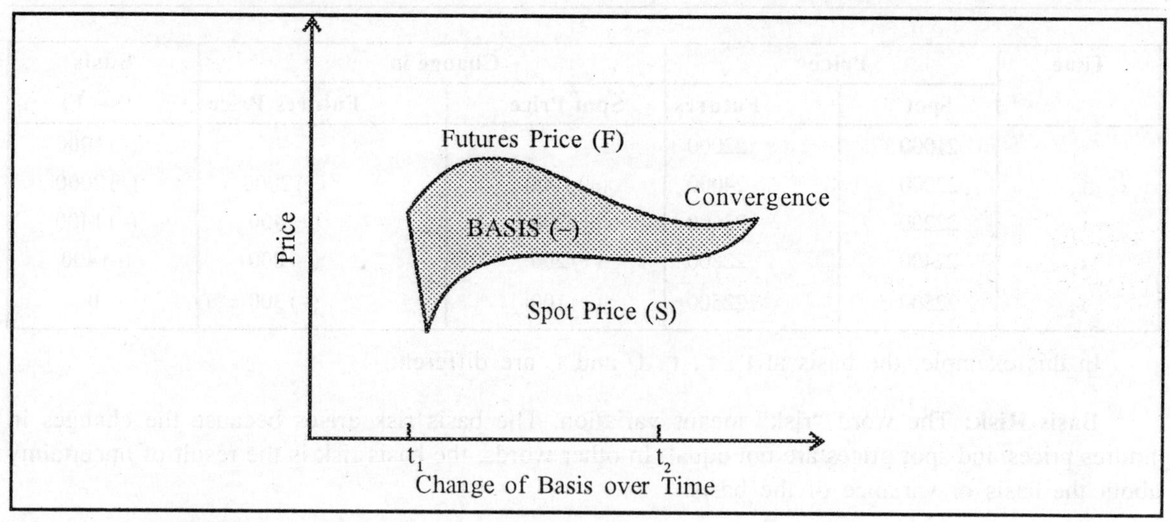

Points to Note:

(i) Hedge starts at time t_1.

(ii) Hedge closes at time t_2.

(iii) If S > F, then basis is positive. For example if the underlying is high-interest-rate currency, then basis will be positive.

(iv) If F > S, then basis is negative. For example if the underlying is low-interest-rate currency, then the basis will be negative.

(v) If F = S, then basis is zero.

(vi) Prior to expiration the basis may be positive or negative.

(vii) On maturity, both spot price and futures price converge and the basis is zero, if the asset to be hedged and the asset underlying the futures contract are same.

Consider the following examples:

Example 1

Time	Price		Change in		Basis
	Spot	Futures	Spot Price	Futures Price	(S – F)
t_1	21000	22000	–	–	(–) 1000
t_2	22000	23000	(+) 1000	(+) 1000	(–) 1000
t_3	22200	22800	(+) 200	(+) 200	(–) 600
t_4	22400	22600	(+) 200	(–) 200	(–) 200
t_5	22500	22500	(+) 100	(–) 100	Nil

In the above table, the basis is negative, i.e., 1000 at t_1, since futures price is higher than spot price. The basis at t_2 is (–) 1000 which is equal at t_1. It means there is no basis risk. At t_5, the basis is zero.

Time	Price		Change in		Basis
	Spot	Futures	Spot Price	Futures Price	(S – F)
t_1	21000	22000	–	-	(–) 1000
t_2	22000	24000	(+) 1000	(+) 2000	(–) 2000
t_3	22200	23600	(+) 200	(+) 400	(–) 1400
t_4	22400	22800	(+) 200	(–) 800	(–) 400
t_5	22500	22500	(+) 100	(–) 300	0

In this example, the basis at t_1, t_2, t_3, t_4 and t_5 are different.

Basis Risk: The word "risk" means variation. The basis risk arises because the changes in futures prices and spot prices are not equal. In other words, the basis risk is the result of uncertainty about the basis or variance of the basis.

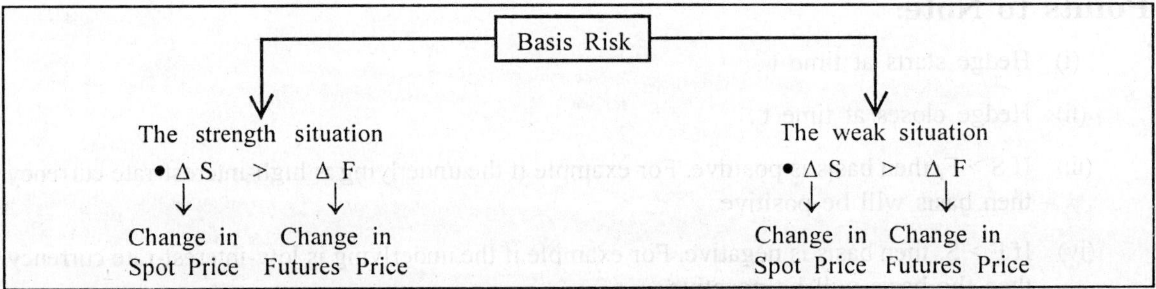

Determination of Cost of Assets under Long Hedge and Price Realisation under Short Hedge:

(i) Cost of Asset under Long Hedge:

Let F_1 = Initial Futures Price

F_2 = Final Futures Price

S_2 = Final Asset Price

A = Cost of Asset

When a trader hedges the future purchase of an asset by entering into a long futures contract, then the cost of the asset will be determined by the following formula:

$$P = S_2 - (F_2 - F_1) = S_2 - F_2 + F_1$$
$$= (\text{Basis}) + F_1 = F_1 + \text{Basis}$$

(ii) Price Realisation under Short Hedge:

When a trader hedges the future sale of an asset by entering into a short futures contract, then the price will be calculated by using the following formula:

$$P = S_2 + (F_1 - F_2) = F_1 + (S_2 - F_2) = F_1 + \text{Basis}$$

Thus, it is observed that, changes in the futures price and cash price of an asset are not equal in normal cases. This situation brings basis risk to the trader.

The above concept can be understood from the following example:

Time	Price		Change in		Basis
	Spot	Futures	Spot Price	Futures Price	
t_1	21000	22000	0	0	(–) 1000
t_2	21200	22300	(+) 200	(+) 300	(–) 1100
Change	(+) 200	(+) 300	(+) 200	(–) 300	(–) 100

Here Spot price at time $t_1 = S_1 = 21000$

Spot price at time $t_2 = S_2 = 21200$

Futures price at time $t_1 = F_1 = 22000$

Futures price at time $t_2 = F_2 = 22300$

Basis at time t_1 = (–) 1000

Basis at time t_2 = (–) 1100

Now we examine the following two situations:

Situation I

Let, the trader plans that he will buy the asset at time t_2 and use Long Hedge at time t_1. The price paid for the asset say P will be calculated as:

S_2 + loss on the hedge, i.e., $F_1 - F_2$

or $S_2 + (F_1 - F_2)$

or $S_2 - F_2 + F_1$ or $(S_2 - F_2) + F_1$

= Basis + F_1 or F_1 + Basis

Here price under long hedge = P

= F_1 + Basis = 22000 – 1100 = 20,900

Situation II

Let, the trader plans that he will sell the asset at time t_2 and use Short Hedge at time t_1. The price to realised under this situation will be calculated as:

$$P = S_2 + (F_1 - F_2) = F_1 + (S_2 - F_2)$$

$$= F_1 + \text{Basis}$$

Here P = 22000 – 1100 = 20,900

In both the situation the basis, i.e., 1100 is considered as BASIS RISK.

7.6 FORMULATION OF A HEDGING STRATEGY TO MANAGE BASIS RISK

Risk is a condition in which there is a possibility of an adverse deviation from a desired outcome that is expected or hoped for.

Futures derivative is used to hedge (manage the risk) the market risk from a future sale or purchase of an asset. The process of hedging strategy using futures are as follows:

I. Defining the objective, i.e., the expected optimal result.

II. Analysing the environment/situation.

- Market – To identify the opportunities and threats.
- Internal – To know the strengths and weakneses.

III. Formulation of an appropropriate futures contract to hedge.

IV. Managing the strategy to get the optimal result.

In this section, we will discuss the first 3 steps.

I. Objective of Using the Futures Derivative as Strategy: To basic objective of hedging strategy to manage the market risk, i.e., to minimise risk or maximise hedging effectiveness. For minimising the market risk, a market participant has to consider the following guidelines:

- To select appropriate futures contract, the correlation between the spot price and futures price must be very high.
- To select the suitable contract month, the trader has to select the specific month in which the futures prices and spot prices are highly correlated. In general, the prices of the near month contract are the most highly correlated with spot price which should be selected.

II. Environmental/Situation Analysis

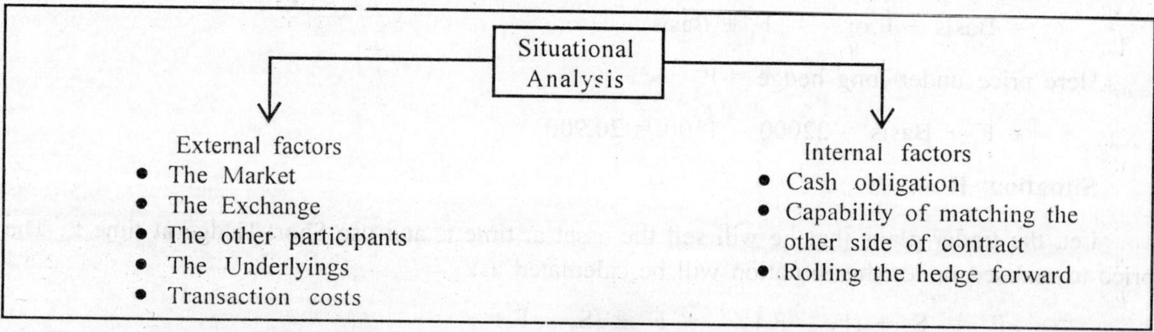

III. Formulation of an Appropriate Hedging Strategy: The next step in hedging is to devise a hedging strategy. The strategic way to devise a hedge strategy is based on the concept of HEDGE RATIO. This hedge ratio is important for investors in futures contracts, as it will help to identify and minimise BASIS RISK.

What is a Hedge Ratio?

A ratio comprising the value of a position protected via a hedge with size of the entire position itself.

Example: Mr. X holds ₹ 1,00,000 in foreign equity, which exposes him to currency risk. If he hedges ₹ 50,00,000 worth of equity with a currency position, his hedge ratio is 0.5 (50/100). This means that 50% of his equity position is sheltered from exchange rate risk.

A hedge ratio is a ratio comprising the value of futures contracts transacted (purchased/sold) to the value of the cash commodity being hedged.

Mat! ematical Expression of General Hedge Ratio:

$$HR = \frac{\text{Futures positions}}{\text{Cash market positions}} = \frac{Q_F}{Q_S}$$

Where, HR = Hedge Ratio

Q_F = Quantity (or units) of assets represented by the futures position

Q_S = Quantity (or units) of the spot (cash) asset that is being hedged.

Thus, the hedge ratio is a measure of the proportion of an investment which is protected by a related hedging action.

Example:

Long position in spot = 10,000 kg

Long position in futures = 6000 kg

$$\therefore HR = \frac{6000}{10000} = 0.60$$

As it is already mentioned that the objective of hedger is to minimise the basis risk, so we now define the hedge ratio which minimises the basis risk.

Hedge Ratio Which Minimises the Risk

$$HR^{mr} = \frac{Q_F^{mr}}{Q_S^{mr}}$$

Where, H^{mr} = Hedge Ratio that minimises the risk.

mr = Minimisation of risk

Q_F^{mr} = Quantity (or units) of futures that minimises risk

Q_S^{mr} = Quantity (or units) of spot assets that minimises risk.

Point to Note:

- The hedge ratio that minimises the risk is known as optimum hedge ratio or minimum variance hedge ratio.

Derivation of Optimal Hedge Ratio

The conceptual derivation of HR^{mr} (optimal hedge ratio) is as follows:

Let $\Delta V_H = (\Delta SP \times Q_S) - (\Delta FP \times Q_F^{mr})$

Where, ΔV_H = Change in the value of the total hedged position

ΔSP = Change in the spot price

ΔFP = Change in the futures price

Q_S = Quantity of the spot asset that is being hedged

Q_F^{mr} = Quantity of futures that minimises risk.

Let the variability is zero. Then

$\Delta SP \times Q_S = \Delta FP \times Q_F^{mr}$

$$\Rightarrow \frac{\Delta SP}{\Delta FP} = \frac{Q_F^{mr}}{Q_S}$$

$$\text{or } Q_F^{mr} = \frac{\Delta SP}{\Delta FP} \times Q_S$$

$$\text{or } Q_F^{mr} = Q_S \times HR$$

Example: If the charge in spot price, i.e., ΔSP = 80 and change in future price, i.e., ΔFP = 80 and change is futures price, i.e., ΔFP = 100, then

HR = 80/100 = 0.80.

Estimating Optimal Hedge Ratio

The optimal hedge ratio can be estimated by using the following formulae:

$$HR^{Opt} = r\frac{\sigma_S}{\sigma_F}$$

Where,

HR^{Opt} = Optimal Hedge Ratio that minimises the variance of the hedgers position

r = Co-efficient of correlation between ΔS and ΔF

σ_S = Standard deviation of ΔS

σ_F = Standard deviation of ΔF.

Δ_S = Change in spot price S, during a period of time equal to the life of the hedge

Δ_F = Change in futures price F, during a period of time equal to the life of the hedge.

Example 1. Find out optimal hedge ratio from the following data:

Correlation coefficient between ΔS and ΔP = 0.93

Standard deviation of ΔF = ΔS = σ_s = 0.04

Standard deviation of ΔF = σ_F = 0.05

Solution:

$$HR^{opt} = r\frac{\sigma_S}{\sigma_F}$$

$$= 0.93 \times \frac{0.04}{0.06} = 0.62$$

Optimal Number of Contracts

The hedger should now how many number of futures contracts to be hedged and what is the total value?

The number of futures contracts will be determined by using the following formula:

$$N^{OPT} = \frac{HR^{Opt}.N_H}{Q_F}$$

Where

N^{opt} = Optimal number of futures contracts for hedging

HR^{opt} = Optimal Hedged Ratio

N_H = Quantity of the position being

Q_F = Quantity (units) of one futures contract.

Example 2. Calculate the optimal number of futures contracts to be hedged from the following data:

Optimal hedge ratio = 0.85

Quantity of long position = 40.000 kg

Quantity for every contract = 100 g

Solution:

$$N^{opt} = \frac{HR^{Opt}.N_H}{Q_F}$$

$$\Rightarrow \frac{0.85 \times 40000}{100} = 340$$

Thus, the number of optimal long futures contract is 340.

7.7 IMPLEMENTATION OF A HEDGING STRATEGY

A hedger assumes a position in a futures market when price moves adversely against his spot market position. **Consequently, his hedge position will be opposite of the position that he already has in the spot market or expected to have later.** Essentially, the implementation of a hedging strategy will be:

- The hedge will be short in the futures if spot position is long. This is known as **Short Hedge**. It is implemented only when the hedger expects that there will be a fall in the prices on the spot market.
- The hedge will be long in the futures if spot position it short. This is known an **Long Hedge**. It is implemented only when the hedger expects that there will be a rise in the prices on the spot market.

The current position, the hedge position and the behaviour of the market can be understood from the following table:

Current Position	Future trend in the asset price	Hedge Position
Possession of the underlying asset	Expected to fall	Short
Sold the asset	Expected to rise	Long

The next issue is which futures contract is to be implemented. There are two choices of a hedger?

(i) If a future contract is traded on a particular asset, then he has the choice to implement hedge strategy for the same commodity.

Example: Gold price risk can be hedged using gold futures. The logic is the futures price and cash price of gold are generally highly corrected.

(ii) If a futures contract is not traded on the asset whose price risk is being attempted to cover, there he has the choice to implement the hedge strategy for such asset whose spot price and futures price are highly corrected.

Finally, the hedger should select the near month contract to be an ideal. Further he should roll over the hedge before the expiry (before 5-10 days) since futures expiry will be very volatile.

7.8 EVALUATION AND CONTROL OF A HEDGING STRATEGY USING FUTURES

After implementation of hedging strategy, the market participant has to manage it effectively through continuous monitoring and adjustments. Systematic evalution of the effectiveness of the hedge must be made to see that the objective of minimisation of a risk must be achieved. In case of negative **remarly**, reasons should be identified and necessary steps must be initiated to minimise the basis risk in future. The "MAE" model to be followed for effectiveness of hedging. The MAE:

M : Monitoring

A : Adjustments

E : Evaluation

The MAE model is an effective tool for a hedger to get the ultimate expected result. The conceptual framework of MAE model is presented below.

MAE MODEL

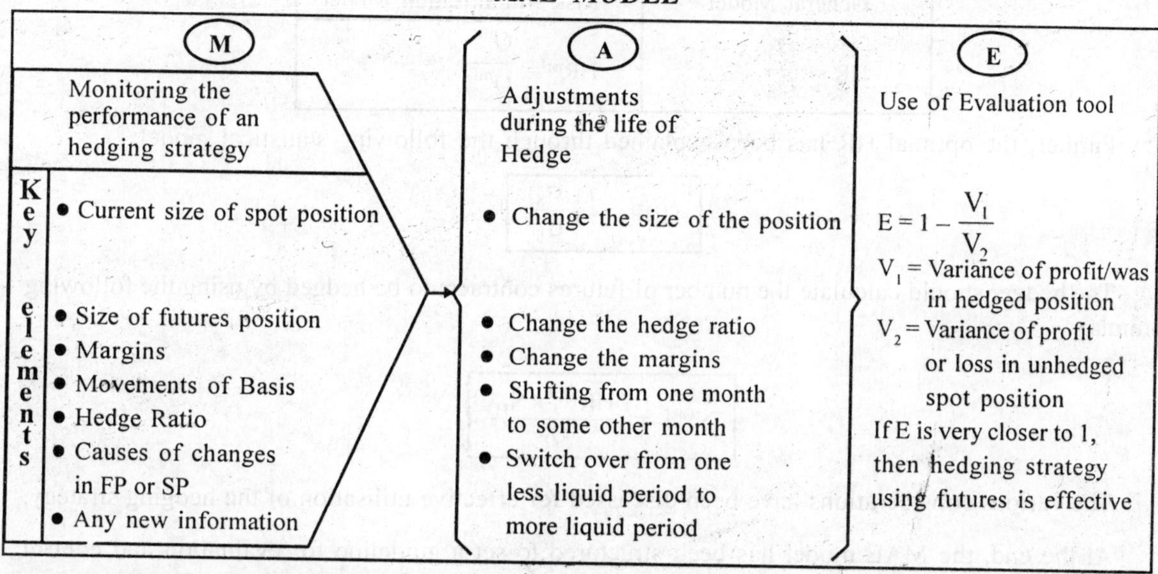

CHAPTER SUMMARY

Hedging is a method of reducing risk. It is an act of protecting a market participant against probable losses. Futures can be used as an effective risk management tool to minimise price risk or market risk. There are various types of futures, i.e., stock index futures, short-term interest rate futures, long-term interest rate futures and foreign currency exchange futures. These futures are used as hedging strategy.

This chapter elaborates two types of hedges, i.e., long hedges and short hedges. A long hedge is a hedge that involves a long (buying) position in futures contract. Similarly, a short position is a hedge that involves a short (selling) position in a futures maret. A long futures hedge is suitable when an hedger purchases an asset in the future and wants to lock in the price now. Similarly, a short futures hedge is suitable when the hedger has to sell an asset in the futures and wants to lock in the price now.

This chapter explained the concept of BASIS and BASIS RISK. Basis is the difference between the spot price and futures price. The basis risk arises because the unequal changes in futures prices and spot prices.

The cost of an asset under long hedge or the amount to be realised under short hedge can be easily worked out by using the following model:

$$P = F_1 + \text{Basis}$$

Strategic management of hedge strategy using futures have been explained in a logical, sequential and systematic manner. The various steps like defining the objective of hedging, situational analysis, formulation of an appropriate hedging strategy have been discussed in detail. The concept of Hedge Ratio (HR) in general and Hedge Ratio in particular to minimise the risk have been modelled in an easy understandable way. These are:

General Model	Risk Minimisation Model
$HR = \frac{Q_F}{Q_S}$	$HR^{mr} = \frac{Q^{mr}_F}{Q^{mr}_s}$

Further, the optimal HR has been explained through the following statistical model:

$$HR^{Opt} = r\frac{\sigma_S}{\sigma_F}$$

The hedger should calculate the number of futures contracts to be hedged by using the following formula:

$$N^{OPT} = \frac{HR^{Opt} \times N_H}{Q_F}$$

The various considerations have been discussed for effective utilisation of the hedging strategy.

At the end, the MAE model has been structured to set a guideline for evaluation and control of the hedging strategy using futures.

SUGGESTIONS FOR FURTHER READINGS

1. Nielsen, Lars Tyge, *Pricing and Hedging of Derivatives Securities,* Oxford University Press, 1999.
2. Chicago Board of Trade, *Introduction to Hedging.*
3. Jayanth Rama Varma, *Derivatives and Risk Management,* Tata McGraw-Hill Edn, New Delhi, Third Reprint 2010.

EXERCISES

Quiz

1. State Whether the Following Statements are True or False.

(a) A long hedge is a hedge in which the buyer buys a futures contract to protect himself against the risk of arising from a possible of hike in prices in future.

(b) A short hedge is a hedge in which the hedger sells a futures contract to protect himself against the loss liely to arise from a fall in asset prices in future.

(c) Hedging strategy using futures can secure protection against a potentially adverse outcomes.

(d) A long futures hedge is suitable when a trader has to purchase an asset in the futures and wants to lock in the price now.

(e) Long hedge is concerned with buying while short hedge is concerned with selling.

(f) Prior to expiration, the basis may be positive or negative.

(g) The basis risk arises because the changes in futures prices and spot prices are not equal.

(h) The price to be paid under long hedge or the amount to be realised under short hedge is calculated by the same formula, i.e., F_1 + Basis, where F_1 = initial futures price

(i) The hedge ratio is the ratio of the size of the position taken in the futures contracts to the size of the exposure.

(j) MAE model represents Monitoring, Adusting and Evaluating the hedging strategy by using futures.

Ans: (a) True, (b) True, (c) True, (d) True, (e) True, (f) True, (h) True, (i) True, (j) True.

A. Short Type Questions

1. What is price risk? Explain.
2. What do you mean by the concept "hedging"?
3. Define the concept "hedging".
4. What are the two steps in hedging?
5. What is Long Hedge?
6. What is Short Hedge?
7. Under what circumstances are: (a) a short hedge and (b) a long hedge suitable?
8. Explain the term basis.
9. What is basis risk?
10. Write short notes on the following:

    (a) Basis Risk (b) Price Risk
11. How to calculate the cost of asset under long hedge?
12. How to calculate the amount to be realised under short hedge?
13. What is the objective of hedging strategy using futures?
14. What are the external factors of situational analysis while hedging strategy by using futures is formulated?

15. What is Hedge Ratio?
16. What is Hedge Ratio for minimising the risk?
17. What is optimum hedge ratio?
18. What is minimum variance hedge ratio?
19. What is the formula for estimating optimal hedge ratio?
20. How to calculate optimal number of contracts while hedging is to be planned?
21. What are the factors to be considered for implementing the hedging strategy?
22. What is MAE? Explain.

B. Long Type Questions

1. Define the term hedging? What are the two important hedging strategies? Discuss.
2. What is basis risk? How it will be calculated?
3. How to calculate cost of an asset under long hedge? Explain the method with the help of futures price and basis.
4. How to calculate the amount to be realised under short hedge? Explain the method with the help of futures price and basis.
5. What is Hedge Ratio? How it will be calculated? Explain.
6. What is Hedge Ratio? How it will be estimated?
7. Discuss the following steps in hedging strategy by using futures:
   (a) Formulating the strategy
   (b) Implementing the strategy
   (c) Evaluating and controlling the strategy
8. What is MAE? Give a conceptual framework of MAE?

OPTION: THE BASICS

Learning Objectives

After studying this chapter, you will be able to:

- Understand the concept and different types of option contract/derivative
- Distinguish between options and futures contracts
- Know about intrinsic value and time value of options
- Understand four option positions, i.e., long call position, long put position, short call position and short put position
- Calculate the pay-off and profit/loss of each option positions

Chapter Outline

8.1 INTRODUCTION

An option is a special type of contract which gives its holder the right (but not obligation) to buy or sell an asset at a fixed price at some future date. There are only two basic types of options, i.e., ***call options*** and ***put options***. A call option is the right to buy an underlying asset at a specified price over a given time period, while a put option is a right to sell an underlying asset at a specified price over a given time period. According to the language of option contract, the owner who obtains (buys) the right to trade (buy/sell) an asset is known as ***option holder***. The counterparty who grants (sells) the right is known as *option writer*.

Conceptually, the option contract is shown below:

(a) Right to Buy Option

Parties →	Buyer of the Asset	Seller of the Asset
Status →	Option Holder	Option Writer
Right →	Yes	No
Obligation →	No	Yes

(b) Right to Sell Option

Parties →	Buyer of the Asset	Seller of the Asset
Status →	Option Writer	Option Holder
Right →	No	Yes
Obligation →	Yes	No

Thus, the option holder is the buyer of the option and the option writer is the seller of the option.

Definitions

The Conceptual Definition of Option is as Follows:

1. "An option is a derivative contract or instrument that gives the option holder the right, but not obligation, to trade an underlying asset for a specific price on or before a specified time period."

2. Option in finance may be defined as the right, but not obligation, to buy or sell a specific amount of a given stock, commodity, currency, index or debt, at a specified price during a specified period of time.

3. Option is a financial derivative that represents a contract sold by one party (option writer) to another party (option holder). The contract offers the buyer the right, but not obligation to buy (call) or sell (put) a security or other financial asset at an agreed upon price (the strike price) during a certain period of time or on a specific date.

8.2 TYPES OF OPTIONS

Options may be classified on the basis of right to trade without obligation, style of exercise and nature of trading.

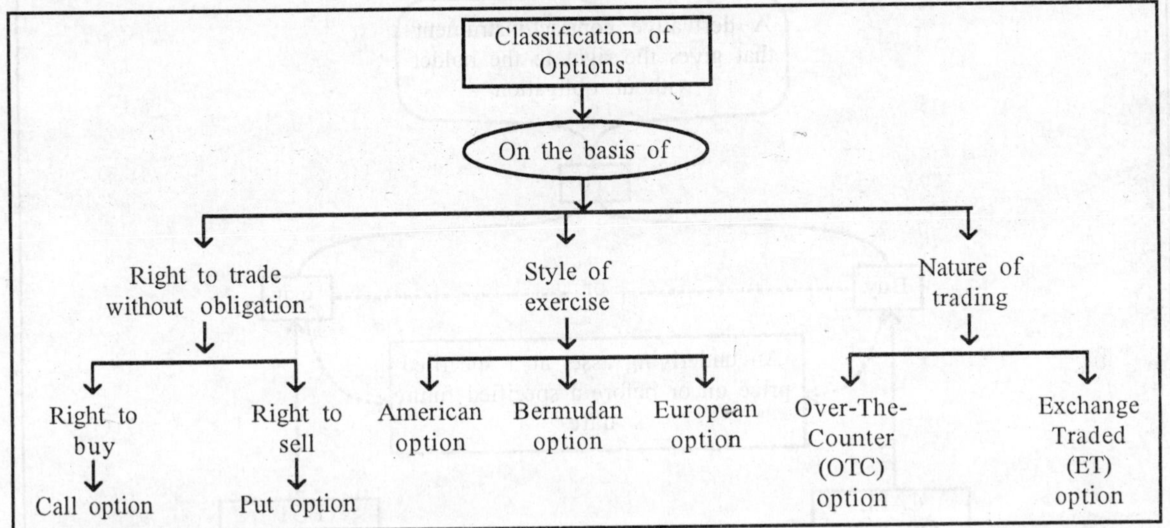

8.2.1 Types of Option on the Basis of Right

On the basis of *"right to trade without obligations"*, options may be classified as call options and put options:

(i) **A call option:** An option which conveys the right to buy something is called a **Call.** A call option gives the holder the right but not obligation to **buy** an underlying asset at a specified price on or before a certain date, i.e., over a given time period.

(ii) **A put option:** An option which conveys the right to sell something is called a **Put.** A put option gives the holder the right to sell an asset at a specified price on or before a certain date, i.e., over a given time period.

Conceptually, these two types cf options are shown below:

Option type	Buyer of the right	Seller of the right
Call	Right to buy at the specified price	Obligation to sell at the specified price
Put	Right to sell at the specified price	Obligation to buy at the specified price

Conceptual Framework of Option Derivative

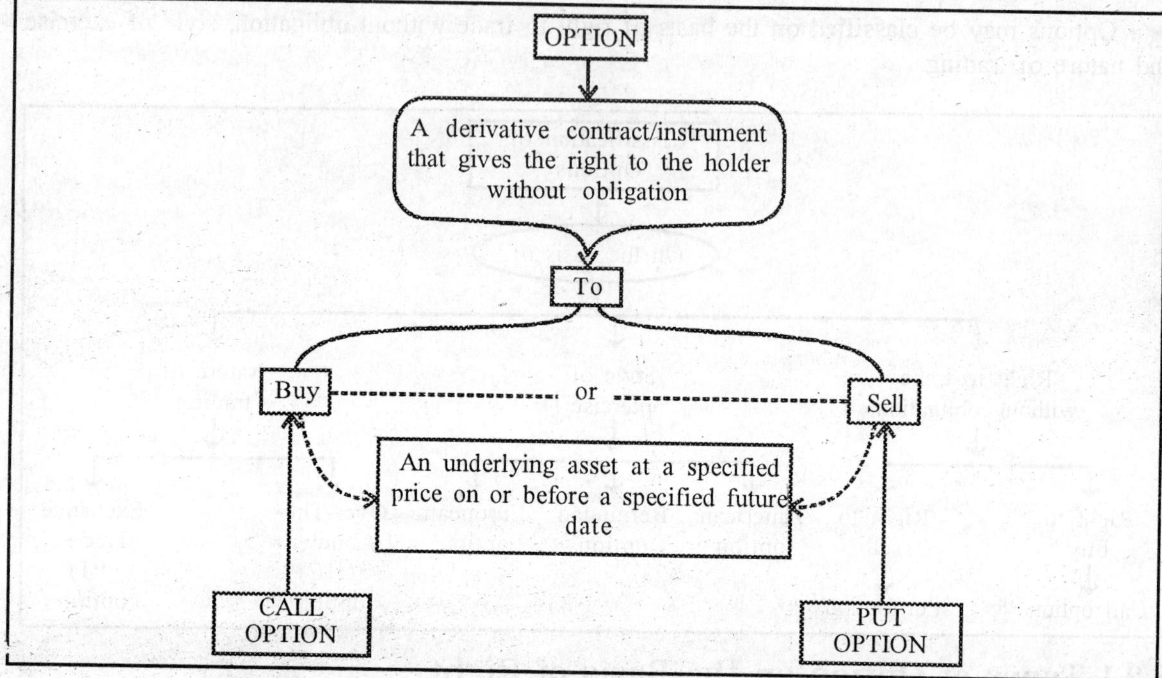

Fig. 8.1: Conceptual Framework of Derivative Contract

8.2.2 Types of Options on the Basis of "Style of Exercise"

In finance, the style of an option denotes the date on which the option may be exercised. Depending on when an option can be exercised, it is classified in to the following three categories:

(i) American Style Option or American Option: In this style, the option can be exercised by the option holder during any time during the life of the contract, i.e., on or before the expiration date. Thus, in an Americal style, the option holder has right to exercise his right to buy/sell any time before the expiry date.

(ii) European Style Option or European Option: In this style, the option may be exercised only on the expiry date of the option, i.e., at a single pre-defined point of time.

Points to Note:

(a) The origins of the names "American" or "European" in the context of option style are not known. Further these names have significance with geographical region.

(b) With American style, the option can be exercised at any time upto the date of maturity while with European style of exercise, the option can be exercised only on the expiration date.

(iii) Bermudan Style Option or Bermudan Option: In this style of exercise, the option can be exercised on a few specific dates prior to expiry.

Notes: (a) The place "Bermuda" is half way between America and Europe. The Finance professionals have chosen this title to justify the significance of style of exercise.

(b) It is occasionally used with OTC options.

8.2.3 Types of Options Trading Practices

There are two types of option tradings, i.e., Exchange traded options and Over-the-Counter traded options.

The options can be traded on an organised exchange or on the over-the-counter (OTC) market. An exchange traded option contract is very similar with Futures while an OTC option is like a Forward contract. However, these two types of options are different in the following points:

Distinguish between ET options and OTC Options

Points of Distinctions	Exchange Traded Options	Over-the-Counter Traded Options
Sort of market	Exchanges	OTC markets
Norms	Specified and standardised.	Negotiated between two counterparties.
Restricted terms	Uniform underlying assets, limited number of strike prices, limited maturity dates, etc.,	No restriction in underlying quantity, strike prices and maturity dates, etc.
Default risk	Very low	Very high
Deposite of margin money	Obligatory on part of the option writer	Not required
Transaction cost	Very low	Moderate and high

8.3 BASIC CONCEPTS OR TERMS USED IN OPTION TRADING

Trading through option derivative based on the following basics:

1. The Option Contract 2. Underlying Asset 3. Exercise Price or Strike Price 4. Option Style 5. Expiration Date or Date of Maturity 6. Exercise Date 7. Exchange Traded or OTC Traded Options 8. Option Premium 9. Option Moneyness 10. Position of an Option Participant 11. Covered and Naked Options 12. Open Class 13. Open Interest.

Options markets are quite complicated and risky. Options are used to eliminate the risks. But if one party makes money then the other party must loose money. But the holder of an option contract must understand the following basics or fundamentals so that he can bet against the seller or writer of the option:

1. **The Option Contract:** An option is a contract. It gives the buyer the right, but not obligation, to buy or sell, an underlying asset at a specific price on or before a certain date.

2. **Underlying Asset:** The underlying asset of an option contract may be stock, commodity, currency, index or debt. Thus, the specific asset which is exchanged if the option is exercised called underlyings.

3. **The Agreed Contract Price:** The price at which the option may be exercised and the underlying assets bought or sold is called **Strike Price or Exercise Price**. The exchanges decide the strike price at which call and put options are traded.

4. **Style of Option:** An option style refers to whether the option contract can be exercised before the expiration date or not. On the basis of the timing of the possible exercise, an option contract may have any one of the following style:

   (i) *American Style:* In this style, the option can be exercised by the option holder any time during the life of the contract, i.e., on or before the expiration date.

   (ii) *European Style:* In this style, the option can be exercised only on the expiration date. It cannot be exercised before the expiration date of the option contract.

   Notes: (a) The origins of the names "American" and "European" in the context of option contract are not known. Further they are unrelated to practices common in any particular geographical region.

   (b) With American style of exercise the option can be exercised at any time upto the expiration date while with European style of exercise, the option can be exercised only on the expiration date.

   (iii) *Bermudan Style:* In this form of exercise, the option can be exercised on a few specific dates prior to exercise.

   Notes: (a) This name "Bermunda" is titled because it is half way between America and Europe.

   (b) It is occasionally used with OTC options.

5. **Expiration Date:** All options have a maturity or expiry date after which the option to trade cannot be exercised. The date when the option expires or matures is referred to as **expiration date**. In case an option is not exercised, it expires automatically.

6. **Exercise Date:** The date on which the option holder exercises his option is called Exercise date. In case of European style of option, both expiration date and exercise date are same. But in case of American style, the exercise date may be any date on or before the date of maturity.

7. **Exchange-traded Options and Over-the-Counter Options:** Options which are traded on exchanges are called Exchange-traded options. These options are standardised in terms of quantity, trading cycle, expiration date, strike prices, type of option, style of option and mode of payments, etc.

   Options which are not traded on exchanges are called over-the-counter options.

8. **Option Premium:** In an option contract, the option holder buys the **right** from the option writer. To buy such right, he has to pay certain amount to the option writer as consideration. The price which is paid by the option holder to the option writer for acquiring the right

to trade (buy/sell) is known as option premium. Once it is paid, it remained with the option writer whether the option is exercised or not. The option premium is to be paid upfront.

Points to Note:

(i) The option premium is quoted in the market on a per share basis.

(ii) Option premium is not similar to down payment or margin.

(iii) Option premium is the consideration for acquiring right by the option holder from the option writer (seller). So, he has to pay premium amount to the option writer.

(iv) Option premium is the consideration for conferring right by the option writer to the option holder. So, he has to receive the premium amount from the option holder. In other words, it is received by the option writer from the option holder against the obligation undertaken.

9. **Option Moneyness: At-the-money (ATM), In-the-money (ITM) and Out-of-the-money (OTM):** A call option gives the holder the right to buy at the exercise price while a put option gives the holder the right to sell at the exercise price. At a particular time, the market price of the underlying may be greater, equal or lesser than the Exercise Price. In such situations, the options are said to be at-the-money (ATM) or in-the-money (ITM) or out-of-the-money (OTM). These situations are as shown below:

Call Option	Option is said to be	Put Option
Exercise Price = Market Price	At-the-money	Exercise Price = Market Price
Exercise Price < Market Price	In-the-money	Exercise Price > Market Price
Exercise Price > Market Price	Out-of-the-money	Exercise Price < Market Price

10. **Position of an Option Participant**

There are four types of options participants depending on the positions they take. They are:

1. Buyers of calls, i.e., call option buyers
2. Sellers of calls, i.e., call option sellers
3. Buyers of puts, i.e., put option buyers
4. Sellers of puts, i.e., put option sellers

These four types of option positions are shown below:

Option	Buyer	Seller
Call	Right to buy (Buyer of the call)	Obligation to sell (Seller of the call)
Put	Right to sell (Buyer of the put)	Obligation to buy (Seller of the put)

11. Covered and Naked Options:

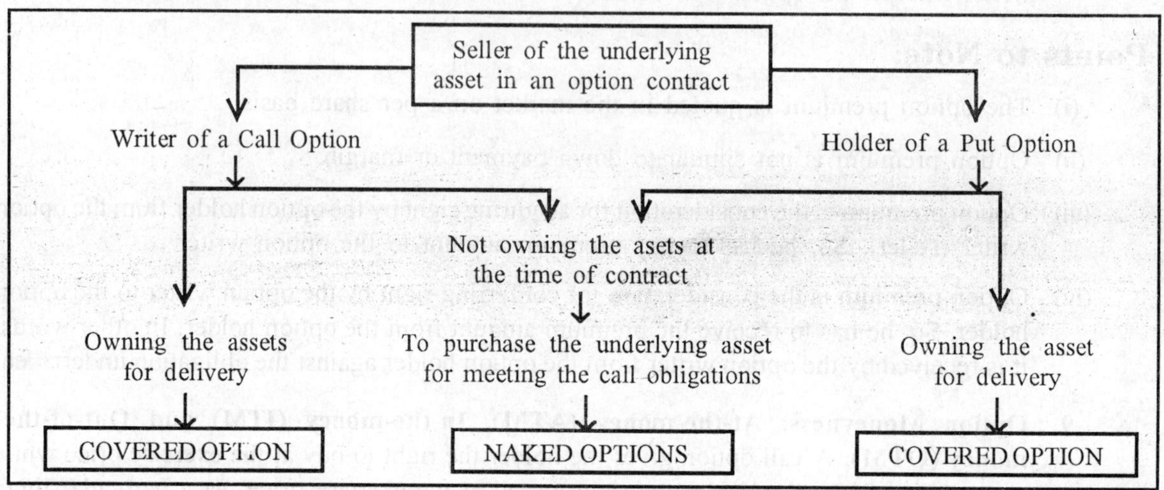

From the above presentation, it is very clear that a call option position which is covered by an opposite position in the underlying instrument, i.e., securities, commodities, etc., is called a covered call. Thus, writing covered calls involve writing call options when the underlying assets might have to be delivered (if the option holder exercises his right to buy), are already owned.

Writing a call generates income in the form of premium paid by the option buyer (holder). If the price of the underlying remains stable or decreases the option holder will not exercise his option, then the writer will be able to keep this income as a profit, even though the profits may not have been higher. If the asset price increases, then the call writer will likely to loose money. But if the call writer owns the underlying asset, he can avoid such risk. Otherwise, if the writer of the call option does not own the underlying security, he will be exposed to extreme risk because the price of the underlying heads dramatically higher and he will be obliged to sell the underlying to the buyer at the predetermined strike price.

A covered position refers to a situation in which a trader sells an option contract with holding a position in the underlying security as protection from an adverse shift in price.

A naked position refers to a situation in which a trader sells an option contract without holding a position in the underlying security as protection from an adverse shift in price.

For a better understanding, the concept of covered and naked options, study the following two situations:

Situation I

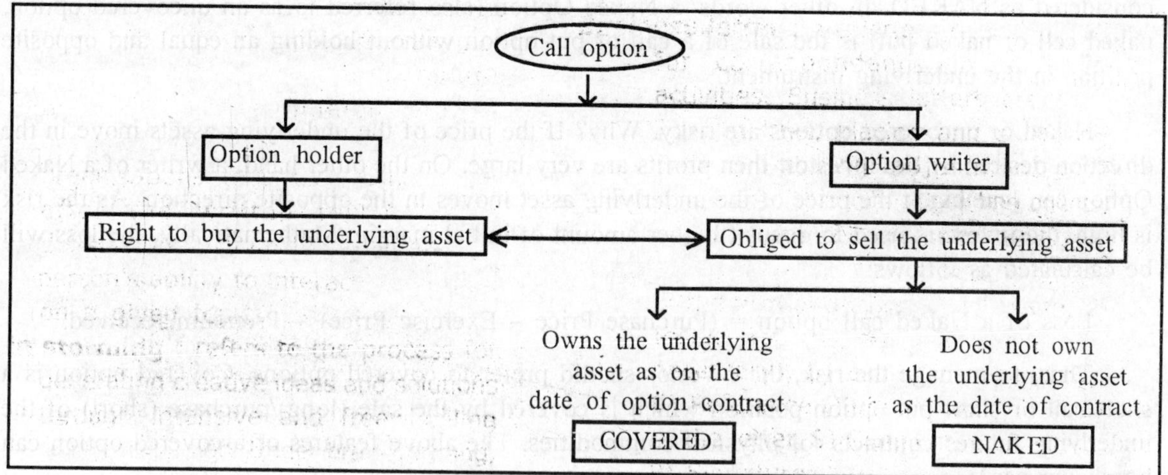

Fig. 8.2: Call Writer and Covered Option

A call option is considered *covered* when the call writer owns the assets of the underlying equal to the contract quantity which will be delivered at the time when the calls are exercised.

Example: Let Mr X is a call writer. He owns 1,000 shares of P Ltd. and writes 10 P Ltd. call contracts, the calls are covered by the shares. If Mr X writes 15 contracts (one contract is equal to 100 shares), then 10 contracts would be covered and 5 would be naked.

Situation II

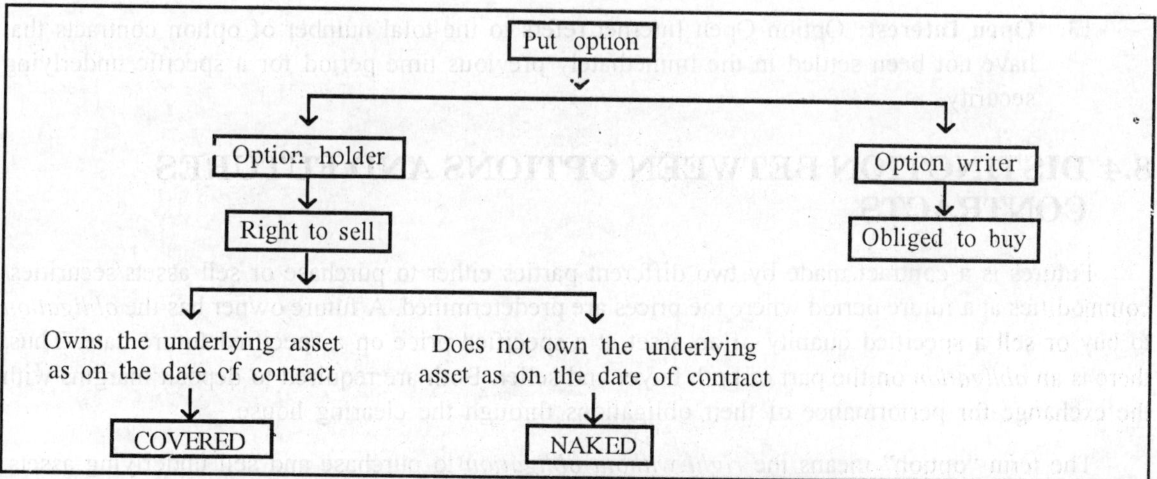

Fig. 8.3: Put Holder and Covered Option

A put option (right to sell) is considered *covered* when the put holder owns the assets of the underlying equal to the contract quantity which will be delivered when the calls are exercised.

An option position where the buyer or seller has no underlying security position, then it is considered as NAKED. In other words, a Naked Option (also referred to as an uncovered option, naked call or naked put) is the sale of a call or put option without holding an equal and opposite position in the underlying instrument.

Naked or uncovered options are risky. Why? If the price of the underlying assets move in the direction desired by the investor, then profits are very large. On the other hand, a writer of a Naked Option can lose big if the price of the underlying asset moves in the opposite direction. As the risk is high, the investors need to deposit higher amount of initial margin. Mathematically, the loss will be calculated as follows:

Loss of a Naked call option = (Purchase Price – Exercise Price) – Premium received.

Thus, to manage the risk, the investor should prefer to covered options. Covered option is a short call or short put option position which is covered by the sale (long)/purchase (short) of the underlying futures contracts for physical commodities. The above features of a covered option can be shown as:

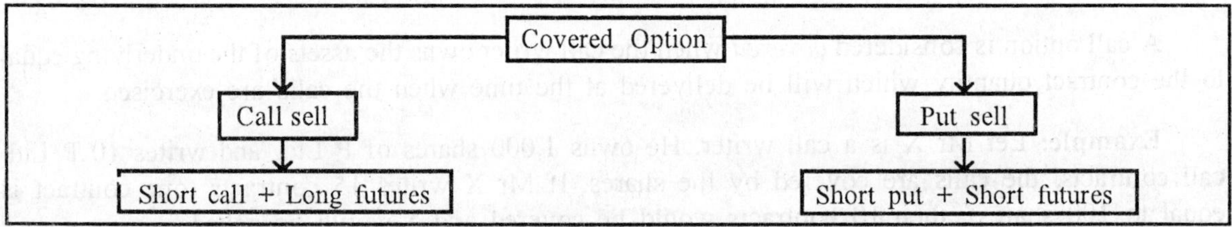

12. **Option Class:** It means all listed options of a particular type (i.e., call or put) on a specific asset with a particular exchange.

13. **Open Interest:** Option Open Internet refers to the total number of option contracts that have not been settled in the immediately previous time period for a specific underlying security.

8.4 DISTINCTION BETWEEN OPTIONS AND FUTURES CONTRACTS

Futures is a contract made by two different parties either to purchase or sell assets/securities/ commodities at a future period where the prices are predetermined. A future owner has the *obligation* to buy or sell a specified quanity of an asset at a specified price on a specified future date. Thus, there is an *obligation* on the part of both buyer and seller. Both are required to deposit margins with the exchange for performance of their obligations through the clearing house.

The term "option" means the *right without obligation* to purchase and sell underlying assets. Call option stands for the right without obligation to buy the underlying asset and the buyer may refuse the contract prior to its maturity. Put option means the opposite of call option. Thus, an option holder has the right (but not the obligation) to buy or sell a specified quanity of an asset at a particular price over a specified time period.

Both are considered **"Derivatives"** as they derive their value from an underlying security or commodity. The fundamental difference between these derivatives is that option gives the holder the right to buy or sell the underlying asset at (or, if the option is an American style, before) expiration, while the holder of a futures contract is obliged to fulfill the terms of his contract.

It is an interesting feature of an option contract is that the cost to the option holder is limited to the premium paid while the profit is unlimited. However, for an option writer the cost (risk) is unlimited while profits are limited to the premium received from the holder. Thus, the cost-benefits of both the parties of an option contract are:

Parties	**Cost/Risk**	**Benefit**
Option buyer (holder)	Limited	Unlimited
Option seller (writer)	Unlimited	Limited

However, the gain in the futures trading is automatically linked to the daily fluctuations in the market, i.e., "Marked to market" daily.

Another technical difference between options and futures is the pricing methods or models. The various models for pricing these two derivatives are as follows:

Pricing Models

Futures	**Options**
• Expectation model	• Binomial model
• Expectation model	• Black-Scholes model
• Normal Backwardation	• Finite Difference model
• Capital Asset Pricing model	• CAPM

From the above discussions, there are five distinction criteria between futures and options as follows:

1. Right and Obligations
2. Premium and Margins (cash flows)
3. Pay-off, i.e., profit and loss position
4. Users of derivatives
5. Pricing methods/models.

Now we summarise the differences between futures and options in the following table:

Difference between Options and Futures

Distinction	*Options*	*Futures*
1. Right and Obligation	An option gives the buyer (holder) the **right** but not the **obligation** while the seller has an obligation to comply with the contract. It represents a **right** to one partly and an **obligation** on the other.	In case of futures, there is an **obligation** on the part of the buyer and the seller. It represents an **obligation** to both a buyer and a seller.
2. Premium and Margins	Buyer of the option contract pays **premium** to the seller of the contract for obtaining the right. It is non-refundable whether the option is exercised or not.	Both buyer and seller have to deposit upfront **margin** with the exchange. Different types of margins like initial margin, maintenance margin and variation margins, etc are to be deposited by the traders.
3. Pay-off (Profit/Loss)	The buyers (holders) of option contracts have the possibility of unlimited profit but their losses are restricted to the premium paid. Sellers (writers) of the option contracts have the possibility of limited profit only to the extent of the premium received but they are exposed to the possibility of unlimited losses.	In case of rise in futures prices, the buyer gains and *vice verse*. The position is opposite in case of the seller of the futures contract. Thus, both buyers and sellers face the possibility of unlimited gain or loss.
4. Common Users in the Derivative Market	Options are preferential derivative contracts for the hedgers in the derivative market to minimise risk. Normally they are the covered call writers.	Futures are the preferential contracts for the speculators in the derivative market to maximise profit. Normally they are the call holders.
5. Pricing Methods/ Models	Binomial option pricing model and Black-Scholes models are used.	Cost-of-carry model, Expectation model, Normal Backwardation model and CAPM are used.

8.5 VALUE OF AN OPTION

The buyer of the option pays premium to the seller (or writer) of the option. In return, the writer of the call option is obligated to deliver the underlying asset to the buyer of the option if the call is exercised. In case of put option, the holder of the option will buy the underlying asset if the put is exercised.

The price of an option can be decomposed into two parts: Intrinsic value and Time value (Extrinsic value). Thus,

Option Value = Intrinsic Value + Time Value (Extrinsic Value)

8.5.1 Intrinsic Value

Intrinsic Value of the option that can be realised if the option is exercised. Therefore, only in-the-money (ITM) options have intrinsic value. In other words, the value that can be made by exercising the option is known as intrinsic value. As a matter of trade practice, the owner (the holder) of the option will never choose to loss money by exercising his option. Therefore, an option can never have a negative value, i.e., > 0.

The intrinsic value of an option is the difference between its exercise price (X) and the current spot price of the underlying asset (S_T).

Symbolically, the intrinsic value of an option is given as follows:

Intrinsic Value of a Call Option (C_T) :	Max [(S_T – X), O] OR $(S_T - X)^+$

Intrinsic Value of Put Option (P_T) :	[Max (X – S_T), O] OR $(X - S_T)^+$

The intrinsic value is realised only when the option is exercised. The following table makes the concept clear:

Let Spot Price of the underlying asset on exercise date = S_T

Exercise or Strike Price = X

Market Condition	Call Option	Put Option
$S_T > X$	In-the-money Intrinsic value > 0	Out-of-the-money Intrinsic value = 0
$S_T < X$	Out-of-the money Intrinsic value = 0	In-the-money Intrinsic value > 0
$S_T = X$	At-the-money Intrinsic Value = 0	At-the-money Intrinsic Value = 0

Graphic Presentation: The intrinsic value of a call option and put option can be shown in the following graphs:

Call Option Intrinsic Value

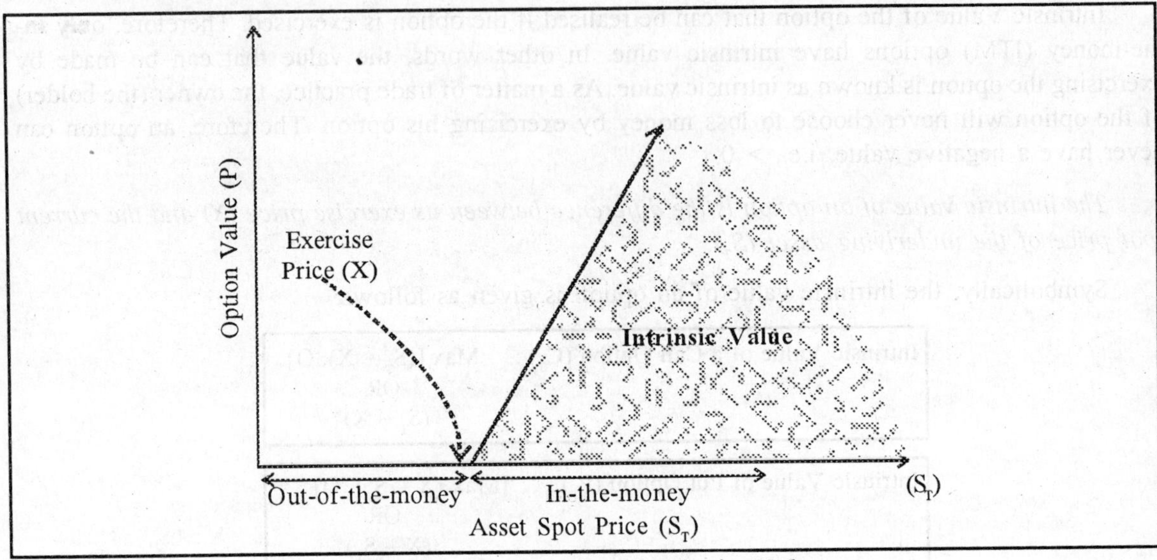

Fig. 8.4: Call Option Intrinsic Value

Put Option Intrinsic Value

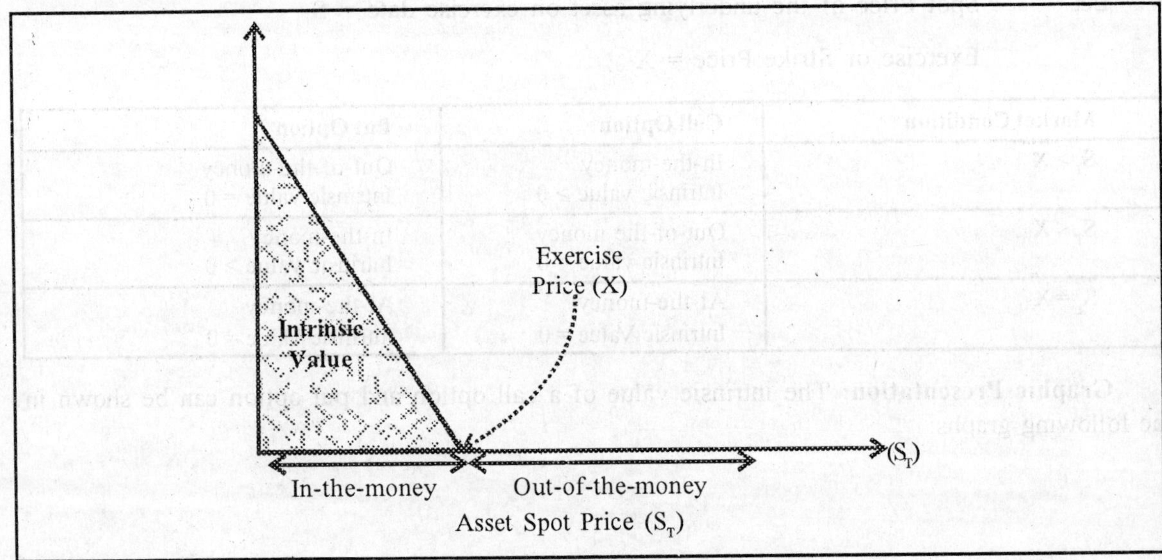

Fig 8.5: Put Option Intrinsic Value

As seen in the graph, the intrinsic value of a call option is positive when underlying asset's spot price (S_T) exceeds the option's strike price (X). Similarly, the intrinsic value of a put option is positive when option's strike price (X) exceeds the spot price of the underlying asset. However, the fact that the option cannot have negative value and also works in the owner's favour.

Option value can be determined via a predictive formula such as **Black-Scholes** or using a numerical method such as the **Binomial model**. These models will be discussed later part of this chapter.

Example 8.1: Intrinsic value of a call option.

Spot Price (S_T)	110	120	130	140	150	160	165	167	170	175	180
Exercise Price (X)	150	150	150	150	150	150	150	150	150	150	150
Intrinsic Value (C_T)	0	0	0	0	0	10	15	17	20	25	30

As spot price of the underlying asset increases, the intrinsic value of the option also increases.

Example 8.2: Intrinsic value of a put option.

Exercise Price (S_T)	150	150	150	150	150	150	150	150	150	150	150	150
Spot Price (X)	180	175	170	165	160	155	150	145	140	135	130	125
Intrinsic Value (C_T)	0	0	0	0	0	0	0	5	10	15	20	25

As spot price of the underlying asset decreases, the option price (intrinsic value) increases.

8.5.2 Time Value of an Option

When an option trading at more than the intrinsic value, the difference is known as Extrinsic value, or more commonly known as *Time Value.*

Consider the following call options:

Case (a): Underlying: P. Ltd. Stock

Underlying Price: ₹ 150 per share

Type: Call option

Style: American

Exercise Price: ₹ 145

Expiry Date: 31st December

Let assume the current spot price of this stock is ₹ 160 on 30th September. So this particular call option is traded at ₹ 15 (i.e., ₹ 160 – ₹ 145).

On 30th September, we understand that the option has the following values:

(i) Intrinsic value – ₹ 150 – ₹ 145 = ₹ 5

(ii) Actual value on trading = ₹ 160 – ₹ 145 = ₹ 15

Here the difference between these two value, i.e., ₹ 15 – ₹ 5 = ₹ 10 is the Time value.

Point to Note:

The difference between the value of an option (American) at the particular time on or before the expiration and its intrinsic value is known as TIME VALUE of an option.

Mathematically,

Time Value = Option Price – Intrinsic Value

- Option Price is the option premium.

The following examples make clear of the computational aspect of Time value:

Example on Call Option

Option	Strike Price	Option Premium	Spot Price	Intrinsic Value	Time Value
Call	130	5	128	2	3
Call	125	2	125	0	2
Call	115	3	120	0	3

Example on Put Option

Option	Strike Price	Option Premium	Spot Price	Intrinsic Value	Time Value
Put	150	4	152	2	2
Put	160	8	165	5	3
Put	140	20	155	15	5

Note: In the above examples, we find that the intrinsic value plus the time value equals the total premium of the option.

8.5.3 Factors Influencing Time Value of an Option

There are certain factors which are influencing the time value of an option. These are:

1. **The Expected Volatility in the Futures Spot Price of Underlying Instrument**

   We know that:

   Option Time Value = Option Price – Option Intrinsic Value

   Intrinsic Value = (Spot Price – Strike Price) for Call Option

   Intrinsic Value = (Strike Price – Spot Price) for Call Option

   Thus, spot price of the underlying instrument is a determinant of intrinsic value. So, the expected volatility in the future spot price influences the time value of an option. However, volatility in the prices of the underlying instrument can stimulate option demand and enhance its value.

2. **Time to Expiration (Remaining Life Span of the Option)**

   The second influencing factor on time value of an option is the length of the period remaining to the expiry date of an option. It may be noted that the more time that remains in the life span of an option, the time value tends to be higher.

Numerically, time value depends on the time until the expiration date and volatility of the underlying instrument's price.

8.6 OPTIONS POSITIONS

Options are two types — calls and puts. Calls give the buyer the right but not the obligation to buy an asset at a prespecified price on, or before, a specified date in the future. Puts give the buyer the right but not obligation to sell an asset at a prespecified price on, or before, a specified date in the future. Thus, there are two sides to every option contracts. As there are two types of options, so there are four basic option positions.

Call Options:

1. Call options give the holder (buyer) the right (but not the obligation) to buy the underlying asset at the exercise/strike price any time until the expiry date.
2. Call options obligate the writer (seller) to sell the underlying asset at the exercise/strike price any time until the expiry date.

Thus, the option writer has the exact opposite position in comparison to the option holder, this is because they are on opposite sides of the same contract.

Put Options:

3. Put options give the holder (buyer) the right (but not the obligation) to sell the underlying asset at the exercise/strike price any time until the expiry date.
4. Put options obligate the writer (seller) to buy the underlying asset at the exercise/strike price any time until the expiry date.

Thus, the writer has the exact opposite in comparison to the holder, this is because these are on opposite sides of the same contract.

Summary of the Four Basic Options Positions

	Holder (The buyer of the right)	Writer (The seller of the right)
Call Options	Right buy (1)	Obligation to sell (2)
Put Options	Right to sell (3)	Obligation to buy (4)

In the language of option derivatives, these four positions are called as:

1. A long position in a call option
2. A short position in a call option
3. A long position in a put option
4. A short position in a put option

Summary of Transaction through Option (European Style)

Option Position	Now	At Expiration Let X = Strike Price, S_T = Market Price of the underlying asset
Buyer (Holder) of a call (Long call) → Right to buy	The option holder pays premium and acquires the right to buy the underlying asset at the strike price on the expiration date.	• If $S_T > X$, the option holder exercises the option. Then Gross pay-off = $S_T - X$ and Net Profit = $S_T - X -$ Premium. • If $S_T < X$, the option holder does not exercise the option, then Net Profit = Zero – Premium.
Buyer (Holder) of a put (Long put) → Right to sell	The option holder pays the premium and acquires the right to sell the underlying asset at the strike price on the expiration date.	• If $S_T < X$, the option holder exercises the option. Then Gross pay-off = $X - S_T$ and Net Profit = $X - S_T -$ Premium. • If $S_T > X$, the option holder does not exercise the option, then Net Profit = Zero – Premium.
Seller (Writer) of a call (Short call) → Obliged to sell	The option writer receives the premium and commits to delivery the underlying asset at the strike price on the expiry date, if the holder exercies the option and demands the delivery.	• If $S_T > X$, the option holder exercises the option, then Net Loss = $(X - S_T)$ + Premium. • If $S_T < X$, the holder does not exercise the option. Then, Net Profit = Premium.
Seller (Writer) of a put (Short put) → Obliged to buy	The option writer receives the premium and commits to buy and take delivery of the underlying assets at the exercise price on the expiration date if the holder exercises the option and give delivery of the underlyings.	• If $S_T < X$, the option holder exercises the option. Then Net Loss = $(S_T - X)$ + Premium. • If $S_T > X$, the holder does not exercise the option. Then, Net Profit = Premium.

8.7 PAY-OFF PROFILES OF OPTION POSITIONS

There are two sides to every option contract. In case of call (right to buy) option, the holder exercises his right only when the future outcome is favourable (in the money) to him. The writer of a call option, being the owner of the asset, obliged to sell to the option holder in such situation. Therefore, the buyer of the call option (holder) must pay upfront a price, called premium to the option seller (writer). The writer of an option receives cash upfront but has potential liabilities later.

In case of put (right to sell) option, the holder exercises his right only when the future outcome is favourable (in the money) to him. The writer of a put option, being the buyer of the asset, is obliged to buy in such situation. Therefore, the buyer of the put option, being the holder of the right, must pay upfront a price, called premium to the option writer. The writer of an option receives cash upfront but he has potential liabilities later.

Now we illustrate the pay-off of the following four positions:

1. pay-off of the call option buyer
2. pay-off of the call option seller
3. pay-off of the put option buyer
4. pay-off of the put option seller

Besides, pay-off diagrams are also drawn to show how option will pay out prior to expiry and at the time just before expiration.

The pay-off of a call option or put option depends on the following factors:

(i) Spot price of underlying asset just before the expiration.

(ii) Exercise price

(iii) The option value, i.e., option premium.

I. Pay-off of a Call Option Buyer (Long Call) at Expiration

Consider the following basics of a call option:

Underlying : Reliance share

Type of option : Call option

Style of option : European

Position : Long (Buyer)

Exercise Price = ₹ 150 per share

Option premium = ₹ 5 per share

Spot price at expiration say ₹ 130, ₹ 140, ₹ 150, ₹ 160, ₹ 170, ₹ 180 per share.

Now we calculate the pay-off of the call option holder in the following table:

Table 8.1: Pay-off of the Call Option Holder at Expiration

	₹	₹	₹	₹	₹	₹	₹
(a) Spot price (S_T)	130	140	150	155	160	170	180
(b) Exercise price (X)	150	150	150	150	150	150	150
(c) Option exercise	No	No	–	Yes	Yes	Yes	Yes
(d) Pay-off (S_T – X)	–	–	0	5	10	20	30
(e) Call premium (paid)	–5	–5	–5	–5	–5	–5	–5
(f) Profit/Loss : (d) + (e) (Net pay-off)	–5	–5	–5	0	5	15	25

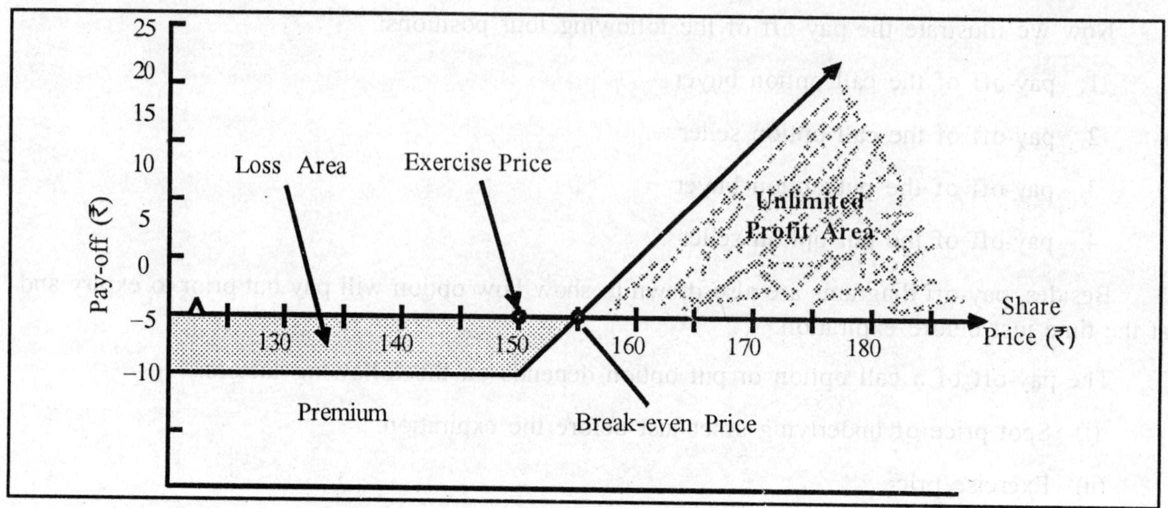

Fig. 8.6: Pay-off of the Call Option Buyer

II. Pay-off of a Call Option Seller (Short Call) at Expiration

Consider the following basics of a call option:

Underlying: Reliance stock

Type of option: Call option

Style of option: European

Position: Short (Seller)

Exercise price = ₹ 150 per share

Option premium = ₹ 5 per share

Spot price at expiration say: ₹ 130, ₹ 140, ₹ 150, ₹ 160, ₹ 170, ₹ 180 per share.

Now we calculate the pay-off of the call option seller writer in the following table:

Table 8.2: Pay-off of the Call Option Writer (Seller) at Expiration

	₹	₹	₹	₹	₹	₹	₹
(a) Strike price (X)	150	150	150	150	150	150	150
(b) Current spot price (S_T)	130	140	150	155	160	170	180
(c) Option exercise by holder	No	No	No	Yes	Yes	Yes	Yes
(d) Option pay-off	–	–	0	–5	–10	–20	–30
(e) Option premium (received)	+5	+5	+5	+5	+5	+5	+5
(f) Profit or Loss : (d) + (e) (Net pay-off)	5	5	5	0	–5	–15	–25

Pay-off Diagram:

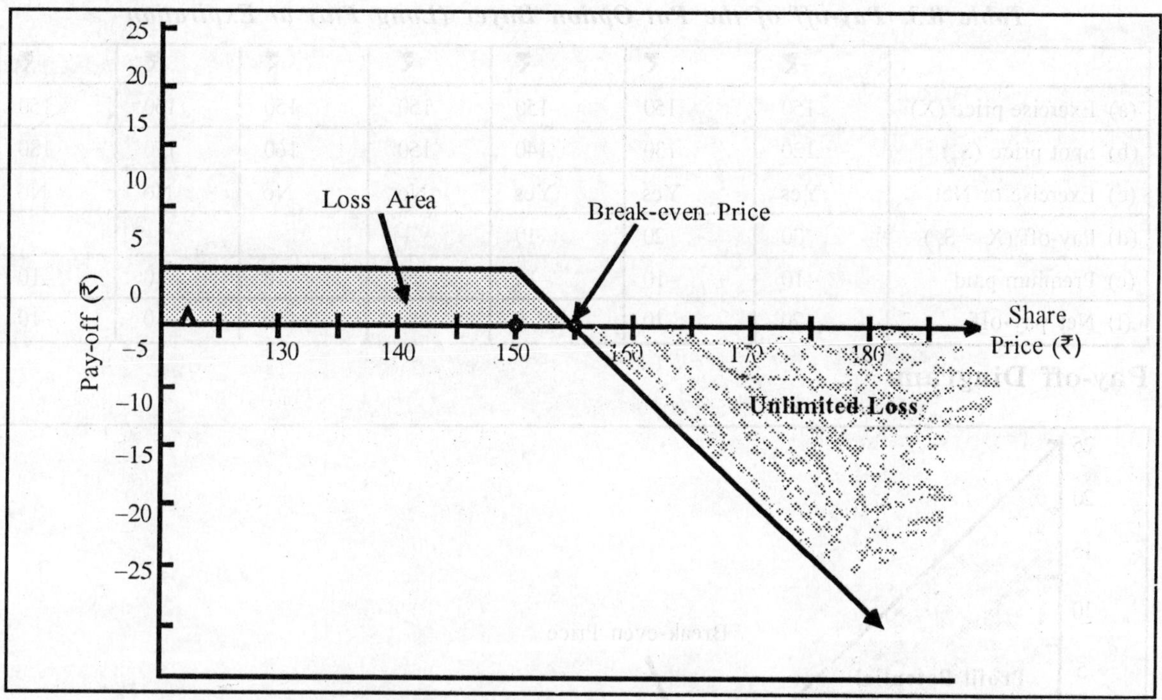

Fig. 8.7: Pay-off of the Call Option Seller

III. Pay-off of a Put Option Buyer (Long Put) at Expiration

Consider the following basics of a put option:

Underlying: Reliance stock

Type of option: Put option

Style of option: European

Position: Long (Buyer)

Exercise price = ₹ 150 per share

Option premium = ₹ 10 per share

Spot price at expiration say: ₹ 120, ₹ 130, ₹ 140, ₹ 150, ₹ 160, ₹ 170 per share.

Now we calculate the pay-off of the put option buyer in the following table:

Table 8.3: Pay-off of the Put Option Buyer (Long Put) at Expiration

	₹	₹	₹	₹	₹	₹	₹
(a) Exercise price (X)	150	150	150	150	150	150	150
(b) Spot price (S_T)	120	130	140	150	160	170	180
(c) Exercise or Not	Yes	Yes	Yes	No	No	No	No
(d) Pay-off ($X - S_T$)	30	20	10	–	–	–	–
(e) Premium paid	–10	–10	–10	–10	–10	–10	–10
(f) Net pay-off	20	10	0	–10	–10	–10	–10

Pay-off Diagram:

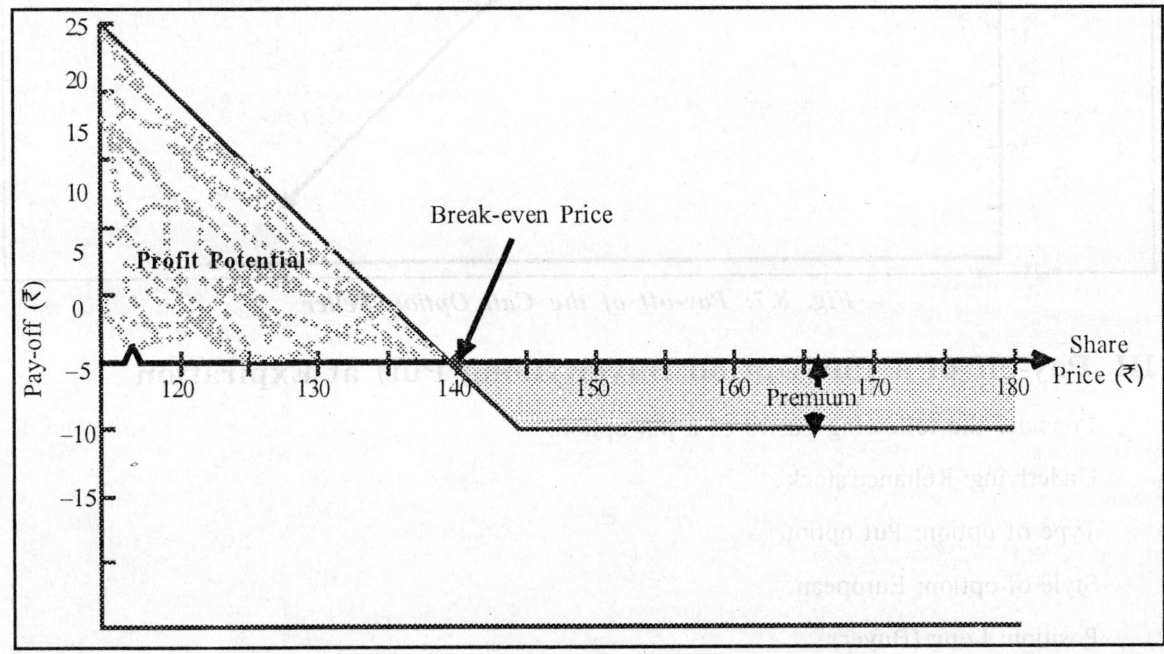

Fig. 8.8: Pay-off of the Put Option Buyer

IV. Pay-off of a Put Option Seller (Short Put) at Expiration

Consider the following basics of a put option:

Underlying: Reliance stock

Type of option: Put option

Style of option: European

Position: Long (Seller)

Exercise price = ₹ 150 per share

Option premium = ₹ 10 per share

Spot price at expiration say: ₹ 120, ₹ 130, ₹ 140, ₹ 150, ₹ 160, ₹ 170, ₹ 180 per share.

Now we calculate the pay-off of the put option seller in the following table:

Table 8.4: Pay-off of the Put Option Seller (Short Put) at Expiration

	₹	₹	₹	₹	₹	₹	₹
(a) Spot price (S_T)	120	130	140	150	160	170	180
(b) Exercise price (X)	150	150	150	150	150	150	150
(c) Exercise or Not	Yes	Yes	Yes	No	No	No	No
(d) Pay-off = (a) – (b)	–30	–20	–10	0	–	–	–
(e) Option premium (received)	+10	+10	+10	+10	+10	+10	+10
(f) Net pay-off (Profit loss)	–20	–10	0	+10	+10	+10	+10

Pay-off Diagram:

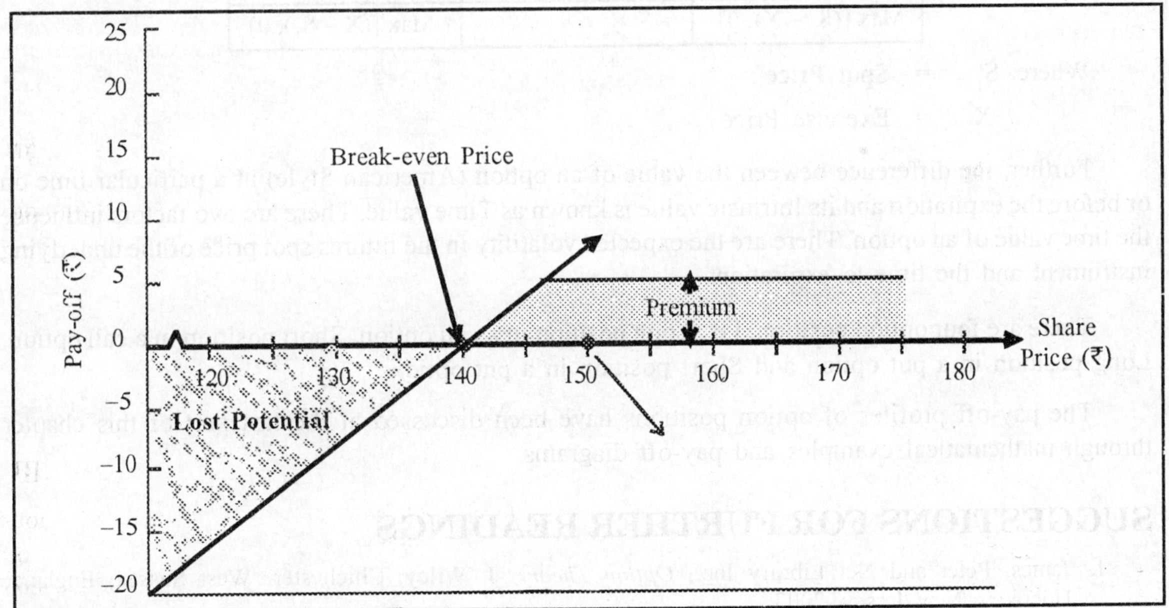

Fig. 8.9: Pay-off of the Put Option Seller

CHAPTER SUMMARY

An option is a special type of contract between two parties where one party grants the other party the right to buy or sell a specific asset or commodity (or instrument) at a specified price within a specific time period. There are only two basic types of options, i.e., ***call option*** and ***put option.***

Call option means right to buy without obligation while put option means right to sell without obligation. To get the right, the buyer has to pay premium to the seller of the option. The buyer of the option is known as option holder while the seller of the option is known as writer. There are two distinctive styles of option contract, i.e., European style and American style.

This chapter has highlighted the various terminologies which are commonly used in option contract. There are the Option contract, Underlying asset, Strike (Exercise price) Expiration date, Option premium, Option moneyness (At-the-money, In-the-money and Out-of-the-money), Covered and Naked options, Option class and Open Interest, etc.

Distinction between futures and options have been discussed at 8.4. There are five points of distinctions between options and futures. These points are right and obligation, premium and margins, pay-off positions, uses of contracts and the pricing models.

At 8.5, the value of an option has been discussed. There are two components of option value, i.e., Intrinsic value and Time value. Intrinsic value of a call option and put option can be calculated as follows:

Intrinsic value		
Call option		Put option
Max $[(S_T - X), 0]$		Max $[(X - S_T), 0]$

Where S_T = Spot Price

X = Exercise Price

Further, the difference beween the value of an option (American Style) at a particular time on or before the expiration and its Intrinsic value is known as Time value. There are two factors influence the time value of an option. There are the expected volatility in the futures spot price of the underlying instrument and the time to expiration.

There are four option position, i.e., Long position in a call option, Short position in a call option, Long position in a put option and Short position in a put option.

The pay-off profiles of option positions have been discussed at the last part of this chapter through mathematical examples and pay-off diagrams.

SUGGESTIONS FOR FURTHER READINGS

1. James, Peter and Net Library Inc., *Option Theory,* J. Wiley, Chichester, West Sussex, England, Hoboken, New Jersey, 2003.
2. Williams, Michaels and Hoffman, *Fundamentals of the Options Market,* McGraw-Hills, New York, 2004.
3. *www.theoptions.net/pay-off-diagrams for options.*
4. *www.learnmoney.co uk/options.*

SOLVED PROBLEMS

Illustration 1

Mr X, the holder of 10 call options

Mr Y, the call option writer

Underlying asset: 1000 shares

Option size: 1 option = 100 shares

Mr Y has purchased 1000 shares on the date of option contract @ 140 per share.

Exercise price = ₹ 150 per share.

Option premium = ₹ 10 per share

Calculate the profit or loss of the covered option writer if the market price on the date of exercise is as follows:

(a) ₹ 135 per share

(b) ₹ 165 per share

Solution:

(a) When the Spot Price on exercise date is lower than the strike price, then Mr. X will not exercise his option. Further, the price paid by Mr Y is ₹ 140 per share.

Hence, his profit/loss will be:

Premium – (Purchase Price – Spot Price) – Premium

= 10 – (140 – 135) = ₹ 5 profit per share

Therefore, total profit = 5 × 1000 = ₹ 5000

Illustration 2

Mr X, the writer of a Naked call option has furnished the following data:

Exercise Price: ₹ 1,00,000

Option premium received: ₹ 5,000

Option style: American

Date of Expiry: 31st December

On 15th December, the option holder exercised his option to buy. On this date, the cash price of the underlying asset is ₹ 1,13,000. Find the loss of Mr X.

Solution:

Loss of Naked call option = (Purchase Price – Exercise Price) – Option Premium

= (1,13,000 – 1,00,000) – 5,000 = 8,000 – 5,000 = 3,000

Note: When a physical delivery of naked call is assigned on exercise, the writer will have to purchase the underlying asset to meet his call obligation and his loss will be the excess of the purchase price over the exercise price of the call reduced by the premium received for waiting the call.

(b) When the spot price is 165 per share Mrs X will exercise his option. In such price Mr. Y will not suffer any loss because the loss will be covered by the shares already he has.

His Profit = (Strike Price – Purchase Price) + Premium

= (₹ 150 – ₹ 140) + ₹ 10

= ₹ 10 + ₹ 10 = ₹ 20 per share

His total profit = ₹ 20 × 1000 = ₹ 20,000.

EXERCISES

Quiz

State Whether the Following Statements are True or False.

(a) An option which conveys the right to buy something is called a put; an option which conveys the right to sell is called a call.

(b) The process of activating an option and thereby trading the underlying at the agreed upon price is referred as exercising.

(c) Over-the-Counter options are standardised contracts and settled through a clearing house.

(d) Exchange Traded Options are listed options.

(e) An option that may only be exercised on or before expiry is known as European option.

(f) Option Open Interest refers to the total number of option contracts that have not been settled in the immediately previous time period for a specific underlying security.

(g) An option may have a negative value.

(h) Moneyness is the term which describes the relationship between the strike price of an option and the current trading price of its underlying security.

(i) The person in an option contract who acquires the right is known as option buyer or holder.

Ans: (a) False, (b) True, (c) False, (d) True, (e) False, (f) True, (g) False, (h) True, (i) True.

Match the Following:

(j) In case of price rises:

(i) Call buyer	(a) Limited gain
(ii) Call seller	(b) Limited loss
(iii) Put buyer	(c) Unlimited loss
(iv) Put seller	(d) Unlimited gain

(k) In case of price falls:

(i) Call buyer	(a) Unlimited loss
(ii) Call seller	(b) Unlimited gain
(iii) Put buyer	(c) Limited gain
(iv) Put seller	(d) Limited loss

A. Short Type Questions

1. Define the term "option" is the language of finance.
2. What is a call option?
3. What is a put option?
4. What is an Americal style of an option?
5. What do you mean by European style of an option?
6. What is the difference between on American style and European style of an option?
7. Define the following concepts in the language of option finance.
   (a) Underlying Asset (b) Style of an option
   (c) Bermudan style of an option (d) Strike price or Exercise price
   (e) Option premium (f) At-the-money (ATM)
   (g) In-the-money (ITM) (h) Covered option
   (i) Naked or Uncovered option (j) Moneyness of an option
8. What is option value?
9. What is Intrinsic value of an option?
10. Is there any difference between option price and option premium?
11. How to calculate Time value of an option?
12. Name two factors which are affecting Time value of an option.
13. Explain the followings:
    (a) Long call (b) Long put
    (c) Short call (d) Short put
14. What is pay-off of an option ?
15. How to calculate the pay-off of the following option positions?
    (a) Call option (b) Call option writer
    (c) Put option buyer (d) Put option seller

B. Long Type Questions

1. What is an "option" in the language of derivatives? Briefly discuss the features of an option.
2. What is an option? Briefly discuss the various types of options.
3. What is an option style? Discuss various styles of an option contract with suitable example.
4. Distinguish between:
   (a) Covered option and Naked option
   (b) Exchange traded options and Over-the-Counter traded options

5. What is option moneyness? Explain the following concepts in contest of option moneyness:
   (a) In-the-money
   (b) Out-of-the-money
   (c) At-the-money
6. Distinguish between Options and Futures contracts.
7. What is option value? Explain how to calculate Intrinsic value and Time value of an option.
8. What is option position? Explain the basic four positions of an option contract?
9. What is option pay-off? How to calculate pay-off of the following option position?
   (a) Call option buyer (b) Call option writer
   (c) Put option buyer (d) Put option seller
10. Draw the pay-off diagrams of the following option positions:
   (a) Call option buyer (b) Call option writer
   (c) Put option buyer (d) Put option seller

PRACTICAL PROBLEMS

1. Exercise price = ₹ 150
   Spot price of instrument at expiration = ₹ 170
   Option premium = ₹ 10
   Find option In-the-money of a call option.
2. Exercise price = ₹ 150
   Spot price of instrument at expiration = ₹ 140
   Option premium = ₹ 5
   Type of option = Put option
   Find-out-in-the-money.
3. Spot price at exercise date = ₹ 160
   Exercise price = ₹ 150
   Option premium = ₹ 5
   Find the Intrinsic value of an option.
4. Option premium = ₹ 10 per share
   Intrinsic value per share = ₹ 7 per share
   Calculate Time value of an option.
5. Fill in the blanks:

Option price	Strike premium	Option price	Spot value	Intrinsic value	Time
Call	140	10	130	?	?
Call	140	10	125	?	?
Call	150	6	160	?	?
Put	160	4	162	?	?
Put	170	8	175	?	?
Put	150	20	165	?	?

6. Calculate the pay-off of a Long call from the following data and draw the pay-off diagram.
   Underlying: X Ltd stack
   Type of option: Call option
   Style of option: European
   Position: Long
   Exercise price: ₹ 120 per share
   Option premium: 2 per share
   Assume spot price at expiration is ₹ 100, ₹ 110, ₹ 120, ₹ 130, ₹ 140, ₹ 150 per share.
7. The ITC stock is selling at ₹ 4,000. Mr. X. has a negative view about the stock. He decides to go through the option route to take advantage of the situation. He buys an option from Mr. A which will entitle him to sell 100 shares on on before 30th December at ₹ 3,500 per share for which he has to pay ₹ 200 per share today.
   You are required to identify:
   (i) Type of Option
   (ii) Exercise Price
   (iii) Expiry Date
   (iv) Option Premium
   (v) Buyer of the Option
   (vi) Writer of the option
   (vii) Underlying Assets
   (viii) Current Market Price [ICWA June 2010, Final Stage III]

Hints: (i) American put option
(ii) ₹ 3,500 per share
(iii) 30th December
(iv) ₹ 20,000 (at ₹ 200 per share for 100 shares)
(v) Mr. X
(vi) Mr. A
(vii) ITC Shares
(viii) Current Market Price: ₹ 4,000.

Option Pricing: Basics (Determinants, Bounds and Put-Call Parity)

Learning Objectives

After studying this chapter, you will be able to:

- Know the basics of option pricing
- Record in your memory the six determinants of option pricing
- Express the upper limit and lower limit of call option as well as put option price
- Know the fundamentals of put-call parity

Chapter Outline

9.1 AN INTRODUCTION TO OPTION PRICING

A call option gives the holder the **right to** buy an asset (say stock) at a fixed (strike) price while the put option gives the holder the **right to sell** at a fixed (strike) price. Let us consider a stock option. A call option holder pays option premium to the writer of the option. In return, the option writer is obliged to sell the shares if the option is exercised by the option holder. If the stock price (S_t) at the time of exercise is less than the exercise price (X), the option holder will not exercise the option. In this case the liability of the option writer is nil. On the other hand, if the stock price (S_t) is higher than the exercise price (X), the option holder will exercise the option. The reverse situation is in case of put option. Thus, in option trading :

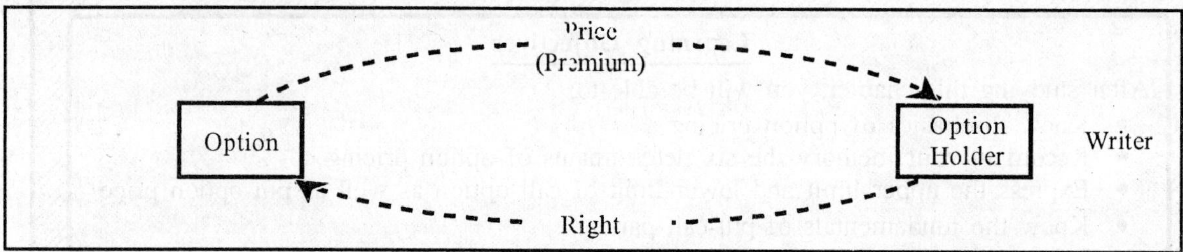

It is very clear that the option holder pays certain price which is otherwise known as option premium to the option writer to obtain the right to trade, i.e., to buy or sell.

Option prices (or Premiums) have two components; prices are determined by six factors; and the way prices change are measured by six indicators (called Greeks).

There are various models used to determine the option price.

To understand the option pricing one has to conceptualise each element of the following figure:

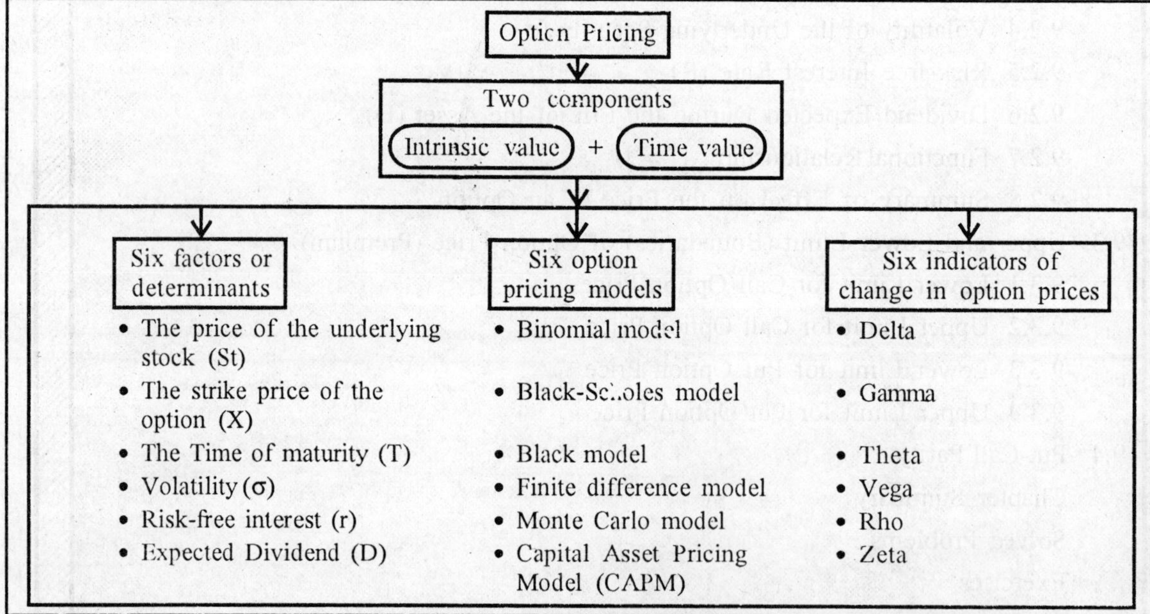

Fig. 9.1: The Fundamentals of Option Pricing

In this chapter, we will discuss the six determinants of option pricing.

9.2 DETERMINANTS OF OPTION PRICE

There are six factors influencing the value of an option. These are:

1. Current price of the underlying security (S_t) at maturity.
2. Strike price (X).
3. Time to maturity (T).
4. Volatility of the underlying security price (σ).
5. Risk-free interest rate (r).
6. The expected dividends during the life of the asset (D).

These factors influence the value of an option depending upon the type (call option or put option) and style (American or European) of an option. We shall now discuss these determinants.

9.2.1 Current Price of the Underlying Security (S_t) at Maturity

We know that pay-off an option is calculated by comparing the current price (S_t) of the underlying asset with its strike price (X). Thus:

Option	Call option	Put option
Pay-off	$(S_t - X)$	$(X - S_t)$

In case of increase in the value of underlying asset, the value of call option will increase and the value of put option will decrease. In case of decrease in the value of underlying asset, the value of call option will decrease and the value of put option will increase.

Thus, the higher the asset price, the higher is the chance that it will rise above the exercise price and therefore, the higher the premium for call option. On the other hand, the higher the asset price, the lower is the chance that it will fall below the strike price and therefore, the premium for a put option would be lower.

Example:

Call Option

Current Stock (S_t)	Strike Price (X)	Pay-off ($S_t - X$)
150	150	0
155	150	5
160	150	10
165	150	15
170	150	20
175	150	25

Put Option

Strike Price (X)	Current stock Price (S_t)	Pay-off ($X - S_t$)
175	150	25
175	155	20
175	160	15
175	165	10
175	170	5
175	175	0

These above stated data can be presented is the following Figures 9.2 and 9.3 to show the manner in which call option and put option prices depend on the price of the current price of the underlyings.

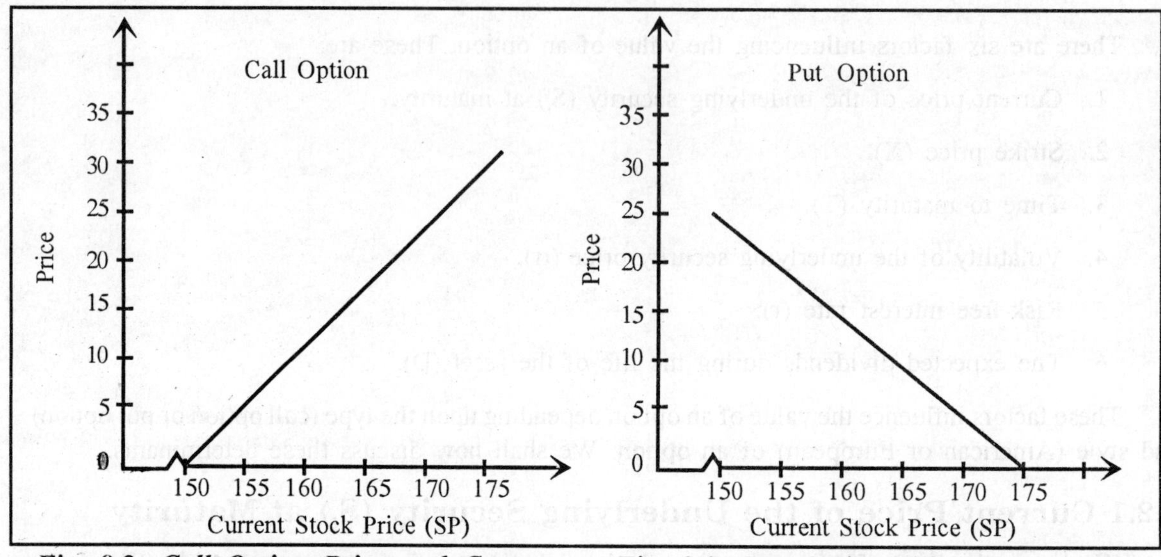

Fig. 9.2: Call Option Price and Current Price of the Underlying

Fig. 9.3: Put Option Price and Current Price of the Underlying

Remarks:

1. Increase in the current price of underlying asset results higher pay-off for a call option. Thus, a call option becomes more valuable as the price of the underlying increases. The reverse situation will be for a put option.
2. Decrease in the current price of underlying asset results lower pay-off for a call option and higher pay-off for a put option. Thus, a call option becomes less valuable and a put option becomes more valuable as the price of the underlying decreases.

9.2.2 Strike (Exercise) Price of an Option (X)

A call option will be exercised only when the price of the underlying asset at maturity (S_t) exceeds the strike price (X). A put option will be exercised only when the strike price (X) exceeds the price of the underlying asset at maturity (S_t). The pay-off in both options may be summarised in the following table:

Type of Option	Option Buyer (Holder)	Option Seller (Writer)
Call Option	Max [0, $(S_t - X)$]	Min [0, $(X - S_t)$]
Put Option	Max [0, $(X - S_t)$]	Min [0, $(S_t - X)$]

Keeping all other variables (determinants) constant, if we change strike price, what is the impact on pay-off *vis-à-vis* value of on option? Consider the following example.

Example:

Call Option

Current Stock (S_t)	Strike Price Price at Maturity (X)	Pay-off (S_t – X)
180	155	25
180	160	20
180	165	15
180	170	10
180	175	5

Put Option

Current Stock (S_t)	Current Price Price at Maturity (X)	Pay-off (X – S_t)
150	155	5
150	160	10
150	105	15
150	170	20
150	175	25

The strike price of an option contract is just like an insured value of the underlying asset.

In case of call option, the lower the strike price, the higher would be the pay-off. This means the value of the call will be higher and ultimately the option premium will be higher. Logically, if the strike price of an option contract is lower, then the asset price will easily exceed this level. Accordingly, the option seller (writer) will demand for higher premium because the probability of exercising the option by the option holder is very less. The situation is the reverse for a put option.

From the above, it is very clear that there is a negative correlation between strike price and option value in case of call option and positive correlation between call option and positive correlation between strike price and option value in case of put option.

The following diagram depicts the above features.

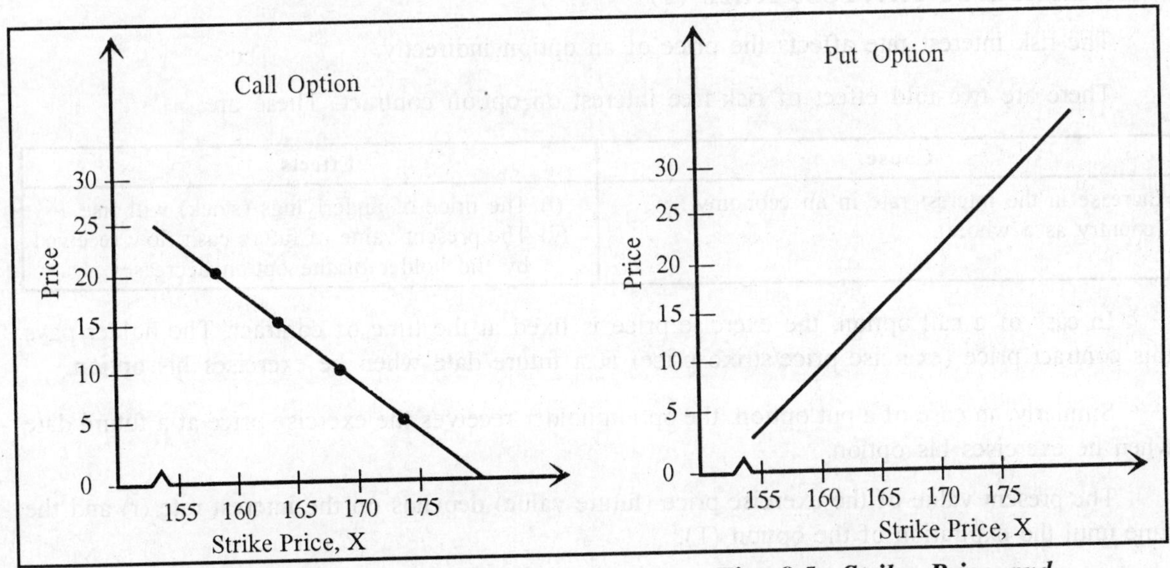

Fig. 9.4: Strike Price and Call Option Value

Fig. 9.5: Strike Price and Put Option Value

Remark: Keeping all other factor constant, call option is less valuable as the strike price increases and *vice versa.* Similarly, put option is more valuable as the strike price increases and *vice versa.*

9.2.3 Time to Maturity (T)

Time to maturity is one of the important factor which influences the option value. Generally, the longer the time taken for maturity, the higher is the option value. Because, the longer the life of an option, the greater the chances of price fluctuations and *vice versa.*

Option value is the aggregate of its intrinsic value and time value. As an option's expiration date approaches, its time value diminishes and ultimately becomes zero.

Remark: Longer the time to expiration, higher is the value of call as well as put.

9.2.4 Volatility of the Underlying Security (σ)

Volatility (i.e., price variability) of the underlying asset influences the value of an option. The fluctuation in the price of an asset brings risk to the investors (the option holders). Options are used to manage such risk. For example, the call option protects the option holder against upward movement of the price and a put option protects against downward movement of price. But the degree of variability (i.e., volatility) in the prices of the underlying assumes risk contents in the dealings. This volatility is measured by Standard Deviation (σ). Both call options and put options become more valuable when volatility of the underlying asset increase.

Remark: Higher the volatility, higher is the option value (Premium).

9.2.5 Risk-free Interest Rate (r)

The risk interest rate affects the price of an option indirectly.

There are two-fold effect of risk-free interest on option contract. These are:

Cause	Effects
Increase in the interest rate in an economy (country as a whole).	(i) The price of underlyings (stock) will rise. (ii) The present value of future cash flow received by the holder of the option decreases.

In case of a call option, the exercise price is fixed at the time of contract. The holder pays this contract price (exercise price/strike price) at a future date when he exercises his option.

Similarly, in case of a put option, the option holder receives the exercise price at a future date when he exercises his option.

The present value of the exercise price (future value) depends on the interest rate (r) and the time until the expiration of the option (T).

Consider the following example:

Exercise Price	Risk-free Interest Rate	Time to Expiration	Present Value of Exercise Price
240	10%	1 year	$\frac{240}{1.10} = 218.18$
240	11%	1 year	$\frac{240}{1.10} = 216.22$
240	12%	1 year	$\frac{240}{1.12} = 214.29$

From the above example, it is very clear that if the interest rate rises, the present value declines. This situation will be favo-rable to the call holder (the partly who pays) and unfavourable to the put holder (the party who receives). Thus, the call option price increases as the risk-free interest rate increases and *vice versa.* Similarly, the put option price declines as the risk-free interest rate increases. See the following figures:

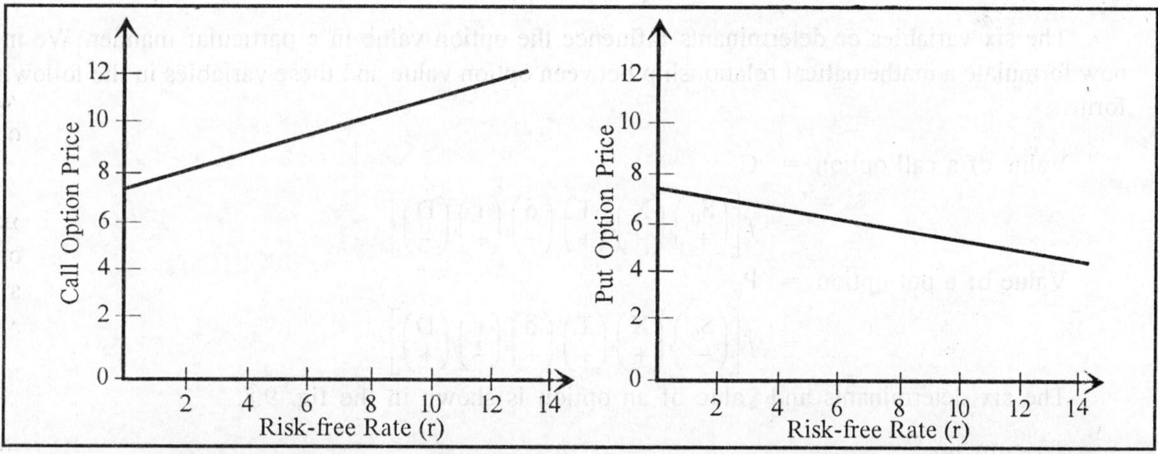

Fig 9.6: Effect of Changes in Risk-free Interest on Call Option Price

Fig. 9.7: Effect of Changes in Risk-free Interest on Put Option Price

9.2.6 Dividends Expected During the Life of the Asset (D)

The most common popular type of call option is the option on **stocks.**

Sometimes, stocks can be sold just before the declaration of dividend, i.e., dividend has become due to the shareholder but has not been received by him. In such circumstances, if the market price includes the accrued dividend, then the price will be higher to the extent of such dividend. In this case, the buyer will receive such dividend as and when the dividend will be paid by the company. Thus, when the stock price includes dividend, the price is called **cum-dividend price.**

Contrary to this, if the market price of stock does not include such dividend, then the buyer pays only the normal market price and ultimately the seller receives the accrued dividend as it is due to him. Thus, when the stock price does not include the amount of dividend, then such price is called **ex-dividend price.**

In option trading, dividends that are expected during the life of the option are another determinant of the option price. Particularly, in case of Ex-dividend price, the call value will decrease and put value will increase. To provide protection to the option holder, the option contract generally specifies that the exercise price and the number of shares will be adjusted for stock splits and stock dividends.

The reasons are as follows:

(i) In case of call option, when the dividend amount goes to the option writer, ultimately it reduces the probability of rising the asset price above the exercise price and therefore decreases the value of the call option.

(ii) In case of put option, when the dividend is received by the option holder, the stock price would fall below the exercise price and therefore enhances the option value or premium.

Remark: The value of the call option decreases and the value of put option increases when the dividend is paid on the underlying asset under ex-dividend option contract.

9.2.7 Functional Relationship

The six variables or determinants influence the option value in a particular manner. We may now formulate a mathematical relationship between option value and these variables in the following forms:

$$\text{Value of a call option} = C_0 = f\left[\binom{S_0}{+},\binom{X}{-},\binom{T}{+},\binom{\delta}{+},\binom{r}{+},\binom{D}{-}\right]$$

$$\text{Value of a put option} = P_0 = f\left[\binom{S_0}{-},\binom{X}{+},\binom{T}{+},\binom{\delta}{+},\binom{r}{-},\binom{D}{+}\right]$$

The six determinants and value of an option is shown in the fig. 9.8.

To sum up,

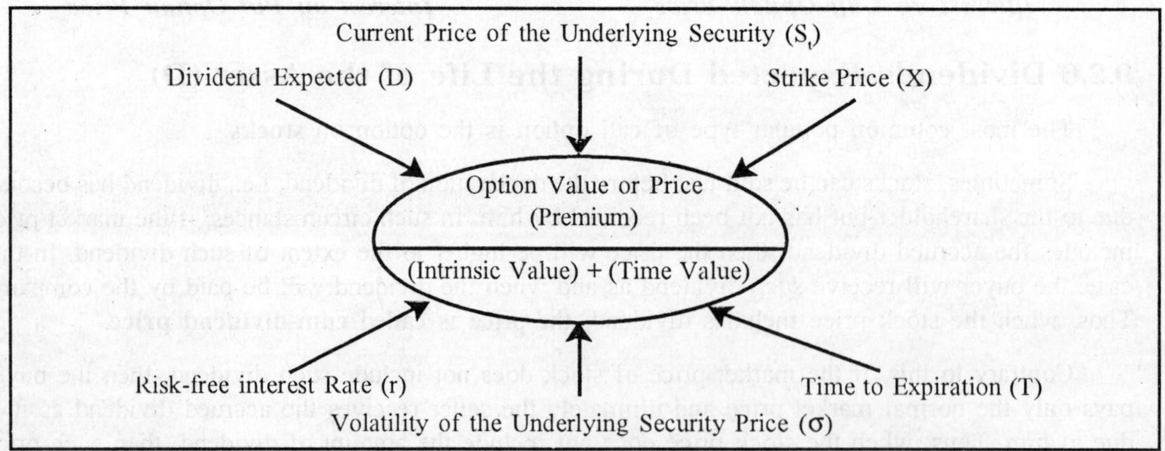

Fig. 9.8: Six Major Factors Influencing Option Price (Premium)

9.2.8 Summary of Effect on the Price of an Option

Summary of the effect on the price of an option (call and put) of increasing one determinant keeping other determinants constant.

Table 9.1: Determinants of Option Price

Factor (Determinant)	Effect of an Increase in One Factor Keeping All Other Factors Constant			
	European Option		American Option	
	Call	Put	Call	Put
Current Price of Stock (S_t)	Increase	Decrease	Increase	Decrease
Strike Price (X)	Decrease	Increase	Decrease	Increase
Time to Expiration (T)	Uncertain	Uncertain	Increase	Increase
Volatility (Variance) of Underlying Price (σ)	Increase	Increase	Increase	Increase
Risk-free Interest Rate (r)	Increase	Decrease	Increase	Decrease
Dividend (D)	Decrease	Increase	Decrease	Increase

9.3 UPPER AND LOWER LIMIT (BOUNDARIES) OF OPTION PRICE (PREMIUM)

Let S_t = Price of the underlying asset at maturity

X = Strike Price

In case of call option, the option holder exercises his option when St > X or $(S_t - X) > 0$. If $S_t < X$ or $(S_t - X) < 0$, the option holder does not exercise his option. So the pay-off of the option holder (buyer) and option writer (seller) would be as follows:

Call Option	Option Holder	Option Writer
Pay-off	Max $(0, S_t - X)$	Min $(0, X - S_t)$

Similarly, in case of put option, the option holder exercises his option when $X > S_t$ or $(X - S_t) > 0$. If $X < S_t$ or $(X - S_t) < 0$, the option holder does not exercise his option. So, the pay-off of the put option holder (buyer) and put option writer (seller) would be as follows:

Put Option	Option Holder	Option Writer
Pay-off	Max $(0, X - S_t)$	Min $(0, S_t - X)$

It may be noted that pay-off of an option is always positive considering the above stated pay-off, we will now discuss the boundaries on option price.

9.3.1 Lower Limit for Call Option Price

Consider the following example:

Type of option:	Call option
Style of option:	American
Date of option contract:	1st January 2012
Date of maturity:	31st March, 2012
Underlying Asset:	Stock of Z Ltd.
Exercise Price (₹) per share:	160
Stock Price at maturity (₹) per share:	140

Since it is an American option, the option holder has a right to exercise his option on or before 31st March 2012. Let on 1st March, the stock price is 157. Accordingly the value Max (0, S – X) is the lower limit on the current price S = 157. Here Max (0, 157 – 140) or, 17 is the lower limit of the American call option price. If the option holder expects higher value in future till the date of maturity like European option, the lower limit would be the same i.e., Max (0, S – X). We may assume that the stock or other underlying for the option does not give any dividends.

Point to Note:

Option is a right, but not obligation. In case S < X, the option holder will not exercise. Then the value of an option is zero. It cannot be negative.

Motives of an Option Holder

When the stock price is in rising trend, the option holder of an American style keeps the option as such instead of exercising it immediately. He hopes further increase for a better pay-off. There are three advantages in keeping the option instead of exercising it immediately:

(i) **To Postpone Immediate Cash-out Flow:** In case the option holder exercises before the date of maturity, he has to make payment at the predetermined exercise price, i.e., X. But if he waits further, the payment will be deterred. An American option holder may wait till maturity to avail this benefit.

(ii) **To Save Interest:** If an American option is exercised on the date of maturity, then interest on exercise price (X) can be saved till the maturity date. However, in case of European option, this is not applicable.

(iii) **Chance of Less Investment at Maturity:** Sometimes the price of stock decreases as on maturity date. In such case, the option holder will not exercise his option and simultaneously purchase the stock at a lesser price than the exercise price (X). Hence, there is a chance of less investment in case an option holder waits till maturity.

From the above analysis, we find that the American option holder ultimately waits till the date of maturity. Eventually, there is no difference between an American option and European option. Further the value of an option is always positive and equal to Max (0, S – X).

As it is already explained that there are two components of option value, these are intrinsic value and time value. The quantity Max (0, S – X) is known as the intrinsic value of the call option. The time value is influenced by the factors like interest and time to maturity.

Let Mr. P is an investor. He has the following two alternative strategies:

Strategy I (without option)	Strategy II (with option)
Buy the stock now by paying its price say S.	Buy a call option contct by paying premium say C.
• Immediate cash out flow. • No cash out flow at maturity.	Invest the sufficient money to ensure that the principal plus interest will be equal to exercise price say X at the maturity.

In strategy II, how much amount to be invested to get X at the maturity?

It is the present value of X which is calculated as follows:

PV of $X = Xe^{-rt}$

Where r = Rate of interest continuously compounded

t = Time to maturity

Thus, the total investment at present in strategy II would be as follows:

Price of the call option $= C$

Present value of X $= Xe^{-rt}$

Total amount $C + Xe^{-rt}$

There may be two situations at maturity:

Situation (1)

Stock price is greater than exercise price, i.e., $S > X$. In this situation, the option holder exercises his option at price X. He is able to pay the amount X by realising from his invested amount, i.e., Xe^{-rt}.

Situation (2)

Stock price is less than the exercise price. In this situation, the option holder will not exercise his option. He will purchase the stock from the open market at price S.

The price for such stock will be paid out of the amount realised from investment. Since the amount realised is equal to X and the stock price S is less than X, so some surplus will be available with the option holder.

Which Strategy is Better?

The second alternative is better than the first. In both alternatives, the stock remains at the maturity of the option. But the second alternative is in advantage position because there is a chance of surplus of cash as well. Therefore, the cost of second alternative ($C + Xe^{-rt}$) must be greater than the cost of the first alternative, i.e.,

Mathematically,

$$C + Xe^{-rt} \geq S$$

$$\Rightarrow C \geq S - Xe^{-rt}$$

This is another approach to determine the lower limit of call option. Since the value of call option is alway positive, hence lower bound of the call option can be expressed as $C \geq$ Max (0, $S - X^{-rt}$).

9.3.2 Upper Limit for Call Option Price

Consider the following two examples:

	Example I	Example II
Type of option	Call	Call
Style of option	American	European
Date of option contract	1st January	1st January
Date of maturity	31st March	31st March
Underlying asset	Stock of Z Ltd.	Stock of Z Ltd.
Exercise price (₹)	160 per share	160 per share
Stock price as on 1st January (₹)	140 per share	140 per share
Option premium (₹)	5 per share	5 per share

One point must be clear that the amount of Premium (Price of the option) is always less than the stock price itself. Because, an option holder has to invest an additional amount to buy the underlying stock at maturity. The additional amount is the exercise price if the option is exercised on maturity when stock price is higher than the exercise price. But the additional price is the stock price if the option is not exercised, i.e., when stock price is less than exercise price. Thus, the additional amount is either the exercise price or the stock price at maturity, whichever is lower.

In the previous section, the concept of lower bound of call option has already expressed in the following form:

$$C \geq \text{Max } (0, S - X^{-rt})$$

Where C = Call option price

S = Stock price at maturity

X = Strike price

r = Rate of interest continuously compounded

t = Time to expiration

Since upper bound is higher than the lower bound, now we express their relationship in the following mathematical forms:

(i) Upper bound ≤ Lower bound

$\Rightarrow$ Max (O, S – X) ≤ Max O S – X^{-rt}

(ii) Lower limit ≤ Option price

$\Rightarrow$ Max (O, S – X) ≤ C

Here C = Call option price (American/European)

(iii) Option price ≤ Stock price

$\Rightarrow$ C_A = Call price of American style

C_E = Call price of European style

We may now summarise the upper limit of call option price considering the above stated three conceptual relations:

$$\text{Max } (O, S - X) \leq \text{Max } (O, S - X^{-rt}) \leq C \leq S$$

9.3.3 Lower Limit for Put Option Price

Let P is an investor. He is holding certain stocks. He has the following two alternative strategies:

Strategy I	Strategy II
Sell the stock now by realising its price say S. • Immediate cash in flow. • No cash in flow at maturity.	Buy a put option contract by paying premium say C. Borrow sufficient money to ensure that the amount (principal + interest) will be equal to X at the maturity of the option.

In strategy II, how much money to be borrowed so that the borrowing amount plus interest will be equal to exercise price, i.e., X. It is the present value of X which is calculated as follows:

PV of X = Xe^{-rt}

Where r = Rate of interest continuously compounded

t = Time to maturity

Thus, the total amount required at present for strategy II would be calculated as follows:

Borrowing amount (Present value of X)	Xe^{-rt}
Less put option premium received (say P)	P
Net amount required	$= Xe^{-rt} - P$

On maturity, the option holder will sell the stock, realise the amount and able to repay the borrowing amount. But there may be two situations at maturity.

Situation (1)

When stock price at maturity is less than X, i.e., S < X. The option holder will exercise the option at price X and repay the loan.

Situation (2)

When the stock price at maturity is greater than X, i.e., S > X. In this situation, the option holder will not exercise his option. He will sell his stock at open market at price S and repay the loan. Since the sale proceeds is higher than the amount of loan, some surplus money will be available with the option holder.

Which Alternative is Better?

The second alternative is better than the first because there is a possibility of cash surplus at the time of maturity of option. This possibility of additional cash flow in future can be strategically done by borrowing a lesser amount.

We examine the cash inflows at the time of option or before maturity we get the following results.

Strategy I	Strategy II
Cash inflow at the time of Where S = Stock price X = Strike price P = Put option premium	S option contract = $Xe^{-rt} - P$

Since 2nd strategy is better than the first strategy, so the cash inflow under second must be less than the immediate cash inflow under first strategy.

Mathematically,

$$(Xe^{-rt} - P) \leq S$$

$$\Rightarrow P\ ^{3}\ Xe^{-rt} - S$$

As an option price cannot be negative so we may define the lower bound for a put option in the following mathematical expression:

$$\boxed{P \geq \text{Max } (O, S - X^{-rt} - S)}$$

Points to Note:

(i) American put is more valuable than European put because it can be exercised before maturity.

(ii) In case of American put, immediate exercise is possible. This implies that it has definitely some intrinsic value.

9.3.4 Upper Bound for Put Option Price

Consider the following two examples.

Particulars	Example I	Example II
Type of option	Put	Put
Option style	American	European
Date of option contract	1st January	1st January
Date of maturity	31st March	31st March
Underlying Asset	Stock of Z Ltd.	Stock of Z Ltd
Exercise Price (₹) (per share)	160	160
Stock price as on 1st January (₹)	140	140
Option premium (₹) per share	6	6

(a) American Put Option

An American put option is always of less value than the exercise price. Thus,

$$P_A \leq X$$

Where P_A = American put option

X = Exercise price

In this above example, $P_A = 6$ and $X = 140$. So, $P_A < X$. Thus, the upper bound is X.

In the previous section, we have expressed the lower bound of American option as:

$$P_A \geq \text{Max}\ (O, Xe^{-rt} - S)$$

Now we combine the above limits and obtain the bounds as follows:

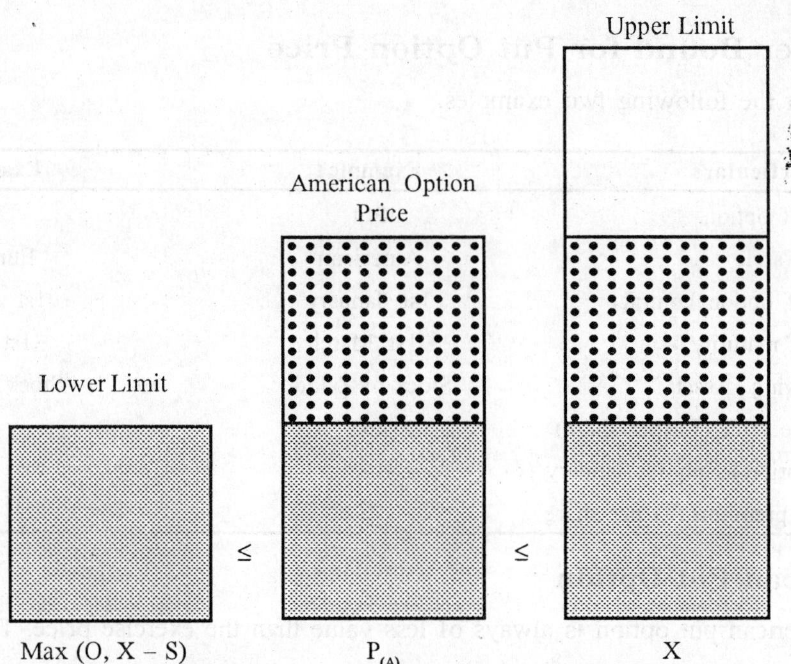

Thus, the upper limit of an American put option can be expressed as:

$$\text{Max } (O, X - S) \leq P_{(A)} \leq X$$

European Put Option: Like American put option, we may now combine the lower limit and upper limit of an European option and summarise the bounds as follows:

$$\text{Max } (O, Xe^{-rt} - S) \leq P_E \leq Xe^{-rt}$$

9.4 PUT-CALL PARITY

Meaning: Put-call Parity is a financial relationship between the price of a put option and a call option on the same underlying instrument with identical strike price and expiry.

Application: To derive the **put-call parity** relationship, the assumption is that the options are not exercised before the date of maturity. Thus, the **put-call parity** is a concept related to European call and put options.

Concept: The put-call parity is an option pricing concept that requires the values of call and put options to be in ***equilibrium*** to prevent arbitrage.

Relationship: Put-Call Parity: A close relationship among the price of a call, price of a put and the price of the underlying stock. Thus:

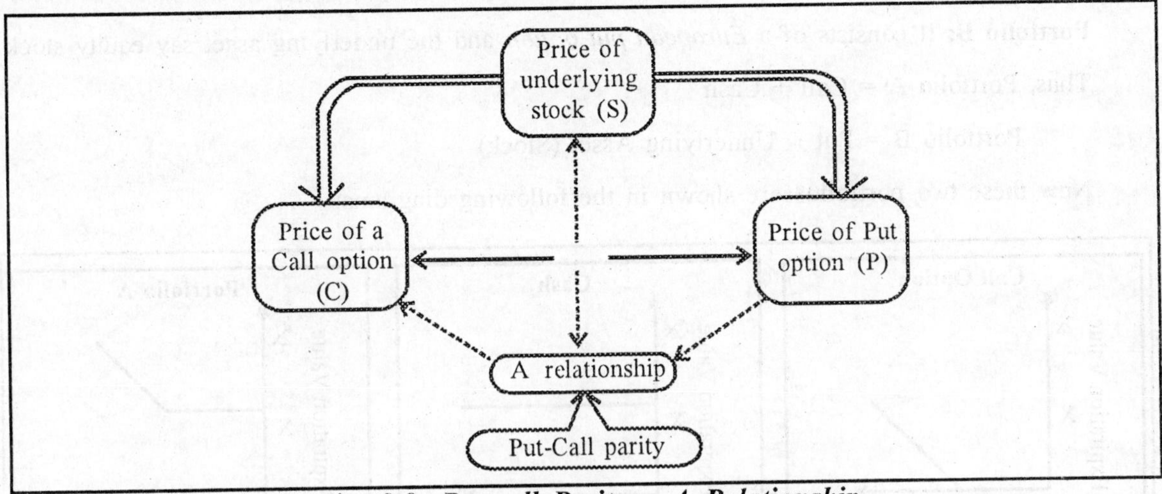

Fig. 9.9: Put-call Parity – A Relationship

As a matter of fact, there is a close relationship among the prices of put options, call options and their underlyings. A change in the price of the underlying stock affects the price of both call and put options that are written on the stock. Put-Call parity defines this relationship.

It states that the premium (price) of a call option implies a certain fair price for the corresponding put option having the same strike price and expiration date, and the *vice versa.*

Prevent Arbitrage

Arbitrage opportunities would prevail if there is a divergence between the value of calls and puts. Arbitrageurs would come into make profitable, riskless trades until the put-call parity is restored. Consider these cases:

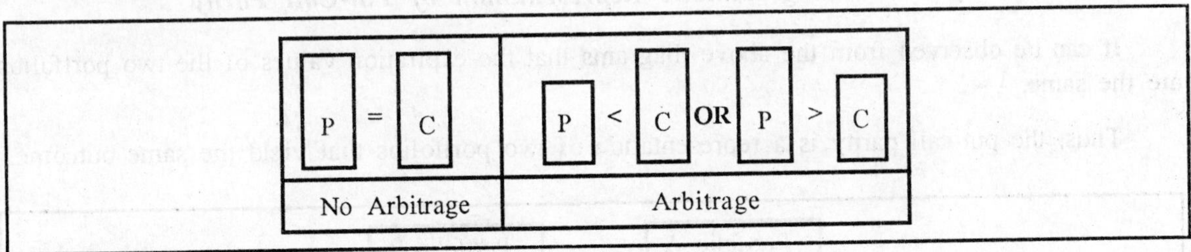

Here P = Price of the put option, C = Price of the call option.

The *put-call parity* implies that if the price of a put option, price of a call option and price of the underlying stock are in the equilibrium, there is no opportunity for arbitrage. This relationship is strictly for European style options.

Put-Call Parity Formula

To understand the put-call parity relationship, let's consider the following two portfolios:

Portfolio A: It consists of a *European call option* and cash. The cash component is equal to the number of shares covered by the call option multiplied by the call's strike price.

Portfolio B: It consists of a *European put option* and the underlying asset say equity stock.

Thus, Portfolio A = Call + Cash

Portfolio B = Put + Underlying Asset (Stock)

Now these two portfolios are shown in the following diagrams:

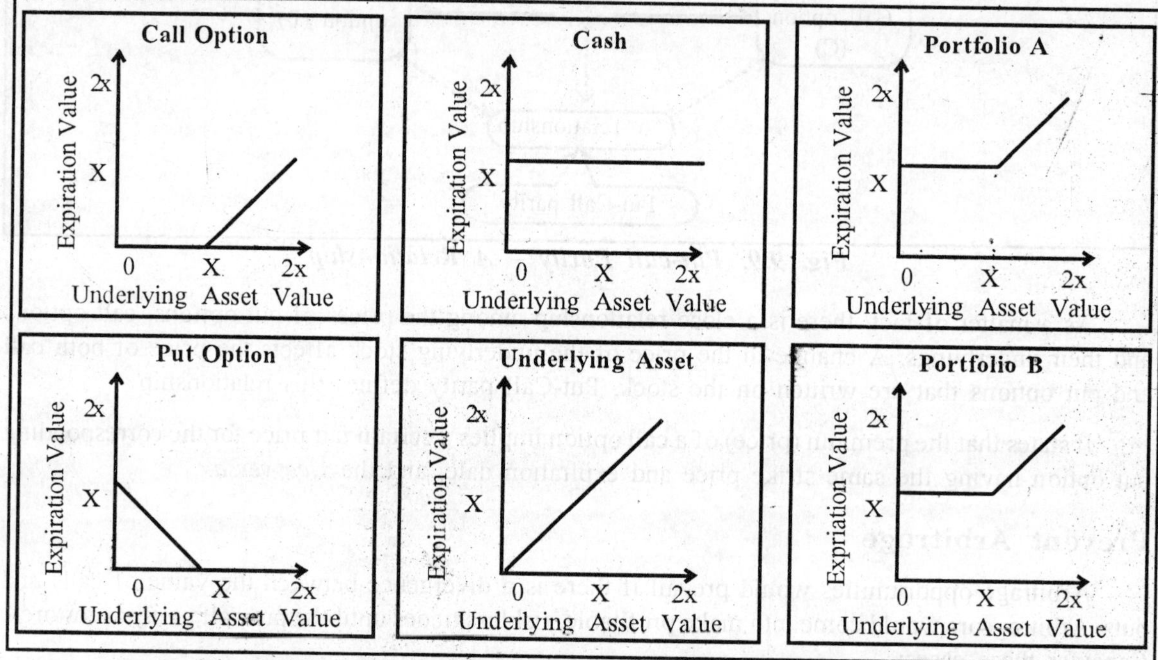

Fig. 9.10: Diagrammatic Representation of Put-Call Parity

It can be observed from the above diagrams that the expiration values of the two portfolios are the same.

Thus, the put-call parity is a representation of two portfolios that yield the same outcome.

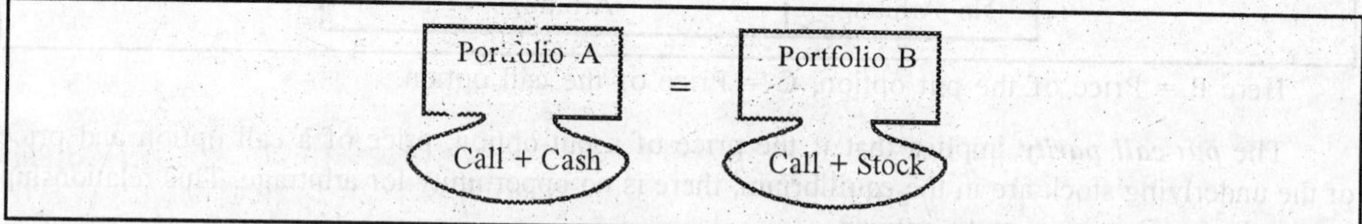

If the two portfolios have the same expiration value, then they have the same present value. Otherwise, an arbitrage trader can go long on the undervalued portfolio and short the overvalued portfolio to make a risk-free profit on maturity.

Put-Call Parity Relationship on the Date of Option Contract

Now we have to calculate the present value of the above stated two portfolios basing on the following assumptions:

(i) Interest rate does not change in time. It is constant for both borrowing and lending.

(ii) The dividend to be received (in case of portfolio B) are known and certain.

(iii) The underlying stock is highly liquid and no transfer barriers exist.

Put-Call Parity Equation:

$$C + \frac{X}{(1+r)^t} = S_0 + P$$

Where C = Call premium r = Annual Interest Rate

P = Put premium t = Time in years

X = Strike price of call and put S_0 = Initial price of underlying

If we calculate interest compounded continuously, then the put-call parity equation will be expressed as follows:

$$C + Xe^{-rt} = P + S_0$$

Point to Note:

Put-Call Parity and American Option

Some American style options allow early exercise, put-call parity will not hold for such American options unless they are held to expiration. Early exercise will result in a departure in the present values of the two portfolios. However, we may derive some outcomes for American option prices in the following mathematical forms:

$$\{S_0 - X\} \leq \{C - P\} \leq S_0 - Xe^{-rt}$$

CHAPTER SUMMARY

Option is a derivative instrument wich gives the holder the right without an obligation to do so. There are four types of options:

Right to Trade ↓	Exercise of an Option	
	Only on maturity date	**On or before maturity date**
To buy an asset (Call option)	European call option	American call option
To sell an asset (Put option)	European put option	American put option

The buyer of the call option pays premium for the option to buy a specified quantity at a specified price any time prior to the maturity of the option. Similarly, the buyer of the put option pays a premium for the option to sell a specified quantity at a specified price at any time prior to maturity of the option. The premium which is paid by the buyer of the option (holder) to the seller of the option (writer) is called option price.

There are six factors affecting the option price. These are the current stock price (S_0), Exercise price of option (X), Time to expiration (T), Volatility of the stock price (d), Risk-free interest (r) and cash dividends (D).

In this chapter we have discussed the effect on the price of an option (particularly stock option) when one of the daterminant increases and all other five remain constant.

Determinant	Increase (↑)	Call option Price	Put Option Price
Stock Price	↑	↑	↓
Exercise Price	↑	↓	↑
Time to expiration	↑	↑	↑
Volatility	↑	↑	↑
Risk-free interest	↑	↑	↑
Cash Dividend	↑	↑	↓

↑ : Increase, ↓ : Decrease

The call option price as well as put option price have both lower and upper bounds. Using the following notations, these bounds are expressed as follows:

C_E = Price of the European call option

C_A = Price of the American call option

S = Stock price on the date of trade

X = Strike price

Xe^{-rt} = Present value of strike price

The mathematical definitions of the limits or bounds of the option prices are:

(i) $\text{Max}(O, S - X) \leq \text{Max}(O, S - Xe^{-rt}) \leq C_E = C_A \leq S$

(ii) $\text{Max}(O, Xe^{-rt} - S) \leq P_E \leq Xe^{-rt}$

(iii) $\text{Max}(O, X - S) \leq P_A \leq X$

In the last part of the chapter, the concept of put-call parity has been explained. Put-call defines the relationship between put prices and call prices that must exist to avoid possible arbitrage profits. It is a principle referring to the static price relationship, given a stock's price, between the prices of European put and call options of the same classs (i.e., same underlying, strike price and expiration date). This relationship is shown from the fact that combinations of options can create positions that are the same as holding the stock itself. These option and stock positions must all have the same return otherwise an arbitrage opportunity would be available to traders. Any option pricing model that produces put and call prices that don't satisfy put-call parity should be rejected as unsound because arbitrage opportunities exist. In general, the put-call parity is expressed as follows:

Let S = Current stock price

P = Put price

C = Call price

r = Continuously compounded rate of interest

X = Strike price

t = Time to maturity

Xe^{-rt} = Present value of strike price

$$S + P = C + Xe^{-rt}$$

$$P = C - S + Xe^{-rt}$$

SOLVED PROBLEMS

Problem 1

1. Calculate lower bound from the following data:

Stock price: ₹ 270 per share

Style of option: European

Type of option: Call

Strike price ₹ 265 per share

Interest Rate = 10% p.a.

Time to expiration = 6 months

Dividend: Nil

Solution:

A lower bound for the price of a European call option on a non-dividend paying is calculated by the following formula:

$$S - Xe^{-rt}$$

Where S = Stock price = ₹ 270

X = Strike price = ₹ 265

r = 10%

$t = 6 \text{ months} = \frac{6}{12} = 0.5$

Now the lower bound of call option will be:

$$S - Xe^{-rt} = 270 - 265\, e^{-(.10 \times .5)}$$
$$= 270 - 265\, e^{-0.05}$$
$$= 270 - 265 \times 0.9512$$
$$= 270 - 252$$
$$= 18$$

Problem 2

A one-year call option with an exercise price of ₹ 180 is available at a premium of ₹ 18. Further a one-year put with an exercise price is available with an exercise price of ₹ 165 at a premium of ₹ 9.

Set up a portfolio combining both put and call. Also calculate the pay-off if the share price after one year is (a) ₹ 174 (b) ₹ 135 or (c) ₹ 225.

Solution:

(a) At share price ₹ 174, neither call option, not put option will be exercised.

Thus, profit/loss = – ₹ 18 – ₹ 9 = – ₹ 27.

(b) At share price ₹ 135, call option will not be exercised, but put option can be exercised.

Thus, profit/loss = (₹ 165 – ₹ 135) – ₹ 27

= ₹ (30 – 27) = ₹ 3

(c) At share price ₹ 225, call will be exercised but not put.

Thus, profit/loss = (₹ 225 – ₹ 180) – ₹ 27

= ₹ (45 – 27) = + ₹ 18

Problem 3

The current market price of a share is ₹ 155. The volatility of the share is measured as 20%. The risk free interest rate is currently 8% per annum. There is a call option and put option on the share. Time to expiration is 6 months with exercise price ₹ 150. Calculate put option price using put-call parity of call price is ₹12.

Solution:

By using the put-call parity relation model, we have

$$P = C - S + Xe^{-rt}$$

Where P = Put price

C = Call price = 12

S = Current stock price = ₹ 160

r = Rate of interest continuously compounded

t = Time to expiration = 6 months

Now we can calculate

$$P = 12 - 155 + 150\ e^{(.08 \times \frac{6}{12})}$$

$$= 12 - 155 + 150 \times 0.9608$$

$$= 12 - 155 + 144.12$$

$$= 1.12$$

Problem 4

Calculate the call option price from the following data by using put-call parity theory:

Present value of Exercise price = ₹ 128

Value of put option = ₹ 10

Current stock price = ₹ 125

Solution:

Put-call parity relation is:

$C + PV(X) = P + S$

Where C = Call Price

P = Put Price

X = Exercise Price

S = Stock Price

Putting the values in the above equation, we get,

$C + 128 = 10 + 135$ or $C = 135 - 128 = 7$

EXERCISES

Quiz

State Whether the Following Statements are True or False.

(a) The premium of an option has two main components, i.e., intrinsic value and time value.

(b) Prior to expiration, any premium in excess of intrinsic value is called time value.

(c) If the value of the underlying security rises the price of call option will generally increase and the price of put option will decrease.

(d) As expiration approaches, the level of an options time value, for both puts and calls decreases or erodes.

(e) Volatility is a measure of risk (uncertainty), or variability of price of an options underlying security.

(f) The option premium is primarily affected by the difference between stock price and the strike price, the time remaining for the option to be exercised and the volatility of the underlying stock.

(g) Option price whether American or European style is always non-negative, i.e., an option must be worth at least zero.

(h) The strike price of an option contract is just like an insured value of the underlying asset.

(i) On the expiry date, the value of a call option obeys the following correlation

$$C + X \geq S$$

or, $$C \geq S - X$$

Where C = Value of a call option

S = Stock price

X = Exercise price

(j) The put-call parity relationship is expressed mathematically as Value of put + Value of a share = Value of a call + PV of exercise price.

(k) The lower bound of a American call option which is exercised before the maturity can be calculated by the following formula:

$$C + Xe^{-rt} \geq S$$

$$\Rightarrow \quad C \geq S - Xe^{-rt}$$

Where C = Call price

S = Stock price at the time of exercise

X = Strike price

r = Rate of interest continuously compounded

t = Time to maturity

(l) On the expiry date, the value of a put option obeys the following correlation:

$$(P + S) \geq X$$

or, $$P \geq X - S$$

(m) Any day before the maturity, the value of a put obeys the following correlation:

$$P + S \geq Xe^{-rt}$$

or, $$P \geq Xe^{-rt} - S$$

Where S = Stock price

X = Strike price

r = Rate of interest continuously compounded

t = Time to maturity

Ans: (a) True, (b) True, (c) True, (d) True, (e) True, (f) True, (g) True, (h) True, (i) True, (j) True, (k) True, (l) True, (m) True.

A. Short Type Questions

1. What is option price?
2. What are the two components of option value?
3. What are the six variables affect option price.
4. How to define the lower bound of a call option?
5. How to define the lower bound of a put option?
6. How to define the upper bound of a put option?
7. How to define the lower bound of a call option?
8. What is put-call parity?
9. Give a mathematical formula of a put-call parity.
10. Can put-call parity relationship be established for an American option?

B. Long Type Questions

1. There are number of factors influence option pricing. Discuss.
2. Briefly discuss the following in relation with option pricing:
   (a) Lower bound of call option
   (b) Upper bound of call option
   (c) Lower bound of put option
   (d) Upper bound of put option
3. What do you mean by put-call parity? Explain with suitable example. Show the relationship in diagrams.

PRACTICAL PROBLEMS

1. Calculate lower bound from the following data:

   Stock Price: ₹ 300 (per share) Style of option: European

   Type of option: Call Strike price: ₹ 280

   Interest rate: 8% p.a. Time to expiration: 3 months

   Dividend: Nil

2. Examine the following diagrams on bounds of option prices and explain with suitable example.

C = Call option price, P = Put option price, S = Stock price, X = Exercise price.

(i) Option prices are always positive:

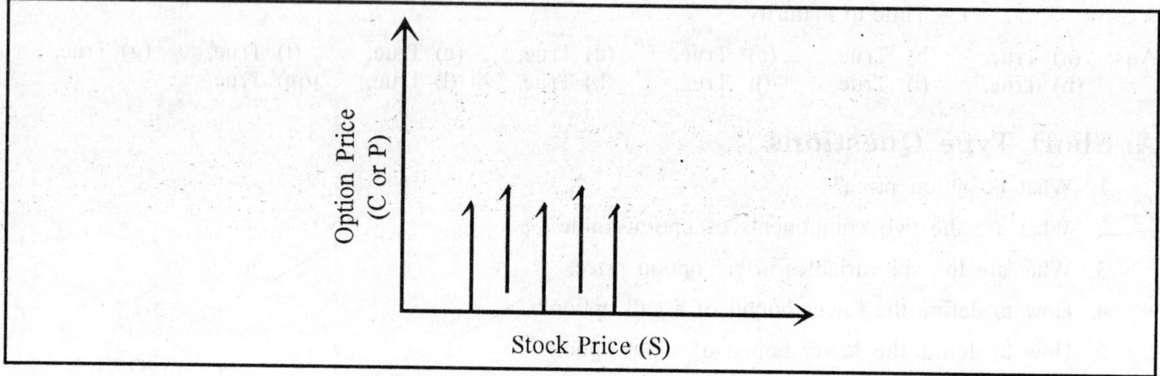

(ii) An option price must be less than or equal to the value of the underlying asset price:

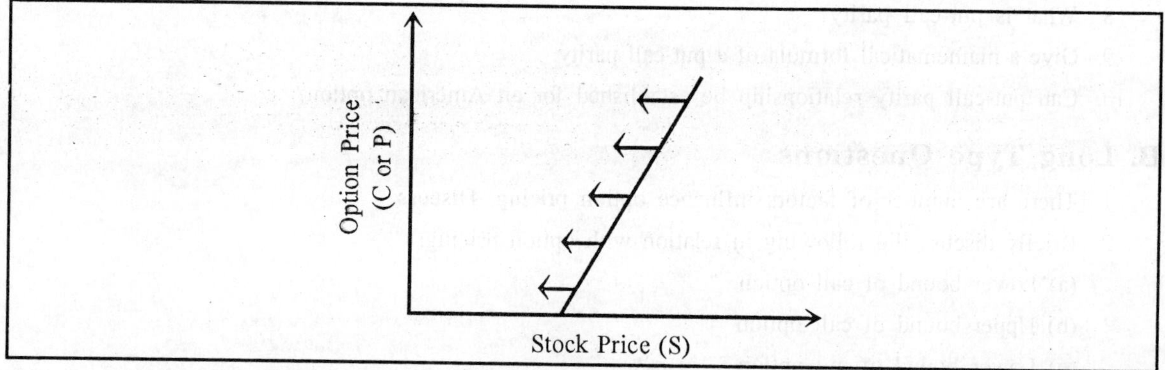

(iii) The prices of an American option must be greater than or at least equal to its intrinsic value:

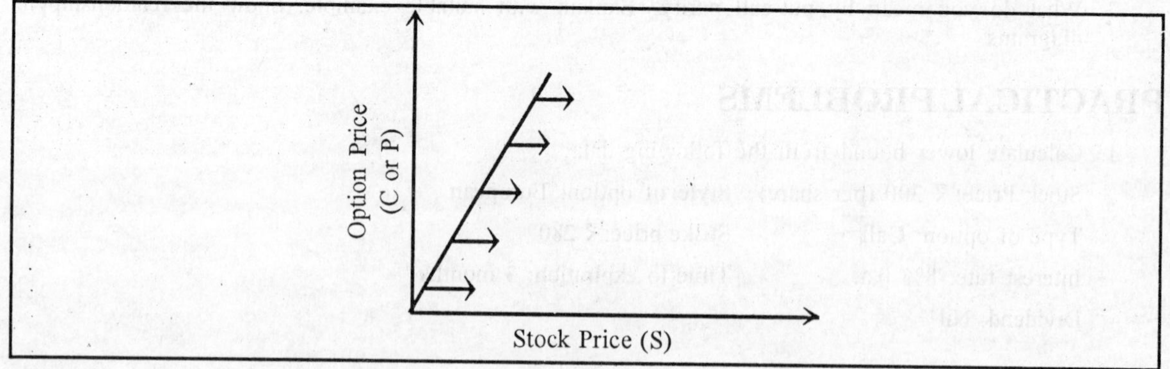

3. (a) Find out arbitrage profit from the following data of a call option:

   Exercise price: ₹ 115

   Current stock price: ₹ 125

   (b) Find the arbitrage profit from the following data of a put option:

   Exercise price: ₹ 125

   Current stock price: ₹ 115

4. Calculate the call option price from the following data by using put-call parity theory:

   Present value of Exercise price = ₹ 185

   Value of put option = ₹ 87

   Current stock price = ₹ 184

5. The current market price of a stock is ₹ 123 (per share). The risk-free interest rate is currently 8% per annum. There is a call option and put option on the same share. Time to expiration is 6 months with exercise price of ₹ 120 per share. Call option price is ₹ 10. Calculate put option price by using put-call parity theory.

   (*Ans.* 2.30)

6. The current market price of a stock is ₹ 123 (per share). The risk-free interest rate is currently 8% per annum. There is a put option and call option on the same stock. Time to expiration is 6 months. The exercise price is ₹ 120 per share. Put option price is ₹ 2.30. Calculate call option price by using put-call parity theory.

   (*Ans.* 10)

The Binomial Option Pricing Model (BOPM)

Learning Objectives

After studying this chapter, you will be able to:

- Understand the concept of Binomial option pricing model
- Know the assumptions and characteristics of BOPM
- Draw a binomial tree
- Calculate stock prices at each node by using forward induction method
- Calculate option value at each final node
- Determine option values at earlier nodes
- Know the strengths and limitations of BOPM
- Be a Strategic master in option valuation

Chapter Outline

10.1 INTRODUCTION

In finance, the *Binomial Option Pricing Model (BOPM)* provides a generalisable numerical method for the valuation of options. The original version of this Binomial model was developed by John Cox, Stephen Ross and Mark Rubinstein in 1979. This model is also known as C-R-R model.

This model is a "discrete-time" model, because it breaks down the total time to expiration into potentially a very large number of time intervals or steps. In other words, the total time of the option is divided into discrete bits or time steps. These steps form a tree like format. At each step, it is assumed that the price of the underlying asset say stock will move *up or down* by an amount calculated using volatility and time to expiration. Thus, this model is based on binomial approach. This approach assumes that the price of the stock at every point of time may have only two possible states, i.e., move up or move down.

Initially, a tree of stock prices is drawn showing the possible stock prices at every point of time in a forward form (left to right). This tree is commonly known as Binomial Tree. Fig. 10.1 shows a binomial tree.

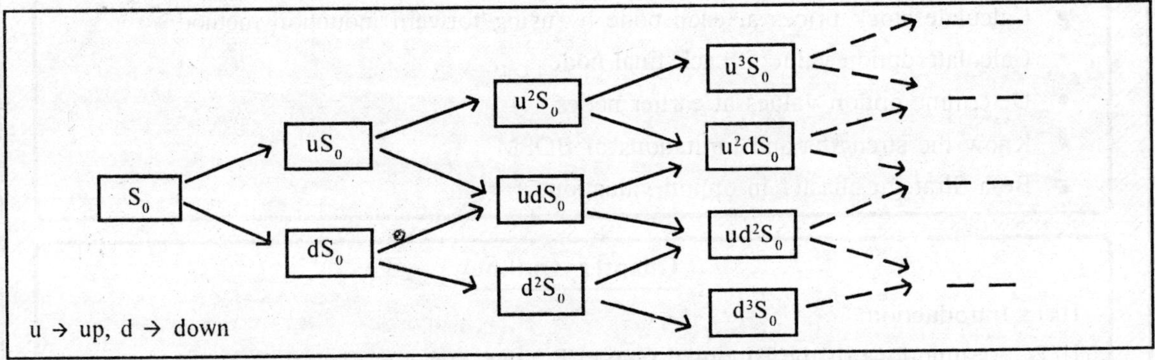

Fig. 10.1: The Binomial Process and Binomial Tree

Points to Note:

(i) This Binomial tree produces a binomial distribution of underlying stock prices.

(ii) The Binomial tree represents all the possible paths that the stock price could take during the life of the option.

From the above concept, we may define a BOPM tree as follows:

"A BOPM tree is an option pricing model, obeys a binomial generating process, in which the underlying stock can assume one of only two possible discrete values in the next time period, for each value that it can take in the proceeding time period."

The tree must be systematically structured and ended at the expiration of the option. The most important concept of this model is that all the terminal option prices for the final possible stock prices are known as they simply equal to their intrinsic value. Thus, the option values at the final point of times are calculated first.

Next option prices at each step of the tree are calculated working back from expiration to present. The option prices at each step are used to derive the option prices at next step of the tree. For calculating the option prices, this BOPM uses "Risk Neutial Valuation" method.

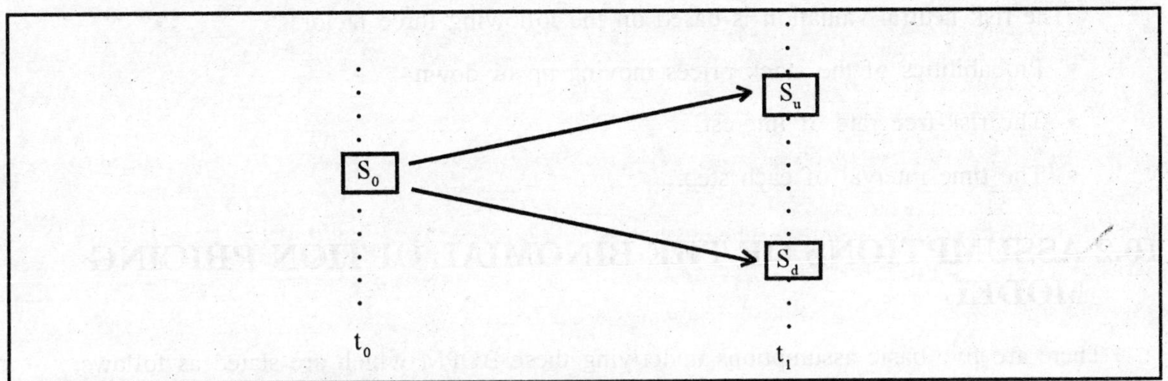

Fig. 10.2: Conceptual Framework of Binomial Tree

Example 1. The current market price of a stock is ₹ 160. It is expected that the price may either move up by 10% or move down by 5% by the end of the month.

Here S_0 = 160 up factor (u) = 10%, down factor (d) = 5%.

Now we represent the above facts in the following binomial tree.

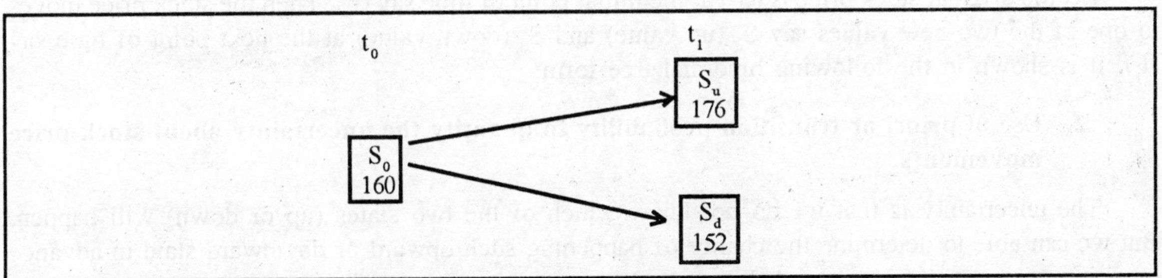

Fig. 10.3: One Step Binomial Tree

In the above example, we may calculate u factor and d factors:

$$\text{u factor} = \frac{S_u}{S_0} = \frac{176}{160} = 1.10$$

$$\text{d factor} = \frac{S_d}{S_0} = \frac{152}{160} = 0.95$$

Points to Note:

By definition $u \geq 1$, and $0 < d \leq 1$.

The risk neutral valuation is based on the following three factors:

- Probabilities of the stock prices moving up or down.
- The risk-free rate of interest.
- The time interval of each step.

10.2 ASSUMPTIONS OF THE BINOMIAL OPTION PRICING MODEL

There are five basic assumptions underlying these BOPM which are stated as follows:

1. Stock price movements obeys the binomial process in short periods.

This BOPM assumes that during a short interval of time, the stock can take only two values – the up move or the down move. Thus, the underlying stock price will either:

- Increase by a factor of u% (an up tick)
- Decrease by a factor of d% (a down tick)

Let the original stock price is (S_0) at the initial point of time say (t_0). Then the stock price moves to one of the two new values say S_u (up value) and S_d (down value) at the next point of time say (t_1). It is shown in the following binomial tree form:

2. Use of priori or transition probability to quantity the uncertainty about stock price movements.

The uncertainty is that we do not know which of the two states (up or down) will happen. But we can able to determine the chance of happening such upward or downward state in advance by using *priori* or *transition* probability.

The up (u) and down (d) factor are calculated using the underlying volatility (d) and the time duration of a step (t). Taking the condition that the variance of the log of the price is d²t, we have

$$u = e^{\sigma\sqrt{t}}$$

$$d = e^{-\sigma\sqrt{t}} = \frac{1}{u}$$

Priori or transition probabilities for price movement: The probability of an up movement is assumed to be (P) and the probability of a down movement is assumed to be (1 – P).

Formula:

$$P = \frac{e^{rt} - d}{u - d}$$

Example 1

If u = 1.1, d = 0.9, r = 0.12 and t = 3 months = 0.25. Find probability of up movement and probability of down movement.

Solution:

We denote probability of up movement is P and probability of down movement is (1 – P).

P is calculated by using the following formula:

$$P = \frac{e^{rt} - d}{u - d} = \frac{e^{0.12 \times 0.25} - 0.9}{1.1 - 0.9}$$

$$= \frac{e^{0.3} - 0.9}{0.20} = 0.6523$$

The probability of down movement is 1 – P = 1 – 0.6523 = 0.3477.

Example 2

Current stock price is ₹160 at time (t_0). It will go up by 20% or down by 10% in the next point of time (t_1). Suppose the probability of the up move is 0.6. Find out the expected stock price at time t_1. Use binomial model.

Solution:

Here $S_0 =$ ₹160 $\quad S_u = 160 \frac{120}{100} = 192 \quad S_d = 160 \times \frac{90}{100} = 142$

$P = 0.6 \quad 1 - P = 0.4$

Now we draw the binomial tree:

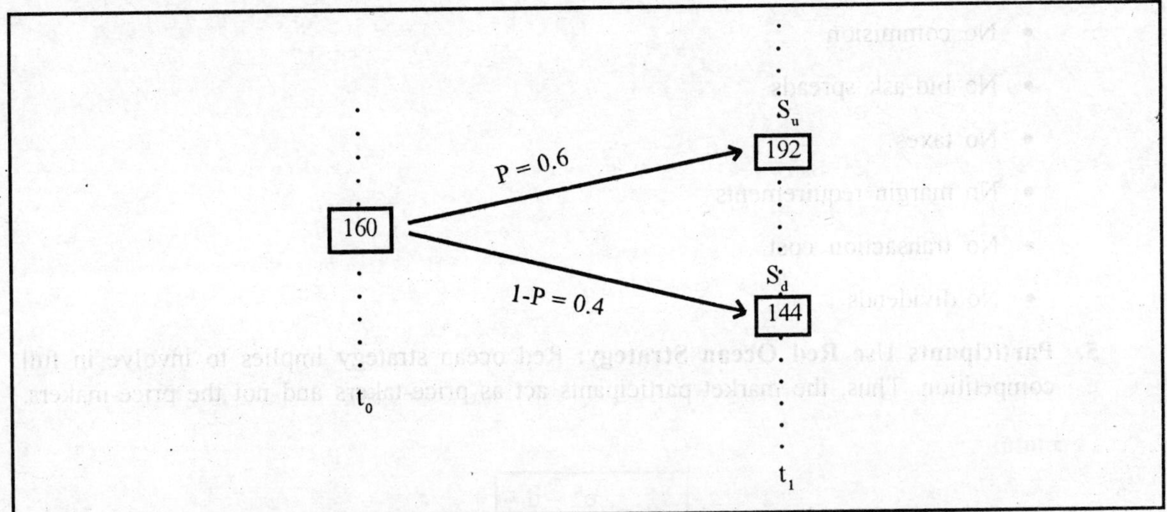

Fig. 10.4: Binomial Tree – The Stock Pricing Process

Expected stock price $= (S_u \times P) + S_d (1 - P)$

$= 192 \times 0.6 + 144 \times 0.4 = 172.80$

Example 3

A stock is currently priced at ₹ 160. In one month, the stock price may go up by 25%, or go down bv 12.5%. The strike price is ₹ 180. Find pay-off of a call option. Use binomial tree.

Solution:

Computation of stock prices at t_1.

Pay-off = ₹ 200 − 180 = 20

3. **Constant Interest Rate (r% Per Period):** It is assumed that there is no interest rate uncertainty. The one period interest rate (r) is constant over the life of the option.

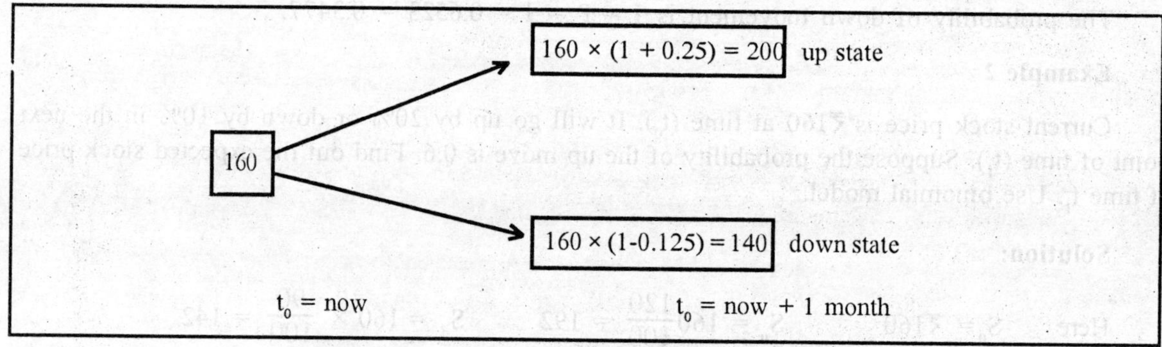

Fig. 10.5: Binomial Tree for Stock Prices

4. **Markets are Perfect:**
   - No arbitrage opportunities
   - No commision
   - No bid-ask spreads
   - No taxes
   - No margin requirements
   - No transaction cost
   - No dividends
5. **Participants Use Red Ocean Strategy:** Red ocean strategy implies to involve in full competition. Thus, the market participants act as price-takers and not the price-makers.

10.3 CHARACTERISTICS OF BINOMIAL OPTION PRICING MODEL

There are five important features of C-R-R option pricing model. These are:

1. **It is a Constant Dicrete-time Model:** This model breaks down the total time of expiration into potentially a very large number of time intervals. The length of such time intervals remain constant throughout the Binomial tree. The end of each time interval is known as 'node'.

2. **Volatility Remains Constant throughout the Model:** Volatility is the variability about the mean value of the stock price. It is measured by standard deviation (σ). The volatility represented by standard deviation remains constant throughout the binomial tree.

3. **The Probability of an Up Movement and Down Movement Remain Constant throughout the Model.**

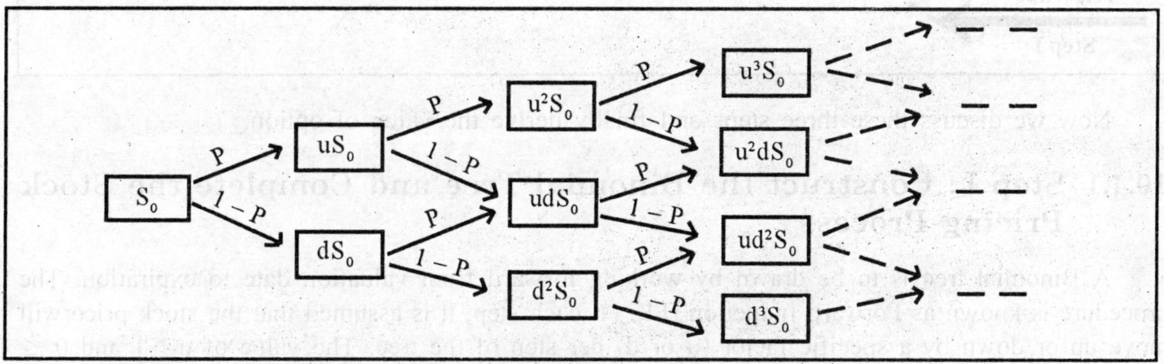

Fig. 10.6: Probability in Binomial Tree

4. **The Binomial Tree is Recombinant:** The Binomial model ensures that the tree is recombinant, i.e., if the underlying asset moves up and then down (u, d) the price will be same as if it had moved down and then up (d, u). Here the two paths merge or recombine. The following figure shows the above concept:

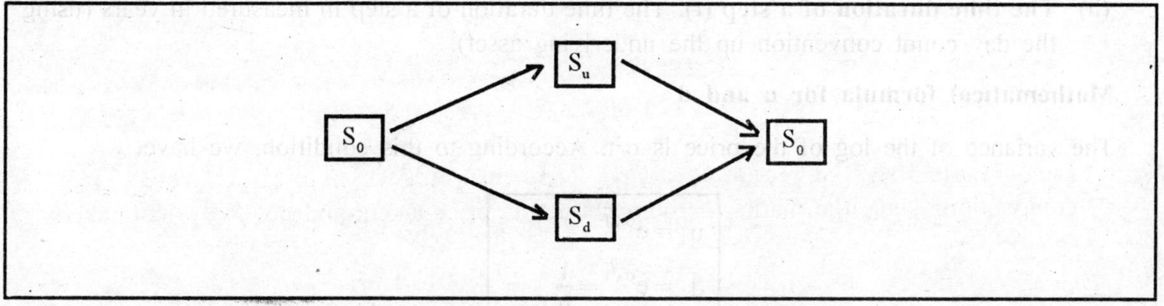

Fig. 10.7: A Combining Tree

5. **Option Price is Determined by Backward Process Calculation:** The option price at each step of the tree are calculated working back from expiration to the present. The option prices at each step are used to derive the option prices at the next step of the tree using risk neutral valuation method. The value computed at each stage is the value of the option at that point in time.

10.4 METHODOLOGY

Option valuation using BOPM is a three-step process as follows:

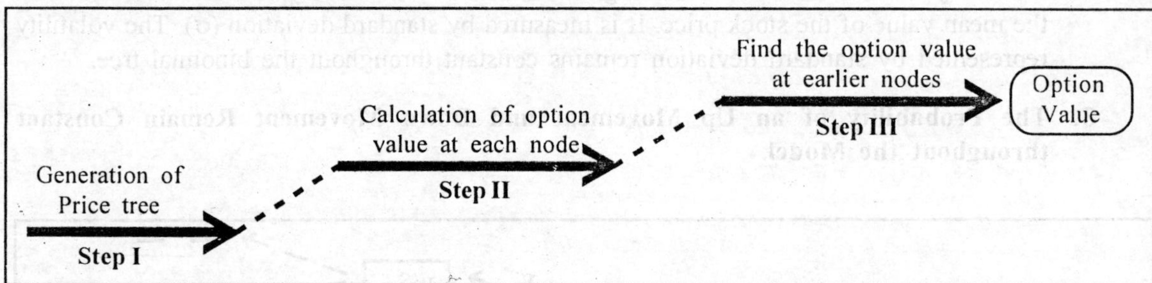

Now we discuss these three steps and finally derive the value of option.

10.4.1 Step I: Construct the Binomial Tree and Complete the Stock Pricing Process

A Binomial tree is to be drawn by working forward from valuation date to expiration. The procedure is known as Forward Induction (FI). At each step, it is assumed that the stock price will move up or down by a specific factor (u or d) per step of the tree. The value of $u \geq 1$ and $0 \leq d \leq 1$. Take the initial current price S. Then in the next period, it will either be $S_{up} = S \cdot u$ or $S_{down} = S \cdot d$.

How to calculate up and down factors?

The up and down factors are calculated using the following two determinants:

(i) The volatility in the price of the stock i.e., σ.

(ii) **The time duration of a step (t).** The time duration of a step in measured in years (using the day count convention up the underlying asset).

Mathematical formula for u and d

The variance of the log of the price is $\sigma^2 t$. According to this condition, we have,

$$u = e^{\sigma\sqrt{t}}$$

$$d = e^{\sigma\sqrt{t}} = \frac{1}{u}$$

While we construct binomial tree, we must ensure that the tree is recombinant. The condition 'recombinant' implies that if the stock moves up and then down (u, d) the price will be same as it had moved down and then up (d, u). Accordingly the two paths merge or recombine. This property reduces the number of tree nodes and thus accelerates the computation of the option price.

The Stock Pricing Process: Direct Method

The value of the underlying asset say stock at each node can be calculated directly by using the following formula and does not require that the binomial tree be constructed first. The formula for the node value will be:

$$S_n = S_0 \times u^{N_u - N_d}$$

Where N_u = Number of up ticks

N_d = Number of down ticks

Binomial tree representation:

Let S_0 = Initial stock price

u = Up factor

d = Down factor

t_0 = Present time

t_1 = One-step time interval (say 3 months)

t_2 = Two-step time interval (say 6 months)

We may now draw one-step binomial tree and two-step binomial trees.

One-step Binomial Tree

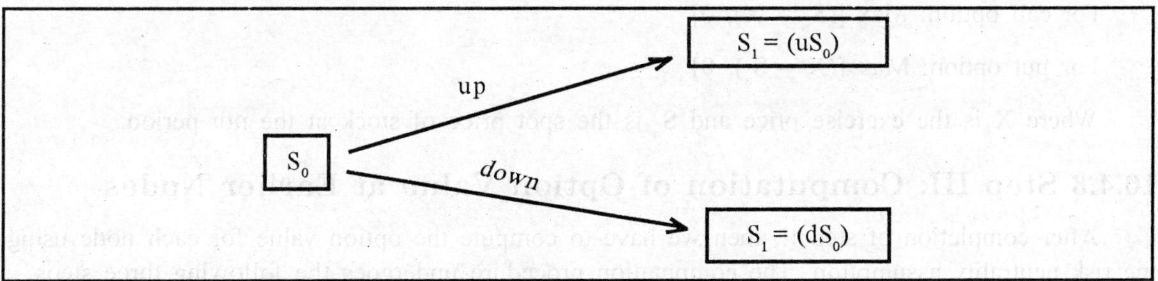

Fig. 10.8: One-step Binomial Tree

Two-step Binomial Trees

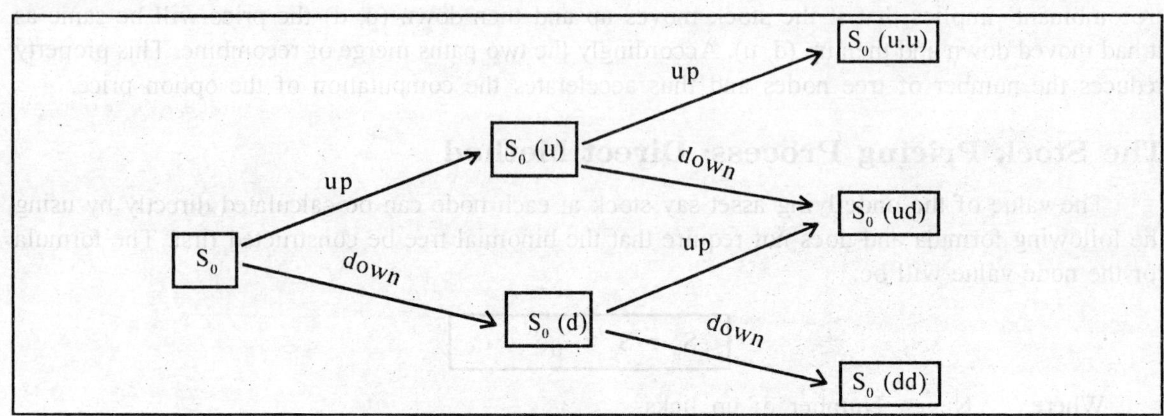

Fig. 10.9: Two-step Binomial Tree

Similarly, we can draw three steps and multi steps binomial trees.

10.4.2 Step II: Computation of Option Value at Each Final Node

At each final node of the tree (i.e., at expiration of the option), the option value is simply its **intrinsic or exercise value**. The intrinsic value of an option is the gain to the holder of an option on immediate exercise.

It may be pointed out here that option holder cannot exercise the option before maturity in European option, hence the **intrinsic** value will be just notional and not actual. But in case of American option, the option holder can exercise his right at any time before the maturity date.

Mathematically, the value of an option will be defined as follows:

For call option: Max $[(S_n - X), 0]$

For put option: Max $[(X - S_n), 0]$

Where X is the exercise price and S_n is the spot price of stock at the nth period.

10.4.3 Step III: Computation of Option Value at Earlier Nodes

After completion of step II, then we have to compute the option value for each node using the risk neutrality assumption. The computation procedure undergoes the following three steps:

Step A

Computation of Binomial Option Values: Under the risk neutrality assumption, today's fair price of an option is equal to the expected value of its future pay-off discounted by the risk-free interest. Thus:

- Fair of value an option today = Present value of its future pay-off.
- Present value of future pay-off = Discounted value of expected pay-off.
- Discounted value is computed at risk-free interest.

Expected value is calculated using the option values from the later two nodes (option up and option down) weighted by their respective probabilities. It is already explained that the probability of an up move in the underlying is denoted by "P" and probability of a down move is denoted by "(1–P)". The expected value is then discounted at (r), the risk-free rate corresponding the life of the option.

Formulas:

1. $$\text{Binomial Option Value} = (\text{Expected Option Value})\, e^{-rt}$$

2. $$(\text{Expected Option Value}) = \{(\text{Option up value}) \times P\} + \{(\text{Option down value}) \times (1 - P)\}$$

3. $$p = \frac{e^{rt} - d}{u - d}$$

Here P is the probability of on up tick in a risk-neutral world. In a risk-neutral world, all assets (including the stock and the option) will be priced the same riskless rate of return (·).

Step B

Continue the procedure of computing the Binomial option values by using backward induction method. The binomial option value represents fair price of an option at a particular point in time (i.e., at each node).

Step C

Evaluation of Possibility of Early Exercise: There are three styles of option – European, American and Bermudan. Depending on the style of option, evaluate the possibility of early exercise at each node subject to the following criterion:

(i) **European Option:** For European option, there is no option of early exercise. Hence, the binomial value applies at all nodes.

(ii) **American Option:** American option can be exercised at any time prior to expiry. As it is already discussed that option values at each previous node is determined by backward induction process. At each intervening node, i.e., the nodes other than the final nodes and initial node, the option value from early exercise is compared with the option value. For an American option, since the option may either be held or exercised prior to expiry the value at node is: **Max {Binomial value, Exercise value).**

(iii) **Bermudan Option:** For a Bermudan option, the binomial value at nodes (where each exercise is allowed) is: Max {Binomial value, Exercise value).

At nodes where early exercise is not allowed, only the binomial value is applied.

10.5 REPLICATING PORTFOLIO STRATEGY FOR OPTION VALUATION

A strategic (option) player always takes a decision in such a way so that he can able to hedge the risk in future and always be "In-the-Money". He has two alternatives:

1. Directly buy a call option by paying the call premium, or
2. Go for a **replicating portfolio** without holding an option.

In both the cases, he will have the same pay-off at maturity.

In the second case "Replicating Portfolio", the investor will go for investing certain portion of shares out of his own fund and invest certain amount by borrowing. At the maturity, he will sell the shares and repay the loan and have a surplus which is equal to a call pay-off.

The methodology is explained as follows:

Example 1

(i) Current stock price = ₹ 140 = ₹ 140 per share.

(ii) In one year, the stock price may:

- go up by 25%, or
- go down by 10%.

(iii) Strike price = ₹ 160 per share

(iv) Risk-free interest = 6% p.a.

(v) Option period = 1 year.

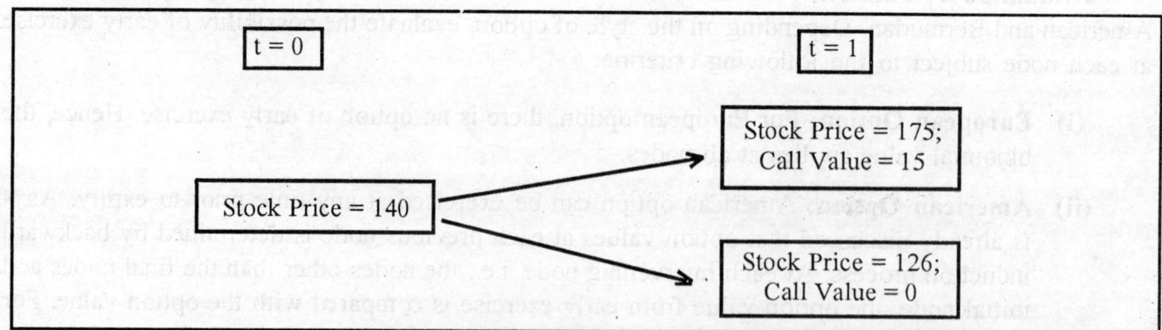

Fig. 10.10: Binomial Tree of Stock Prices and Option Values

Consider a Portfolio: Δ Shares of stock + ₹ B invested in risk-free securities.

So, the present value of this portfolio = Δ S + B = 140 Δ + B

Now, we draw the Binomial tree for portfolio value:

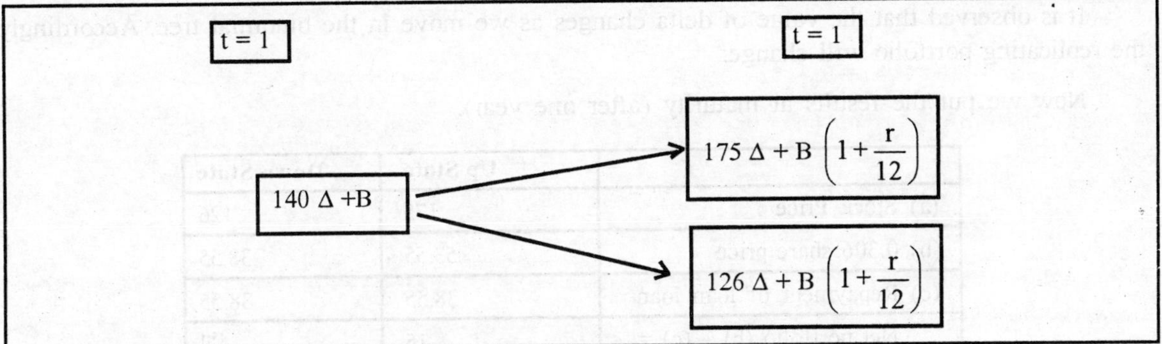

Fig. 10.11: Binomial Tree of Portfolio

Determining the Value of Δ and B

We have the following figures

Portfolio of Pay-off = Option Pay-off

$175\Delta + B\left(1+\frac{r}{12}\right) = 15$ Up state .... (1)

$175\Delta + B\left(1+\frac{r}{12}\right) = 0$ Down state .... (2)

Solving these equation; we get

$175\Delta - 126\Delta = 15 - 0$

$\Rightarrow 49\Delta = 15$ or $\Delta = \frac{15}{49} = 0.306$

Taking $= 175\Delta + B\left(1+\frac{r}{12}\right) = 15$

$\Rightarrow 175\Delta \times 0.306 + B\left(1+\frac{r}{12}\right) = 15$

$\Rightarrow 53.55 + B\left(1+\frac{r}{12}\right) = 15$

or $B\left(1+\frac{r}{12}\right) = 15 - 53.55 = -38.55$

$\Rightarrow B = {-38.55}\Big/\left(1-\frac{r}{12}\right) = \frac{-38.55}{1.06} = -36.37$

(i) 0.306 shares of stock. So, the current value of stock = 140 × 0.306 = 42.84

(ii) Partially financed by borrowing the amount B = ₹ 36.37

Point to Note:

It is observed that the value of delta changes as we move in the binomial tree. Accordingly, the replicating portfolio will change.

Now we put the results at maturity (after one year).

	Up State	Down State
(a) Stock Price	175	126
(b) 0.306 share price	53.55	38.55
(c) Repayment of loan loan	38.55	38.55
Net portfolio (b) – (c) =	15	Nil

Finding: The replicating has the same portfolio in all states as the call portfolio, the two must also have the same price.

For further understanding, consider the second example.

Example 2

Consider the following two binomial trees:

A. (i) Type of option: European call.

(ii) Current stock price = 100

(iii) Exercise price = 110

(iv) Time to expiration = 1 year

(v) In one year, the stock price may.

— go up by 25%

— go down by 20%

(vi) Risk-free interest = 5% p.a.

(vii) No Dividend

(viii) $e^{0.5}$ = 1.0513

Now, we construct a binomial tree for stock price.

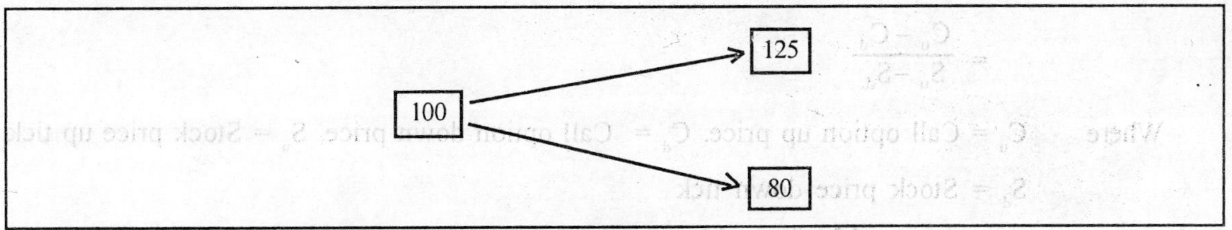

Fig. 10.12: Binomial Tree of Stock Price

When the stock price goes up, option worth is Max (0,125 – 110) = 15

When the stock goes down, option worth is Max (0.80 – 110) = 0

B. After computing the stock prices as above now, we have to construct the binomial tree of option prices.

Assume the Risk neutral probability, P = 0.6

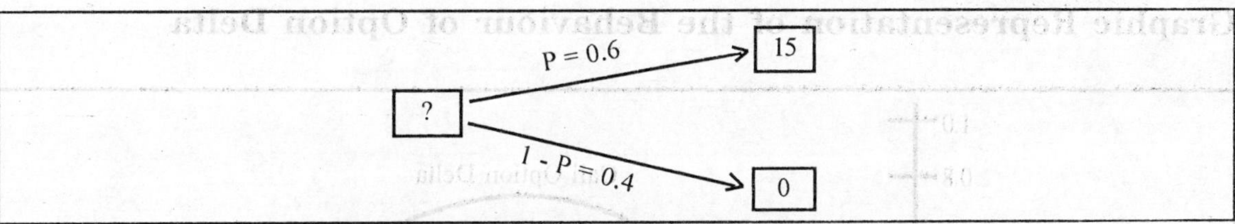

Fig. 10.13: Binomial Tree of Option Price

Expected value of option = 15 × 0.6 + 0 × 0.4 = 9

Value of option = $9\ e^{-rt} = 9\ e^{(-0.5\times1)} = 9 \times 0.9512 = 8.56$

In the above example, the stock price can be either 125 or 80 (Figure 10.12). Corresponding to these, the call option values are 15 and 0 respectively (Figure 10.13).

Observation: Change in stock prices = 125 – 80 = 45

Change is option prices = 15 – 0 = 15

When stock prices changes ₹ 45, then the corresponding change in option price is ₹ 15. If the change in stock price is 1, then the corresponding change in option price is $\frac{15}{45}$ = 0.3334.

What is Option Delta?

The delta of an option is the sensitivity of an option price relative to changes in the price of the underlying asset. Thus, it is the change in the option value when the stock price changes, by 1.

Mathematically, Option Delta $C_\Delta = \dfrac{\text{Change in option value}}{\text{Change in stock price}}$

$$= \frac{C_u - C_d}{S_u - S_d}$$

Where C_u = Call option up price, C_d = Call option down price, S_u = Stock price up tick

S_d = Stock price down tick

In this example, $C_\Delta = \frac{15-0}{125-80} = \frac{15}{45} = 0.3333$

The option delta is usually have a decimal value. It indicates how fast the price of the option will change as the underlying stock moves.

Points to Note:

1. Option Delta values range between 0 and 1 for call options and –1 to 0 for put options.
2. Call options and put options have opposite delta.

Graphic Representation of the Behaviour of Option Delta

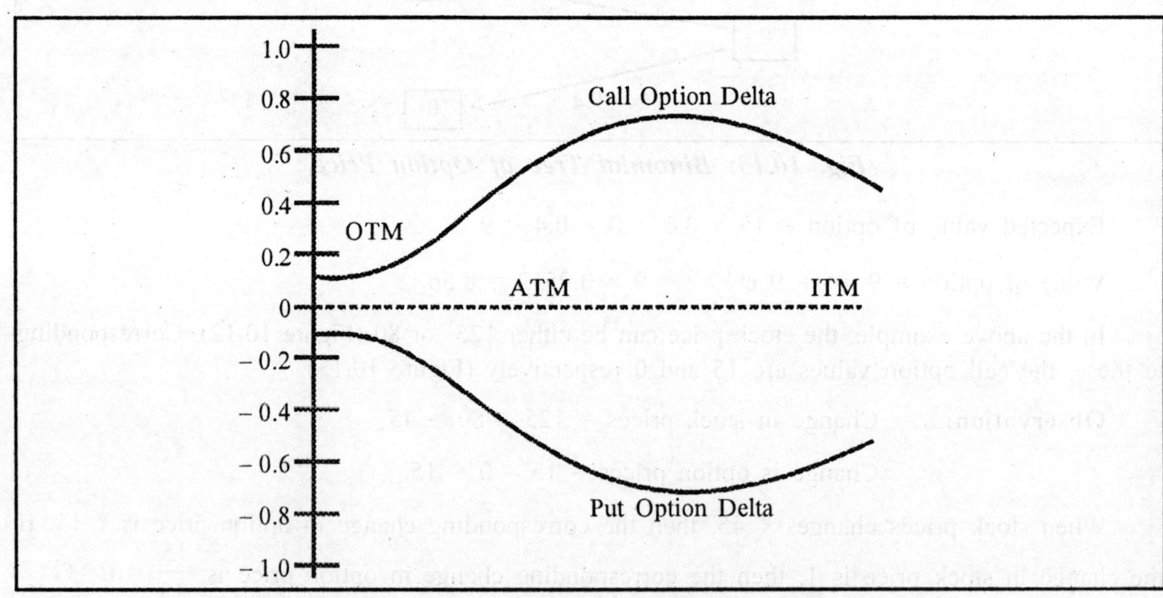

Fig. 10.14: Behaviour of Option Delta

What is Replicating Portfolio?

In the above example, we get the following values:

- Value of Call Option = ₹ 8.56
- Value of Call Delta = 0.3333 = 1/3

If the call option holder holds $\frac{1}{3}$ of the share, then he will have the same exposure. In other words, the trader only involves investing in cash for the following two forms:

- Option price, i.e., ₹ 8.56
- $\frac{1}{3}$ of underlying stock, i.e., $\frac{1}{3} \times 100 = 33.33$

Thus, the intial investment for a call option should be 33.33 – 8.56 = 24.77. This amount will be borrowed.

Here the option holder has the following composite position at present.

$\frac{1}{3}$ share @ 100 option with ₹ 8.56. (one call)

This composite position is known as **Replicating portfolio**.

The call option holder has to repay the borrowed fund of ₹ 24.77. Hence, the repayment amount will be = 24.77 e^{rt} = 24.77 × 1.0513 = 26.04

The value of replicating portfolio is shown as follows:

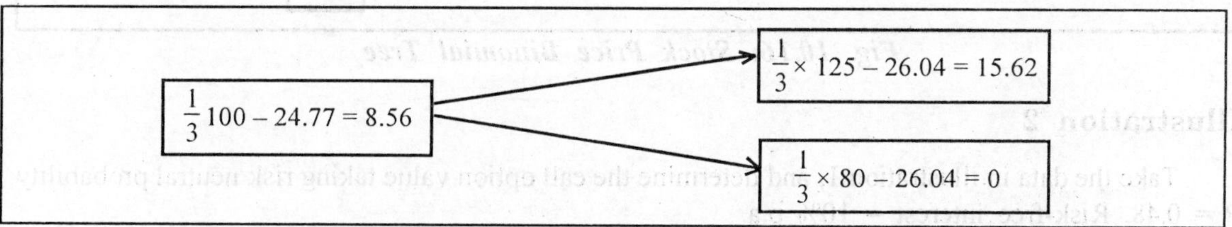

Fig. 10.15: Valuation of Option by Replicating Portfolio Strategy

What is Dynamic Portfolio?

When the Stock Price go on changing in subsequent sub-periods, we have to continuous adjustment in the replacing portfolio. This process is known as dynamic delta hedging or dynamic portfolio.

10.6 DYNAMIC APPROACH TO BOPM – STRATEGIC ILLUSTRATIONS

Illustration 1

Draw binomial trees from the following date and show the stock prices:

Parameter	**European**	
	Call option	**Put option**
Stock price	100	100
Strike price	120	80
Maturity	1 year	1 year

Sub-periods (t)	Two	Two
u factor	1.40	1.40
d factor	0.80	0.80

Solution

The stock price tree for the both option will be same as shown in the following figure.

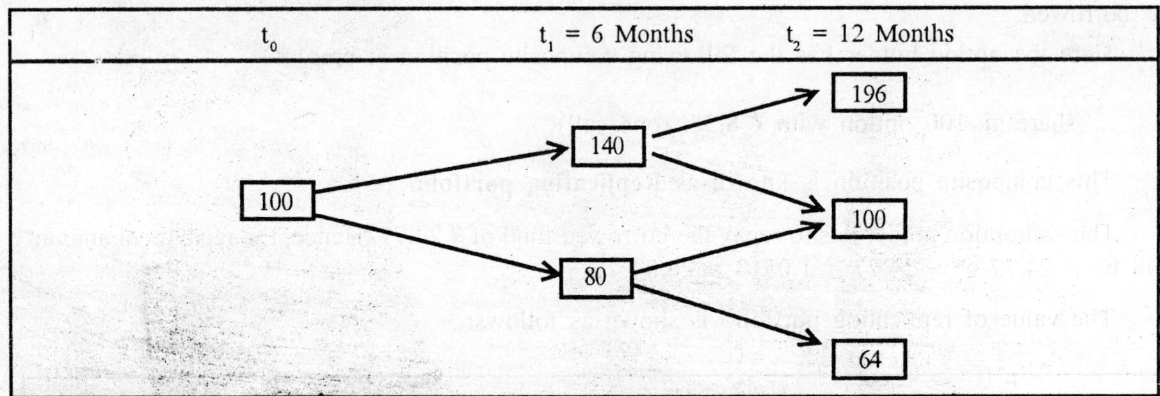

Fig. 10.16: Stock Price Binomial Tree

Illustration 2

Take the data in illustration 1, and determine the call option value taking risk neutral probability P = 0.48. Risk-free interest = 10% p.a.

(a) Computation European call option value by backward induction process:

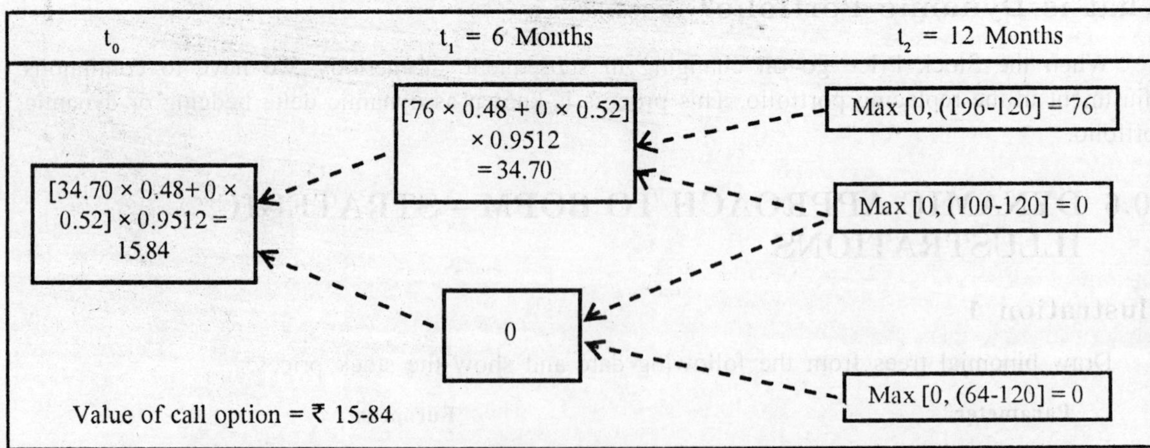

Fig. 10.17: Binomial Tree for European Call Option Values

(b) Computation of European put option value by backward induction process:

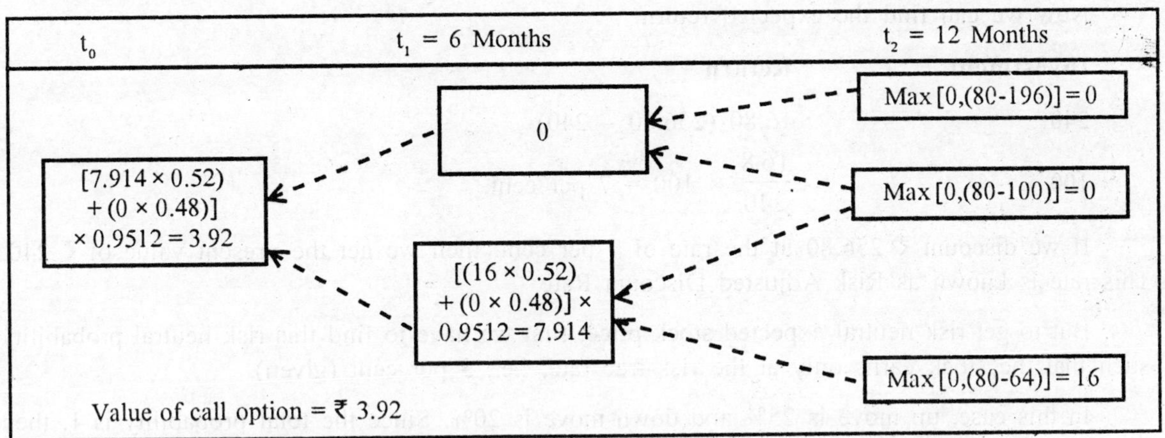

Fig. 10.18: Binomial Tree for European Put Option Values

Illustration 3

From the following data, calculate: (a) Expected stock price, (b) Value of an option, (c) Option Delta.

(i) Type of option:	European
(ii) Stock price at the intial point of option =	₹ 240
(iii) Option period (Time):	one year
(iv) Stock price movement in the next year.	
— go up by 25%	
— go down by 20%	
(v) Exercise price =	₹ 260
(vi) Risk-free interest rate =	5% p.a.

(vii) Risk neutral probability of up move is 0.60 and down move is 0.40.

Solution:

Binomial Tree of Stock Prices

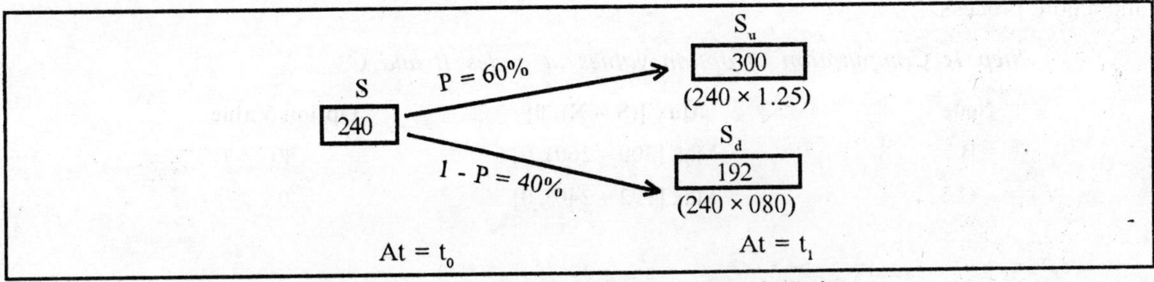

Fig. 10.19: Binomial Tree for Stock Prices

The expected stock price at t_1 = (300 × 0.60) + 192 × 0.4) = 180 + 76.80 = 256.80

Now we can find the expected return:

Investment	**Return**
240	16.80 (256.80 – 240)
100	$\frac{16.8}{240} \times 100 = 7$ per cent.

If we discount ₹ 256.80 at the rate of 7 per cent, then we get the present value of ₹ 240. This rate is known as Risk Adjusted Discount Rate.

But to get risk neutral expected stock price, first we have to find this risk neutral probability such that the stock earns only at the risk-free rate, i.e., 5 per cent (given).

In this case, up move is 25% and down move is 20%. Since the total probability is 1, then

$$P = \frac{25}{25+20} = \frac{3}{9} = \frac{5}{9} \text{ and } 1 - P = 4/9$$

Taking these risk neutral probabilities, we may now draw the binomial tree and calculated the stock price.

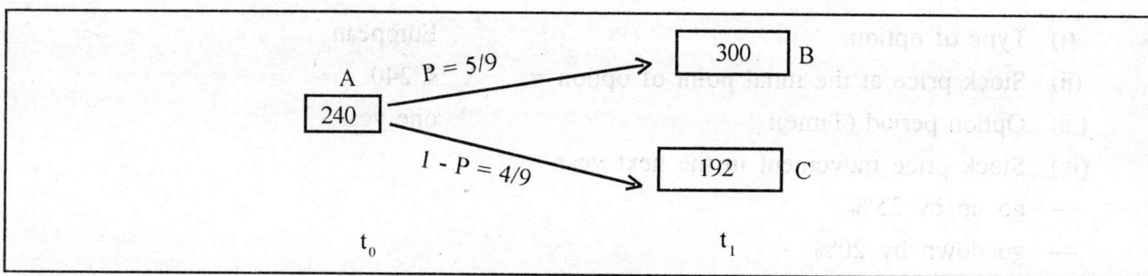

Fig. 10.20: Binomial Tree for Stock Prices

$$\text{Expected Stock Price at } (t_1) = 300 \times \frac{5}{9} + 192 \times \frac{4}{9} = 166.66 + 85.33 = 251.99 = 252$$

Determination of European Call Value

Now we have to calculate the option price by using the binomial free approach and backward induction process.

Step 1: Computation of option values at nodes B and C.

Node	**Max [(S – X), 0]**	**Option Value**
B	Max [300 – 260), 0]	40
C	Max [192 – 240), 0]	0

Step 2: Computation of option values at the preceeding node A by backward induction process:

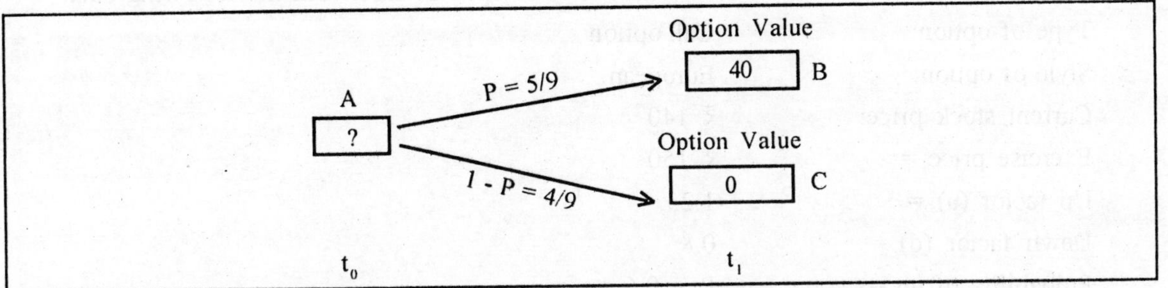

Fig. 10.21: Binomial Tree for Stock Prices

$$\text{Expected value of option} = 40 \times \frac{5}{9} + 0 \times \frac{4}{9} = 22.22$$

Now to calculate the option value at A node A, i.e., at the initial point of time. We have to find out the present value of 22.22 by discounting at this risk-free rate 5% p.a.

Thus, the present value of the European call option $= 22.22\ e^{-rt} = 22.\ 22\ e^{-0.5 \times 1}$

$= 22.22 \times .9512 = 21.14$ (Approx.)

Binomial tree representation:

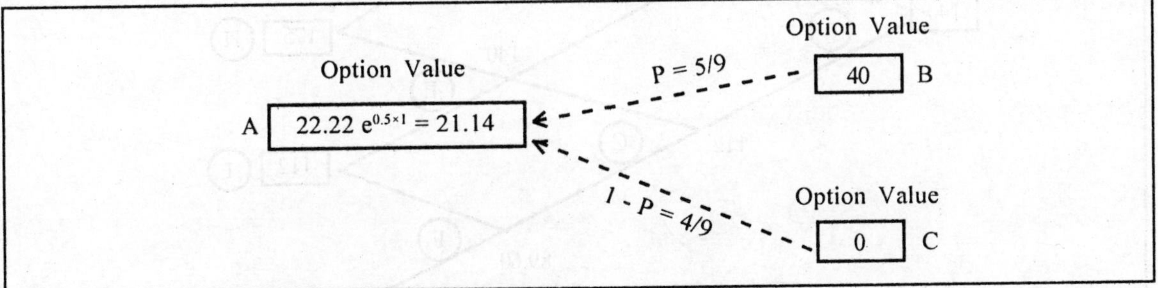

Fig. 10.21: Computation of Call Option Value

(c) Call Option Delta

$$C_{\Delta} = \frac{\text{Change in option price}}{\text{Change in stock price}}$$

$$= \frac{C_u - C_d}{S_u - S_d}$$

$$= \frac{40 - 0}{3000 - 192} = \frac{40}{108} = 0.3704$$

Illustration 4

Use three-step binomial model and determine the option value from the following data:

Type of option:	Call option
Style of option:	European
Current stock price:	₹ 140
Exercise price =	₹ 150
Up factor (u) =	1.25,
Down factor (d) =	0.8
Probability of up =	P = 0.6
Probability of down =	1 − P = 0.4
Risk-free interest rate =	10% p.a.

Solution:

Now, we first draw the binomial tree of stock prices for three time intervals:

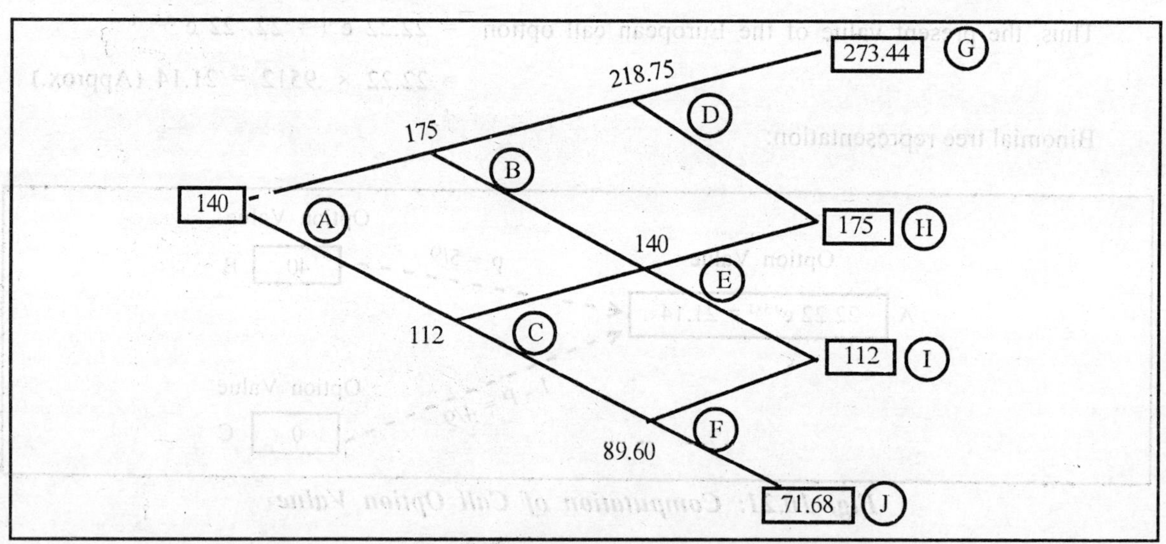

Next we calculate the option prices by backward induction process.

Step 1: Computation of option values at the final nodes G, H, I and J.

Node	Max [(S – X), 0]	Option Value
G	Max [273.44 – 150), 0]	123.44
H	Max [175 – 150), 0]	25
I	Max [112 – 150), 0]	0
J	Max [71.68 – 150), 0]	0

Step 2: Computation of option value of the proceeding nodes at D, E and F.

(a) Option Value at D.

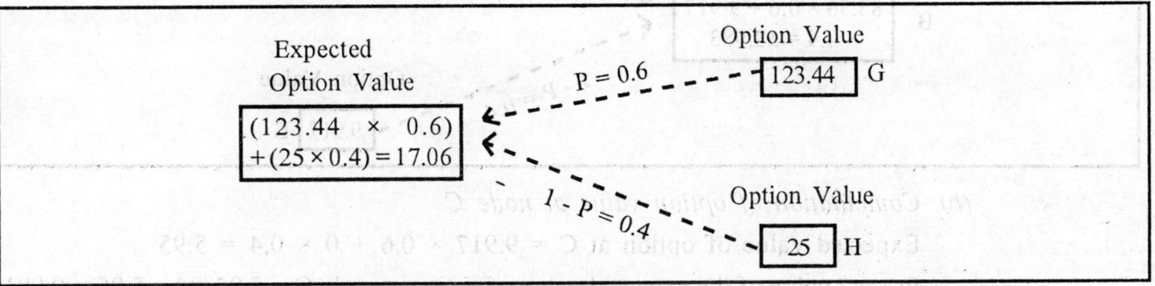

Expected value of option = 123.44 × 0.6 + 25 × 0.4 = 84.06

Present value of the expected option value at D = 84.06 e^{-rt} = $84.06 e^{-0.10\times\frac{1}{12}}$

= 84.06 × 0.9917 = 83.36

(b) Option Value at E.

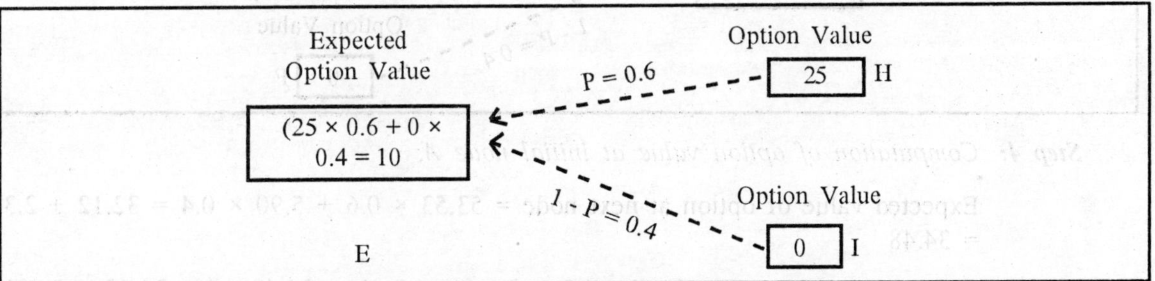

Present value of the expected option value at node E.

= 10 e^{-rt} = $10\ e^{-0.10\times\frac{1}{12}}$ = 10 $e^{-0.183}$

= 10 × 0.9917 = 9.917

(c) Option Value at F = 0

Step 3: (a) Computation of option value at node B

Expected value of option at B

= 83.36 × 0.6 + 9.917 × 0.4 = 53.983

Present value of the expected option value at B = 53.983 e^{-rt} = 53.983 × 0.9917 = 53.53

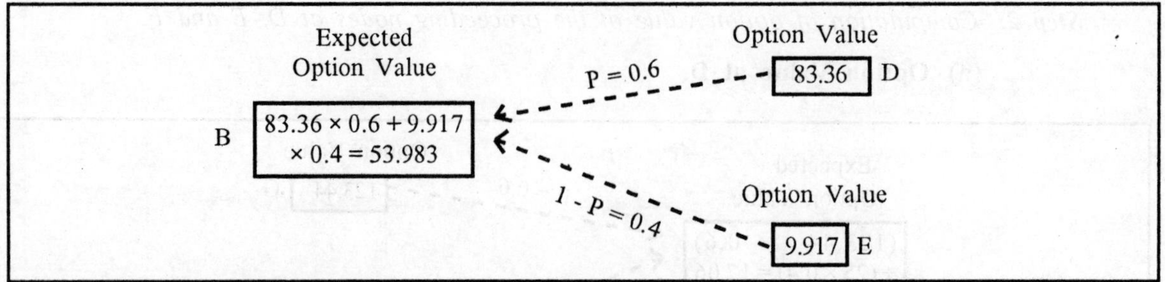

(b) Computation of option value at node C

Expected value of option at C = 9.917 × 0.6 + 0 × 0.4 = 5.95

Present value of the expected value of option at node C = 5.95 e^{-rt} = 5.95 × 0.9917 = 5.90

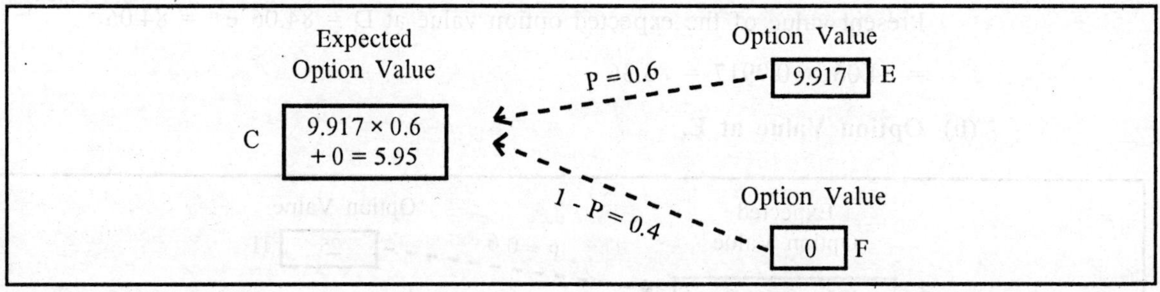

Step 4: *Computation of option value at initial node A:*

Expected value of option at next node = 53.53 × 0.6 + 5.90 × 0.4 = 32.12 + 2.36 = 34.48

Present value of expected value of option at node A = 34.48 e^{-rt} = 34.48 × 0.0017 = 34.19

Thus, the current value of European option is ₹ 34.19.

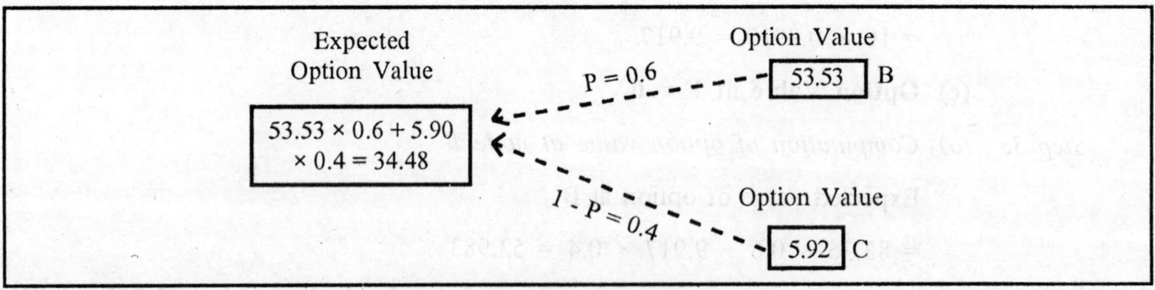

10.7 ADVANTAGES AND LIMITATIONS

Binomial Option Pricing Model (BOPM) was originally developed by Cox, Ross and Rubinstein in 1974. It is a numerical method. This option pricing model has the following advantages and limitations:

Advantages

1. It is more accurate pricing model for American style option.
2. It facilitate the possibility of early exercise because with the binomial model it is possible to check at every point in an options life (i.e., at every step of the binomial tree).
3. This model uses simple mathematical calculations for stock prices as well as option prices.
4. It is easy to calculate the option price with a computer spreadsheet.

Limitations

1. It is relatively slow speed. It is very difficult to calculate thousands of option prices quickly for a multi-step binominal model.
2. It is much more complex than the Black-Scholes model.

CHAPTER SUMMARY

The Binomial Option Pricing Model (BOPM) was developed by Cox, Ross and Rubinstein in 1979. This a very versatile numerical method for valuing American and European Options.

This model is a "discrete-time" model. Total time of the option is divided into a number of sub-periods. It is assumed that during a time period the stock price can move in only two ways, i.e., an up move by a multiplicative factor u or a down move by a multiplicative factor d. For this reason the model is known as Binomial Model.

Under this method, first we have to draw a binomial tree which obeys the binomial generating process. Then we proceed in the following three steps:

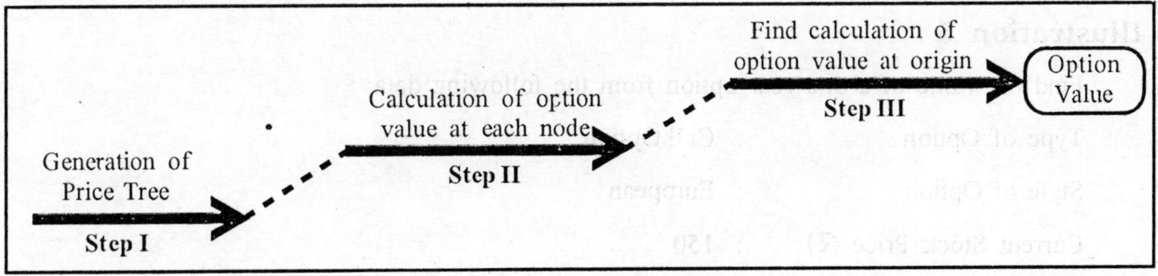

For computing the stock prices as well as option prices at various nodes of a Binomial Tree, we have to depend on the following parameters:

1. The volatility of stock prices measured by Standard Deviation (σ)
2. The risk-free interest rate (r) continuously compounded
3. The number of sub-periods or bits.

The Binomial Model is suitable when the length of each sub-period in high. But where time period and the share price movements can be made very small, then we have to use Black-Scholes Option Pricing Model. The steps for computing the value of a European call option are as follows:

In Step I, we have to construct a Binomial Tree and complete the stock pricing process. Then in Step II, we have to compute option value at each node. The option values for the different possible future stock prices at maturity can be determined. Then value of the option at each node is determined moving back one step at a time. Such option value is obtained as the discounted expected value of the values at the two possible nodes in the next period. This process will continue until we come to time t = 0. The value that we get at t = 0 (at the initial point of time of binomial tree) is the **value of the option.**

To compute the value of an American Option, we have to compare the value of immediate exercise of the option (Exercise Value) with the value of holding the option (Binomial Value) and select the higher one. Thus, **Max (Binomial Value, Exercise Value)** will be the value of the **American Option.**

This chapter also explained the concept of option delta and replicating portfolio. The delta of an option in the sensitivity of an option price relative to changes in the price of the underlying asset.

Mathematically, option delta is defined as:

$$\Delta = \frac{\text{Change in option value}}{\text{Change in stock price}}$$

The trader has to construct a portfolio with number of shares equal to option delta. But when the stock price go on changing in subsequent time periods, an attempt has to make continuous adjustment in the portfolio. This strategy is known as dynamic delta hedging or dynamic portfolio.

SOLVED PROBLEMS

Illustration 5

Find the value of a one-year option from the following data:

Type of Option	:	Call Option
Style of Option	:	European
Current Stock Price (₹)	:	150
Exercise Price (₹)	:	160
Up factor (u)	:	20%
Down factor (d)	:	10%
Option period	:	One year
Rise-free interest rate	:	9% p.a

Use Replicating Portfolio Strategy of Binomial Model.

Solution:

Let us set up a portfolio of one call option (Short) and Δ shares (long). Now we draw the binomial tree:

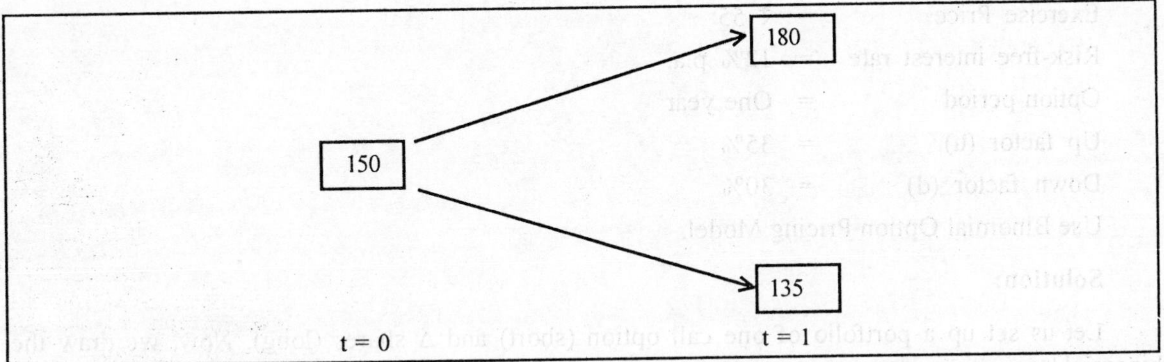

If the price increases to ₹ 180, then the value of portfolio at t = 1 (after one year) will be: $180\ \Delta - (180 - 160) = 180\ \Delta - 20$

If the price decreases to ₹ 135, the European call option is worth nothing and the portfolio will be 135 Δ only. The pay-off will be equal if

$$180\ \Delta - 135\ \Delta = 20 - 0$$

$$\Rightarrow 45\ \Delta = 20 \text{ or } \Delta = \frac{20}{45} = 0.4444$$

The value of portfolio after one year:

OR	
180 Δ – 20	135 Δ – 0
⇒ 180 × 0.4444 – 20	135 × 0.4444
= 79.99 – 20	
= 59.99 or ₹ 60	= 59.99 or ₹ 60

The current share price at t = 0 is ₹ 150

Therefore, the present value of call option (C) will be:

150 Δ – C = Present value of ₹ 60

$$\Rightarrow 150 \times 0.4444 - C = \frac{60}{1.09} = 55.05$$

$$\Rightarrow 66.66 - C = 55.05$$

$$\text{or } C = 66.66 - 55.05 = 11.61$$

Illustration 6

From the following data, calculate the European call option price:

Current Stock Price	=	₹ 60
Exercise Price	=	₹ 55
Risk-free interest rate	=	12% p.a.
Option period	=	One year
Up factor (u)	=	35%
Down factor (d)	=	30%

Use Binomial Option Pricing Model.

Solution:

Let us set up a portfolio of one call option (short) and Δ shares (long). Now, we draw the binomial tree:

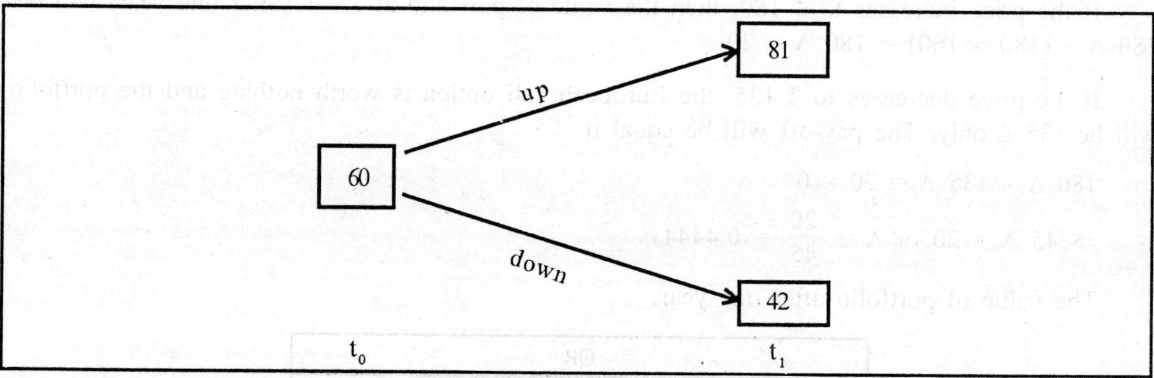

If the price increases to ₹ 81, then the value of portfolio at t_1 = 1 (after one year) will be:

81 Δ – (81 – 55) = 81 Δ – 26

If the price decreases to ₹ 42, the call option is worth nothing and the portfolio will be 42 Δ only. The pay-off will be equal if

81 Δ – 42 Δ = 26 – 0

⇒ 39 Δ = 26 or Δ = $^{26}/_{39}$ = 0.666

The value of portfolio after one year

OR	
81 Δ – 26	42 Δ – 0
⇒ 81 × 0.6666 – 20	⇒ 42 × 0.6666
= 41.472 – 20	= 23
= 28	

The current share price at t = 0 is ₹ 60 Therefore, the present value of call option (C) will be:

$60\ \Delta - C$ = Present Value of ₹ 28

$$\Rightarrow 60 \times 0.6666 - C = \frac{28}{1.12} = 25$$

$$\Rightarrow C = 40 - 25 = 15$$

Therefore, the value of the call option is ₹ 15.

Problems on American Call Option

Illustration 7

Calculate the value of an American Call option from the following data:

Current Market Price	=	₹ 180
Exercise Price	=	₹ 190
Volatility	=	30% p.a
Risk-free interest rate	=	12% p.a
Interval period	=	Monthly
Time to Expiration	=	3 months

Solution:

First, we have to calculate the values of up movement factor (u), down movement factor (d) and the probability of up movement factor (P) by using the formula as follows :

$$u = e^{\sigma\sqrt{t}} = e^{0.30\times\sqrt{\frac{1}{12}}} = e^{0.30 \times 0.2887}$$

$$e^{0.0866} = 1.0905$$

$$d = \frac{1}{u} = \frac{1}{1.0905} = 0.9170$$

$$P = \frac{e^{rt} - d}{u - d} = \frac{e^{0.12\times\frac{1}{2}} - 0.9170}{1.0905 - 0.9170}$$

$$= \frac{1.0101 - 0.9170}{0.1735} = \frac{0.0931}{0.1735} = 0.5366$$

So, $(1 - P) = 1 - 0.5366 = 0.4634$

Now we proceed to calculate the value of American option.

Step 1: Now we draw a Binomial Tree and show the stock prices at the end of each month:

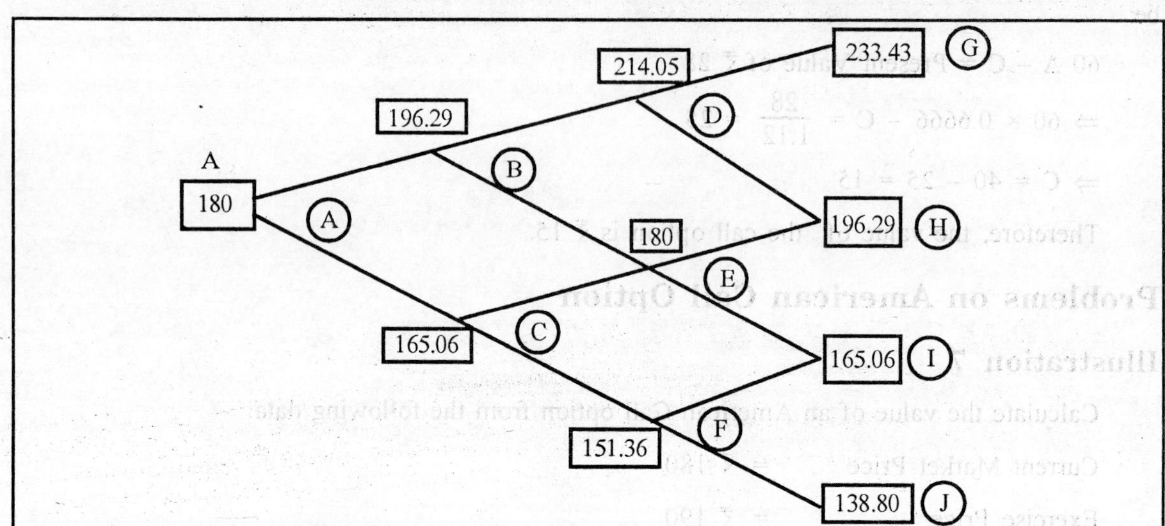

Next we calculate the option prices at the final nodes by backward process as follows:

Node	Max [(S – X), 0]	Option Value
G	Max [233.43 – 190, 0]	43.43
H	Max [196.29 – 190, 0]	6.29
I	Max [165.06 – 190, 0]	0
J	Max [138.80 – 190, 0]	0

Step 2: Determination of Option values at the preceeding nodes at D, E and F.

(a) Option value of node D

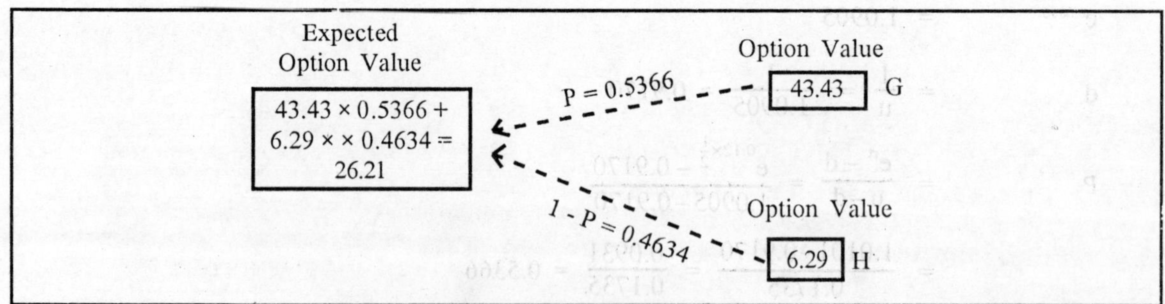

Present value of the expected option value at D = 26.21 e^{-rt} = 26.21 × 0.99005 = 25.95

If the option holder will exercise his option at node D, then the value of the option will be Max [(214.05 – 190), 0] = 24.05

Here at node D, we get two different values. These values are:

- Binomial value = ₹ 25.95
- Exercise value = ₹ 24.05

We have to select the higher one, i.e., 25.95.

Thus, the value of American option at the early exercise point at D is

Max (Binomial value, Exercise value)

= Max (25.95, 24.05) = 25.95

(b) Option value at node E

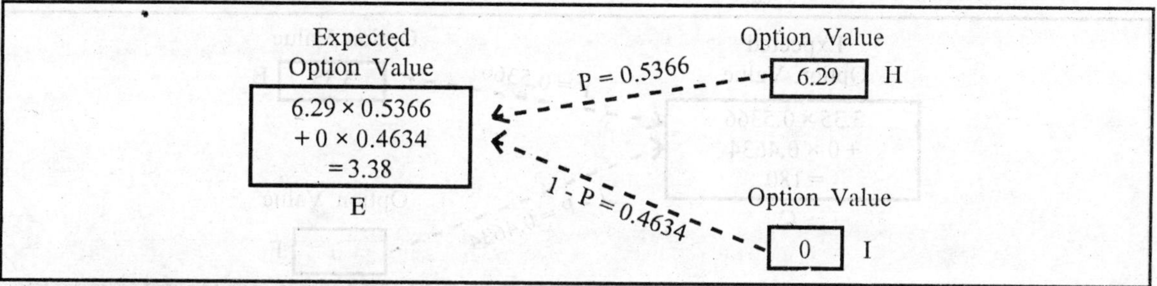

Present value of expected option value at node

E = 3.38 e^{-rt} = 3.38 × 0.99005 = 3.35

Exercise value of option at node E = 0

Thus, the value of American call option at node

E = Max {3.35, 0} = 3.35

(c) Option value at node at F = 0

Step 3: Calculation of option values at the preceeding nodes B and C

(a) Option value at B:

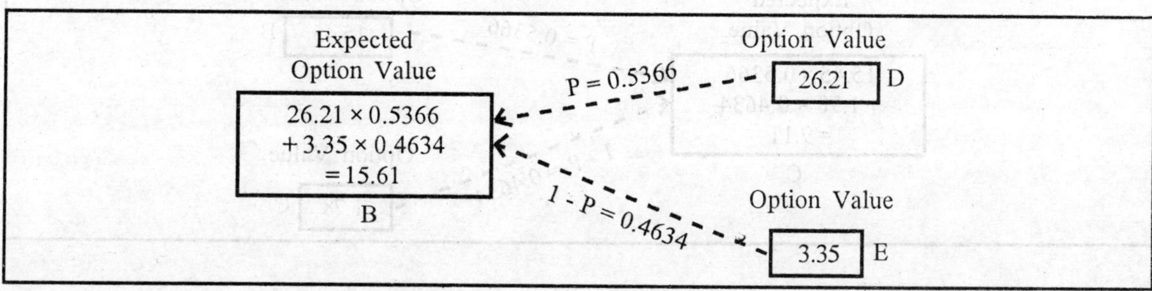

Present value of expected option value at node

B = 15.61 e^{-rt} = 15.61 × 0.99005 = 15.45

Further, if the option holder will exercise his option at node B, then the value of such option will be:

Max [196.29 – 190, 0] = 6.29

Here at node B, we get two different option values. These values are:

- Binomial value = 15.45
- Exercise value = 6.29

The higher of the two, i.e., 15, 45 will be taken as American option value at node B.

(b) Option value at node C

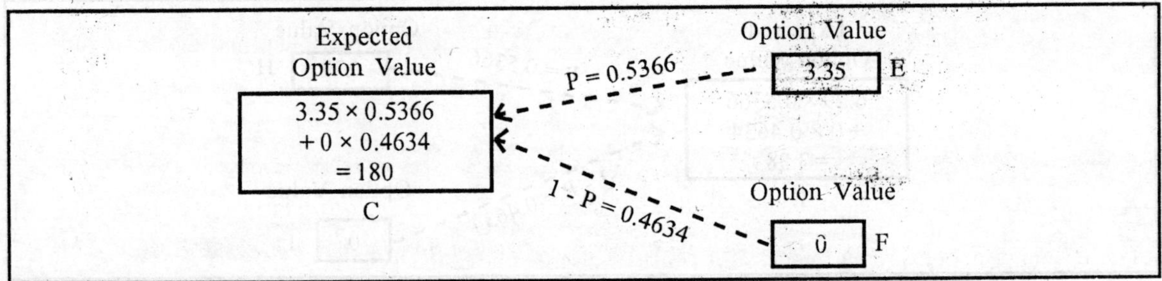

Present value of expected option value at node C

= 1.80 e^{-rt} = 1.80 × 0.99005 = 1.78

Exercise value of the option at node C

= Max [(165.06 – 190), 0] = 0

Thus, the value of American call option at node C = Max (Binomial value, Exercise value)

= Max (1.78, 0) = 1.78

Step 4: Computation of option value at the initial node A:

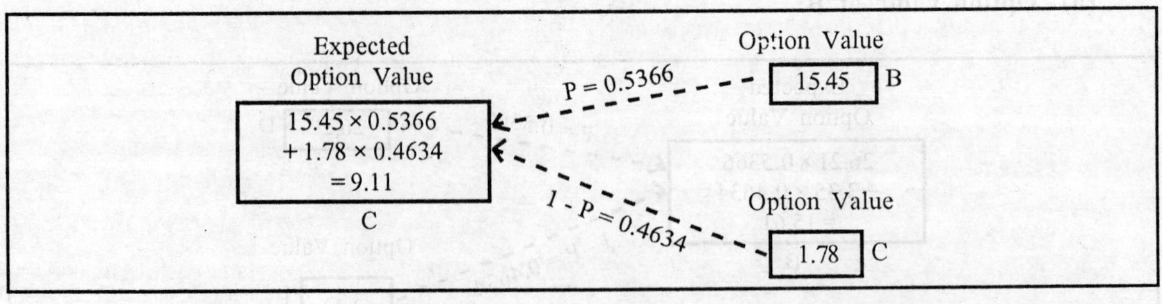

Present value of expected option value at node

A = 9.11 e^{-rt} = 9.11 × 0.99005 = 9.02

Exercise value of option at node A

= Max [(190 – 180), 0] = 10

Thus, the value of American call option at node A = Max (9.02, 10) = ₹ 10

SUGGESTIONS FOR FURTHER READINGS

1. Cox, J ., S. Ross, and M. Rubinstein. *"Option Pricing: A Simplified Approach"*, Journal of Financial Economics, October 1979, pp. 229-64.

EXERCISES

Quiz

1. State Whether the Following Statements are True or False.

(a) Binomial option pricing model is known as C-R-R model.

(b) Binomial option pricing model is a constant discrete-time model.

(c) In Binomial option pricing model, the forward stock prices will be calculated by forward induction process while the option prices will be calculated by backward induction process.

(d) The up movement factor in always ≥ 1.

(e) The down movement factor is always ≤ 1.

(f) The value of a call option is expressed as Max [$(S_n – X)$, 0] where X is the Strike price and S_n is the spot price at the nth period.

Ans: (a) True, (b) True, (c) True, (d) True, (e) True, (f) True.

2. Fill up the Blanks.

(a) If the Binomial value of an American option is ₹ 17 and exercise value is ₹ 16, then the American call option will be ________.

(b) If up factor is = 1.2, then the down factor is ________.

(c) If Volatility of Stock Price is 40%, time interval is one month, then the down movement factor is ________.

(d) If probability of up movement in stock prices is 0.65, then the probability of down movement is ________.

(e) The Binomial model can be used successfully for valuing ________style options which may be exercised early, i.e., before maturity.

(f) Binomial option pricing model is used to determine option value numerically through an ________ process involving several steps.

Ans: (a) £ 17, (b) < 1, (c) $d = \frac{1}{u}$, $u = e^{\sigma\sqrt{t}}$, $u = e^{0.4 \times \sqrt{\frac{1}{2}}}$, (d) 0.35, (e) American, (f) Iterative.

A. Short Type Questions

1. Why Binomial option pricing model is called a discrete time model?
2. What do you mean by Binomial Process?
3. What do you mean "u" factor? How it is calculated?
4. What is 'd' factor in binomial process? How it is calculated?
5. How to calculate the probability of up movement?
6. Why u factor is greater than one and d factor is less than one?
7. What do you mean by the recombinant concept in binomial tree?
8. What are the three steps in Binomial Option Pricing Methodology?
9. What are the advantages of Binomial Option Pricing Model?
10. What are the limitations of Binomial Option Pricing Method?
11. What do you mean by Replicating portfolio?
12. What is option delta?
13. Change in option prices is 10 and change in stock prices is 40. Find out option delta.
14. What is a binomial tree?
15. What is backward induction process?

B. Long Type Questions

1. What do you mean by Binomial Option Pricing Model? What are the assumptions? Briefly discuss its important characteristics.
2. Briefly discuss the methodology of Binomial option pricing model for: (a) European Options, (b) American Options.

PRACTICAL PROBLENS

1. Draw a Binomial tree and compute the Stock Pricing process for two periods from the following data:

   Current Stock Price = ₹ 47
   Up factor = 3.25%
   Down factor = 2.5%

2. From the following data, calculate Option Delta at expiration.

   Type of option : European call
   Current Stock Price = ₹ 160
   Exercise Price = ₹ 150
   Time to expiration = 1 year
   Risk-free interest = 10% p.a
   No dividend

3. Draw binomial trees from the following data and show the stock prices:

Parameters	European	
	Call option	Put option
Stock Price	300	300
Strike Price	360	240
Time to expiration	1 year	1 year
Sub-periods	Two	Two
u factor	0.2	1.2
d factor	0.9	0.9

4. From the following data, calculate: (a) Expected Stock Price (b) Value of an option, (c) Option Delta:
   (i) Type of Option = European
   (ii) Stock Price at (t_0) = ₹ 240
   (iii) Time to expiration (T) = One year
   (iv) Stock price movement in the next year
   – go up by 25%
   – go down by 20%
   (v) Exercise Price = ₹ 260
   (vi) Risk-free interest rate = 5%
   (vii) Risk neutral probability of up move = 0.60
5. The Current Market Price of a stock is ₹ 300 per share. The stock has a volatility of 0.40. The risk-free interest rate is 10% per annum. Using binomial tree with monthly intervals, calculate:
   (a) The three possible prices for the stock after two periods
   (b) The Value of a European call option for the stock with an exercise price of ₹ 320 per share
6. A share is currently selling for ₹ 50. It is expected that in one year it will either raise to ₹ 55 or decline to ₹ 45. If the Strike Price of the underlying share is ₹ 48 and the risk-free interest rate is 9% p.a., determine the value of a European call. [ICWA (F) 2010 June]
7. From the following data, calculate the value of a call option (European style):
   Current Price of the stock = ₹ 100
   Option period = 3 months
   Up movement factor (u) = 1.1
   Down movement factor (d) = 0.9
   Exercise Price = ₹ 105
   Risk-free interest rate = 12% P.a.
   Use Binomial Option Pricing Method.
   (*Ans:* Call Value = 3.16)
8. From the following data, calculate the value of a call option:
   Style of option = European
   Current price of the stock = ₹ 100
   Option period = 6 months
   Time intervals for change at each = 3 months

Up movement factor (u) = 1.1
Down movement factor (d) = 0.9
Exercise Price = ₹ 105
Risk-free interest rate = 12% p.a

Draw a two-step binomial tree, show the stock prices at each node and calculate the option price.

(*Ans:* Call Option Price = ₹ 6.48)

9. From the following data, calculate the value of a call option:

Current Stock Price = ₹ 20
Strike Price = ₹ 21
Option period = 6 months
Time intervals for change = 3 months
Move up factor (u) = 0.10
Move down factor (d) = 0.90
Risk-free rate of interest = 12% p.a

Use Binomial Model.

(*Ans:* Call Price = ₹ 1.28)

10. From the following data, calculate the value of a put option (European Style) from the following data:

Current Stock Price = ₹ 50
Strike Price = ₹ 52
Option Period = 2 year
Time interval for change = 1 year
Move up factor (u) = 1.20
Move down factor (d) = 0.80
Risk-free interest rate = 5% P.a.

Use Binomial Option Pricing Model.

(*Ans:* Put Value = ₹ 5)

11. (a) From the following data, calculate the value of a one-year European call option and value of a one-year European put option:

Current Stock Price (S) = ₹ 100
Strike Price = ₹ 100
Option period = 1 yea
Risk-free interest rate = 8% per annum with continuous compounding.

Expected Stock Price Movements:

(i) Up in each of the next six months = 10%

(ii) Down in each of the next six months = 10%

(b) Verify that the European call option and European put option prices satisfy put-call parity.

Black-Scholes Option Pricing Model (BSOPM)

Learning Objectives

After studying this chapter, you will be able to:

- Understand the Black-Scholes Option Pricing Model (BSOPM)
- Know the BSOPM formula
- Be aware of the eight important assumptions of BSOPM
- Use statistical tables like Natural logarithm, power of e, log normal (l_n) distribution.
- Determine call option price and put option price easily by using BSOP formula.

Chapter Outline

11.1 INTRODUCTION

Professor Fisher Black, Professor Myron Scholes and Professor Robert Merton published an article *"The Pricing of Options and Corporate Liabilities"* in 1973. It was a path-breaking paper published in *"Journal of Political Economy"*. In their article, they have developed a model on *"Pricing of European call Option"*. We should offer hearty regards to these financial engineers.

Myron Scholes and Fischer Black

Fischer Black

Born: 1938 Died: 1995

1964 – Earned Ph. D. from Harvard in applied math
1971 – Joined faculty of University of Chicago Graduate School of Business
1973 – Published "The Pricing of Options and Corporate Liabilities"
19XX – Left the University of Chicago to teach at MIT
1984 – Left MIT to work for Goldman Sachs & Co.

Myron Scholes

Born: 1941

1973 – Published "The Pricing of Options and Corporate Liabilities"
Currently he is working in the derivatives trading group at Salomon Brothers.

The Black-Scholes Model is a mathematical model of a financial market containing certain derivative investment instruments. From this model, we can deduce the Black-Scholes formula for pricing of European style option.

The Black-Scholes formula is widely used by option market participants. Many empirical tests have shown that Black-Scholes price is "fairly-close" to the observed price. To acknowledge the benefits of this model, **Myron Scholes and Robert Merton** were awarded the Nobel Prize in Economics in 1997 for their noble contribution. Sadly Professor Fisher Black died in 1995. Otherwise he would undoubtedly also being one of the recipients of the Nobel Prize.

In this chapter, we will not explain the derivation of this BSOPM. However, we will discuss the assumptions and applications of this model. We have already discussed the various determinants for option pricing in the previous chapter.

11.2 ASSUMPTIONS OF THE BLACK-SCHOLES OPTION PRICING MODEL

1. No Dividends

   The B-S model assumes that the stock pays no dividend during the option's life.

2. No transaction cost or taxes.
3. Shares are infinitely divisible, i.e., all stocks are perfectly divisible.
4. Prices are lognormally distributed.
5. No brokerage or commission to buy or sell options.
6. Interest rates remain constant and known.
7. Borrowing and lending at the same risk-free rate of interest.
8. Market operates continuously, i.e., stock trading is continuous. This assumption suggests that the participants cannot consistently predict the direction of the market or an individual stock. The continuous stock trading follows the Markov Process.

Points to Note:

The BSOPM uses the European exercise terms.

Thus, the assumptions are shown in figure 11.1.

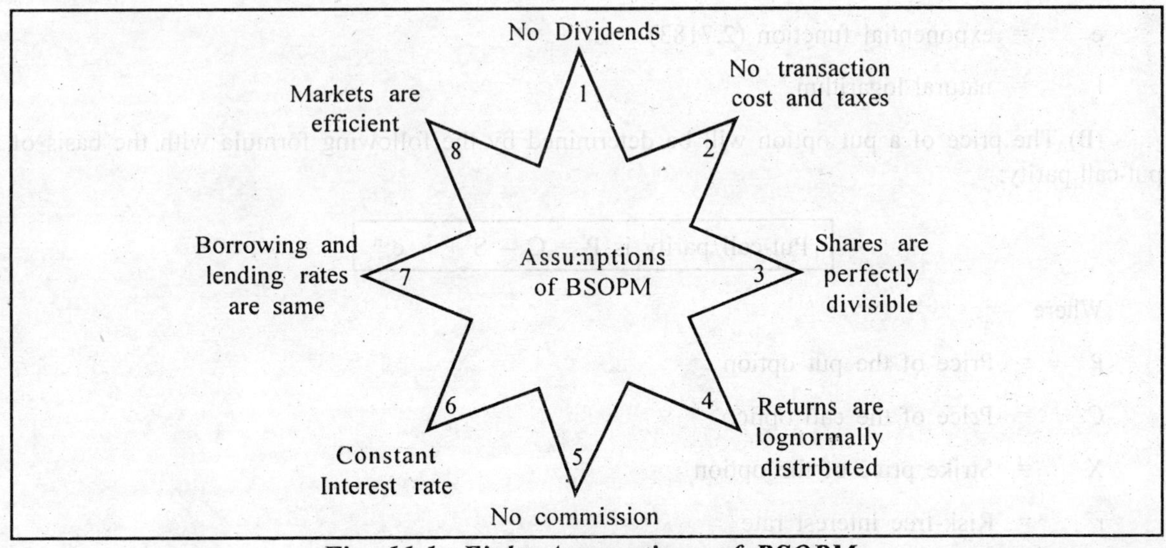

Fig. 11.1: Eight Assumptions of BSOPM

11.3 BLACK-SCHOLES OPTION PRICING FORMULA

(A) The price of a call option will be determined by the following formula:

$$C = SN(d_1) - Xe^{-rT} N(d_2)$$

Where

C = Price of the call option

S = Current Stock price

X = Exercise price of the Option

r = Risk-free interest rate continuously compounded

T = Current time until expiration, expressed as a per cent of a year

N() = Cumulative standard normal distribution i.e., area under the normal curve

σ = Annualised standard deviation of returns on the underlying asset, expressed as decimal

$$d_1 = \frac{\ln(S/X) + (r + \sigma^2/2)T}{\sigma\sqrt{T}}$$

$$d_2 = d_1 - \sigma\sqrt{T}$$

$N(d_1)$ and $N(d_2)$ are cumulative distribution function at d_1 and d_2 respectively

e = exponential function (2.7183)

l_n = natural logarithm.

(B) The price of a put option will be determined by the following formula with the basis of put-call parity:

Put-call parity is $P = C - S + \times e^{-rt}$

Where

P = Price of the put option

C = Price of the call option

X = Strike price of the option

r = Risk-free interest rate

T = Time to expiration

e = Exponential function, i.e., 2.7183

Then the price of the put option is:

$$P = X\,e^{-rt}\,N(-d_2) - SN(-d_1)$$

11.4 USE OF STATISTICS AND MATHEMATICS FOR B-S OPTION PRICING FORMULA

Black-Scholes Option Pricing Model is used to calculate a theoretical call price using the six determinants of an option's price.

The original formula for calculating a European call option (non-dividend) is:

$$C = S\,N(d_1) - Xe^{-rT}N(d_2)$$

Where

S = Current Stock Price

X = Exercise Price

r = Risk-free interest

T = Time to expiration expressed as proportion of a year

But we have to calculate the values of $N(d_1)$, $N(d_2)$ and e^{-rT} for inserting in the above formula.

$$d_1 = \frac{\ln\left(\frac{S}{X}\right) + \left(r + \frac{\sigma^2}{2}\right)T}{\sigma\sqrt{T}}$$

$$d_2 = d_1 - \sigma\sqrt{T}$$

$N(d_1)$ = Cumulative normal probability value of (d_1) which will be identified from the Normal Distribution Table

$N(d_2)$ = Cumulative normal probability value of (d_2) which will be identified from the Normal Distribution Table

The symbol l_n stands for natural logarithm.

So, for correct computation of all elements in the B-S formula, the basic requirements are:

1. Natural Logarithm (l_n)
2. Power of e, i.e., e^x
3. Volatility – historical and implied (σ)
4. Lognormal Distribution
5. Cumulative normal probability value

We will discuss these elements in brief. For details, one may refer any Standard Statistics or Mathematics books on these subjects.

11.4.1 Natural Logarithm (l_n)

The natural logarithm is the logarithm to the base e, where e is an irrational constant approximately equal to 2.718281828. The natural logarithm is generally written as l_n (x) or $\log_e x$.

Mathematicians, Statisticians, and some Engineers generally understand either "$\log_e^{(x)}$ or l_n (x) that is "log x to the base e".

Points to Note:

(i) $l_n\ 1 = 0$ because $e^0 = 1$.

(ii) When x is less than 1, then the natural logarithm will be negative.

(iii) When $n \geq 1$, then the natural logarithm is positive.

Example 1.

$l_n\ 0.01 = -4.60517$

$l_n\ 0.09 = 0.01005$

$l_n\ 1.00 = 0.0000$

$l_n\ 1.1 = 0.09531$

$l_n\ 10 = 2.39789$

Example 2. Find the natural logarithm 1.085.

Solution. From the statistical table of Natural Logarithm Values, we can identify the natural logarithm values of 1.08 and 1.09. These are as follows:

$l_n\ 1.08 = 0.07696$ $l_n\ 1.09 = 0.08618$

By interpolating these two values, we can get the value as:

$$
\begin{aligned}
l_n\ 1.085 &= l_n\ 1.08 + 0.5\ [l_n(1.09) - l_n(1.08)] \\
&= 0.07696 + 0.5\ (0.08618 - 0.07696) \\
&= 0.07696 + 0.5 \times 0.00921 \\
&= 0.07696 + 0.00460 \\
&= 0.08157
\end{aligned}
$$

11.4.2 Power of e, i.e., e^x or e^{-x}

We can calculate the e^x by referring to the statistical table "power of e".

Example 3

If x = 0.00, then e^x = 1.0000

If x = 1.00, then e^x = 2.7183

If x = –1.00, then e^x = 0.36788

Example 4. Find $e^{-0.04}$.

Solution: $e^{-0.04} = 0.96079$

Example 5. Find the values of the following

(a) $e^{0.565}$ (b) $e^{-0.565}$

Solution:

(a) $e^{0.565}$

From the statistical table, we can get the following values directly:

$e^{0.56} = 1.7507$, $e^{0.57} = 1.7683$

$$\text{Now } e^{0.565} = e^{0.56} + 0.5\,(e^{0.57} - e^{0.56})$$

$$= 1.7507 + 0.5\,(1.7683 - 1.7507)$$

$$= 1.7507 + 0.5 \times 0.0176$$

$$= 1.7507 + 0.0088$$

$$= 1.7595$$

(b) $e^{-0.565}$

From the statistical table, we can get the following values directly:

$e^{-0.56} = 0.57121$ $e^{-0.57} = 0.56553$

$$\text{Now } e^{-0.565} = e^{-0.570} + 0.5\,(e^{-0.560} - e^{-0.570})$$

$$= 0.56553 + 0.5\,(0.57121 - 0.56553)$$

$$= 0.56553 + 0.00289$$

$$= 0.56837$$

11.4.3 Volatility – Historical and Implied

Volatility is a measure of the variability in the asset's rate of return. It is estimated by using a statistical measure, i.e., Standard Deviation (σ). The degree of variability and chance of realising the asset's rate of return determine the option's pay-off.

Option prices are very sensitive to changes in volatility. Volatility cannot be directly observed and must be estimated.

Forms of Volatility: There are two types of volatility. These are:

(i) Historical volatility

(ii) Implied volatility

Historical Volatility: It is calculated from the historical stock prices. The historical stock prices may be daily or weekly stock prices. It is estimated by the standard deviation. The historical volatility will be calculated before the computation of option price by B-S formula because this historical volatility is one of the important input variable (determinant) of B-S formula.

Steps in Calculation:

Step 1. *Compute the daily changes in the price of the stock in a market. Then calculate the natural log of the ratio of a Stock's Price S_t its previous day's price S_{t-1}*

$R_t = l_n (S_t/S_{t-1})$

Where

R_t = Changes in the daily return

Step 2. *Computation of average returns over a specified period say a month.*

$$R_m = \frac{\frac{\sum R_t}{n}}{n}$$

Where

R_m = Mean of the daily returns

n = No. of days taken or No. of sample units

Step 3. *Calculate the Standard deviation*

$$\sigma_{daily} = \sqrt{\frac{\sum (R_t - R_m)^2}{n-1}}$$

But in B-S formula, the annualised volatility is used. The daily volatility can be converted into equivalent annual volatility by using the following formula:

$$\sigma_{annual} = \sigma_{daily} \times \sqrt{\text{No of trading days in the year}}$$

- The normal assumption in equity market is that there are 252 trading days per year.

Implied Volatility: By using historical volatility in the Black-Scholes formula, we calculate the option value. In other words, we can find the option value when a volatility (historical) is given. But we can put a different question: What is the volatility (or standard deviation) for the observed option price to be consistent with the Black-Scholes formula? The answer is **"Implied Volatility"**. Thus, when the volatility of the stock implies the current option price, we consider it is **implied volatility**.

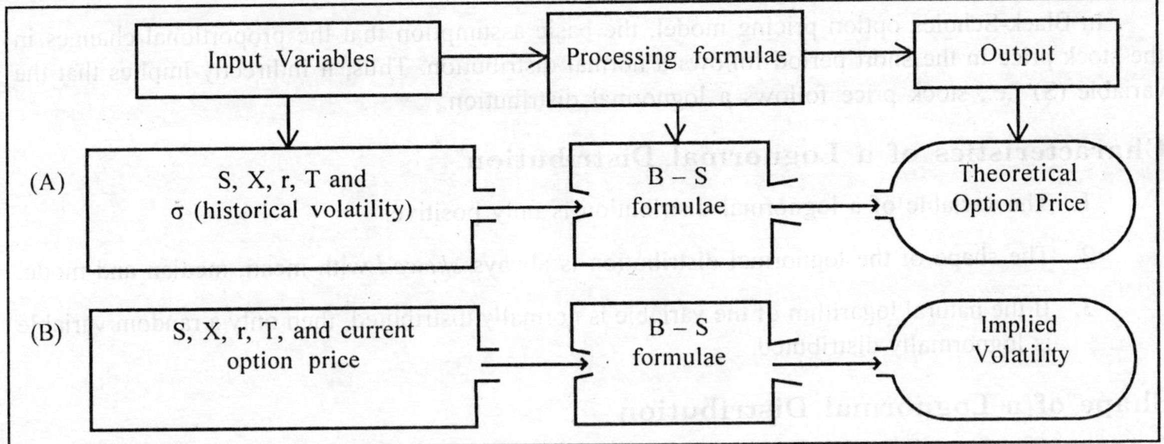

Points to Note:

(i) Basically implied volatility helps in determining the fair option price. while historical volatility helps in determining the theoretical value of an option.

(ii) If the historical volatility truely represents the future (implied) volatility, the actual option prices will be fair and identical to the theoretical prices.

How to Estimate Implied Volatility?

We know that option price is a function of volatility. Thus $C = f(\sigma)$ or $p = f(\sigma)$ where C = call option price, p = put option price and σ = volatility of the stock price. Consider the following two cases:

Case (a): If market price of the call option is greater than the theoretical call price determined by B-S formula, then it is assumed that implied volatility is greater than the historical volatility.

Case (b): If the market price of the call option is greater than the theoretical call price determined by B-S formula, then it is assumed that implied volatility is smaller than the historical probability

To estimate the implied volatility, we have to adopt trial and error method in the B-S formula.

11.4.4 Lognormal Distribution

In probability theory, a lognormal distribution of a random variable whose log is normally distributed is a continuous distribution in which logarithm of a variable has a normal distribution.

Definition: A random variable x is said to have the lognormal distribution with parameter $\beta \in R$ and $\sigma > O$ if logarithm of x has the normal distribution with β and σ. Equivalently if $x = e^y$ where y is normally distributed with mean β and standard deviation σ.

Use: The lognormal distribution is used to model continuous random quantities when the distribution is belived to be *skewed*.

In Black-Scholes option pricing model, the basic assumption that the proportional changes in the stock price in the short period follows a normal distribution. Thus, it indirectly implies that the variable (S) i.e., stock price follows a lognormal distribution.

Characteristics of a Lognormal Distribution

1. The variable of a lognormal distribution is only positive.
2. The shape of the lognormal distribution is always *skewed* with mean, median and mode.
3. If the natural logarithm of the variable is normally distributed, then only a random variable is lognormally distributed.

Shape of a Lognormal Distribution

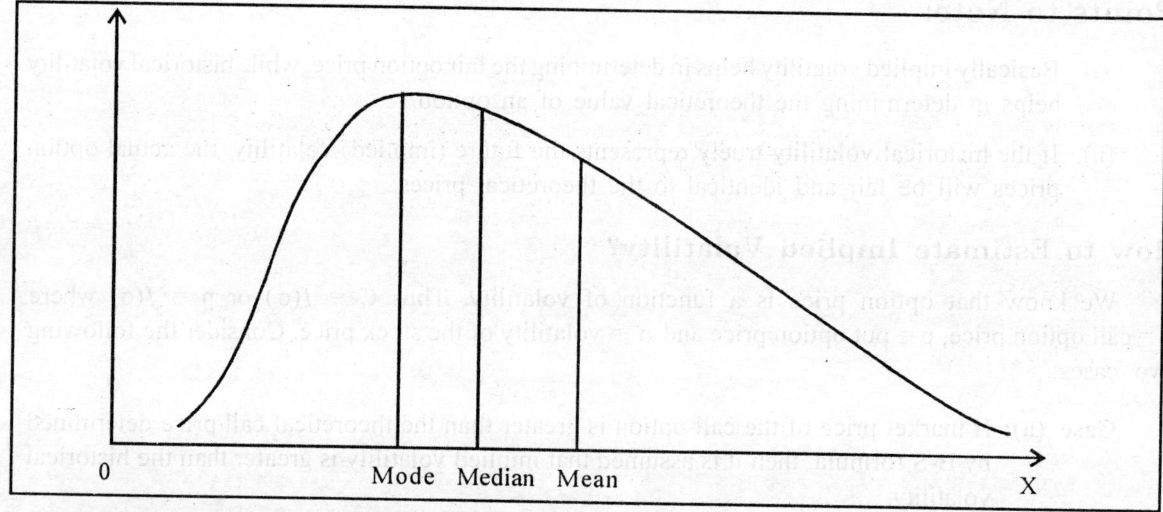

Here Mean > Median > Mode (Positive Skewed)

11.4.5 Cumulative Normal Probability Distribution

To insert the value of $N(d_1)$ and $N(d_2)$ in Black-Scholes formula, one should know the procedure of calculating these values.

$N(d_1)$ = Cumulative normal probability value of (d_1) = The area under the normal distribution to the left of d_1.

$N(d_2)$ = Cumulative normal probability of (d_2) = The area under the normal distribution to the left d_2.

Example 6. Find the value of:

(a) N(d) = N(1.04) (b) N(d) = N(–1.04)

(c) N(d) = N(1.97) (d) N(d) = N(–1.97)

(e) N(d) = N(–0.1082) (f) N(d) = N–(0.2377)

Solution:

(a) N(d) = N(1.04) = 0.5557

(b) N(d) = N(–1.04) = 0.4443

(c) N(d) = N(1.97) = 0.9999

(d) N(d) = N – (1.97) = 0.0244

(e) N(d) = N(–0.1082)

From the table of "Area under the Normal Distribution Curve" (for negative values), we first identify the following two values:

N(–0.10) = 0.4602

N(–0.11) = 0.4562

Then by interpolation, we can calculate the value of N(–0.1082) = N(–0.10) – 0.82

{N(–0.10)} – {N(–0.11)}

= 0.4602 – 0.82 × (0.4602 – 0.4562)

= 0.4602 – 0.0033 = 0.4569 (Ans)

(*f*)N(d) = N(–0.2377)

From the table of "Area under the Normal Distribution Curve" (for negative values), we first identify the following two values:

N(–0.2300) = 0.4090

(N – 0.2400) = 0.4052

Then by interpolation, we can calculate the value of (N – 0.2377) = N(–0.2300) – 0.

Example 7.

(a) If N(d) = 0.9987, find d.

(b) If N(d) = 0.9772 find d.

(c) If N(d) = 0.8483 find d.

Solution:

(a) It is given that N(d) = 0.9987

From the area under the normal distribution curve (for +ve values), we find that the value of d = 3.

(b) It is given that N(d) = 0.9772

From the area under the normal distribution curve (for +ve value), we find that the value of d = 2.

(c) It is given that N(d) = 0.8483

From the area under the normal distribution curve (for +ve values), we find that the value of d = 1.

Example 8: If d = 2, find the value of N(2) + N(–2).

Solution:

N(2) = 0.9772, N(–2) = 0.0228

So, N(2) + N(–2) = 0.9772 + 0.0228 = 1.

11.5 APPLICATIONS OF BSOPM

Illustration 1

From the following information, calculate call option value and put option value:

Current market price (S)	: ₹ 100 per share
Exercise Price (X)	: ₹ 80 per share
Volality of Share Price (S)	: 30%
Risk-free interest rate (r)	: 10% p.a.
Time to expiration (T)	: 3 months

Use Black-Scholes formula.

Solution:

(a) Calculation of Call Option Value

Black-Scholes formula

$C = S.\ N(d_1) - Xe^{-rT} \times N(d_2)$

Where $d_1 = \dfrac{\ln(S/X) + \left(r + \dfrac{\sigma^2}{2}\right)T}{\sigma\sqrt{T}}$

and $d_2 = d_1 - \sigma\sqrt{T}$

Here S = 100, X = 80, l_n = Natural logarithm, r = 0.10, σ = 0.30, T = 3/12 = 0.25

Step 1. Computation of values of d_1 and d_2

$$d_1 = \frac{l_n(100/80)+(0.10+0.030\times0.030/2)\times0.25}{0.30\times\sqrt{0.25}}$$

$$= \frac{l_n(1.25)+(0.10+0.045)\times0.25}{0.30\times0.50}$$

$$= \frac{0.22314+0.03625}{0.15} = \frac{0.25939}{0.15} = 1.7293$$

$$d_2 = d_1 - \sigma\sqrt{T}$$

$$= 1.7293 - 0.30\sqrt{0.25}$$

$$= 1.7293 - 0.15 = 1.5793$$

Step 2. Calculation of the cumulative normal probability values of d_1, d_2. These values can be identified from the Cumulative Normal Distribution Table.

$$N(d_1) = N(1.7293) = 0.9581$$

$$N(d_2) = N(1.5793) = 0.9429$$

Step 3. Calculation of call option value by using BSOPM formula as stated above.

$$C = S \times N(d_1) - Xe^{-rT} \times N(d_2)$$

$$= 100 \times 0.9581 - 80 \times 0.9753 \times 0.9429$$

$$= 95.81 - 73.57 = 22.24$$

(b) Now we compute put option value.

Black-Scholes formula:

$P = Xe^{-rT}\, N(-d_2) - S \times N(-d_1)$

Step 1. Computation of values of d_1, and d_2.

We have already got the values $d_1 = 1.7293$ and $d_2 = 1.5793$

Step 2. Computation of the values of $N(-d_1)$ and $N(-d_2)$

From Normal distribution tables, we find out the areas under the Normal distribution for these values as follows:

Direct Value	**Deductive Value**	
$N(-d_1) = 0.0419$	$1 - N(d_1)$	$= 1 - 0.9581$
		$= 0.0419$
$N(-d_2) = 0.0571$	$1 - N(d_2)$	$= 1 - 0.0429$
		$= 0.0571$

Step 3. Calculation of put option value by using BSOPM formula as stated above.

$$P = Xe^{-rT} N(-d_2) - SN(-d_1)$$
$$= 80\ e^{-0.10 \times 0.25} \times 0.0571 - 100 \times 0.0419$$
$$= 4.4534 - 4.190 = 0.2634 \text{ or}$$
$$\text{say } 0.26$$

Prove by put-call parity:

$C - P = S - X\ e^{-rT}$

LHS = 22.24 – 0.26 = 21.98 say ₹ 22

RHS = 100 – 80 × 0.975 = 100 – 78 = ₹ 29 (Proved)

Illustration 2

Use Black-Scholes formula, calculate call option value and put option value from the following information:

Current Market Price (S)	=	₹ 100 per share
Exercise Price (X)	=	₹ 100 per share
Volatility of Share Price (σ)	=	0.30
Risk-free interest rate (r)	=	10% Per annum
Time to expiration (T)	=	3 months = 0.25 years

Solution:

(a) Calculation of call option value

Black-Scholes formula:

$C = S.N(d_1) - X\ e^{-rT}\ N(d_2)$

Here S = 100; X = 100 r = 0.10, σ = 0.30, T = 3/12 = 0.25

Step 1. Computation of values d_1 and d_2

$$d_1 = \frac{l_n (S/X) + \left(r + \frac{\sigma^2}{2}\right)T}{\sigma\sqrt{T}}$$

$$= \frac{l_n (100/100) + (0.10 + 0.030 \times 0.030/2) \times 0.25}{0.30 \times \sqrt{0.25}}$$

$$= \frac{l_n (1) + 0.3625}{0.15} = \frac{0.0 + 0.03625}{0.15}$$

$= 0.03625 \ / \ 0.15 = 0.2417$

$d_2 = d_1 - \sigma\sqrt{T} = 0.2417 - 0.30 \times 0.30\sqrt{0.25}$

$= 0.2417 - 0.15 = 0.0917$

Step 2. Calculation of the cumulative normal probability values of d_1 and d_2. These values can be identified from the Cumulative Normal Distribution Table.

$N(d_1) = N(0.2417) = 0.5955$

$N(d_2) = N(0.0917) = 0.5365$

Step 3. Calculation of call value.

$C \ . \ N(d_1) - Xe^{-rT} N(d_2)$

$= 100 \times 0.5955 - 100 \ e^{-0.1 \times 0.25} \times 0.5365$

$= 59.55 - 100 \times 0.9753 \times 0.5365$

$= 59.55 - 52.32 = 7.23$

(b) Computation of put option value by Black-Scholes Formula:

Step 1. Computation of d_1 and d_2.

We have $d_1 = 0.2417$, $d_2 = 0.0917$

Step 2. Computation of the values of $N(-d_1)$ and $N(-d_2)$

From the Normal distribution table, we can obtain the areas under the Normal distribution for these values as follows:

Direct value	**Deductive value**
$N(-d_1) = N(-0.2417)$ $= 0.4045$	$1 - N(d_1) = 1 - 0.5955$ $= 0.4045$
$N(-d_2) = N(-0.0917)$ $= 0.4635$	$1 - N(d_2) = 1 - 0.5365$ $= 0.4635$

Step 3. Calculation of put value

$P = X \ e^{-rT} N(-d_2) - S \ N(-d_1)$

$= (100 \ e^{-0.1 \times 0.25} \times 0.4635) - (100 \times 0.4045)$

$= (100 \times 0.9749 \times 0.4635) - 40.45$

$= 45.19 - 40.45 = 4.74$

Prove by put-call parity:

$C - P = S - X\ e^{-rT}$

LHS : $C - P = 7.23 - 4.74 = 2.49$

RHS : $S - X\ e^{-rT} = 100 - 100 \times 0.9749$

$= 100 - 97.49 = 2.51$

Therefore, LHS ~ RHS (Proved)

Illustration 3

From the following information, calculate call option value and put option value:

(i)	Style of Option	=	European
(ii)	Current Stock Price (S)	=	₹ 100 per share
(iii)	Exercise Price	=	₹ 120 per share
(iv)	Volatility of Share (σ)	=	0.30
(v)	Risk-free interest rate	=	10% p.a.
(vi)	Option period (T)	=	3 months

Use Black-Scholes formula.

Solution:

(a) Calculation of call option value

Formula: $C = S \times N(d_1) - X\ e^{-rT} \times N(d_2)$

Step 1. *Computation of d_1 and d_2*

$$d_1 = \frac{l_n (S/X) + \left(r + \frac{\sigma^2}{2}\right)T}{\sigma\sqrt{T}}$$

$$= \frac{l_n (100/120) + \left\{0.10 + \frac{(0.030)^2}{2}\right\} \times \frac{3}{12}}{0.30 \times \sqrt{0.25}}$$

$$= \frac{l_n\ 0.8333 + 0.10 \times 0.045 \times 0.045}{0.30 \times 0.50} = \frac{-0.1463}{0.15}$$

$= 0.9742$

Then $d_2 = d_1 - \sigma\sqrt{T} = -0.9742 - 0.30 \times \sqrt{0.25}$

$= -0.9742 - 0.15 = -1.1242$

Step 2. *Calculation of the cumulative normal probability values of d_1 and d_2.*

$N(d_1) = N(-0.9742) = 0.1652$

$N(d_2) = N(-1.1242) = 0.1305$

Step 3. *Calculation of call option value by using BSOPM formula:*

$C = S \,.\, N(d_1) - X\, e^{-rT} \times N(d_2)$

$= 100 \times 0.1652 - 120 \times 0.9753 \times 0.1305$

$= 16.52 - 15.27 = 1.25$

(b) Computation of put option value formula:

$P = X\, e^{-rT}\, N(-d_2) - S\, N(-d_1)$

Step 1. *Computation of d_1 and d_2*

$d_1 = -0.942$ and $d_2 = -1.1242$

Step 2. *Computation of $N(-d_1)$ and $N(-d_2)$*

$N(-d_1) = 1 - N(d_1) = 1 - 0.1652 = 0.8348$

$N(-d_2) = 1 - N(d_2) = 1 - 0.1305 = 0.8695$

Step 3. $P = (120 \times e^{-0.10 \times 0.25} \times 0.8695) - 83.48$

$= 101.72 - 83.48 = 18.24$

Illustration 4

Take the Current Stock Price, Exercise Price, Computed call values and put value of illustration 1, illustration 2 and illustration 3 and interpret the result and comment on the intrinsic value and time value.

Solution:

Illustration	Current Stock Price (S)	Exercise Price (X)	Call Value (C)	Put Value (P)
1	100	80	22.24	0.26
2	100	100	7.23	4.74
3	100	120	1.25	18.24

Interpretation on Call Option

(a) When S = 100, X = 80, then the intrinsic value of the call is 20 (= 100 – 80)

Time value of call = 22.24 – 20 = 2.24

(b) When S = 100, X = 100, then the intrinsic value = 0

Time value = 7.23

(c) When S = 100, X = 120, then the call is out-of-money. The entire call value represents the time value.

Interpretation on Put Option

(a) When X = 80 and S = 100, then the intrinsic value of the put is zero. The entire value of put option, i.e., 0.26 represents the time value.

(b) When X = 100 and S = 100, then the intrinsic value is zero. The time value is 4.74.

(c) When X = 120 and S = 100, then the intrinsic value of put is 20. The Present Value of X (exercise price) is ₹ 117.04 so the minimum value of put option will be ₹ 17.04. Thus, the remaining value, i.e., ₹ 18.24 – ₹ 17.04 = ₹ 1.20 represents the time value.

11.6 BLACK-SCHOLES OPTION PRICING MODELS — TWO EXTENSIONS

The original Black-Scholes Model was developed for European Style Options of Stocks paying no dividends. Now we discuss the application of B-S model in the following two cases:

(a) Early exercise of American option

(b) Expected dividend (or cash inflows) during the tenor of the option

11.6.1 BSOPM for Early Exercise of American Option

American style options can be exercised at any point of time till the maturity date. In practice, an American call option on a non-dividend paying stock is exercised on maturity to avail the full benefit of exercise. Thus, if an American style option on non-dividend paying stock is exercised on the date of maturity, then the basic formula will be applied to calculate the option price.

11.6.2 Expected Dividends (Or Cash Inflows) During the Tenor of the Option

The current stock price is the first determinant of option price. If dividend on stock is expected to be received before the expiry of the option, then it will reduce the value of a call option and increase the value of a put option. First we have to calculate the Adjusted Stock Price by using the following formulas:

(i) For Call Option.

Adjusted Current Stock Price = $S_0 - De^{-rT}$

(ii) For Put Option

Adjusted Current Stock Price = $S_0 + De^{-rT}$

Where, De^{-rT} = Present value of the dividend using continuous discounting at the risk-free rate.

Then we use the basic BSOPM to calculate the option values.

11.7 ADVANTAGES AND LIMITATIONS

The Black-Scholes Option pricing Model (BSOPM) is a landmark in finance literature. This model was developed by Myron Scholes and Fisher Block is 1973. It has the following advantages and limitations.

Advantages: The main advantage of the Black-Scholes model is speed in calculating the option values. In a very short time, we can able to calculate a large number of option prices.

The Black-Scholes model gives a mathematical formula for calculating the theoretical prices of both call option and put option.

Limitations

1. BSOPM cannot be used to accurately price options with an American Style exercise as it only calculates the option price at one point of time, i.e., at maturity. It does not consider the steps along the way where there could be the possibility of early exercise of an American option.
2. All American style options are exchange traded, hence the traders will feel this BSOPM is useless.
3. It cannot accurately calculate the theoretical value of a dividend paying stock option.

11.8 BLACK-SCHOLES MODEL AND BINOMIAL MODEL — A RELATIONSHIP

Black-Scholes Option Pricing Model was developed in 1973. But the Binomial Option Pricing Model was developed by Cox, Ross and Rubinstein in 1979.

The Black-Scholes model is a mathematical model which is commonly used as it gives an analytical result. It is based on six variables. Though this model was first developed for European option (non-dividend paying stock) but subsequently further developments were made for American style as well as dividend paying stocks. But Binomial option pricing model is very suitable for American style options. Binomial model involves an interative process. It does not give any analytical solution. However, both BSOPM and Binomial Option Pricing Model have their own importance in the world of financial derivatives.

CHAPTER SUMMARY

Black-Scholes option pricing model is the first and most commonly used pricing model in finance. It was initially developed by two financial engineers, Fischer Black and Myron Scholes in 1973. The BSOPM was originally designed to price European option for non-dividend paying stocks. This model is used to calculate a theoretical call option price (ignoring dividends, paid during the life of the option. The key determinants of option price are: Stock price (S), Strike Price (X), Volatility (σ), time to expiration (T) and Short-term (risk-free) interest rate.

The original formula for calculating the theoretical option price is as follows:

Call Option Price = C = $SN(d_1) - Xe^{-rT} N(d_2)$

Put Option Price = P = $X e^{-rT} N(-d_2) - SN(d_1)$

Where $d_1 = \dfrac{\ln(S/X) + (r + \sigma^2/2)T}{\sigma\sqrt{T}}$

$d_2 = d_1 - \sigma\sqrt{T}$

This chapter explained the use of some Statistical Measures and Mathematical formula for BSOPM. These are Natural logarithm (l_n), Power of e, i.e., e_x, Volatility (σ), Lognormal Distribution and Cumulative normal probability values. For easy and quick valuation of option price, these above stated statistics and mathematics are absolutely essential. This chapter explains in a very simple way to make the reader most competent. Interestingly, how to calculate implied volatility is explained in a logical way.

In section 11.5, four illustrations have been given to explain the computational strategy of BSOPM for both call option and put option. The put-call parity has also been highlighted.

In section 11.6, two major extensions in Black-Scholes i.e., early exercise of American option and options for the stocks when expected dividend is likely to be received before the maturity of the option have been discussed.

The main advantage of Black-Scholes model is speed. We can be able to calculate a very large number of option prices in a very short time. However, it suffers one major limitation, i.e., it cannot be used to accurately price options with an American Style exercise as it only calculates the option price at one point of time—at expiration. Besides, it does not consider the steps along the way where there could be the possibility of early exercise of an American option.

SOLVED PROBLEMS

Illustration 5

From the following information, calculate call option value and put option value. Use Black-Scholes formula:

S = ₹ 280, X = ₹ 260, r = 8% p.a., T = 0.6667, $N(d_1)$ = 0.6336, $N(d_2)$ = 0.4470

Assume that no dividend is expected during life of the option.

Solution:

(a) Computation of call option value

C $= S\ N(d_1) - X\ e^{-rT}\ N(d_2)$

$= (280 \times 0.6336) - (260 \times e^{-0.08 \times 0.6667} \times 0.4470)$

$= 177.40 - (260 \times 0.94817 \times 0.4470$

$= 177.40 - 110.20 =$ ₹ 67.20

(b) Computation of put option value

P $= X\ e^{-rT}\ N(-d_2) - S\ N(-d_1)$

$= (260 \times 0.94817 \times 0.5530) - (280 \times 0.3664)$

$= 136.33 - 102.59 =$ ₹ 33.74

Workings:

$N(-d_1) = 1 - N(d_1) = 1 - 0.6336 = 0.3664$

$N(-d_2) = 1 - N(d_2) = 1 - 0.4470 = 0.5530$

Illustration 6

From the following information, calculate call value by using Black-Scholes formula:

S = ₹ 280, X = ₹ 260, r = 0.08, T= 8 months, $N(d_1) = 0.5998$, $N(d_2) = 0.4122$, Expected Dividend = ₹ 12 after 6 months

Solution:

(a) First, we have to determine adjusted S:

S_A $=$ S(Adjusted) $= S - D\ e^{-rT} = 280 - 12\ e^{-rT}$

$= 280 - 12 \times e^{-0.08 \times \frac{8}{12}} = 280 - 12 \times 0.96079$

$= 280 - 11.52 = 268.48$

Now, we use the basic B-S formula to calculate call value

C $= S_A\ N(d_1) - X\ e^{-rT}\ N(d_2)$

$= 268.48 \times 0.5998 - 260 \times 0.94817 \times 0.4122$

$= 161.03 - 101.62 =$ ₹ 59.41

Note: When dividend is expected during the life of option, the call value will be less and put value will be more. The reason is the current price of the stock will be reduced by th present value of expected dividend. In case of put option, it will be reversed.

Illustration 7

Calculate the value of a call option from the following data by using Black-Scholes option pricing formula:

$S = 100 \qquad X = 100$

$r = 0.05 \qquad \sigma = 0.10$

$T = 90 \text{ days} = 0.25 \text{ years}$

Solution:

$C = S\,N(d_1) - X\,e^{-rT}\,N(d_2)$

Where

$$d_1 = \frac{l_n\,(S/X) + \left(r + \frac{\sigma^2}{2}\right)T}{\sigma\sqrt{T}}$$

$$= \frac{l_n\left(\frac{100}{100}\right) + \left\{0.05 + \frac{0.10^2}{2}\right\}T}{0.10 \times \sqrt{0.25}}$$

$$= \frac{l_n\,1 + (0.05 \times 0.005 \times 0.25)}{0.10 \times 0.5} = \frac{0 + 0.01375}{0.05} = 0.275$$

Then $d_2 = d_1 - \sigma\sqrt{T} = -0.275 - 0.1 \times \sqrt{0.25} = 0.225$

Now we have to calculate the cumulative normal probability values of d_1 and d_2. These values can be identified from the cumulative Normal Distribution Table:

$N(d_1) = N(0.275) = 0.6084$

$N(d_2) = N(0.225) = 0.5891$

In the final step, we have to compute the call option value by using BSOPM formula.

$C = S\,N(d_1) - X\,e^{-rT}\,N(d_2)$

$= 100 \times 0.6084 - 100\,e^{-0.05 \times 0.25} \times 0.5891$

$= 60.84 - (100 \times 0.98759 \times 0.5891) = 60.84 - 58.18 = 2.66$

Illustration 8

Take all the data in example 7 and calculate put option price by using Black-Scholes formula and test the result with put-call parity.

Solution:

(a) Put Value: $P = X\ e^{-rT}\ N(-d_2) - SN\ (-d_1)$

Step 1. Computation of values of $N(-d_2)$ and $N\ (-d_1)$

$N\ (-d_2) \quad = 1 - N\ (d_2) = 1 - 0.5891 = 0.4109$

$N\ (-d_1) \quad = 1 - N\ (d_1) = 1 - 0.6084 = 0.3916$

By putting these values in the formula, we get the put option value as:

$$P = \{100\ e^{-0.05 \times 0.25} \times 0.4109\} - \{100 \times 0.3916\}$$

$$= (100 \times 0.98759 \times 0.4109) - 39.16$$

$$= 40.58 - 39.16 = 1.42$$

(b) Put-Call Parity

$$P = C - S + X\ e^{-rT}$$

$$P = 2.66 - 100 + 100 \times 0.98759$$

$$= 2.66 - 100 + 98.76$$

$$= 101.42 - 100 = 1.42$$

Illustration 9

From the following data, calculate the price of the call option and the put option by using Black-Scholes option pricing formula:

(i) Current stock price = ₹ 160 per share

(ii) Volatility of the share = 20%

(iii) Risk-free interest rate = 8% p.a.

(iv) Exercise price = ₹ 150

(v) There is a call option as well as put option on the share, expiring in 6 months.

Solution:

Given S = ₹ 160, X = ₹ 150, $r = 0.06$, $\sigma = 0.20$, $T = 6/12 = 0.5$

(a) Call value: $\boxed{C = SN(d_1) - Xe^{-rT}\ N(d_2)}$

Step 1. Computation of values of d_1 and d_2.

$$d_1 = \frac{\ln(S/X) + (r + \sigma^2/2)T}{\sigma\sqrt{T}}$$

$$= \frac{l_n(160/150)+\left(0.08+0.5(0.20)^2\right)0.5}{0.20\sqrt{0.5}}$$

$$= \frac{l_n(1.0667)+(0.1)0.5}{0.20\times 0707}$$

$$= \frac{0.06456+0.05}{01414} = \frac{0.11456}{0.1414}$$

$$= 0.8102$$

$$d_2 = d_1 - \sigma\sqrt{T}$$

$$= 0.8102 - 0.20\sqrt{0.5}$$

$$= 0.8102 - 0.1414 = 0.6688$$

Step 2. *Calculation of the cumulative normal probability values of d_1 and d_2. These values can be identified from the Cumulative Normal Distribution Table:*

$N(d_1) = N(0.8102) = 0.7910$

$N(d_2) = N(0.6688) = 0.7482$

Step 3. *Computation of call value using BSOPM formula as stated above.*

$$C = S\ N(d_1) - \times\ e^{-rT}\ N(d_2)$$

$$= 160 \times 0.7910 - 150\ e^{-0.08 \times 0.5} \times 0.7482$$

$$= 126.56 - 150 \times 0.96079 \times 0.7482$$

$$= 126.56 - 107.83$$

$$= 18.73$$

(b) Put Value: $\boxed{P = Xe^{-rT}\ N(-d_2) - SN(-d_1)}$

Step 1: *Computation of values of $N(-d_2)$ and $N(-d_1)$*

By referring the Cumulative Normal Distribution Table, we can determine the values of

$N(-d_1) = 1 - N(d_1) = 1 - 0.7910 = 0.2090$

$N(-d_2) = 1 - N(d_2) = 1 - 0.7482 = 0.2518$

By putting these values in this formula, Put value will be calculated as:

$$P = 150\ e^{-0.08 \times 0.5} \times 0.2518 - 160 \times 0.2090$$

$$= 150 \times 0.96079 \times 0.2518 - 33.44$$

$= 36.29 - 33{,}44$

$= 2.85$

Illustration 10

Find out put option price from the following data:

Current stock price = ₹ 160

Strike Price = ₹ 150

Call Option Price = ₹ 18.73

Risk-free interest rate = 8% p.a.

Time to expiration = 6 months

Use put-call parity relation formula.

Solution:

The Put-Call parity relation is

$$C - P = S - X\,e^{-rT}$$

or

$$P = C - S + X\,e^{-rT}$$

Where

P = Put Option Price

C = Call Option Price

S = Current Stock Price

X = Strike Price

Now we calculate P as:

$$P = 18.73 - 160 + 150\,e^{-0.08 \times 0.5}$$

$$= 18.73 - 160 + 150 \times 0.96079$$

$$= 18.73 - 160 + 144.12 = 2.85$$

Remember: "The difference between the price of a call and the price of a put on the same stock, with the same strike price and time to expiration" is equal with the current price of the underlying stock minus the present value of the strike price calculated using continuous compounding. See the following figure:

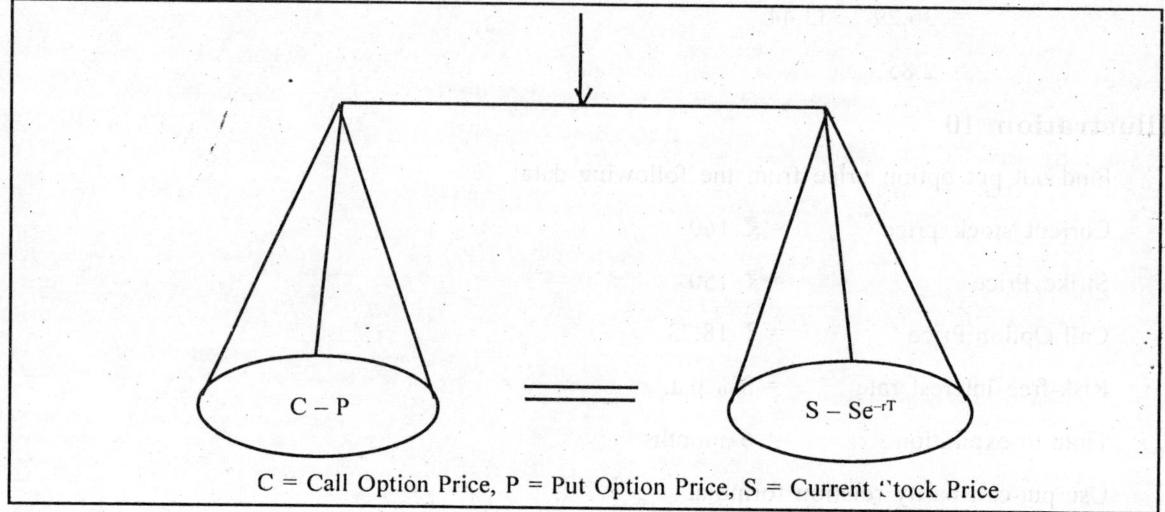

Fig. 11.2: Put-call Parity Relation

SUGGESTIONS FOR FURTHER READINGS

1. Neil A. and Ira Kawaller, "*Black-Scholes & Beyond Option Pricing Model*".
2. Sheldon Nattenburg, "*Option Volatility and Pricing*".
3. Lawnence Mimillan, "*Options as a Strategic Management*"
4. Epsen Haug, "*The Complete Guide to Option Pricing Formulas*".
5. Paul Wilmott, "*The Mathematics of Financial Derivatives*".

EXERCISES

Quiz

1. State Whether the Formulas are True or False.

(a) The value of a call option assuming that the stock pays no dividend during the option life is

$C \quad {}_1) - X e^{-rT} N(d_2)$

Where S = Current Stock Price

X = Exercise Price

r = Risk-free interest rate

T = Time to expiration

(b) $N(d_1)$ and $N(d_2)$ used in the Black-Scholes formula are cumulative distribution function at d_1, and d_2 respectively.

(c) $e^{-0.565} = 0.56837$

(d) Implied volatility helps in determining the fair option price while historical probability helps in determining the theoretical value of an option.

(e) If σ daily = volatility of daily stock price, then

$$\sigma_{annual} = \sigma_{daily} \sqrt{\text{No. of trading days in the year}}$$

(f) If d = –1.5 then $N(d_1)$ = 0.0668

(g) If $N(d_1)$ = 0.0022, then $N(d_1)$ = –2.8

(h) If d = 2.3 then $N(d_1)$ = 0.9993

(i) If d = 1.11 then $N(d_1)$ = 0.8665

(k) If d_1 = –0.9742, = 0.30, T = ½ = then d_2 = –1.1242

(l) For a call option, the Adjusted Stock Price (S) will be calculated when dividend is expected to be received before the expiry of the option is

$S = S_0 - De^{-rT}$

Where S_0 = Current Stock Price, D = Dividend, r = risk-free interest, T = Time to get dividend

Ans: (a) True, (b) True, (c) True, (d) True, (e) True, (f) True, (g) True, (h) True, (i) True, (k) True, (l) True.

A. Short Type Questions

1. What are the determinants of Black-Scholes formula for option pricing?
2. What is BSOPM?
3. Give an equation of put-call parity.
4. How to calculate d_1 and d_2 for Black-Scholes formula of option pricing?
5. How to calculate $N(d_1)$ and $N(d_2)$?
6. What do you mean by natural logarithm?
7. Find $e^{-0.565}$.
8. What is historical volatility?
9. What is implied volatility?
10. Which volatility gives fair value of option?
11. What in Black-Scholes formula for put option?
12. Give two extensions of Black-Scholes option pricing model.
13. What is the best utility of Black-Scholes option pricing formula?
14. What is the main drawback in Black-Scholes option pricing formula?
15. When a stock yields a dividend before the maturity how to calculate adjusted Stock Price?

B. Long Type Questions

1. What is Black-Scholes formula for option pricing? What are the assumptions? Discuss.
2. How to calculate call value and put value by using Black Scholes option pricing model? Discuss.
3. What are the advantages and limitations of Black-Scholes option pricing model? Discuss.

PRACTICAL PROBLEMS

1. From the following data, determine call option price

Current stock price	= ₹ 1260
Strike Price	= ₹ 1280
Time to expiration	= 3 months
Volatility	= 30 per cent per annum
Annual risk-free rate	= 12%

Use Black-Scholes formula.

(*Hints:* T = 0.25 S = 1260, X = 1280 r = ln(1.12) and = 0.30) (*Ans:* value of call option = ₹ 88.10)

2. From the following data, determine put option price:

Current stock price	= ₹ 1260
Strike Price	= ₹ 1280
Time to expiration	= 3 months
Volatility	= 30% p.a.
Annual risk-free rate	= 12%

Use Black-Scholes formula. (*Ans:* P = 67.35)

3. From the following data, compute the value of a put option by using Black-Scholes formula:

Current stock price	= ₹ 1260
Strike Price	= ₹ 1280
Time to expiration	= 3 months
Volatility	= 30% p.a.
Annual risk-free rate	= 12%
Annual dividend yield	= 5%

(*Ans:* P = 74.60)

4. From the following data for a certain stock, find the value of a call option:

Current stock price	= ₹ 280
Strike Price	= ₹ 75
Volatility	= 40% p.a
Time to expiration	= 6 months
Annual risk-free rate	= 12%

Given

No. of SD from mean (z)	0.25	0.30	0.55	0.60
Area of the left or right one tail	0.4013	0.3821	0.2912	0.2578

$e^{0.12 \times 0..5} = 0.0060$

$l_n\, 1.0667 = 0.0645$

Use Black-Scholes formula.

(***Hints:*** $d_1 = 0.5817$, $d_2 = 0.29$, $N(d_1) = 0.7195$, $N(d_2) = 0.6075$, value of option = ₹ 11.53)

APPENDIX

Table A 11.1: Cumulative Normal Distribution

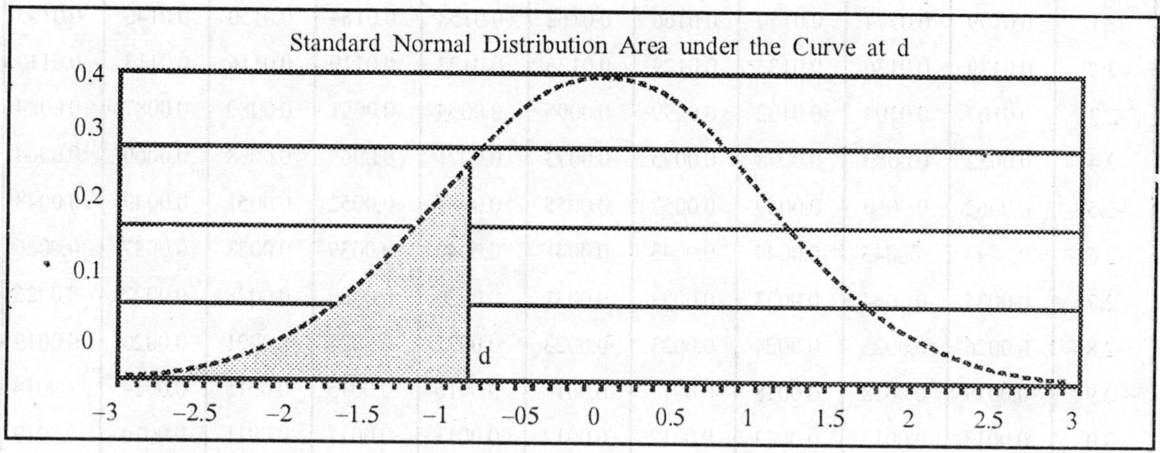

Area Under the Normal Distribution Curve (for Negative Values)

d	0.00	0.01	0.02	0.03	0.04	0.05	0.06	0.07	0.08	0.09
0.0	0.5000	0.4960	0.4920	0.4880	0.4840	0.4801	0.4761	0.4721	0.4681	0.4641
-0.1	0.4802	0.4562	0.4522	0.4483	0.4443	0.4404	0.4364	0.4325	0.4286	0.4247
-0.2	0.4207	0.4168	0.4129	0.4090	0.4052	0.4013	0.3974	0.3936	0.3897	0.3859
-0.3	0.3821	0.3783	0.3745	0.3707	0.3669	0.3632	0.3594	0.3557	0.3520	0.3483
-0.4	0.3446	0.3409	0.3372	0.3336	0.3300	0.3264	0.3228	0.3192	0.3156	0.3121
-0.5	0.3085	0.3050	0.3015	0.2981	0.2946	0.2912	0.2877	0.2843	0.2810	0.2776
-0.6	0.2743	0.2709	0.2676	0.2643	0.2611	0.2578	0.2546	0.2514	0.2483	0.2451
-0.7	0.2420	0.2389	0.2358	0.2327	0.2296	0.2266	0.2236	0.2206	0.2177	0.2148
-0.8	0.2119	0.2090	0.2061	0.2033	0.2005	0.1977	0.1949	0.1922	0.1894	0.1867
-0.9	0.1841	0.1814	0.1788	0.1762	0.1736	0.1711	0.1685	0.1660	0.1635	0.1611
-1.0	0.1587	0.1562	0.1539	0.1515	0.1492	0.1469	0.1446	0.1423	0.1401	0.1379
-1.1	0.1357	0.1335	0.1314	0.1292	0.1271	0.1251	0.1230	0.1210	0.1190	0.1170
-1.2	01151	0.1131	0.1112	0.1093	0.1075	0.1056	0.1038	0.1020	0.1003	0.0985
-1.3	0.0968	0.0951	0.0934	0.0918	0.0901	0.0885	0.0869	0.0853	0.0838	0.0823
-1.4	0.0808	0.0793	0.0778	0.0764	0.0749	0.0735	0.0721	0.0708	0.0694	0.0661
-1.5	0.0668	0.0655	0.0643	0.0630	0.0618	0.0606	0.0594	0.0582	0.0571	0.0559
-1.6	0.0548	0.0537	0.0526	0.0516	0.0505	0.0495	0.0485	0.0475	0.0465	0.0455
-1.7	0.0446	0.0436	0.0427	0.0418	0.0409	0.0401	0.0392	0.0384	0.0375	0.0367

−1.8	0.0359	0.0351	0.0344	0.0336	0.0329	0.0322	0.0314	0.0307	0.0301	0.0294
−1.9	0.0287	0.0281	0.0274	0.0268	0.0262	0.0256	0.0250	0.0244	0.0239	0.0233
−2.0	0.0228	0.0222	0.0217	0.0212	0.0207	0.0202	0.0197	0.0192	0.0188	0.0183
−2.1	0.0179	0.0174	0.0170	0.0166	0.0162	0.0158	0.0154	0.0150	0.0146	0.0143
−2.2	0.0139	0.0136	0.0132	0.0129	0.0125	0.0122	0.0119	0.0116	0.0113	0.0110
−2.3	0.0107	0.0104	0.0102	0.0099	0.0096	0.0094	0.0091	0.0089	0.0087	0.0084
−2.4	0.0082	0.0080	0.0078	0.0075	0.0073	0.0071	0.0069	0.0068	0.0066	0.0064
−2.5	0.0062	0.0060	0.0059	0.0057	0.0055	0.0054	0.0052	0.0051	0.0049	0.0048
−2.6	0.0047	00045	0.0044	0.0043	0.0041	0.0040	0.0039	0.0038	0.0037	0.0036
−2.7	0.0035	0.0034	0.0033	0.0032	0.0031	0.0030	0.0029	0.0028	0.0027	0.0026
−2.8	0.0026	0.0025	0.0024	0.0023	0.0023	0.0022	0.0021	0.0021	0.0020	0.0019
−2.9	0.0019	0.0018	0.0018	0.0017	0.0016	0.0016	0.0015	0.0015	0.0014	00014
−3.0	0.0013	0.0013	0.0013	0.0012	0.0012	0.0011	0.0011	0.0011	0.0010	0.0010

Standard Normal Distribution Area under the Curve at d

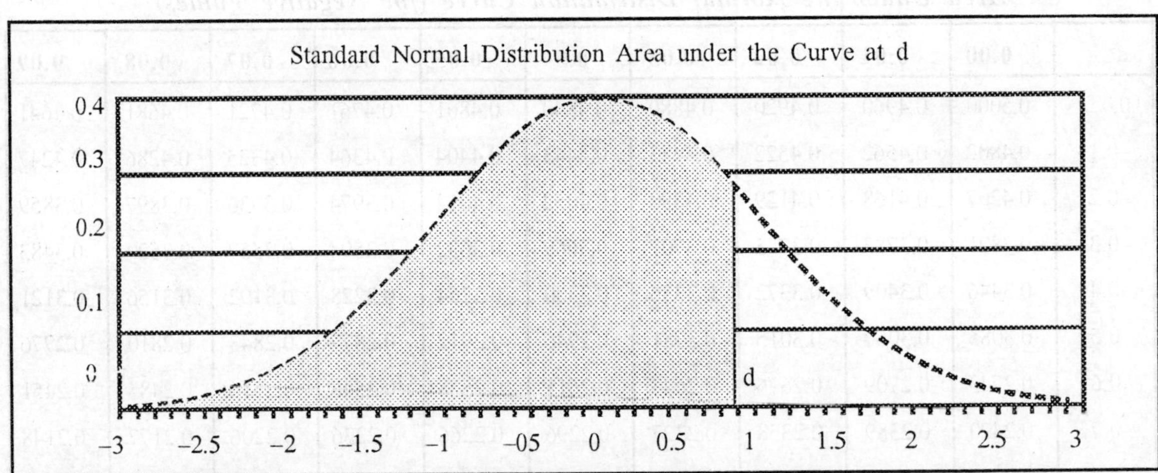

Area Under the Normal Distribution Curve (for Positive Values)

d	0.00	0.01	0.02	0.03	0.04	0.05	0.06	0.07	0.08	0.09
0.0	0.5000	0.5040	0.5080	0.5120	0.5160	0.5199	0.5239	0.5279	0.5319	0.5359
0.0	0.5398	0.5438	0.5478	0.5517	0.5557	0.5596	0.5636	0.5675	0.5714	0.5753
0.2	0.5793	0.5832	0.5871	0.5910	0.5948	0.5987	0.6026	0.6064	0.6103	0.6141
0.3	0.6179	0.6217	0.6255	0.6293	0.6331	0.6368	0.6406	0.6443	0.6480	0.6617
0.4	0.6554	0.6591	0.6628	0.6664	0.6700	0.6736	0.6772	0.6808	0.6844	0.6879
0.5	0.6915	0.6950	0.6985	0.7019	0.7054	0.7088	0.7123	0.7157	0.7190	0.7224

0.6	0.7257	0.7291	0.7324	0.7357	0.7389	0.7422	0.7454	0.7486	0.7517	0.7549
0.7	0.7580	0.7611	0.7642	0.7673	0.7704	0.7734	0.7764	0.7794	0.7823	0.7852
0.8	0.7881	0.7910	0.7939	0.7967	0.7995	0.8023	0.8051	0.8078	0.8106	0.8133
0.9	0.8159	0.8186	0.8212	0.8238	0.8264	0.8289	0.8315	0.8340	0.8365	0.8389
1.0	0.8413	0.8438	0.8461	0.8485	0.8508	0.8531	0.8554	0.8577	0.8599	0.5621
1.1	0.8643	0.8665	0.8686	0.8708	0.8729	0.8749	0.8770	0.8790	0.8810	0.8830
1.2	0.8849	0.8869	0.8888	0.8907	0.8925	0.8944	0.8962	0.8980	0.8997	0.9015
1.3	0.9032	0.9049	0.9066	0.9082	0.9099	0.9115	0.9131	0.9147	0.9162	0.9177
1.4	0.9192	0.9207	0.9222	0.9236	0.9251	0.9265	0.9279	0.9292	0.9306	0.9319
1.5	0.9332	0.9345	0.9357	0.9370	0.9382	0.9394	0.9406	0.9418	0.9429	0.9441
1.6	0.9452	0.9463	0.9474	0.9484	0.9495	0.9505	0.9515	0.9525	0.9535	0.9545
1.7	0.9554	0.9564	0.9573	0.958[illegible]	0.9591	0.9599	0.9608	0.9616	0.9625	0.9633
1.8	0.9641	0.9649	0.9656	0.96[illegible]	0.9671	0.9678	0.9686	0.9693	0.9699	0.9706
1.9	0.9713	0.9719	0.9573	0.9732	0.9738	0.9744	0.9750	0.9756	0.9761	0.9767
2.0	0.9772	0.9778	0.9783	0.9788	0.9793	0.9798	0.9803	0.9808	0.9812	0.9817
2.1	0.9821	0.9826	0.9830	0.9834	0.9838	0.9842	0.9846	0.9850	0.9854	0.9857
2.2	0.9861	0.9864	0.9868	0.9871	0.9875	0.9878	0.9881	0.9884	0.9887	0.9890
2.3	0.9893	0.9896	0.9898	0.9901	0.9904	0.9906	0.9909	0.9911	0.9913	0.9916
2.4	0.9918	0.9920	0.9922	0.9925	0.9927	0.9929	0.9931	0.9932	0.9934	0.9936
2.5	0.9938	0.9940	0.9941	0.9943	0.9945	0.9946	0.9948	0.9949	0.9951	0.9952
2.6	0.9953	0.9955	0.9956	0.9957	0.9959	0.9960	0.9961	0.9962	0.9963	0.9964
2.7	0.9965	0.9966	0.9967	0.9968	0.9969	0.9970	0.9971	0.9972	0.9973	0.9974
2.8	0.9974	0.9975	0.9976	0.9977	0.9977	0.9978	0.9979	0.9979	0.9980	0.9981
2.9	0.9981	0.9982	0.9982	0.9983	0.9984	09984	0.9985	0.9985	0.9986	0.9986
3.0	0.9987	0.9987	0.9987	0.9988	0.9989	0.9989	0.9989	0.9989	0.9990	0.9990

Table A 11.2: Natural Logarithm. Base (e)

The Natural Logarithm Table (Equal to or Less than 1.0)

n	$\log_e n$	n	$\log_e n$	n	$\log_e n$	n	$\log_e n$
0.01	–4.60517	0.26	–1.34707	0.51	–0.67334	0.76	–0.27443
0.02	–3.91202	0.27	–1.30933	0.52	–0.65392	0.77	–0.26236
0.03	–3.50655	0.28	–1.27296	0.53	–0.63488	0.78	–0.24846
0.04	–3.21887	0.29	–.23788	0.54	–0.61618	0.79	–0.23572
0.05	–2.99573	0.30	–1.20397	0.55	-0.59783	0.80	–0.22314

0.06	−2.81341	0.31	−1.17118	0.56	−0.57982	0.81	−0.21072
0.07	−2.65926	0.32	−1.13943	0.57	−0.56212	0.82	−0.19845
0.08	−2.52573	0.33	−1.10866	0.58	−0.54472	0.83	−0.18633
0.09	−2.40894	0.34	−1.07881	0.59	−0.52763	0.84	−0.17435
0.10	−2.30258	0.35	−1.04982	0.60	−0.51082	0.85	−0.16252
0.11	−2.20727	0.36	−1.02165	0.61	−0.49430	0.86	−0.15082
0.12	−2.12026	0.37	−0.99425	0.62	−0.47803	0.87	−0.13926
0.13	−2.04022	0.38	−0.96758	0.63	−0.46203	0.88	−0.12783
0.14	−1.96611	0.39	−0.94161	0.64	−0.44629	0.89	−0.11653
0.15	−1.89712	0.40	−0.91629	0.65	−0.43708	0.90	−0.10536
0.16	−1.83258	0.41	−0.89160	0.66	−0.41551	0.91	−0.09431
0.17	−1.77196	0.42	−0.86750	0.67	−0.40047	0.92	−0.08338
0.18	−1.71480	0.43	−0.81419	0.68	−0.38566	0.93	−0.07257
0.19	−1.66073	0.44	−0.82098	0.69	−0.37106	0.94	−0.06187
0.20	−1.60944	0.45	−0.79851	0.70	−0.35567	0.95	−0.05129
0.21	−1.56065	0.46	−0.77623	0.71	−0.34249	0.96	−0.04082
0.22	−1.51412	0.47	−0.75502	0.72	−0.32850	0.97	−0.03046
0.23	−1.46968	0.48	−0.73397	0.73	−0.31471	0.98	−0.02020
0.24	−1.42711	0.49	−0.71335	0.74	−0.30110	0.99	−0.01005
0.25	−1.38629	0.50	−0.69214	0.75	−0.28768	1.00	−0.00000

The Natural Logarithm Table (Equal to or More than 1.0)

n	$\log_e n$	n	$\log_e n$	n	$\log_e n$	n	$\log_e n$
1.0	0.00000	3.0	1.09861	5.0	1.60944	25.0	3.21887
1.1	0.09531	3.1	1.13140	6.0	1.79176	26.0	3.25809
1.2	0.18232	3.2	1.16315	7.0	1.94591	27.0	3.29583
1.3	0.26236	3.3	1.19392	8.0	2.07944	28.0	3.33220
1.4	0.33647	3.4	1.22377	9.0	2.19722	29.0	3.36729
1.5	0.40546	3.5	1.25276	10.0	2.30258	30.0	3.40119
1.6	0.47000	3.6	1.28093	11.0	2.39789	40.0	3.68888
1.7	0.53063	3.7	1.30833	12.0	2.48491	50.0	3.91202
1.8	0.58779	3.8	1.33500	13.0	2.56495	60.0	4.09434
1.9	0.64185	3.9	1.36097	14.0	2.63905	70.0	4.24849
2.0	0.69314	4.0	1.38629	15.0	2.70805	80.0	4.38202
2.1	0.74193	4.1	1.41099	16.0	2.77259	90.0	4.49981
2.2	0.78845	4.2	1.43508	17.0	2.83321	100.0	4.60517

2.3	0.83291	4.3	1.45861	18.0	2.89037	200.0	5.29832
2.4	0.87547	4.4	1.48160	9.0	2.94444	300.0	5.70378
2.5	0.91629	4.5	1.50408	20.0	2.99573	400.0	5.99146
2.6	0.95551	4.6	1.52605	21.0	3.04452	500.0	6.21461
2.7	0.99325	4.7	1.54756	22.0	3.09104	600.0	6.39693
2.8	1.02962	4.8	1.56861	23.0	3.13549	700.0	6.55108
2.9	1.06471	4.9	1.58923	24.0	3.17805	800.0	6.68461

Table A 11.3: Power of e
The Powers of e for Different Positive and Negative Values

x	e_x	e^{-x}	x	e_x	e^{-x}	x	e_x	e^{-x}
0.00	1.0000	1.00000	0.26	1.2969	0.77105	0.52	1.6820	0.59452
0.01	1.0101	0.99005	0.27	1.3100	0.76335	0.53	1.6989	0.58860
0.02	1.0202	0.98020	0.28	1.3231	0.75578	0.540	1.7160	0.58275
0.03	1.0305	0.97045	0.29	1.3364	0.74826	0.55	1.7333	0.57695
0.04	1.0408	0.96079	0.30	1.3499	0.74082	0.56	1.7507	0.57121
0.05	1.0513	0.95132	0.31	1.3634	0.73345	0.57	1.7683	0.56553
0.06	1.0618	0.94176	0.32	1.3771	0.72615	0.58	1.7860	0.55990
0.07	1.0725	0.93239	0.33	1.3910	0.71892	0.59	1.8040	0.55433
0.08	1.0833	0.92312	0.34	1.4049	0.71177	0.60	1.8221	0.54881
0.09	1.0942	0.91393	0.35	1.4191	0.70469	0.61	1.8404	0.54335
0.10	1.1052	0.90484	0.36	1.4333	0.69768	0.62	1.8589	0.53794
0.11	1.1163	0.89583	0.37	1.4477	0.69073	0.63	1.8776	0.53259
0.12	1.1275	0.88692	0.38	1.4623	0.68386	0.64	1.8965	0.52729
0.13	1.1388	0.87809	0.39	1.4770	0.67706	0.65	1.9155	0.52205
0.14	1.1503	0.86936	0.40	1.4918	0.67032	0.66	1.9348	0.51685
0.15	1.1618	0.96071	0.41	1.5068	0.66365	0.67	1.9542	0.51171
0.16	1.1735	0.85214	0.42	1.5220	0.65705	0.68	1.9739	0.50662
0.17	1.1853	0.84366	0.43	1.5373	0.65051	0.69	1.9937	0.50158
0.18	1.1972	0.83527	0.44	1.5527	0.64404	0.70	2.0!38	0.49659
0.19	1.2092	0.82696	0.45	1.5683	0.63763	0.71	2.0340	0.49164
0.20	1.2214	0.81873	0.46	1.5841	0.63128	0.72	2.0544	0.48675
0.21	1.2337	0.81058	0.47	1.6000	0.62500	0.73	2.0751	0.48191
0.22	1.2461	0.80252	0.48	1.6161	0.61878	0.74	2.0959	0.47711
0.23	1.2586	0.79432	0.49	1.6323	0.61263	0.75	2.1170	0.47237
0.24	1.2712	0.78663	0.50	1.6487	0.60653	0.76	2.1383	0.46767
0.25	1.2840	0.77880	0.51	1.6653	0.60050	0.77	2.1598	0.46301

Table A 11.3: Power of e (Continued)
The Powers of e for Different Positive and Negative Values (Continued)

x	e_x	e^{-x}	x	e_x	e^{-x}
0.78	2.1815	0.45841	0.98	2.6645	0.37531
0.79	2.2034	0.45384	0.99	2.6912	0.37158
0.80	2.2255	0.44933	1.00	2.7183	0.36788
0.81	2.2479	0.44486	1.20	3.3201	0.30119
0.82	2.2705	0.44043	1.30	3.6693	0.27253
0.83	2.2933	0.43605	1.40	4.0552	0.24660
0.84	2.3164	0.43171	1.50	4.4817	0.22313
0.85	2.3396	0.42741	1.60	4.9530	0.20190
0.86	2.3632	0.42316	1.70	5.4739	0.18268
0.87	2.3869	0.41895	1.80	6.0496	0.16530
0.88	2.4109	0.41478	1.90	6.6859	0.14957
0.89	2.4351	0.41066	2.00	7.3891	0.13534
0.90	2.4596	0.40657	3.00	20.086	0.04979
0.91	2.4843	0.40252	4.00	54.598	0.01832
0.92	2.5093	0.39852	5.00	148.41	0.00674
0.93	2.5345	0.39455	6.00	403.43	0.00248
0.94	2.5600	0.39063	7.00	1096.6	0.00091
0.95	2.5857	0.38674	8.00	2981.0	0.00034
0.96	2.6117	0.38298	9.00	8103.1	0.00012
0.97	2.6379	0.37908	10.00	22026.5	0.00005

Hedging Strategies with Options

Learning Objectives

After studying this chapter, you will be able to:

- Understand the basic fundamentals of hedging with options
- Learn, use and trade with the various hedge parameters (option Greeks) such as Delta, Gamma, Theta, Vega and Rho.

Chapter Outline

12.1 INTRODUCTION

The option price for European call non-dividend paying stock is estimated by the following formula derived from Black-Scholes Option Pricing Model:

$$C = SN(d_1) - Xe^{-rT} N(d_2)$$

Where,

$$d_1 = \frac{l_n(S/X) + (r + \sigma^2/2)T}{\sigma\sqrt{T}}, \text{ and}$$

$$d_2 = \frac{l_n(S/X) + (r - \sigma^2/2)T}{\sigma\sqrt{T}} = d_1 - \sigma\sqrt{T}$$

In the above formula, we have used five parameters (determinants or variables) namely current market price of the Stock (S), Strike Price (X), Volatility (σ), Time to expiration (T), and Risk-free rate of interest (r).

We may formulate functional relationship between option price and its determinants in the following expression:

$C = f\ (S, X, \sigma, T, r)$, and

$P = f\ (S, X, \sigma, T, r)$

Where,

C = Call Option Price

P = Put Option Price

S = Current Market Price of Stock

X = Strike Price

σ = Volatility

T = Time to expiry

r = Risk-free interest rate per annum

During the period of option contract, these variables are likely to change. When there is a change in one variable, the value of the option will react to change. In the previous chapter, we have discussed the direction (increase/decrease) of change in the option price due to increase in one variable assuming the other four variables remain as such. The result of such directional change in the option price is reproduced below:

Variable (Determinant)	Notation	Directional Change	
		Increase	Decrease
Current Stock Price	S	Increase	Decrease
Strike Price	X	Decrease	Increase
Time to Expiration	T	Increase	Increase
Volatility of Stock Price	σ	Increase	Increase
Risk-free interest rate	r	Increase	Decrease

The objective of trading with option derivative is to maximise profit or minimise risk of loss. In derivative market, the portfolio managers, individual investors, and corporations are very much inclined to forecast the following two aspects:

(i) The direction of change in the option price due to the influence of change in the value of one determinant.

(ii) The degree or magnitude of change in the option price due to the influence of change in the value of one determinant.

The direction and magnitude of change in the Option Price due to the influence of change in the values of determinants (except the Exercise Price) may be favourable (in-the-money) or unfavourable (out-of-the-money). When the option trader will likely to be out-of-the-money, then he will be at risk. To protect from such adverse situation, he must learn, practice, use and trade with certain risk management tools. There are various types of risks associated with options such as risk of stock price moving up and down, implied volatility moving up and down, the risk-free interest moving up and down or how much money is made or lost as time passes.

Through mathematical formulas, certain numbers are generated to estimate these risks. Collectively, these numbers are known as **"Greeks"**, because these numbers are represented by Greek letters like Δ (Delta), θ (Theta), γ (Gamma), ν (Vega) and ρ (Rho) etc. The Greeks describe how the option price changes when the parameters change. A brief concept on Option Greeks is depicted below:

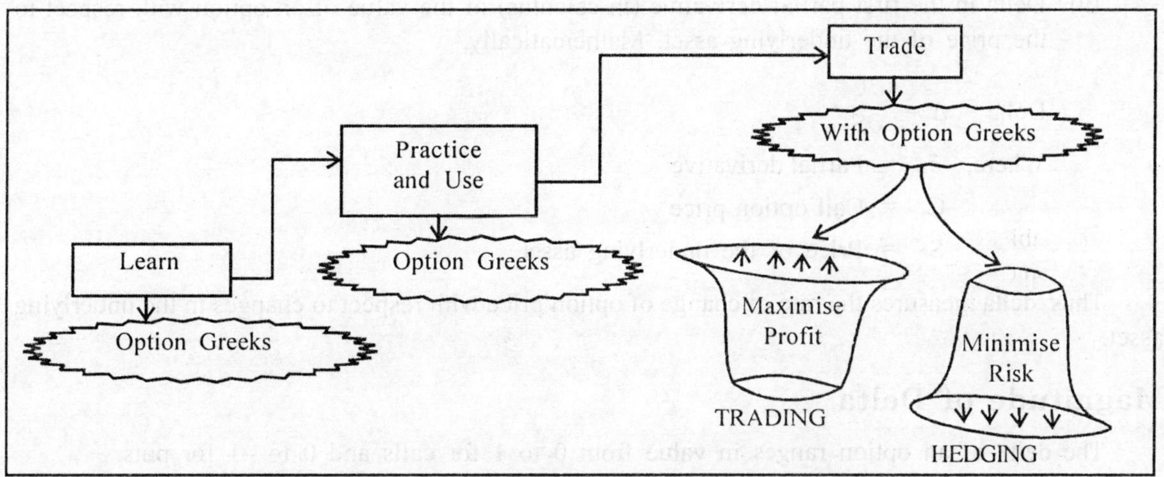

Fig. 12.1: Option Greek, Trading and Hedging

These Greek values are the partial derivatives. Delta, Theta, Vega and Rho are the first order derivatives while Gamma is the second order derivative.

Greeks can help the option traders to better understand the potential risk and reward of an option position. Each Greek measures the risk due to change in the value of one determinant in the following ways:

Delta (Δ): It measures the change in the option price due to change in stock price. It is the sensitivity of an option's theoretical value to a change in the price of the underlying stock.

Theta (θ): It measures the change in the option price due to time passing. Thus, theta is the sensitivity of an option's theoretical value to a change in the amount of time to expiration.

Gamma (γ): It measures the change in the option delta due to change in the stock price. Thus, Gamma is the sensitivity of an option's delta to a change in the price of the underlying asset.

Vega (ν): It measures the change in the option price due to change in the volatility. Thus, Vega is the sensitivity of an option's theoretical value to a change in volatility.

Rho (ρ): It measures the change in the option price due to the change in the interest rates. Thus, Rho is the sensitivity of an option's theoretical value to a change in the rate of interest.

In this Chapter, we will discuss the Greeks and their applications.

12.2 OPTION DELTA (Δ)

Meaning: Option delta is the sensitivity of an option's theoretical price to changes in the value of the underlying asset.

Formula:

(i) $$\text{Option Delta } (\Delta) = \frac{\text{Change in the Option Price}}{\text{Change in the Underlying Price}}$$

Thus, Change in the Option Price = Change in the Asset Price × Delta.

(ii) Delta in the first partial derivative (in calculus) of the value of an option with respect to the price of the underlying asset. Mathematically,

$$\text{Delta} = \Delta = \frac{\partial C}{\partial S}$$

Where, ∂ = Partial derivative

C = Call option price

S = Price of the underlying asset

Thus, delta measures the rate of change of option price with respect to changes in the underlying asset.

Magnitude of Delta

The delta of an option ranges in value from 0 to 1 for calls and 0 to –1 for puts.

Notes: Delta value is always positive for calls and negative for puts.

The delta of an option reflects the increase or decrease in the price of an option in response to 1 point movement (up or down) of the underlying asset price.

Example 1: 100 long calls has a value of ₹ 3 per call. The stock price is ₹ 52 per share with delta 0.45. Estimate the call option price if the stock price moves up to ₹ 53 or moves down to ₹ 51.

Solution:

Stock Price (S)	Call Delta (Δ)	Call Price (C)
52	0.45	3
53	0.45	3.45
51	0.45	2.55

Example 2: 100 long puts on a share has a value of ₹ 3 per put. The stock price is ₹ 52 per share with delta (–)0.45. Estimate the put option price if the stock price moves up to ₹ 53 or moves down to ₹ 51.

Solution:

Stock Price (S)	Put Delta (Δ)	Put Price (P)
52	–0.45	3
53	–0.45	3 – 0.45 = 2.55
51	–0.45	3 + 0.45 = 3.55

Example 3: The change in underlying's price is ₹ 20 and call delta is (+)0.24. Estimate the change in option price.

Solution: Change in Option Price = Change in Asset Price × Option Delta

= 20 × 0.24 = ₹ 4.80

Example 4: The decrease in the underlying assets price is ₹ 10 and put delta is –0.057. Estimate the increase in the put price.

Solution: Change in the Option Price = Change in the Underlying Asset × Option Delta

= 10 × 0.057 = 0.57 (increase)

12.2.1 Moneyness and Behaviour of Option Delta

An option trader should know the relationship between the value of option delta and moneyness of an option. In brief, relationship is summarised as follows:

Call Option		*Put Option*	
Value of Delta	Moneyness Position	Value of Delta	Moneyness Position
1	Deep in-the-money	–1	Deep in-the-money
0.5	At-the-money	–0.5	At-the-Money
Δ → 0 (Approaches to Zero)	Out-of-the-money	Δ → 0 (Approaches to Zero)	Out-of-the-money

It may be noted that calls and puts have opposite deltas, i.e., call option deltas are positive and put option deltas are negative.

The behaviour of both call and put option deltas are depicted in the following graphs:

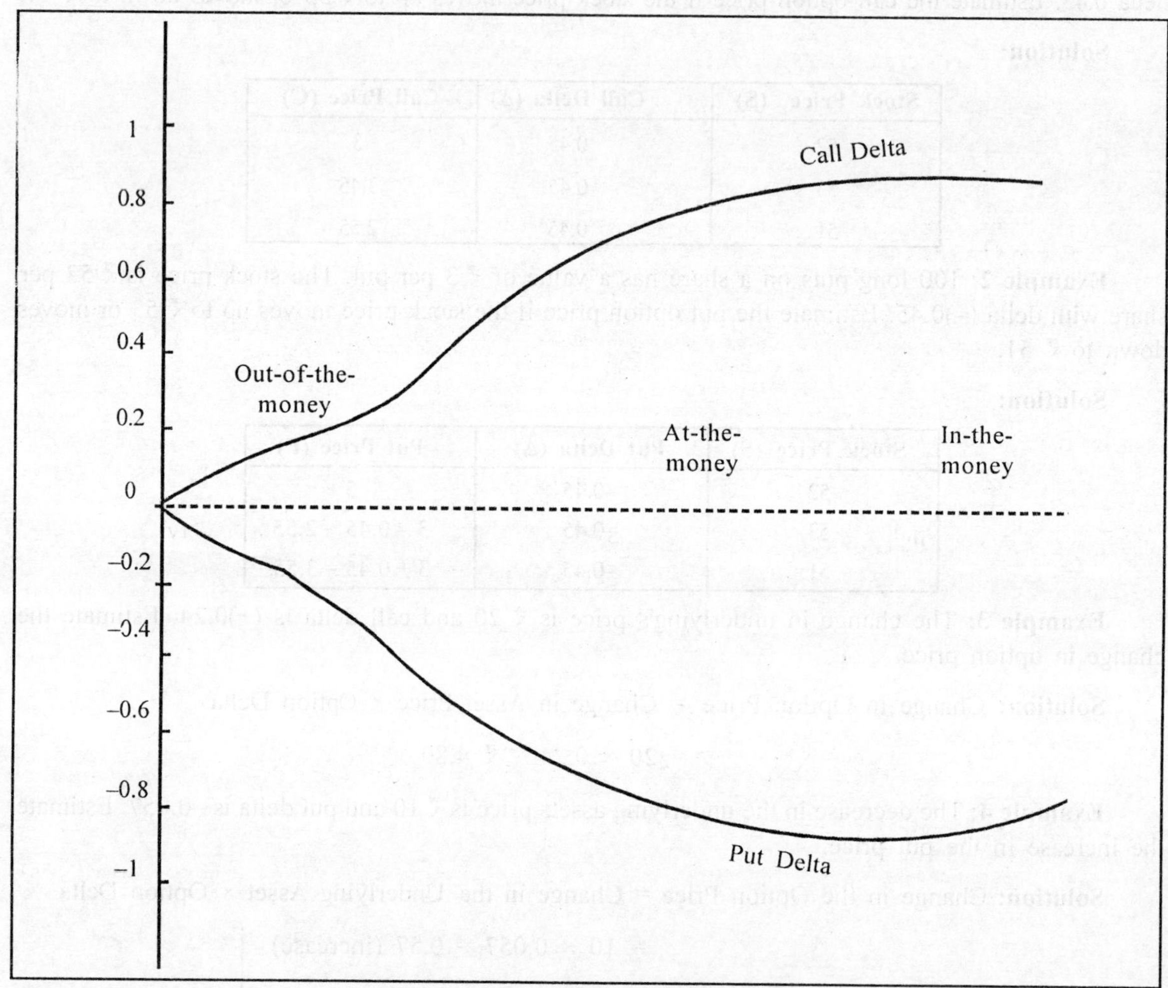

Fig. 12.2: Behaviour of Option Delta

From the above graph, we observe that as both option deltas shift from being out-of-the-money to at-the-money and finally in-the-money.

12.2.2 Stock Price and Option Delta – A Relationship

When the delta is 1, the call is deep in-the-money. This situation will happen when the stock price is very high. At this situation, the put is deep out-of-the-money and the put delta closes to zero.

When the call delta approaches to zero, the call is deep out-of-the money. This situation will happen when the stock price is very low. At this situation, the put is deep in-the-money and the put delta closes to –1.

When the call delta is around 0.5, the call is at-the-money. This situation happens when the stock price is close to strike price. At this situation, the put delta is around –0.5.

Graphic Representation:

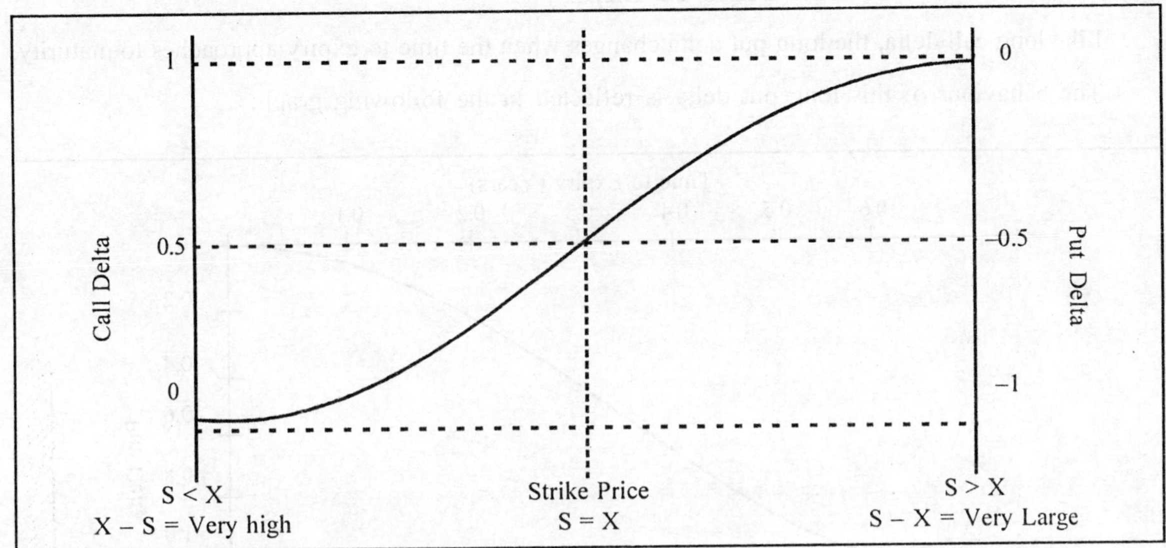

Fig. 12.3: Relationship between Stock Price and Option Delta

12.2.3 Time to Expiry, Option Delta and Moneyness

The delta of an option changes when the time to expiry approaches to maturity. The behaviour of both Long Call Delta and Put Call Delta are reflected in the following graphs:

(A) Long Call Delta and Time to Expiry

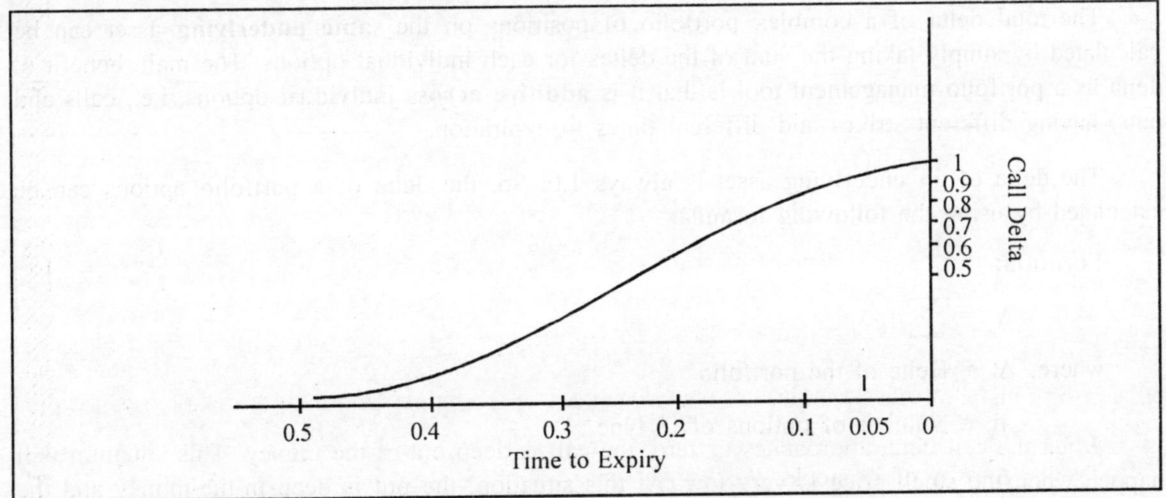

Fig. 12.4: Long Call Delta and Time to Expiry

Findings: As an option approaches expiry date, the call option delta will be very close to 1. In such situation, the call option will be in-the-money. Conversely, when the time to expiry is longer, the option delta approaches to zero. In such situation, the option will be out-of-the-money.

(B) Long Put Delta and Time to Expiry

Like long call delta, the long put delta changes when the time to expiry approaches to maturity.

The behaviour of this long put delta is reflected in the following graph:

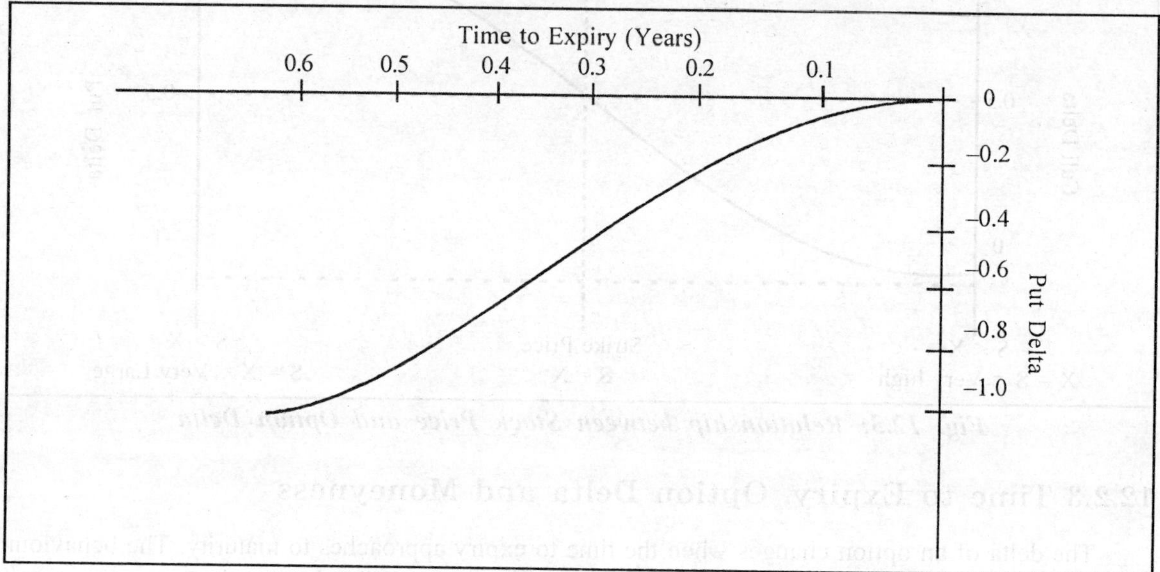

Fig. 12.5: Long Put Delta and Time to Expiry

12.2.4 Delta of a Portfolio Options

The total delta of a complex portfolio of positions on the **same underlying** asset can be calculated by simply taking the sum of the deltas for each individual options. The main benefit of delta as a portfolio management tool is that it is **additive across** individual options, i.e., calls and puts, having different strikes and different times to expiration.

The delta of an underlying asset is always 1.0. So, the delta of a portfolio options can be calculated by using the following formula:

Formula:

$$\Delta_p = \sum n_i \Delta_i$$

where, Δ_p = Delta of the portfolio

n_i = Number of options of ith type

Δ_i = Δ of ith stock.

Example 5: An option trader furnishes the following information of his portfolio relating to a particular type of underlying stock.

Current Stock Price	Strike Price	No. of Options	Option Type	Option Delta
100	118	30	Long Call	+ 0.2567
100	135	42	Long Put	– 0.0412
100	120	18	Short Put	+ 0.5656

Calculate portfolio delta and interpret the result.

Solution: The portfolio delta will be calculated as follows:

$$\Delta_p = (30 \times 0.2567) + (42 \times -0.0412) + (18 \times 0.5656)$$

$$= 7.701 - 1.7304 + 10.1808$$

$$= 16.1514$$

Interpretation:

In this case, the portfolio delta is 16.1514. It indicates that the portfolio of the option is equivalent to holding 16.1514 shares of the underlying stocks. In other words, if the portfolio price rises by ₹ 1, the option trader will get a profit of ₹ 16.1514 and *vice versa.*

12.3 OPTION GAMMA (γ)

Gamma (γ) is an Option Greek. It measures the rate of change in the delta with respect to changes in the underlying price. It is the second derivative of the options value with respect to the underlying price. Mathematically,

Gamma = Change in the Delta/Change in the price of the underlying

$$\text{or, } \gamma = \frac{\partial \Delta}{\partial S} = \frac{\partial^2 C}{\partial S^2}$$

Where, γ = Gamma, Δ = Option Delta, S = Stock Price, C = Call Option Price

Note: In case put option $\gamma = \frac{\partial \Delta}{\partial S} = \frac{\partial^2 P}{\partial S^2}$

Where, P = Put Option Price

Points to Note:

(i) Gamma shows the option delta's sensitivity to market price of the underlying asset changes.

(ii) If delta is the "speed" at which option prices change, gamma will be considered as the "acceleration", i.e., pace of change.

(iii) Gamma may be positive or negative. Positive gamma means delta increases with an increase in price and negative gamma means the opposite.

(iv) Long calls and Long puts have positive gamma while Short calls and Short puts have negative gamma.

12.3.1 Value of Gamma and Moneyness

Gamma is maximum at or near the exercise price, i.e., it is maximum when the option is at-the-money for both long calls and long puts.

Further, for a deep in-the-money option delta (Δ) approaches 1. We know the derivative of any constant is zero. Therefore, when delta approaches to 1 (for a long call), the gamma approaches to zero. Similarly, gamma for the out-of-the-money options will close to zero as delta is already zero.

Graphic Representation:

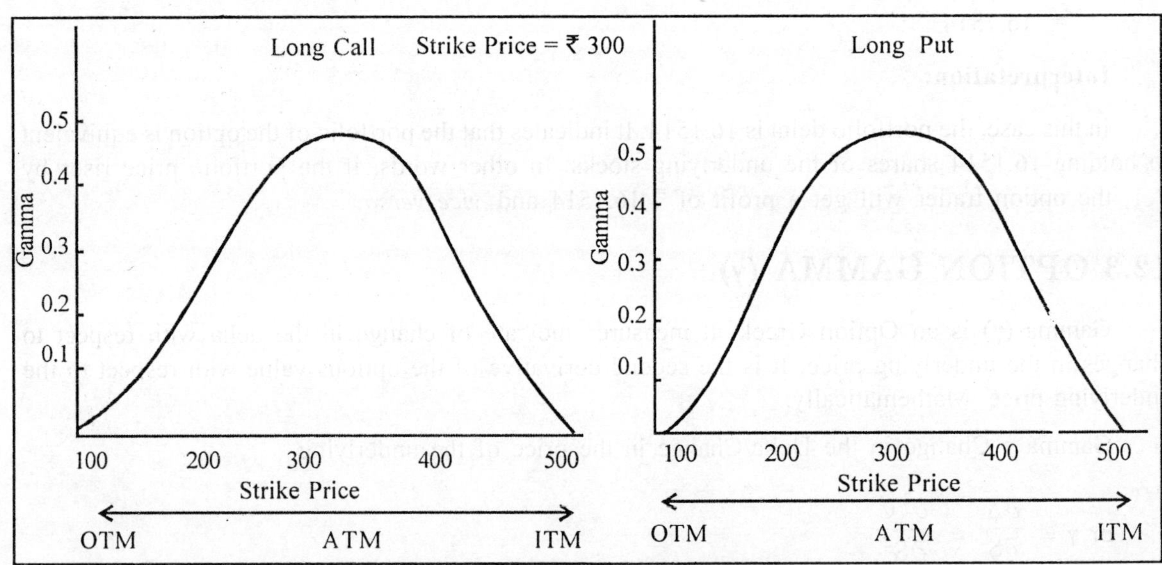

Fig. 12.6: Nature of Gamma

Remember

(i) Gamma = Change in delta/Change in underlying price
Or Change in Δ = γ × Change in underlying price

(ii)

Option Position	Delta	Gamma
Long Call Option	+ve	+ve
Long Put Option	–ve	+ve
Short Call Option	–ve	–ve
Long Call Option	+ve	–ve

12.3.2 Time to Expiration, Gamma and Moneyness

As the time to expiration goes nearer, the gamma of at-the-money options increases while gamma of in-the-money and out-of-the-money option decreases.

Example 6: Consider the three long call options:

	Option A	Option B	Option C
Strike Price	₹ 50	₹ 50	₹ 50
Time to Expiration	9 months	6 months	3 months

The following graph reflects the relationship between time to expiration and gamma.

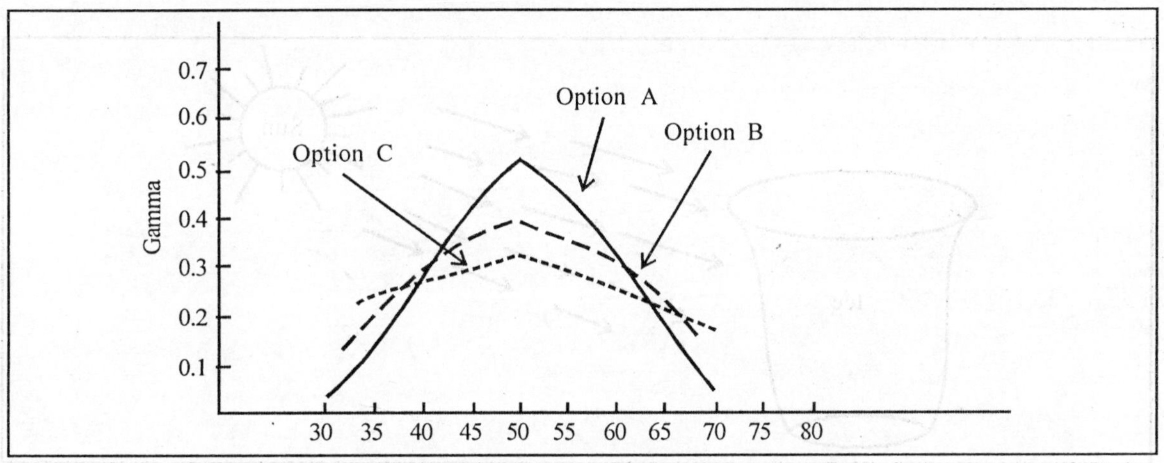

Fig. 12.7: Gamma and Time to Expiry

12.3.3 Changes in Volatility and Its Effect on Gamma

Volatility	Option Moneyness	Value of Gamma
Low	At-the-money	High
Low	In-the-money or out-of-the-money	Zero

When volatility is high, gamma tends to be stable across all strike prices.

12.3.4 Hedging Strategy with Gamma

An option trader may implement the following strategy:

(i) If the option trader is an option buyer, then high gamma is good as long as his forecast is correct.

(ii) If the option trader is an option seller, high gamma is also good as long as his forecast is correct. If forecast is wrong, then he will be out-of-the-money.

12.4 OPTION THETA (θ)

Option theta measures time decay. We know option value has two components, i.e., intrinsic value and time value (extrinsic value). The theta measures the rate at which options lose their value, specially the time value as the expiration date draws nearer. In other words, theta shows how much value the option price will lose for every day that passes.

An option contract has a finite life defined by the expiration date. As the option approaches its maturity date, an option contract's expected value becomes more certain with each day. This time value also called the extrinsic value represents the uncertainty of an option. In the option market, the time to expiration (the passage of time) is similar to the effect of the hot summer sun on a block of ice.

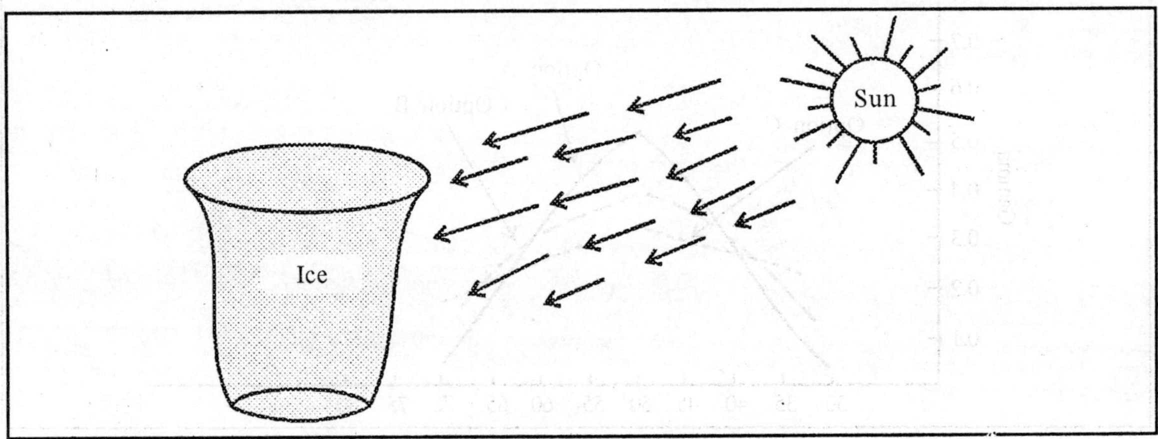

Fig. 12.8: The Nature of Option Theta

Each moment that passes will cause some of the option's time value to "melt away". It means that an option gets closer to expiration, extrinsic value diminishes and only intrinsic value tends to remain. At expiration, intrinsic value is the only value which is left in the option.

What is the Sign of θ?

Thetas are negative as they indicate a loss of value. This will be in case of long call or long put options. The sign of theta is just opposite to that of gamma as well as for the seller of the options.

Whether Theta will be Daily or Annually?

Generally, option valuation formulae give an annual theta number. To compute daily theta, the annual theta is to be divided by the number of days in the year, i.e., 365.

Example: The call option price is ₹ 8 and theta is –0.05 per day. Find out the option price after two days.

Answer: Daily Loss = Option Theta = 0.05

Option Price after two days = ₹ 8 – 2 × 0.05

= 8 – 0.10

= ₹ 7.90

Graphic Representation:

The relationship between the time value of an option and time decay can be better understood from the following graphs:

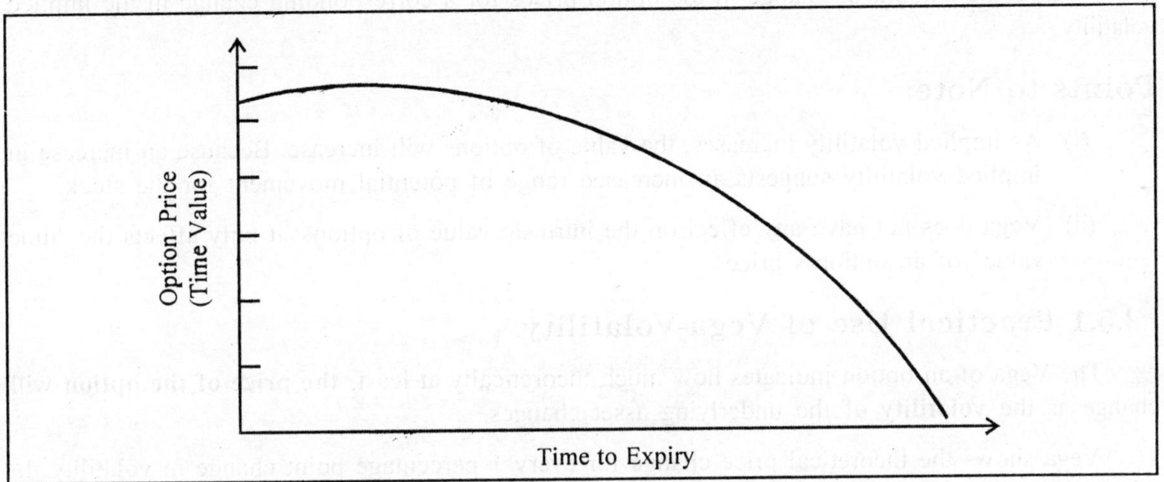

Fig. 12.9: Time Decay for the Option

Point to Note:

Theta is always non-linear. It means option prices do not decline at a constant rate, but accelerate closer to expiration.

12.4.1 Changes in Volatility and Its Effect on the Theta

In general, options of high volatility stocks have higher theta than low volatility stocks. This is because, the time value premium on these options are higher and so they have more to lose per day.

12.5 OPTION VEGA (ν)

Vega measures the sensitivity of the option price with respect to changes in the implied volatility.

It is the derivative of the options value with respect to the volatility of the underlying asset.

Mathematically,

(i) Vega (v) = $\frac{\partial C}{\partial \sigma}$ .... for call option

where C = Call Option Price

(ii) Vega (v) = $\frac{\partial P}{\partial \sigma}$ .... for put option

where, P = Put Option Price.

Vega is the amount of change in the option prices for a corresponding change in the implied volatility.

Points to Note:

(i) As implied volatility increases, the value of options will increase. Because an increase in implied volatility suggests an increased range of potential movement for the stock.

(ii) Vega does not have any effect on the intrinsic value of options; it only affects the "time value" of an option's price.

12.5.1 Practical Use of Vega-Volatility

The Vega of an option indicates how much theoretically at least, **the price of the option** will change as the **volatility** of the underlying asset changes.

Vega shows the theoretical price change for every 1 percentage point change in volatility. In other words, Vega is typically expressed as the amount of money per underlying share that the option's value will gain or lose as volatility rises or falls by 1%.

Example 7: The following particulars are available for an option contract.

Type of Option	: Long call
Current Stock Price	: ₹ 500
Strike Price	: ₹ 500
Vega	: 0.03

If implied volatility increases two point, find the changes in the theoretical price of an option.

Solution:

The value of an option will go up ₹ 0.03 if implied volatility increases one point. In this case, there is an increase of two point in the implied volatility. So, the corresponding increase in the theoretical price of the option is 0.03 × 2 = 0.06.

Example 8: Theoretical price of an option is ₹ 5 and Vega is 0.25. Volatility moves from 20% to 21%. Calculate the new theoretical option price.

Solution:

₹ 5 + 0.25 = ₹ 5.25

12.5.2 Vega and Moneyness

Vega is most sensitivity when the option is at-the-money. It tapers off either side when the market price of stock is above or below the strike price.

The following graph reflects the relationship between Vega sensitivity and moneyness for 3 different options having strike price of ₹ 90, ₹ 100 and ₹ 110 respectively:

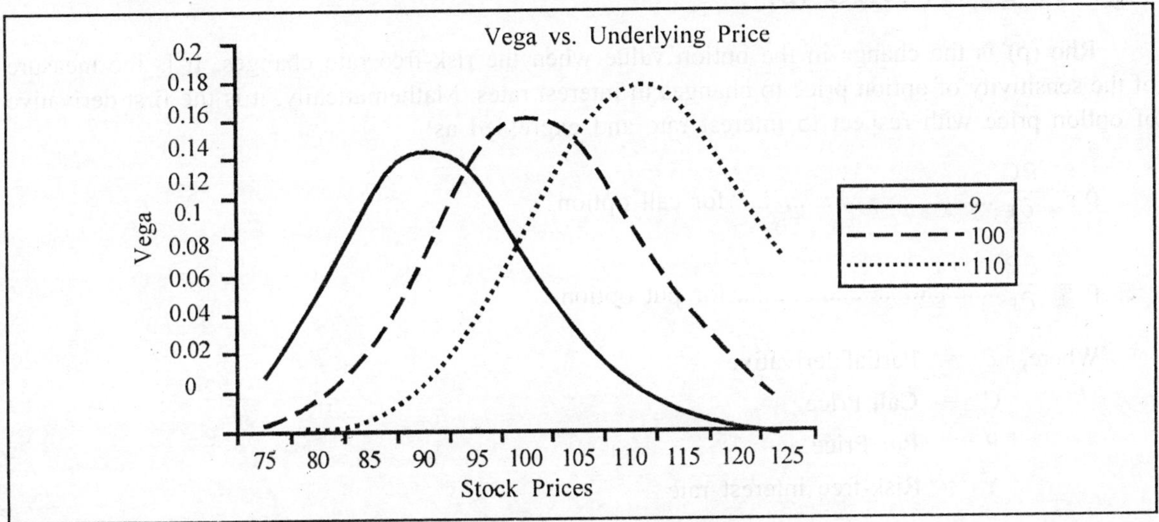

Fig. 12.10: Vega and Moneyness

Further if we draw the graphs of Call Vega and Put Vega, we notice the following shape and behaviour:

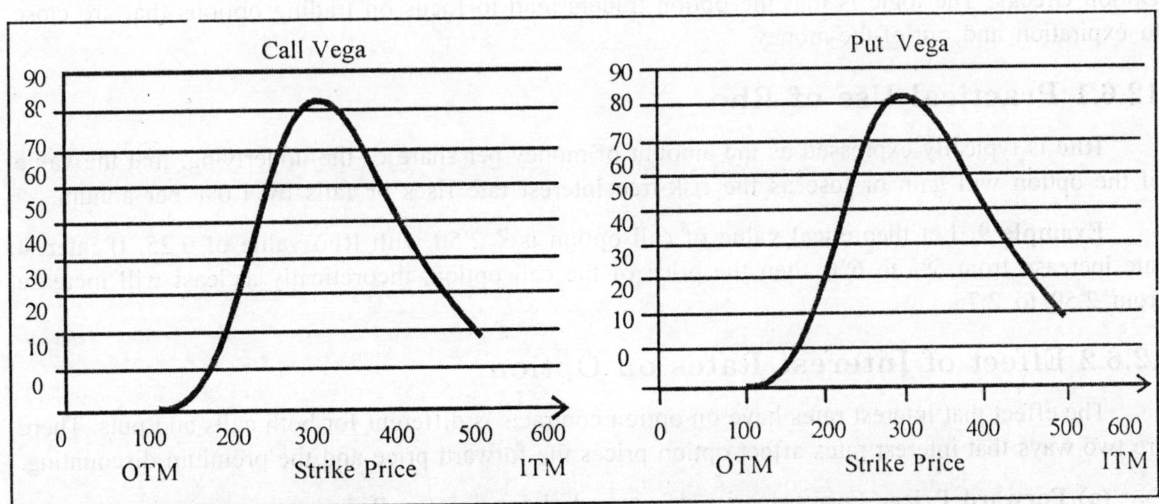

Fig. 12.11: Shape and Behaviour of Call Vega and Put Vega

Findings:

(i) Vega increases as the option moves from being in-the-money to at-the money where it reaches the peak and then decreases as the option moves out-of-the-money.

(ii) Like the Gamma, Vega is the same for Calls and Puts.

12.6 OPTION RHO (ρ)

Rho (ρ) is the change in the option value when the risk-free rate changes. It is the measure of the sensitivity of option price to changes in interest rates. Mathematically, it is the first derivative of option price with respect to interest rate and expressed as:

$$\rho = \frac{\partial C}{\partial r} \text{ .... for call option}$$

$$\rho = \frac{\partial P}{\partial r} \text{ .... for put option}$$

Where, ∂ = Partial derivative

C = Call Price

P = Put Price

r = Risk-free interest rate

The value of Rho is represented as the change in theoretical price of the option for a 1 percentage point movement in the underlying interest rate. Except under extreme circumstances, the value of an option is less sensitive to changes in the risk-free interest rate than to changes in other parameters. For this reason, Rho is the least used of the first order Greeks as well as least important of all the Option Greeks. The logic is that the option traders tend to focus on trading options that are close to expiration and out-of-the-money.

12.6.1 Practical Use of Rho

Rho is typically expressed as the amount of money per share of the underlying, that the value of the option will gain or lose as the risk-free interest rate rises or falls by 1.0% per annum.

Example 9: Let theoretical value of call option is ₹ 2.50 with Rho value of 0.25. If interest rate increase from 5% to 6%, then the price of the call option, theoretically at least will increase from 2.50 to 2.75.

12.6.2 Effect of Interest Rates on Option

The effect that interest rates have on option contracts is different for both calls and puts. There are two ways that interest rates affect option prices the forward price and the premium discounting.

(a) Forward Price: Forward price of an underlying asset = Price at the expiration date.

An option trader can never know what would be the forward price, keeping all other things being equal. But it must be worth at least the cost of holding the asset until the expiration data is to be taken into estimation. This value takes into account the cost of money, i.e., what it would cost in real terms to borrow and invest in the asset until the expiration data. This value, also referred to as the **"cost-of-carry"**, uses the current interest rate to determine how much additional capital a trader needs to hold the asset unit the expiration date. The effect of change in the interest rates on option price is outlined below:

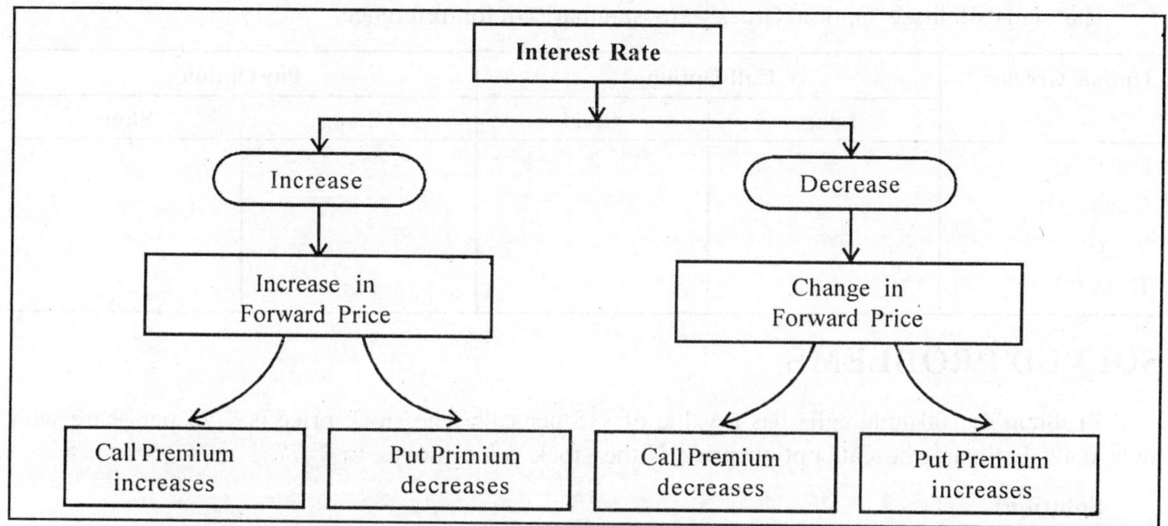

Fig. 12.12: Interest Rate and its Effect on Option Value

From the above, it is very clear that when there is an increase in interest rate, the forward price of the asset increases. But the effect on option price differs for calls and puts. For call options, the premium of the option increases as the forward price increases, but for put options the premium of the put decreases. Conversely, as interest rates decrease, the value of call option will decrease and the value of put option will increase.

(b) Premium Discounting: The second way that interest rates effect the pricing of option contracts is the discounting of the premium. The price of an option contract is a future value. To calculate the present value of an option, we have to do discounting by using a discount factor.

CHAPTER SUMMARY

Price of a call option or put option on non-dividend paying asset is a function of five variables namely current market price of stock (S), strike price (X), volatility (σ), time to expiry (T) and risk-free interest rate (r). If there is any change in any variable or determinant during the option contract, its effect will be on option price. In case the effect is negative, then the option trader will be at risk. Through mathematical formulae, certain numbers are generated to estimate these risks. Collectively, these numbers are known as "Greeks". In this chapter, we have discussed five Greeks namely Delta (Δ), Gamma (γ), Theta (θ), Vega (ν) and Rho (ρ). Delta is the sensitivity of the option price to changes in the price of the underlying. Gamma shows the change in option's delta for a unit of change in the price of the underlying asset. Option theta measures the rate of time decay.

It shows the change in option's price due to elapsing of time if other parameters remain as such. For long call and long put, theta is negative while for short call and short put it is positive. Vega measures the sensitivity of the option price with respect to changes in the implied volatility. Vega affects only the time value of an option's price. Rho (ρ) is the measure of the sensitivity of option's price to changes in interest rates.

The signs of these Option Greeks are summarised for reference.

Option Greeks	Call Option		Put Option	
	Long	Short	Long	Short
Delta (Δ)	+	–	–	+
Gamma (γ)	+	–	+	–
Vega (ν)	+	–	+	–
Theta (θ)	–	+	–	+

SOLVED PROBLEMS

Problem 1: 100 long calls has a value of ₹ 5 per call. The stock price is ₹ 75 per share with delta 0.42. Estimate the call option price if the stock price moves to ₹ 77.

Solution:

Stock Price	Call Delta	Call Value
₹ 75	0.42	₹ 5
₹ 77	0.42	5 + 2 × 0.42 = 5.84

If the stock price increases to 77, then the call option price would be 5.84.

Problem 2: 100 long puts on a share has a value of ₹ 4 per put. The current stock price is ₹ 160 per share with delta of –0.65. Estimate the put price decreases to ₹ 157.

Solution:

Stock Price	Put Delta	Call Value
160	–0.65	4
157	–0.65	4 + 0.65 × 3 = 5.95

If the stock price decreases by 3 rupees, then the put option value will be increased to ₹ 5.95.

Problem 3: The change in the underlying's price is ₹ 10 and call delta in 0.05. Find out the new option price if the original option price is ₹ 6.

Solution: Original Option Price = ₹ 6

New Option Price = ₹ 6 + 10 × 0.05

= 6 + 0.50 = ₹ 6.50

Problem 4: Estimate the new put price from the following data

Decrease in the asset's price = ₹ 8

Put option delta = 0.05

Put price before change = ₹ 5

Solution:

Change in the option price = Change in the underlying asset × Put delta

= 8 × 0.05 = 0.40

The new option price = 5 + 0.40

= ₹ 5.40

Problem 5: An option trader furnishing the following information of his portfolio relating to a particular type of underlying stock.

Current Stock Price	Strike Price	No. of Options	Option Type	Option Delta
150	170	20	Long Call	0.27
150	140	15	Long Call	–0.09
150	160	10	Short Put	0.41

Estimate Portfolio delta.

Solution: The portfolio delta will be calculated as follows:

$\Delta P = 20 \times 0.27 + (15 \times -0.09) + (10 \times 0.41)$

$= 5.4 - 1.35 + 4.1 = 8.15$

Problem 6: The call option price is ₹ 10 and theta is – 0.04 per day. Find out the option price after 3 days.

Solution: Daily Loss = Option Delta = 0.04

So, option price after 3 days = ₹ 10 – 0.04 × 3 = 10 – 0.12 = ₹ 9.88

SUGGESTIONS FOR FURTHER READINGS

1. Lars Tyge, Nielsen, *Pricing and Hedging of Derivative Securities*, Oxford University Press, 1997.
2. Brain, Eales A., *Financial Risk Management*, McGraw-Hill, Maiden Head, 1995.

EXERCISES

Quiz

1. State Whether the Following Statements are True of False.

(a) Delta is a measure of the change in option price for a small change in the spot price of the underlying stock.

(b) The delta of a call option is positive while it is negative for a put option.

(c) If delta is 0.5, then the call option is at-the-money.

(d) Gamma is positive for all long options and negative for all short option positions.

(e) Theta measures the amount of value that is lost from an option due to the passage of time.

(f) The value of theta is negative for long call and long put option.

(g) Vega measures the sensitivity of the option price with respect to changes in the implied volatility.

Ans: (a) True, (b) True, (c) True, (d) True, (e) True, (f) True, (g) True.

2. Fill In the Blanks by Using the Words/Phrases Given in the Brackets.

(a) _____ measures an option's price sensitivity with respect to a unit change in the implied volatility.
(Delta / Gamma / Vega)

(b) Rho is a measure of the sensitivity of option prices to changes in _____.
(Stock Price / Time to expiration / Interest rate)

(c) _____ measures the rate of time decay of an option.
(Volatility / Vega / Theta)

(d) Delta measures the impact of a change in the price of _____.
(Option / Futures / Underlying)

(e) _____ measures the impact of a change in time remaining of an option.
(Delta / Vega / Theta)

(f) Gamma measures the rate of change of _____.
(Vega / Rho / Delta)

(g) Vega measures the impact of a change in _____.
(Underlying Price / Time decay / Volatility)

(h) When volatility is ______, option premiums are relatively expensive.
(Low / Moderate / High)

(i) If an option trader is an option buyer, then _____ gamma is good as long as his forecast is correct.
(Low / Medium / High)

(j) The sign of theta (θ) is just opposite to that of _____.
(Delta / Vega / Gamma)

Ans: (a) Vega, (b) Interest Rate, (d) Underlying, (e) Theta, (f) Delta, (g) Volatility, (h) High, (j) Gammo.

A. Short Type Questions

1. Give a functional definition of call option price.
2. What do you mean by "Option Greeks"?
3. How to calculate option delta?
4. What is Option Gamma?
5. What do you mean by Option Vega?
6. How to calculate option theta?
7. What is Option Rho?
8. What is the range value of an option delta?
9. Why put options have negative deltas?
10. How to calculate portfolio delta?

B. Long Type Questions

1. What are the Greeks of the Black-Scholes model? Discuss.
2. "Hedging strategies with options are based on risk management tools or Greeks." Discuss.
3. "Greeks can help the option traders to better understand the potential risk and reward of an option position". Explain.
4. Explain the following Greeks:
   (a) Delta
   (b) Gamma
   (c) Theta
   (d) Vega
   (e) Rho

PRACTICAL PROBLEMS

1. The spot price of the underlying asset of a call option is ₹ 120. The price of the call is ₹ 5 with delta 0.62. Estimate the call option price if the stock price rises to ₹ 124.

   (*Ans:* ₹ 7.48)

2. The spot price of the underlying stock of a put option is ₹ 120. The theoretical price of the put is ₹ 5 with delta of –0.62. If the stock price falls to ₹ 116, estimate the put option price.

   (*Ans:* ₹ 7.48)

3. The change in the underlying price is (+) ₹ 4 and call delta is 0.05. Estimate the new option price if the initial option price is ₹ 5.

   (*Ans:* ₹ 5.20)

4. The change in the underlying price is (–) ₹ 10 and put delta is –0.02. Estimate the new option price if the initial put price is ₹ 5.

   (*Ans:* ₹ 5.20)

Options Trading Strategies

Learning Objectives

After studying this chapter, you will be able to:

- Understand the basics and principles option trading
- Know about various trading strategies involving options
- Know about the components, characteristics and risk/reward of various strategies for options trading

Chapter Outline

13.1 Introduction

13.2 Option Trading Strategies

13.3 Bullish Options Strategies

- 13.3.1 Long Call
- 13.3.2 Short Put
- 13.3.3 Call Bull Spread
- 13.3.4 Put Bull Spread
- 13.3.5 Long Synthetic
- 13.3.6 Call Back Spread
- 13.3.7 Covered Call
- 13.3.8 Protective Put

13.4 Bearish Options Strategies

- 13.4.1 Short Call (Writing Naked Calls)
- 13.4.2 Long Put (Buying Put Option)
- 13.4.3 Call Bear Spread
- 13.4.4 Put Bear Spread
- 13.4.5 Short Synthetic
- 13.4.6 Put Back Spread

13.1 INTRODUCTION

Option trading means buying and selling options. A trader will go for buying a call option when he expects that the price of the underlying is likely to increase. Similarly, a trader will go for buying a put option when he expects that the price of the underlying is likely to fall. Further, a trader may be the option buyer (holder of the option) or option seller (writer of an option).

An option contract is formed when both the parties (option holder and option writer) agree on a price, i.e., option premium for the option available for trading. The option holder (the buyer) pays the premium to the option writer (the option seller). This premium is the consideration for the option right. Once the premium is paid, the buyer becomes the owner of the option. He can retain this right (ownership) till the expiration of the option contract. *A majority of stock options are American style and they can be exercised anytime between the day they are purchased and the date of official expiration.*

The principle of option trading is to maximise pay-off or minimise the potential risk. The call option holder exercises his option when the current market price of the underlying asset is higher than the sum of the exercise price and option premium. Similarly, the put option holder exercises his option when the current market price is less than the sum of the exercise price and option premium. Thus, the principles of option trading are stated below:

(i) For call option holder: $S > (X + C)$

(ii) For put option holder: $S < (X + P)$

Where S = Current Stock Price; X = Strike Price

C = Call Option Premium; P = Put Option Premium

The option trading is a zero-sum game. The profit of the option holder is equal to the loss of the option writer when the option is exercised. But in case the option is not exercised, the loss of the option holder is equal to the profit of the option writer. In this chapter, we will discuss various types of option trading strategies.

13.2 OPTION TRADING STRATEGIES

Option trading strategies are about the way a trader constructs an option position, or combination of positions. The prime objective of constructing an option position is to maximise profit or minimise risk. There are four factors for developing an option trading strategy. These are as follows:

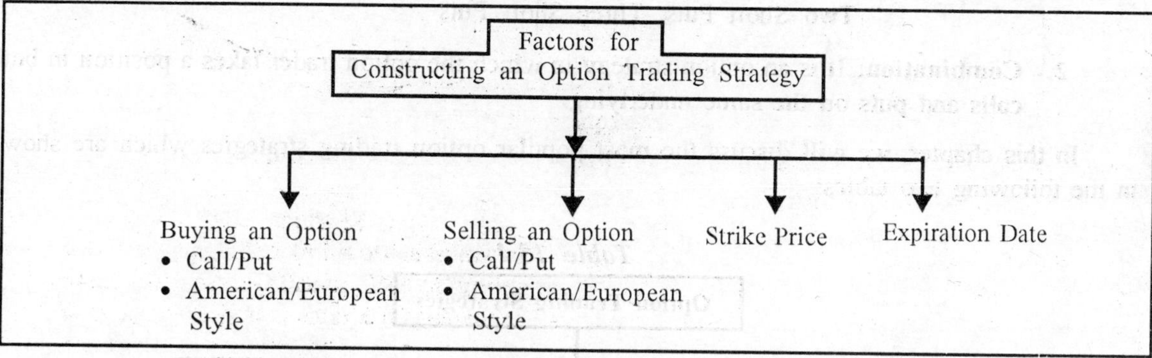

An investor (trader) can construct a combination of long and short positions with different strikes prices and either the same or different expiry dates. These extra dimensions of 'strikes prices', the option expiration date, together with the ability to sell (or write) option contracts as well as buy them, are very criteria that creates an opportunity for designing a number of option trading strategies.

Basically, there are two broad categories of option trading strategies namely, Directional Strategies and Non-directional Strategies. The Directional Strategies are 'Bullish' Strategies and Bearish Strategies. Further, Non-directional or Neutral Strategies are Bullish on Volatility Strategies and Bearish on volatility strategies. The Financial wizards have introduced a number of option trading strategies by giving a suitable name to each for worldwide acceptance.

Broadly, all the option trading strategies are classified into the following categories:

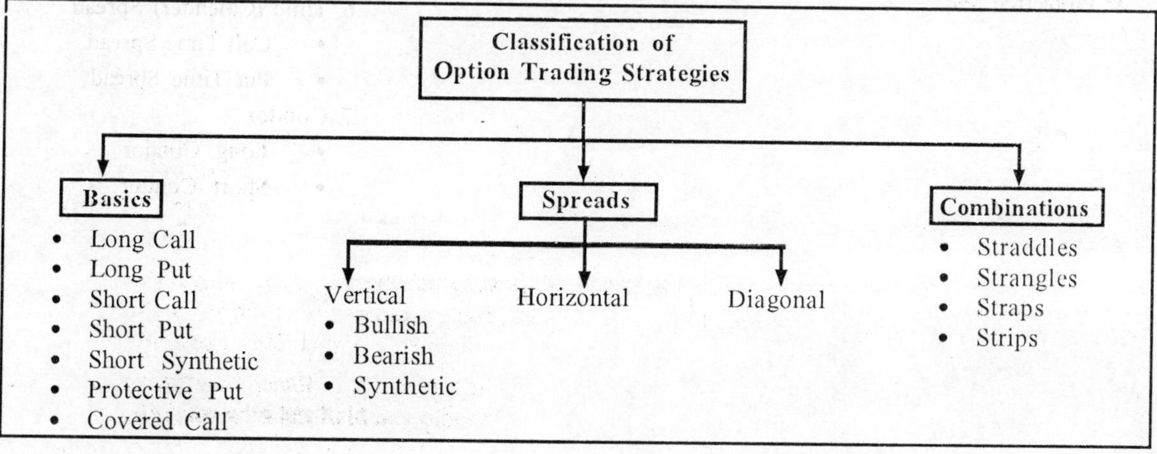

Few Concepts

1. **Spread:** It is an option trading strategy in which the trader takes a position in two or more options of the same type.

   Examples: Two Long Calls, There Long Calls

   Two Short Puts, Three Short Puts

2. **Combination:** It is an option strategy in which the option trader takes a position in both calls and puts on the same underlying.

In this chapter, we will discuss the most popular option trading strategies which are shown in the following two tables:

Table 13.1

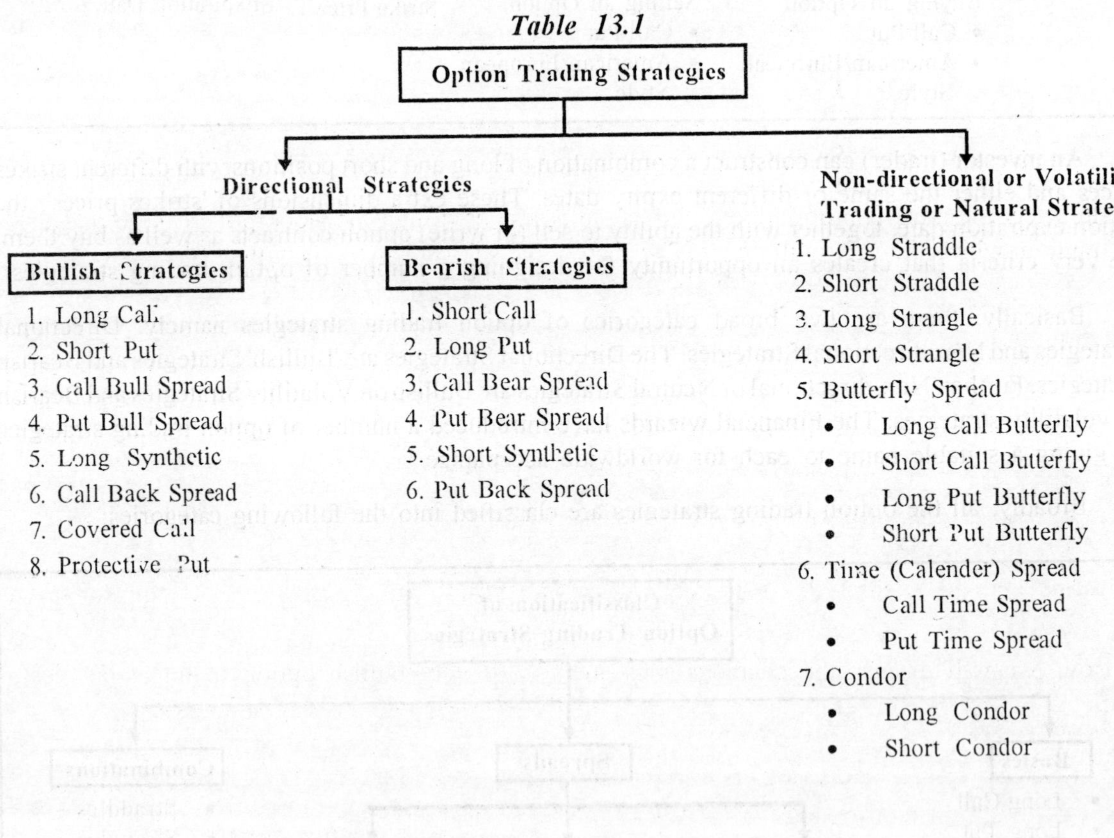

Table 13.2

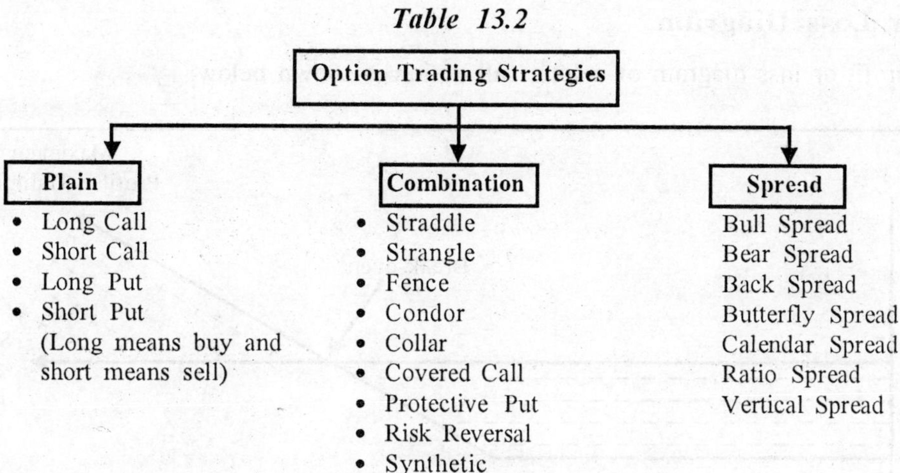

13.3 BULLISH OPTION STRATEGIES

When the option trader expects that the price of the underlying stock will likely to move upwards, then he will implement bullish strategy in option trading. There are series of bullish strategies. In order to select the most appropriate one, he has to assess how high the stock price can go and the time frame in which the rally will occur. There are three sub-categories of bullish strategies. These are as follows:

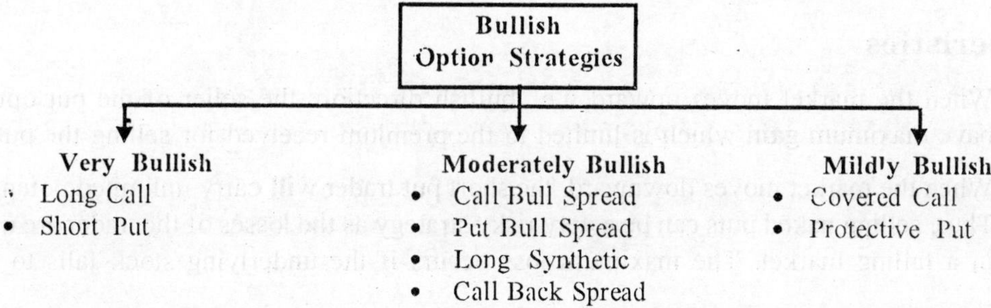

Now, we will discuss the characteristics and use of very bullish option trading strategies, moderately bullish option trading strategies and mildly bullish option trading strategies.

13.3.1 Long Call: Buying a Call Option

The most bullish of options trading strategies is the simple call buying strategy.

Characteristics

(i) When the market moves upward, i.e., bullish trend, the buyer of a call option will exercise his option. Because a long call has unlimited profit potential on the upside.

(ii) When the market moves downward and the stock price is below the strike price, then the call holder will not exercise his option. In such situation, the maximum loss is limited to the premium paid upfront for the option.

Profit or Loss Diagram

The profit or loss diagram of a long call option is shown below:

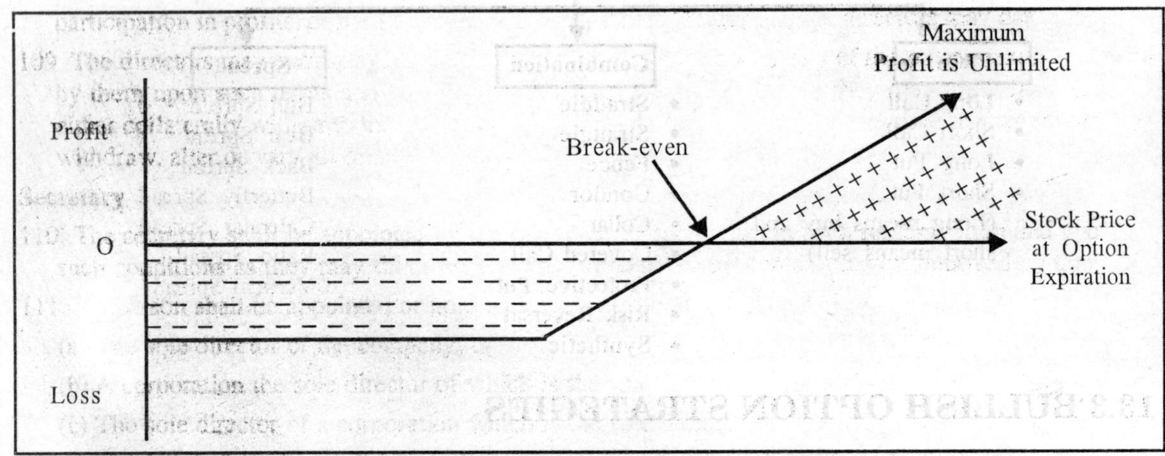

Fig. 13.1: Profit or Loss of a Long Call Option

13.3.2 Short Put: Selling a Put Option

In case of a put option, the holder (buyer) has the right to sell, while the put writer (seller) has the obligation to buy if the option is exercised.

Characteristics

(i) When the market moves upward, i.e., bullish direction, the seller of the put option will have maximum gain which is limited to the premium received for selling the put option.

(ii) When the market moves downward, the short put trader will carry unlimited potential loss. Thus, selling naked puts can be a very risky strategy as the losses of the trader are unlimited in a falling market. The maximum loss occurs if the underlying stock falls to zero.

The profit and loss diagram of a short put is shown below:

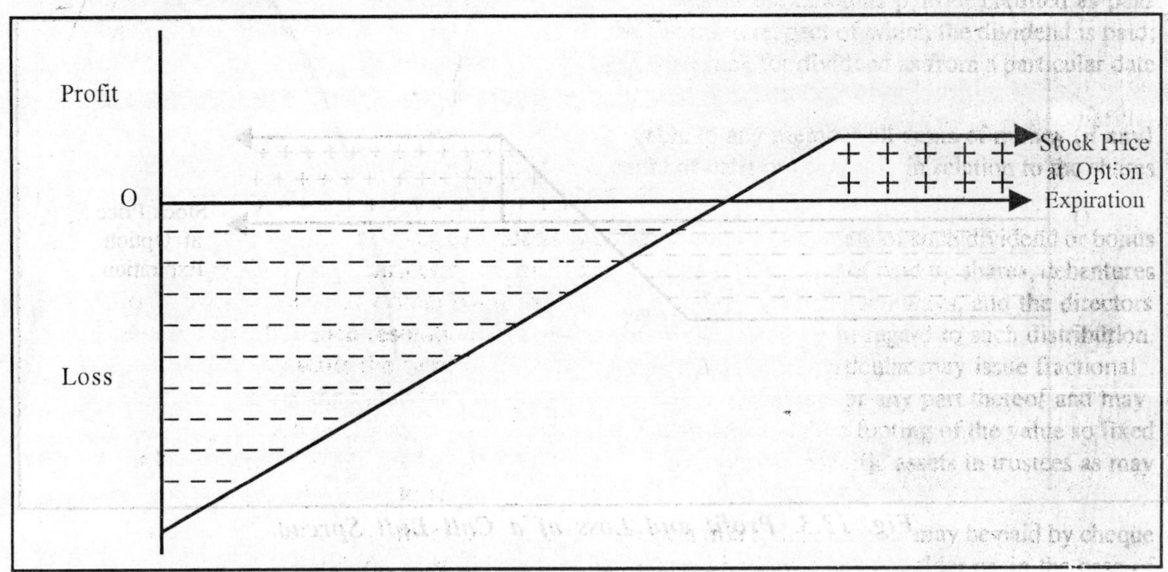

Fig. 13.2: Profit and Loss Diagram of a Short Put Option

13.3.3 Call Bull Spread

A spread is an option trading strategy whereby the option trader will take the position of long and short options simultaneously.

In case of a Call Bull Spread, the option trader will have one long call option with a low strike price and one short call option with a higher strike price.

Option Trading Strategy to Use

When market price and/or volatility is/are mildly bullish, Call Bull Spread is used. Higher the difference between these strike prices higher would be the pay-off maximum profit is limited to the difference between the two strike prices minus the net premium paid for the spread. However, maximum loss is limited to the premium paid for the long call minus the premium received for the short call option.

The following diagram shows the profit or loss position of a Call Bull Spread.

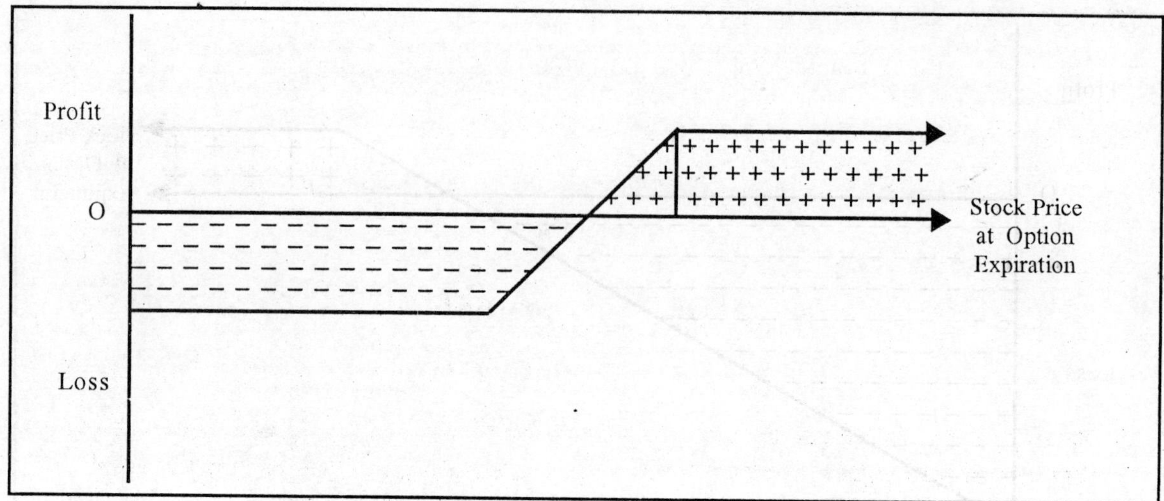

Fig. 13.3. Profit and Loss of a Call Bull Spread

13.3.4 Put Bull Spread

In case of a Put Bull Spread, the option trader will have one long put option with a lower strike price and another short put option with a higher strike price.

Option Trading Strategy to Use

When the market price and/or volatility is/are mildly bullish, this strategy is used. In this case, the profit/risk profile is more favourable in comparison with Call Bull Spread. The maximum profit of Put Bull Spread is limited to the net premium i.e., the premium received for the short put option minus the premium paid for the long put option. However, the maximum loss is limited to the difference between the two strike prices minus the net premium received for the position.

The following diagram shows the Profit or Loss status of a Put Bull spread.

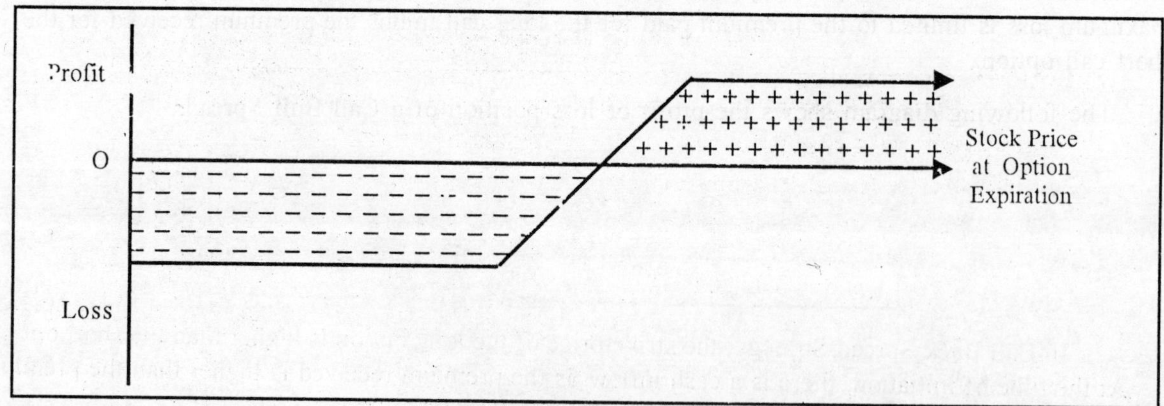

Fig. 13.4: Profit or Loss of a Put Bull Spread

13.3.5 Long Synthetic

In case of a Long Synthetic, a trader buys one call option and sells one put option at the same strike price when the market direction is bullish. The maximum loss is unlimited as well as the maximum profit is also unlimited.

The following diagram shows the profit or loss position of Long Synthetic option trading strategy.

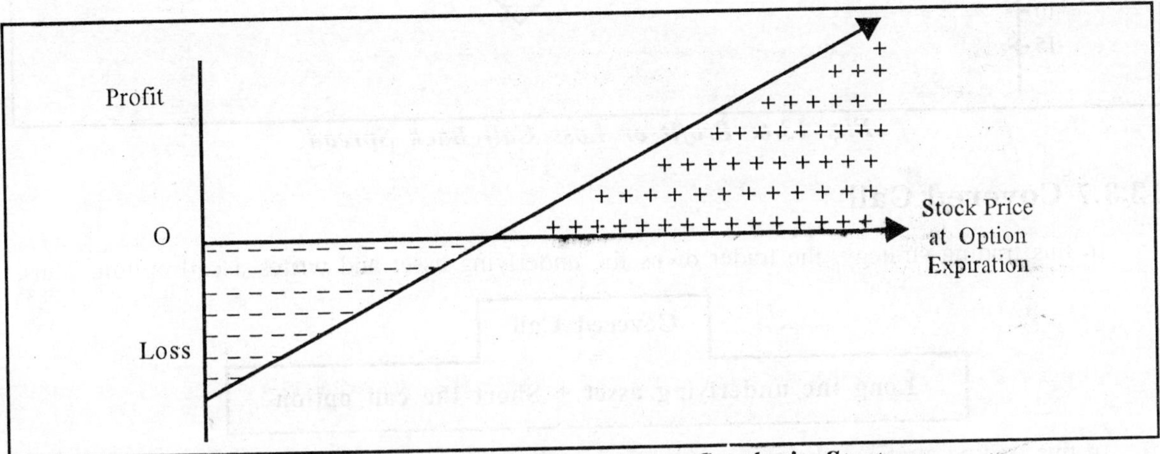

Fig. 13.5: Profit or Loss of Long Synthetic Strategy

13.3.6 Call Back Spread

A Back Spread is formed when the number of Long Options is more than the number of Short Options.

Let n_1 = No. of options purchased

n_2 = No. of options sold.

If $n_1 > n_2$, then it is a case of Back Spread. If $n_2 > n_1$, then it is called Ratio Spread.

Example of a Call Back Spread

	Buy	Sell
Number of Call	2	1
Strike Price	135	120
Option Premium	(–) 5.00	10

In Call Back Spread Strategy, the strike price of the long option is higher than the short option. At the time of initiation, there is a cash inflow as the premium received is higher than the premium paid. Thus, a Call Back Spread is always a "Credit Spread".

The trader expects the stock price will make a large jump so that his profit will be maximised. The following diagram shows the profit or loss status of a Call Back Spread Strategy:

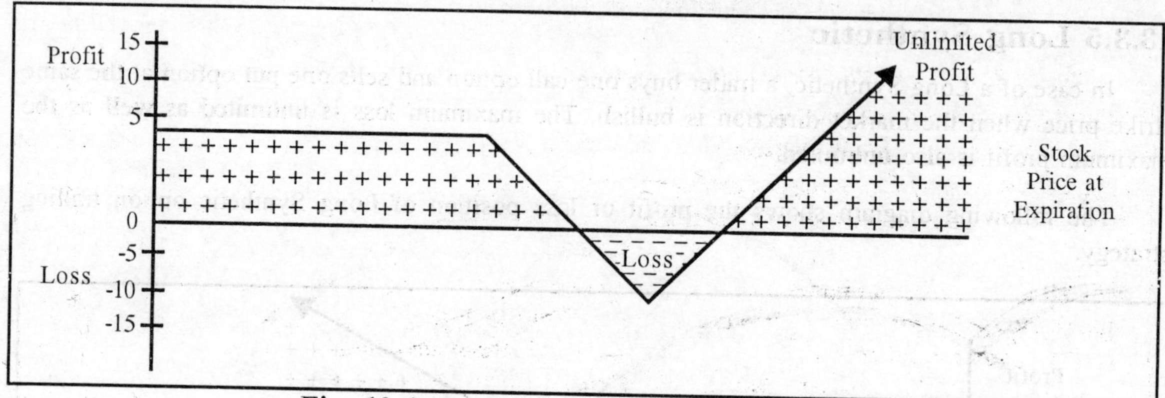

Fig. 13.6: Profit or Loss Call Back Spread

13.3.7 Covered Call

In this trading strategy, the trader owns the underlying asset and writes a call option. Thus,

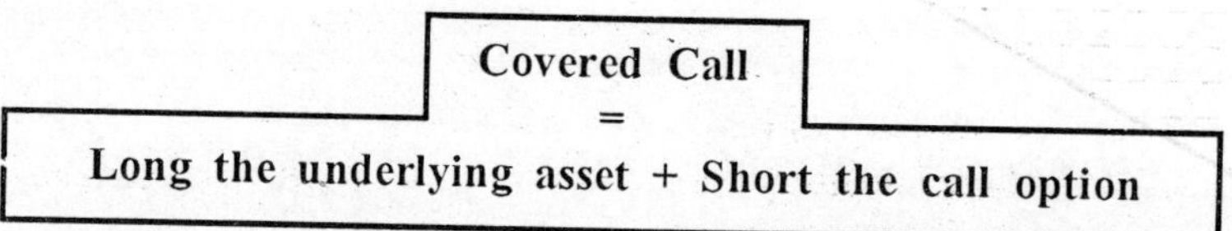

Covered Call
=
Long the underlying asset + Short the call option

In this trading strategy, the maximum loss is unlimited on the downside while the maximum profit is limited to the premium received from the sold call option.

Profit or Loss Diagram

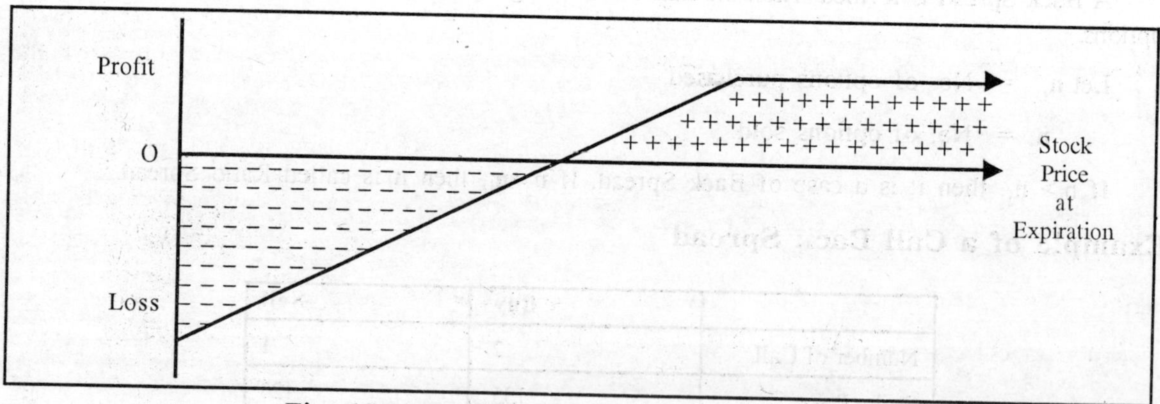

Fig. 13.7: Profit and Loss of a Covered Call

This covered call strategy is used by many traders who hold stock over a long period of time and the stock options strike price may be very high from the purchase price of stock.

Example

Underlying stock purchased @ ₹ 125 per share in January 2011. Current market price is ₹ 175 per share. Strike Price is ₹ 210 per share. Call option premium received ₹ 10 per share. If the option is exercised, then there is a profit of ₹ 85 per share. If the option is not exercised, the call writer will have the profit equal to the premium received.

13.3.8 Protective Put

In this strategy, the trader owns the underlying asset and buys a put option. Thus,

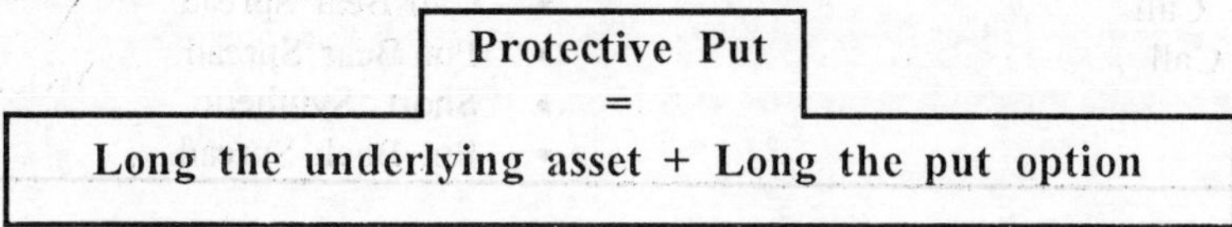

In this strategy, the maximum loss is limited to the premium paid for the put option. But the profit potential is unlimited as the market rallies.

The following diagram shows the profit or loss status of a protective put strategy of an option trading:

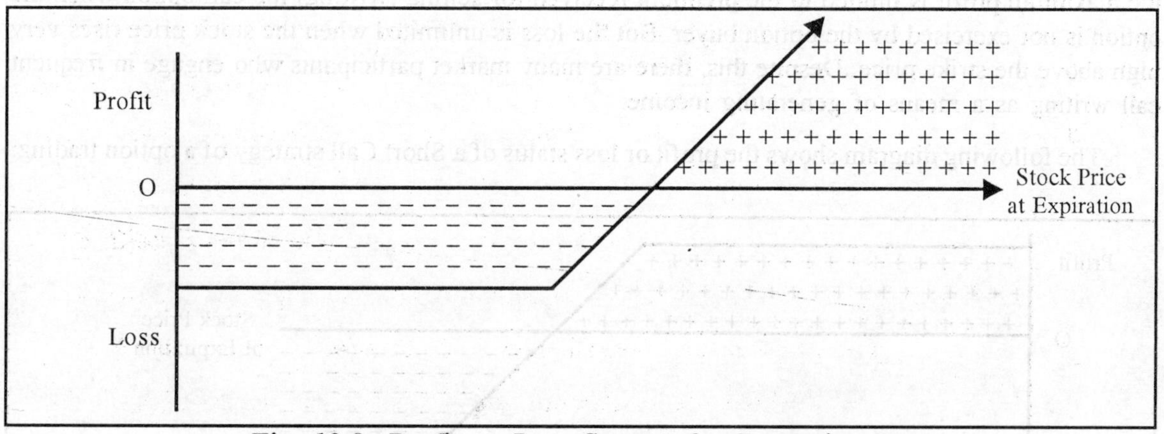

Fig. 13.8: Profit or Loss Status of a Protective Put

Remember: In case of protective put strategy, the losses of the put option and profits from the stock do not offset each other.

13.4 BEARISH OPTION STRATEGIES

When the option treader expects that the price of the underlying stock will likely to move downwards, he decides to employ Bearish Option Strategies. There are series of bearish strategies. In order to select most appropriate in a particular bearish situation, he has to assess how low the stock price can go and the time frame in which the decline will happen. There are three sub-categories of bearish strategies as follows:

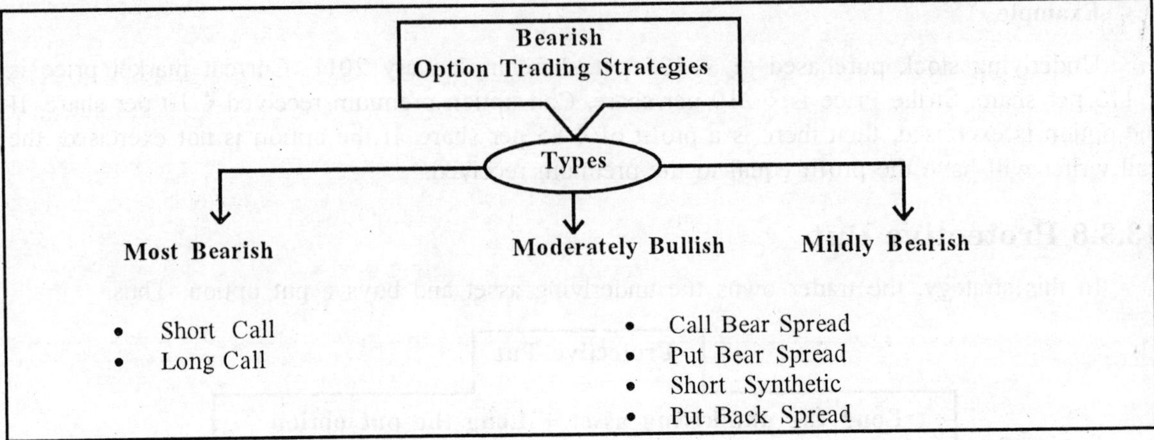

Now, we will discuss the characteristics and use of these above stated bearish option trading strategies.

13.4.1 Short Call (Writing Naked Calls)

A short call option trading strategy means simply selling or writing a call option. In this strategy, the maximum profit is limited to the premium received for selling (writing) the call option when the option is not exercised by the option buyer. But the loss is unlimited when the stock price rises very high above the strike price. Despite this, there are many market participants who engage in frequent call writing as a means of generating income.

The following diagram shows the profit or loss status of a Short Call strategy of a option trading:

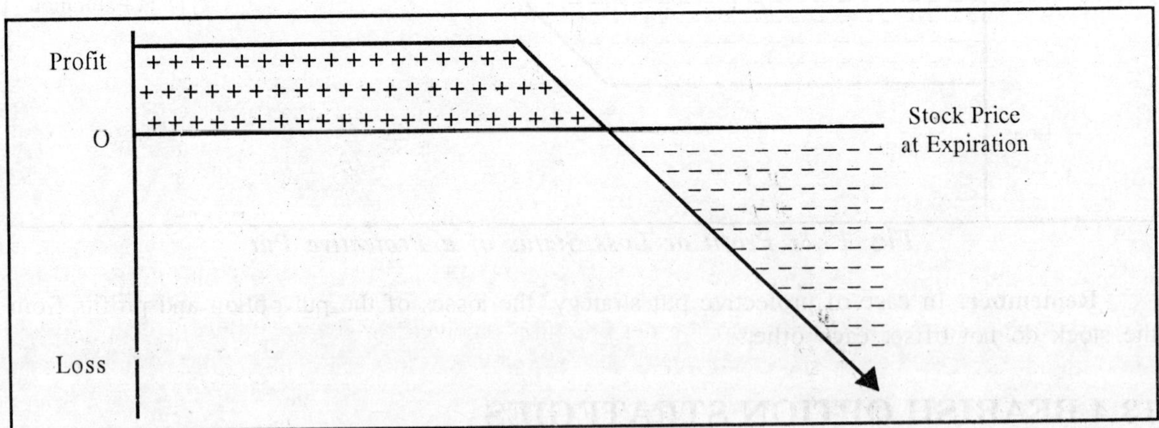

Fig. 13.9: Profit or Loss of a Short Call

The trader uses this simple strategy when he is bearish on market direction and also bearish on market volatility.

Remember: This strategy is very risky because the trader's risk (potential loss) is unlimited.

13.4.2 Long Put (Buying Put Option)

Long put means buying of one put option. The trader uses this long put strategy when he expects bearish on market direction and bullish on market volatility. In this strategy, the maximum loss is limited to the net premium paid for the option.

However, the maximum profit is unlimited the market falls to a large extent. Thus, buying a long put is a best strategy to generate profit from a down turning market without shorting stock.

The following diagram shows the profit or loss status of a long put strategy of an option trading:

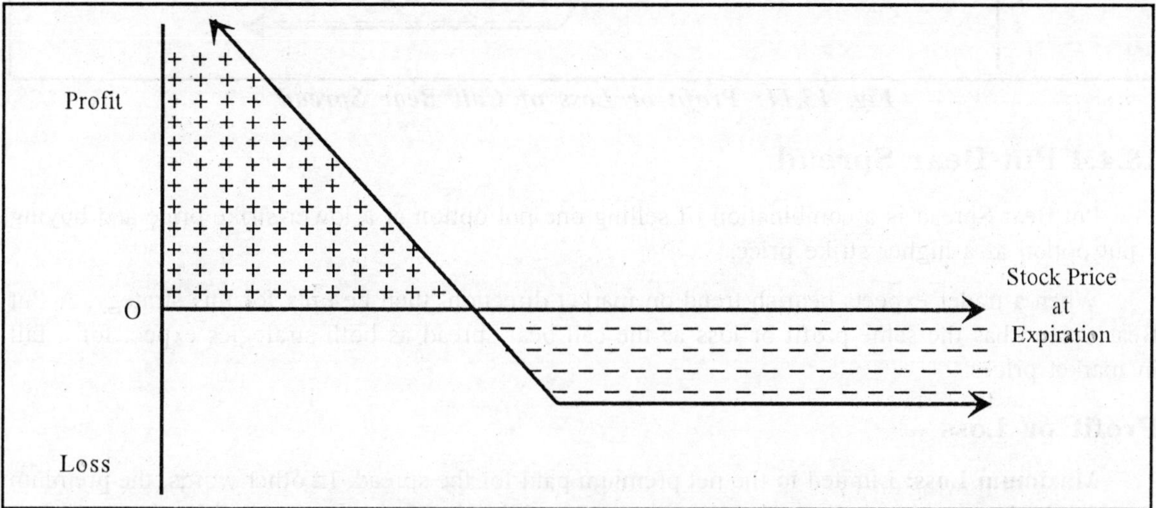

Fig. 13.10: Profit or Loss of Long Put

13.4.3 Call Bear Spread

Call Bear Spread is a combination of selling one call option with a low strike price and buying one call option with higher strike price.

Profit or Loss

Maximum Loss: Limited to the difference between the two strike prices minus the net premium.

Maximum Profit: Limited to the net premium received for the position. In other words, the premium received for the short call minus the premium paid for long call is the maximum gain of a call bear spread strategy.

Points to Note:

(i) Call Bear Spread is always a credit spread.

(ii) It is used when the market direction is mildly bearish.

The following diagram shows the profit or loss status of a Call Bear Spread Strategy of an option trading:

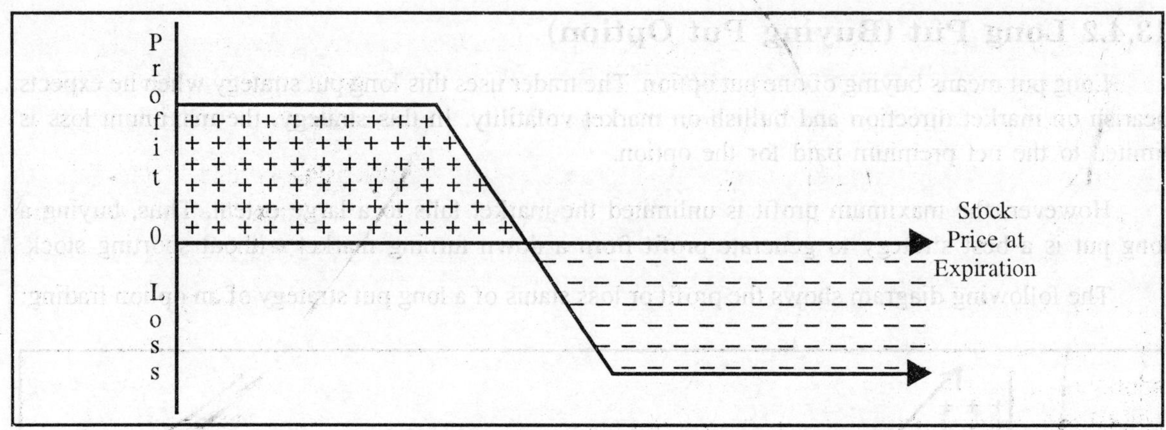

Fig. 13.11: Profit or Loss of Call Bear Spread

13.4.4 Put Bear Spread

Put Bear Spread is a combination of selling one put option at a lower strike price and buying a put option at a higher strike price.

When a trader expects bearish trend on market direction, then he opts for this strategy. A Put Bear Spread has the same profit or loss as the call bear spread as both strategies expect for a fall in market prices.

Profit or Loss

Maximum Loss: Limited to the net premium paid for the spread. In other words, the premium paid for the long position minus the premium received for the short position will be the maximum amount of loss.

Maximum Profit: Limited to the difference between the two strike prices minus the net premium paid for this position.

Diagrammatic Presentation

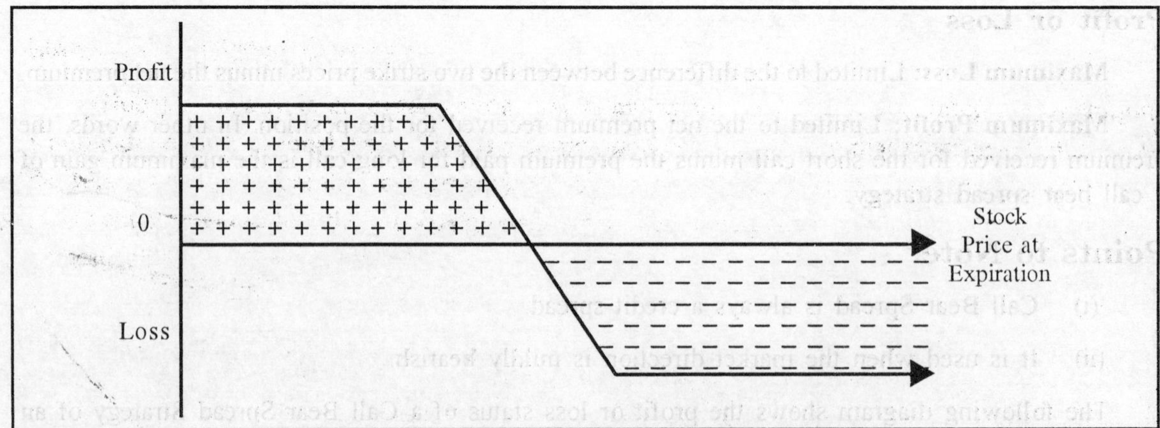

Fig. 13.12: Profit or Loss of Put Bear Spread

13.4.5 Short Synthetic

Short synthetic is a combination of selling one call option and buying one put option at the same strike price.

Profit or Loss

Maximum Loss: Unlimited

Maximum Profit: Unlimited

Diagrammatic Presentation

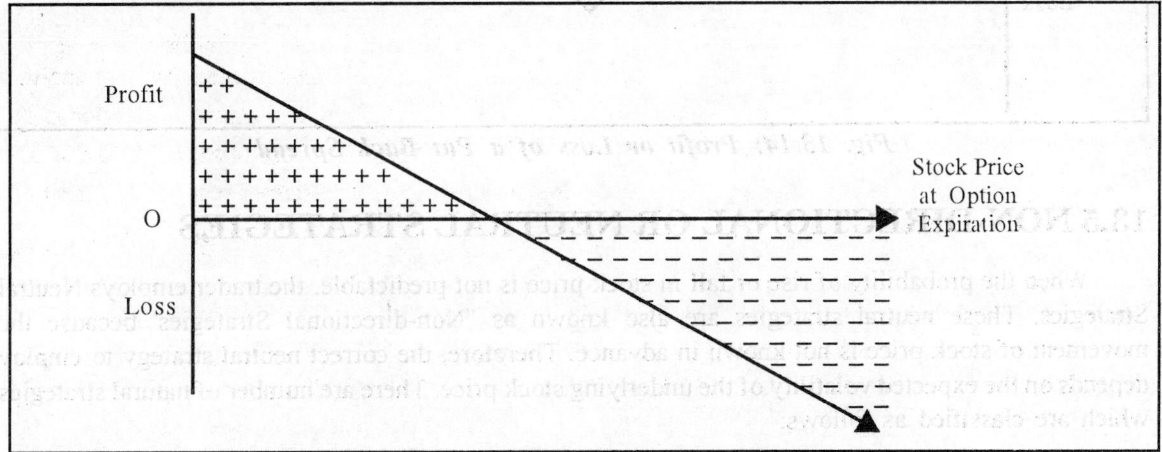

Fig. 13.13: Profit or Loss of a Short Synthetic Strategy

13.4.6 Put Back Spread

A Back Spread is formed when the number of Long positions is greater than the number of Short positions.

Let n_1 = No. of put options purchased

n_2 = No. of put options sold

If $n_1 > n_2$, then it is a case of Put Back Spread. The premium on n_2 put options should be more than the premium on n_1 put options.

Profit or Loss

In this strategy, the maximum loss is limited to the difference between the two strike prices less the premium received. However, the maximum profit is unlimited when the market is downside. But the maximum profit is limited to the net premium received when the market is on the upside.

Diagrammatic Presentation

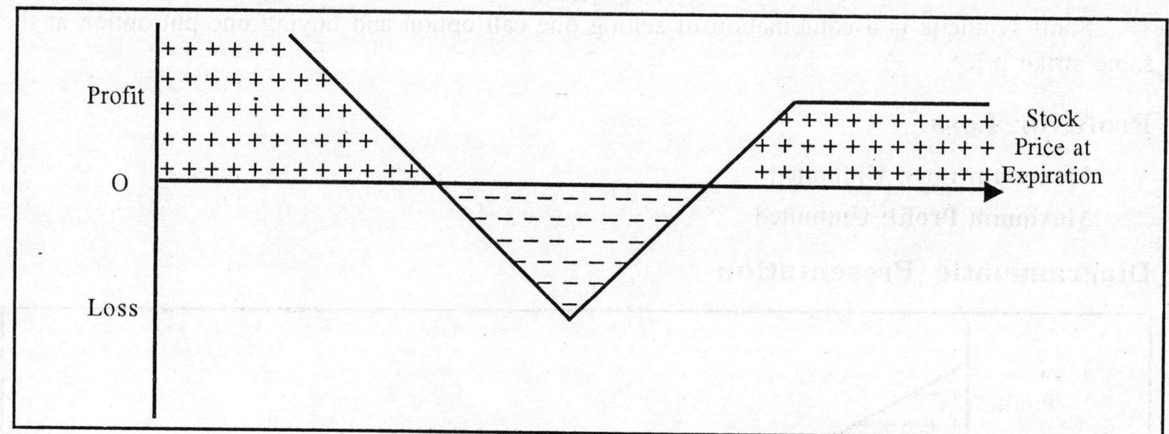

Fig. 13.14: Profit or Loss of a Put Back Spread

13.5 NON-DIRECTIONAL OR NEUTRAL STRATEGIES

When the probability of rise or fall in stock price is not predictable, the trader employs Neutral Strategies. These neutral strategies are also known as "Non-directional Strategies' because the movement of stock price is not known in advance. Therefore, the correct neutral strategy to employ depends on the expected volatility of the underlying stock price. There are number of natural strategies which are classified as follows:

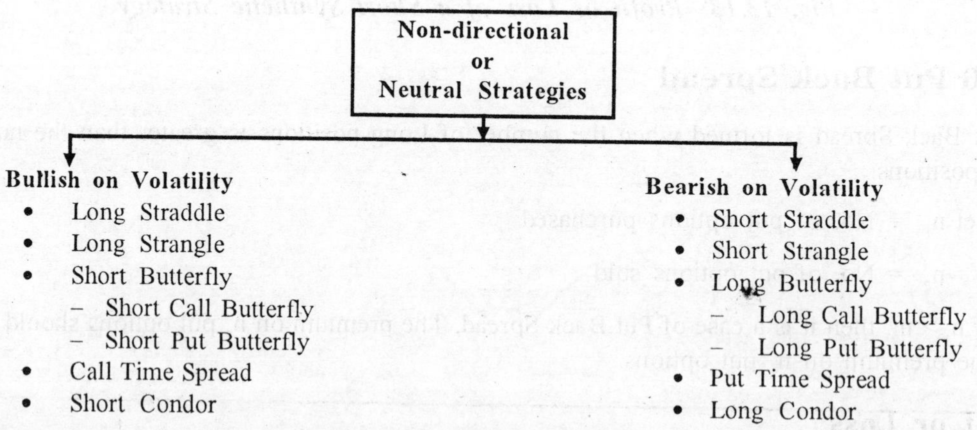

We now discuss these neutral/non-directional option trading strategies.

13.5.1 Long Straddle

A straddle is an option trading strategy. It involves the purchase or sale of particular option derivatives. It creates an opportunity for the trader to generate profit based on how much the price of the underlying security moves, regardless of this direction of price movement.

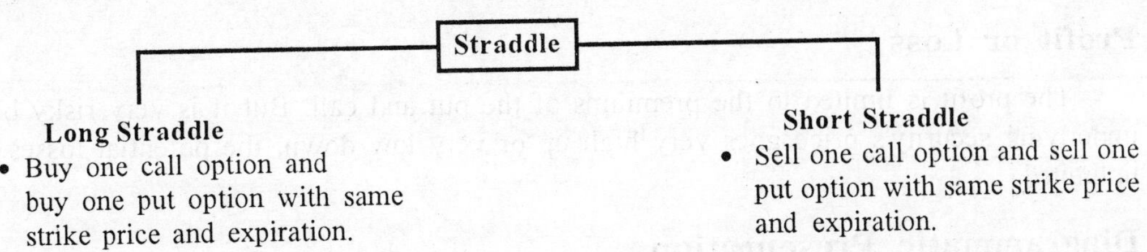

A long straddle involves going long, i.e., buying, both a call option and put option on same stock or other underlying. Both options (call option and put option) are bought at the same strike price and expiring at the same time. The trader of a long straddle makes a profit if the underlying price moves a long way from the strike price, either above or below.

Profit or Loss

Maximum Profit: Unlimited as the market moves in either direction.

Maximum Loss: In this position, the risk of the investor is limited. The purchaser may lose the cost of both option, i.e., the total premium paid for the call and put options.

How to Use: An investor can make money if the market goes up or down. If price goes up enough, he will use call option and ignore the put option. If the price goes down, he will use the put option and ignore call option. If the price does not change enough, he loses money up to the total premium paid for the two options.

Diagrammatic Presentation

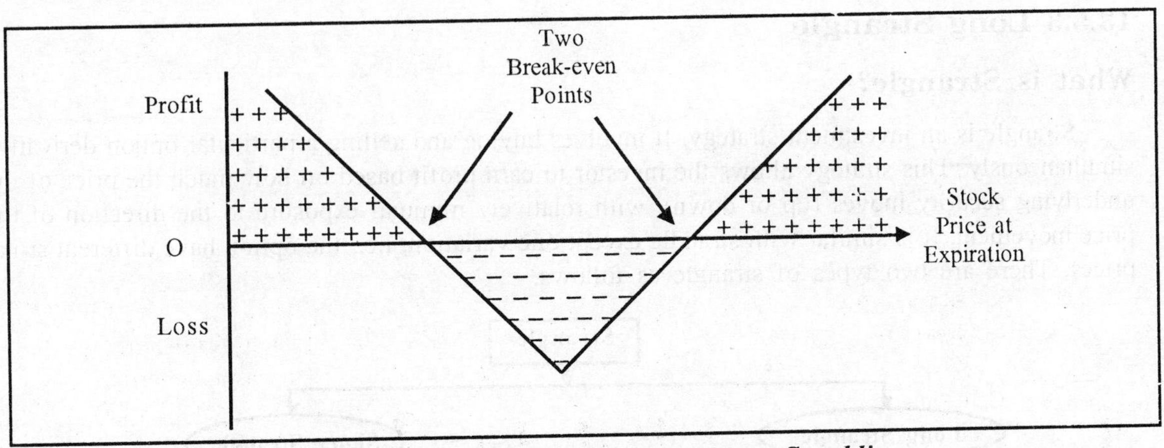

Fig. 13.15: Profit or Loss of a Long Straddle

13.5.2 Short Straddle

A short straddle is a non-directional option trading strategy. It involves simultaneously selling a put and a call of the same underlying asset, strike price and expiration date.

Profit or Loss

The profit is limited to the premiums of the put and call. But it is very risky because if the underlying security's price goes very high up or very low down, the potential losses are virtually unlimited.

Diagrammatic Presentation

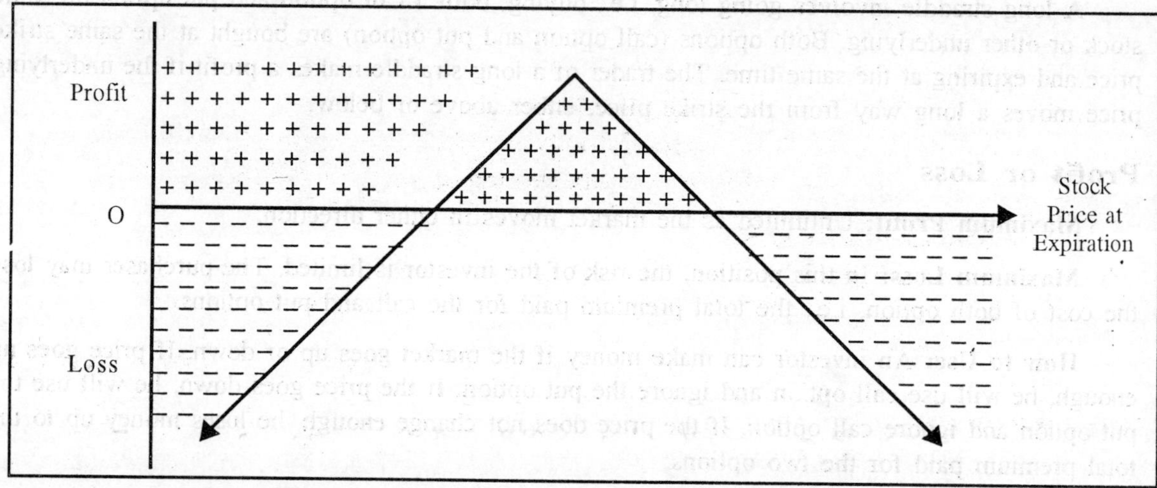

Fig. 13.16: Profit or Loss of a Short Straddle

13.5.3 Long Strangle

What is Strangle?

Strangle is an investment strategy. It involves buying and selling a particular option derivative simultaneously. This strategy allows the investor to earn profit based on how much the price of the underlying security moves (up or down), with relatively minimal exposure to the direction of the price movement. It is similar with straddle except one variation, i.e., the option have different strike prices. There are two types of strangle as follows:

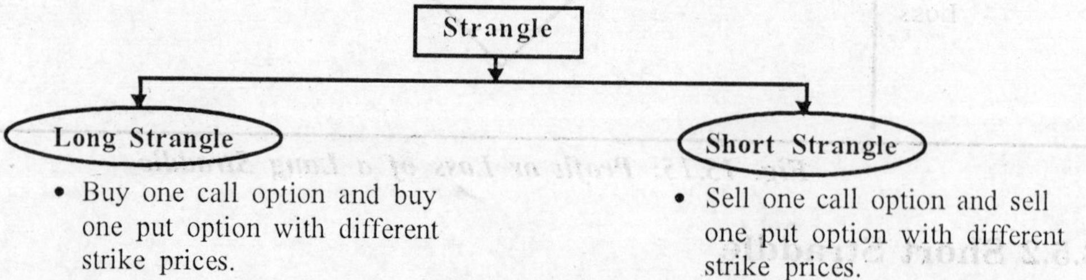

The Long Strangle involves going long (buying) both call option and put option of the same underlying security. But both options have different strike prices. A conceptual framework of a Long Strangle is furnished below:

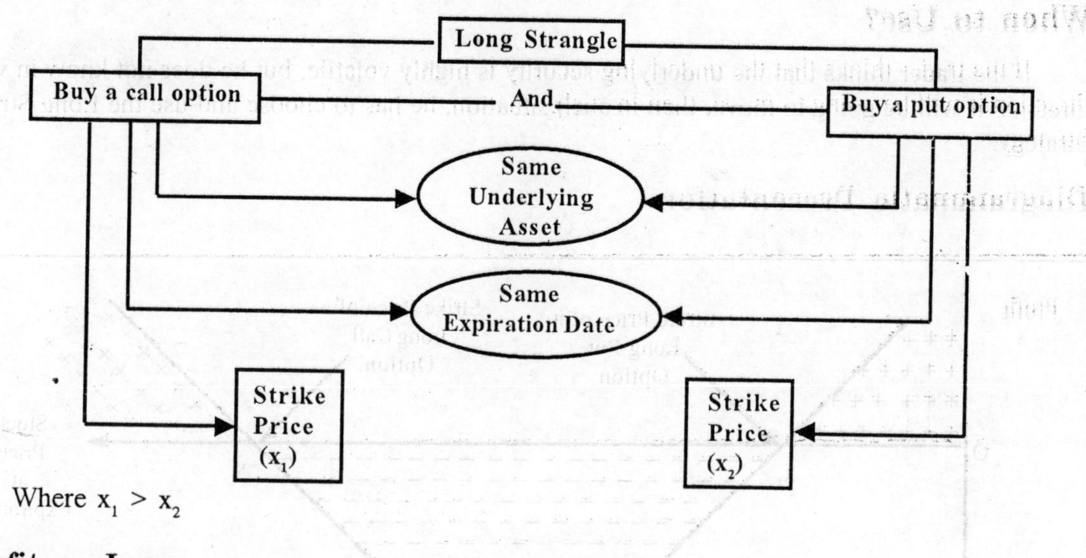

Where $x_1 > x_2$

Profit or Loss

Unlimited Profit Potential: The owner of a long strangle makes a profit if the underlying price moves far enough away from the current price, either above or below. Thus, the maximum profit is unlimited as the market moves in either direction.

The formula for calculating profit is given below:

- Maximum Profit = Unlimited
- Profit is achieved when:

  (i) Price of the underlying > Strike price of Long call + Premium paid

  or

  (ii) Price of the underlying < Strike price of Long put – Net premium paid
- Profit = Price of the underlying – Strike Price of a Long call – Net premium paid

  or

  Profit = Strike Price of Long Put – Price of underlying – Net premium paid

Limited Risk (Loss)

Maximum loss for the long strangle options strategy is hit when the underlying stock price on expiration date is trading between the strike prices of the options bought. At this price, both options expire worthless and the option trader loses the entire initial debit (premiums paid) taken to enter into the trade.

Thus, Long strangle position is a limited risk because the most a purchaser may lose is the cost of both options. In other words, the maximum loss is limited to the total premium paid for the call and put options.

When to Use?

If the trader thinks that the underlying security is highly volatile, but he does not know in which direction it will be going to move, then in such situation, he has to choose and use the Long Strangle Strategy.

Diagrammatic Presentation

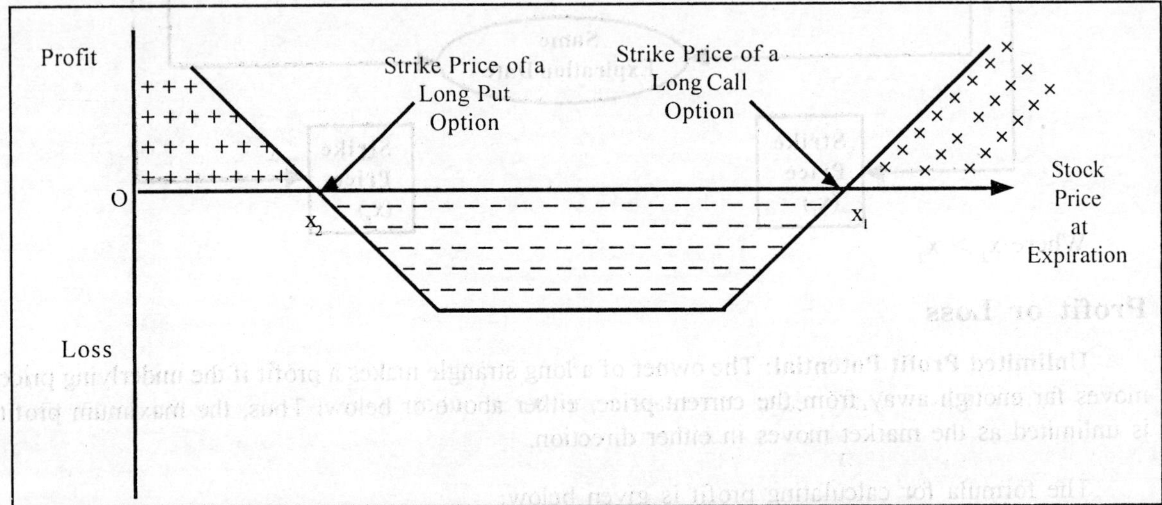

Fig. 13.17: Profit or Loss of Long Strangle Strategy

Break-even Point(s)

There are two break-even points for the long strangle position. The break-even points can be calculated using the following formulae:

(i) Upper Break-even Point = Strike Price of Long Put – Net Premium Paid

(ii) Lower Break-even Point = Strike Price of Long Put – Net Premium Paid

13.5.4 Short Strangle

The short strangle involves going short (selling) both a call option and a put option of the same underlying security with two different strike prices. As a matter of trade practice of a short strangle, the trader sells one put option with a lower strike price and simultaneously sells one call option at a higher strike price. A conceptual framework of a short strangle is furnished below:

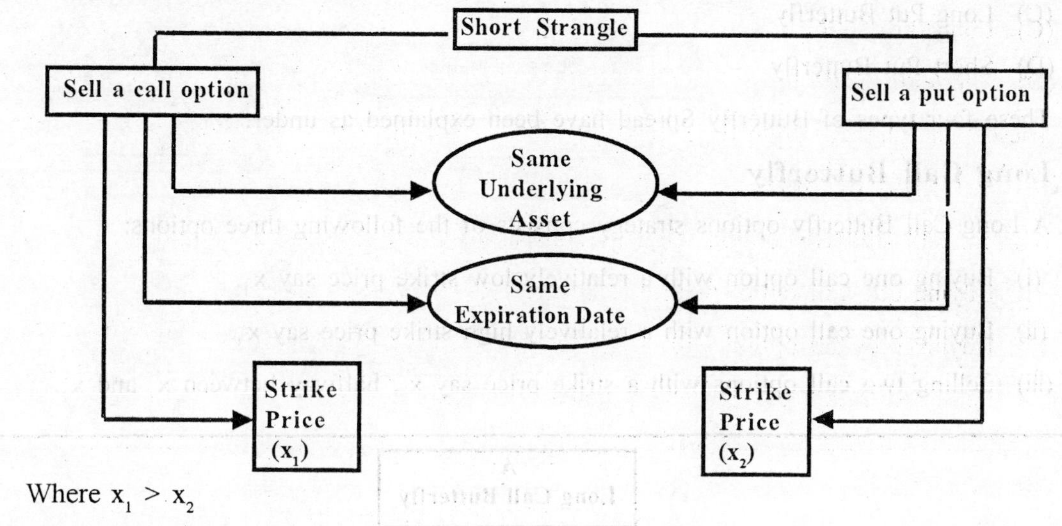

Where $x_1 > x_2$

Profit or Loss

Maximum Profit: Limited to the net premium received for selling the options.

Maximum Loss: Unlimited as the market moves in either upward or downward direction.

Diagrammatic Presentation

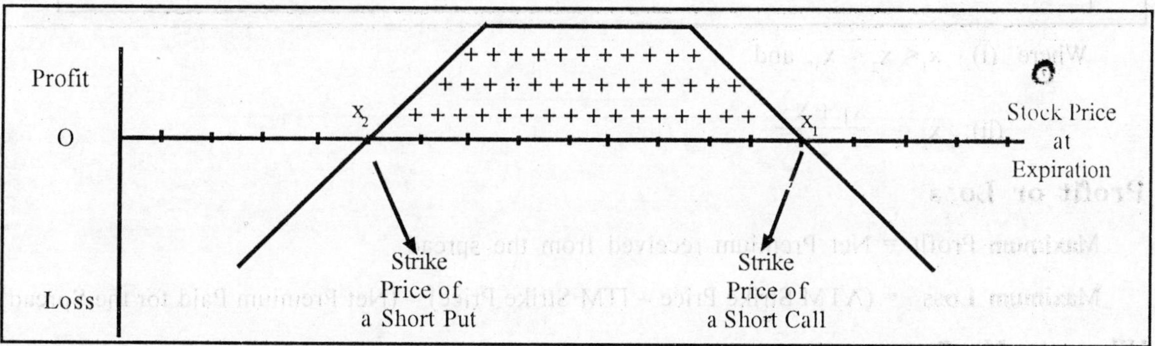

Fig. 13.18: Profit or Loss of Short Strangle Strategy

When to Use Short Strangle Strategy?

Short strangle strategy is suitable when there is bearish on volatility and the trader expects that the market prices will remain stable.

13.5.5 Butterfly Spread

A Butterfly Spread involves positions in options with three different strike prices say x_1, x_2, and x_3. There are four types of Butterfly Spread. These are:

(A) Long Call Butterfly

(B) Short Call Butterfly

(C) Long Put Butterfly

(D) Short Put Butterfly

These four types of Butterfly Spread have been explained as under:

(A) Long Call Butterfly

A Long Call Butterfly options strategy consists of the following three options:

(i) Buying one call option with a relatively low strike price say x_1.

(ii) Buying one call option with a relatively high strike price say x_3.

(iii) Selling two call options with a strike price say x_2, halfway between x_1 and x_2.

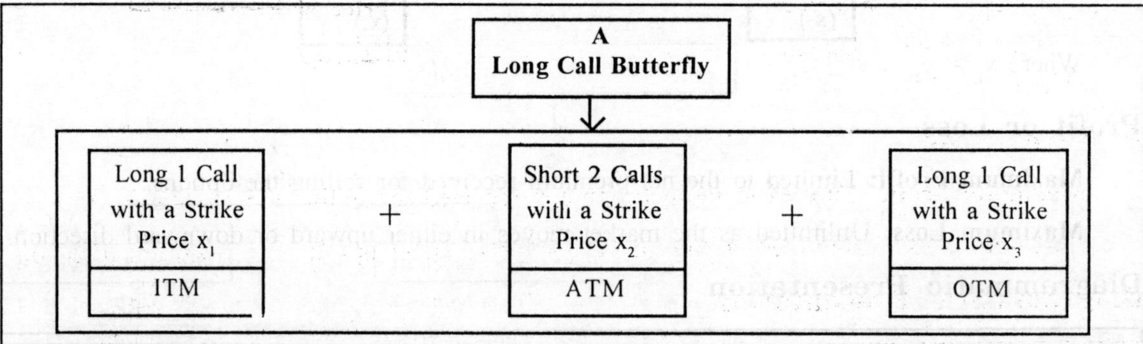

Where (i) $x_1 < x_2 < x_3$, and

(ii) $x_2 = \dfrac{x_1 + x_2}{2}$

Profit or Loss

Maximum Profit = Net Premium received from the spread

Maximum Loss = (ATM Strike Price – ITM Strike Price) – (Net Premium Paid for the Spread)

When to Use?

When the investor is neutral on market direction and bearish on volatility.

Diagrammatic Presentation

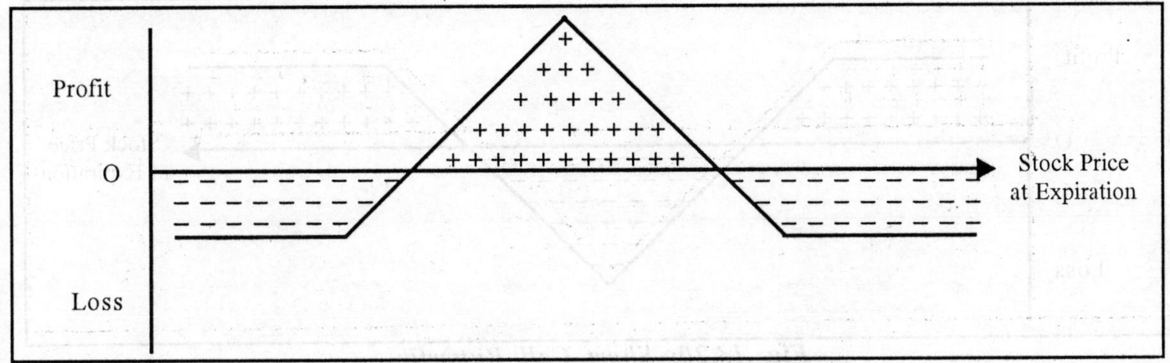

Fig. 13.19: Long Call Butterfly Spread

(B) Short Call Butterfly

A Short Call Butterfly Options strategy consists of the following three options:

(i) Selling one call option with a relatively high strike price say x_1.

(ii) Selling one call option with a relatively low strike price say x_3.

(iii) Buying two call options with a strike price say x_2, halfway between x_1 and x_2.

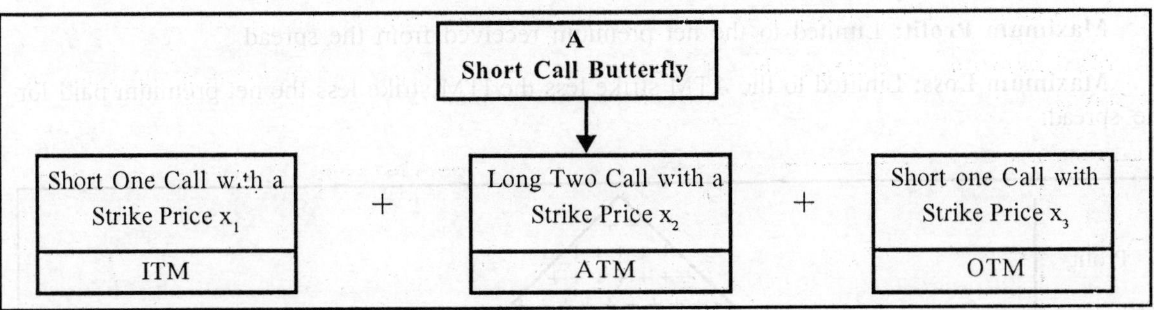

Where (i) $x_1 > x_2 > x_3$, and

(ii) $x_2 = (x_1 + x_2)/2$

Profit or Loss

Maximum Profit = Net premium received for the option spread

Maximum Loss = $x_2 - (x_1 -$ Premium)

= (ATM Strike Price) – (The ITM strike price less premium received for the position)

Diagrammatic Presentation

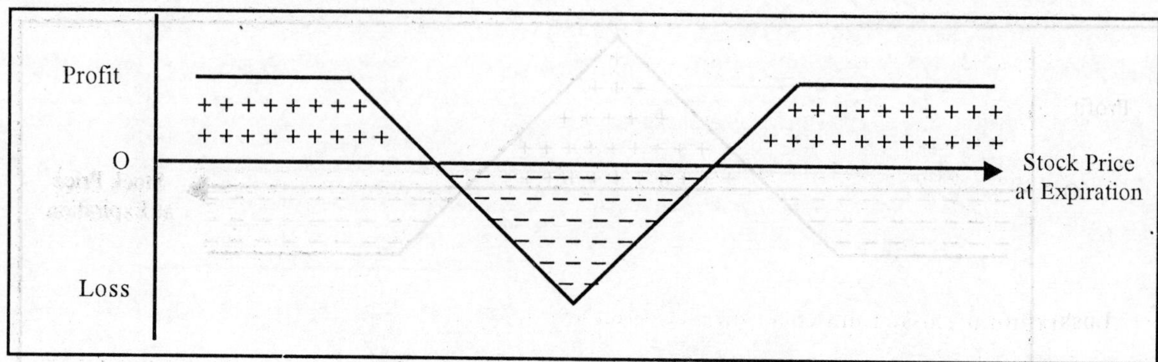

Fig. 13.20: Short Call Butterfly

(C) Long Put Butterfly

A Long Put Butterfly involves the following tradings:

- Selling two ATM put options
- Buying one ITM put option
- Buying one OTM put option

Profit or Loss

Maximum Profit: Limited to the net premium received from the spread.

Maximum Loss: Limited to the ATM strike less the ITM strike less the net premium paid for the spread:

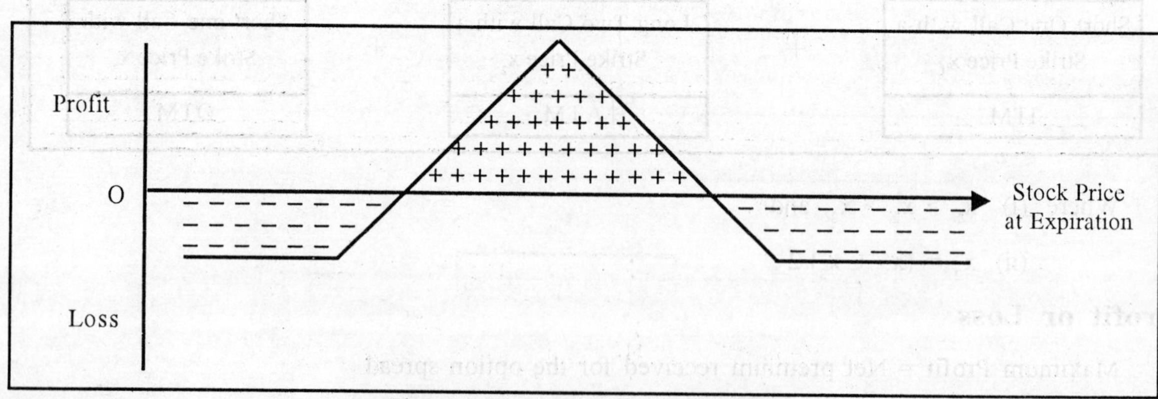

Fig. 13.21: Long Put Butterfly

(D) Short Put Butterfly

A Short Put Butterfly involves the following option tradings:

- Buying two ATM put option
- Selling one ITM put option
- Selling one OTM put option

Profit or Loss

Maximum Profit: Limited to the net premium received for the option spread.

Maximum Loss: Limited to the net difference between the ATM strikes less ITM strike less the premium received for the position.

Diagrammatic Presentation

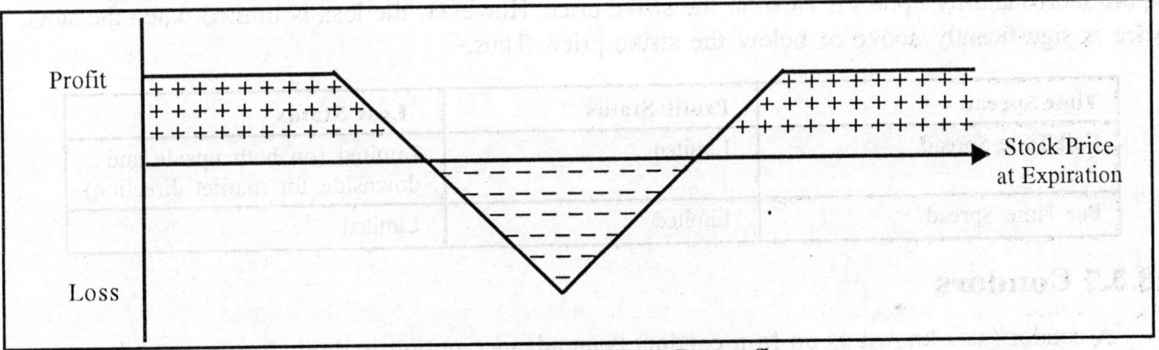

Fig. 13.22: Short Put Butterfly

13.5.6 Time or Calendar or Horizontal Spread

A Time Spread (also called a Calendar Spread or Horizontal Spread) is a spread trade involving the simultaneous purchase of options expiring at a particular date and sell of the same instrument expiring another date. The strike price in both cases is certain and same.

A Time Spread may be a call time spread or a put time spread. The conceptual framework of these Time Spreads are stated.

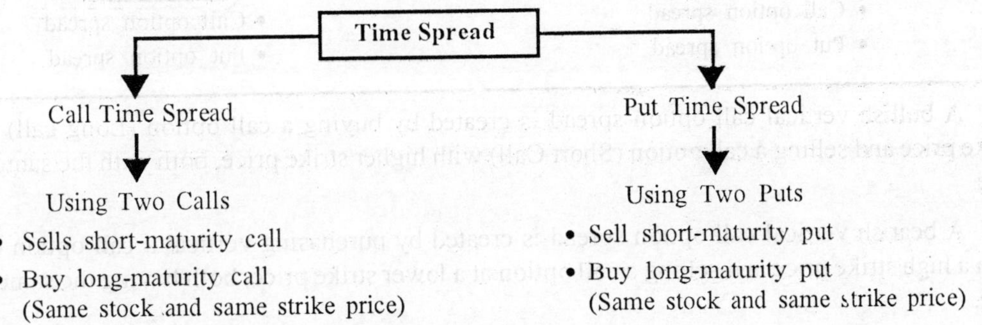

Points to Note:

1. A bullish speculator will buy a call option with a distance expiration and sell the call which is nearer to expiration. A bearish speculator will do the opposite.
2. Option traders use time spreads to take advantage of time decay.
3. It is best to use a time spread when there is less than 30 days to expiration in the front month.
4. Short-maturity option is usually front month option while long-maturity option is called for month option.
5. A time or calendar spread requires an initial investment.

Profit or Loss

An option trader who creates a calendar spread will make profit if the stock price at the expiration of the short-maturity option is close to the strike price. However, the loss is limited when the stock price is significantly above or below the strike price. Thus,

Time Spread	Profit Status	Loss Status
Call Time Spread	Limited	Limited (on both upside and downside for market direction)
Put Time Spread	Limited	Limited

13.5.7 Condors

A condor (also known as on Iron condor) is an advance option trading strategy. It utilises two vertical spreads — a call vertical spread and a put vertical spread.

A vertical spread involves simultaneous buying and selling of options on the same underlying stock for the same expiration date but with different strike prices.

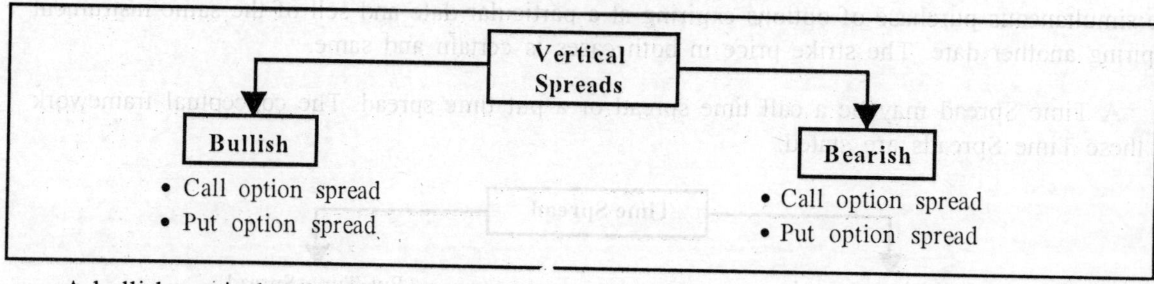

A bullish vertical call option spread is created by buying a call option (Long call) with lower strike price and selling a call option (Short Call) with higher strike price, both with the same expiration date.

A bearish vertical call option spread is created by purchasing vertical a call option (Long call) with a high strike price and selling a call option at a lower strike price, both having the same expiration date.

A bullish vertical put spread is created by buying a put option with a low strike price and selling a put option at a higher strike price, both having same expiration date.

A bearish option put spread is created by buying a put option with a high strike price and selling a put with a low strike price. To sum up:

	Bullish	Bearish
Vertical call spread • Buying a call • Selling a put	 Lower strike price Higher strike price	 Higher strike price Lower strike price
Vertical put spread • Buying a put • Selling a put	 Lower strike price Higher strike price	 Higher strike price Lower strike price

Points to Note:

(i) In case of a bullish spread, the strike price of the option purchased is lower than the strike price of option sold.

(ii) In case of a bearish spread, the strike price of the option purchased is higher than the strike price of the option sold.

Characteristics of a Condor

The literary meaning of "condor" is a very large **South American Vulture**. Here, the option position is so named because of the shape of the Profit/Loss graphs, which resembles a large bodied bird, such as a condor. The traders often refer to the inner options collectively as the "body" and the outer options as the "wings".

Conceptually, a **condor** consists two parts, one part is called the outer strikes and other one is called the inner strikes. To understand the concept and methodology of a condor option trading strategy, one should get an idea about its shape.

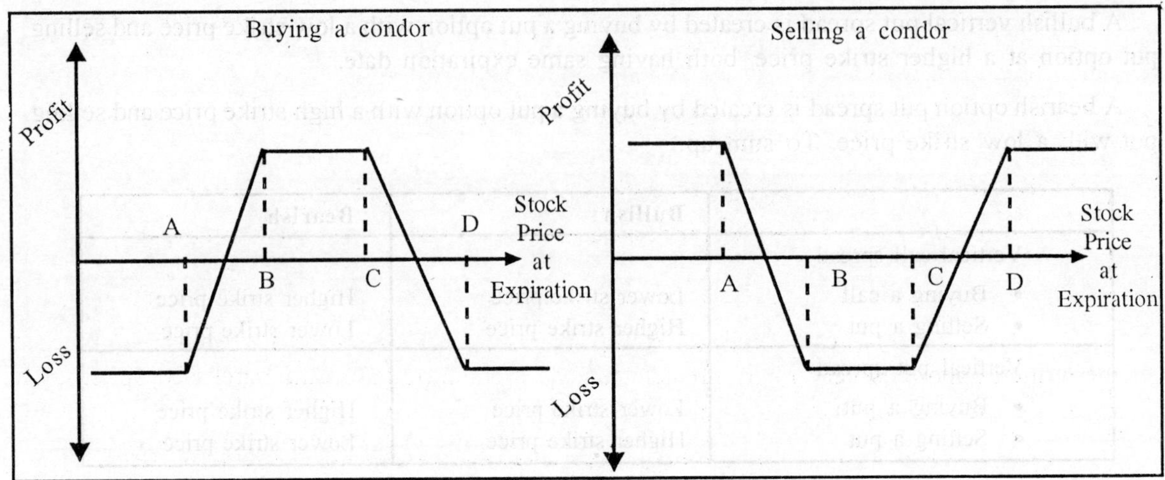

Fig. 13.23: Shape of a Condor

There are two types of condors, i.e., Buying a condor (or Long Condor) and Writing a condor (or Short condor). Each condor uses four strike prices. In the above graphs, these are marketed as A, B, C and D, where A < B < C < D.

Remember: If the outer strikes (A and D) are bought and the inner strikes (B and C) are sold, a Long condor is produced. The converge produces a short condor.

(a) Long Condor

A long condor involves buying option contracts for the outside strike prices and writing the option contracts for the inner strike prices.

Example 1: Let stock price be 100

For outside strike price : Long 97 call

: Long 103 call

For inside strike prices : Short 99 call

: Short 101 call

Example 2: Let stock price be 70

For outside strike price : Long 60 put

: Long 80 call

For inside strike prices : Short 65 put

: Short 75 call

Remember. If a Long condor involves both call and put, then the difference between the put contract strikes will generally be the same as the difference between the call contract strikes.

Example 3: Let the stock price be 80

For outside strikes : Buy 70 call

: Buy 95 put

For inside strikes : Sell 85 call

: Sell 90 put

Profit or Loss

A long condor is typically a net credit transaction. Because the premium received on the sales of the written options is very likely greater than the premium paid on the purchased options. The net credit represents the maximum profit potential for a condor.

Maximum Profit: The maximum profit of a long condor will be realised when the stock is trading between the middle strike prices, i.e., B and C.

Maximum Loss: The maximum loss of a long condor occurs at the wings of the option spread. In other words, the long condor position suffers the maximum loss when the stock is or at or below the minimum strike price (< A), and at or above the highest strike price (> D).

Graphic Presentation

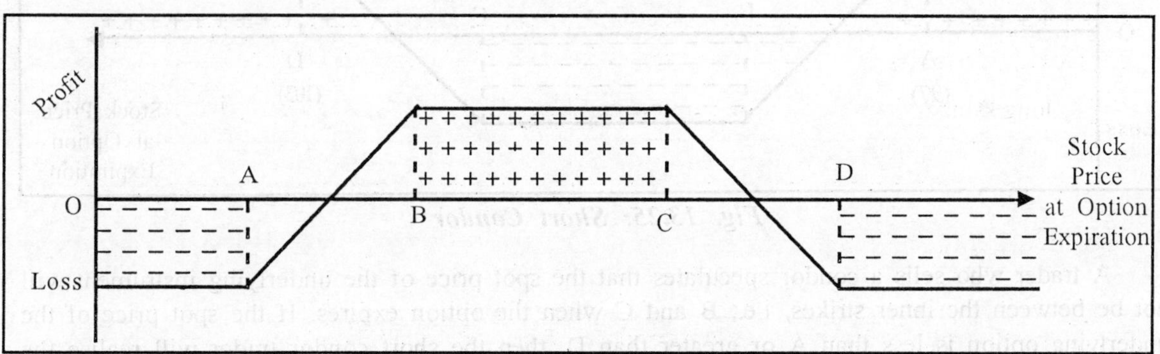

Fig. 13.24: Long Condor

(b) Short Condor (Writing a Condor)

A short condor involves selling option contracts for the outside strike prices and buying the option contracts for the inner strike prices.

Example: Let stock price be 100

For outside strike : Short 97 call

: Short 103 put

For inside strikes : Long 99 call

: Long 101 put

To sell or "go short" a condor, the trader will buy (long) option contracts for the inner strikes using an out-of-the-money (OTM) put and out-of-the-money call options.

Profit or Loss

A short condor is typically a net debit transaction. Because the premium earned on the sales of the written contracts is very likely less than the premium paid for the purchased contracts.

Maximum Profit: The maximum profit of a short condor occurs on the wings, when the underlying asset is trading passed the upper or lower strike price. It in the maximum of the difference between the lower strike call spread less the higher call spread plus the total premium received for the condor.

Maximum Loss: the maximum less is limited to the premium paid. Such maximum loss occurs at the center of the option spread.

Graphic Presentation

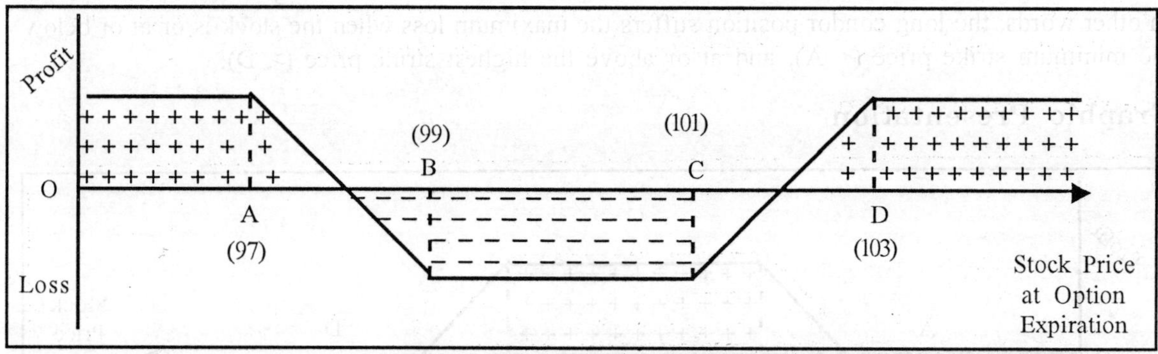

Fig. 13.25: Short Condor

A trader who sells a condor speculates that the spot price of the underlying instrument will not be between the inner strikes, i.e., B and C when the option expires. If the spot price of the underlying option is less than A or greater than D, then the short condor trader will realise the maximum profit potential.

CHAPTER SUMMARY

Option trading strategies are about a way an option trader constructs an option position, or combination of positions. An investor (trader) can construct a combination of long (buy) and short (sell) positions with different strike prices and either the same or different expiry dates. These extra dimensions of "strike prices", "expiration dates" together with the ability to buy or sell an option create an opportunity to construct a number of option trading strategies.

Broadly, there are three categories of option trading strategies. These are basic strategies, spreads and combinations. Each strategy is to be formulated and also implemented with a view to maximise trading profit or minimise potential trading losses. According to the market direction, these strategies may be designated as **Bullish strategies, Bearish strategies** and **Neutral strategies**.

The basic strategies include Long Call, Long Put, Short Call, Short Put, Synthetic, Protective Put, and Covered Call. **Spread** is an option trading strategy in which the trader takes a position in two or more options of the same type. These spreads may be vertical spreads, horizontal spreads and diagonal spreads. In this chapter, various types of spreads like Call Bull Spread, Put Bull Spread, Call Back Spread, Put Back Spread, Call Bear Spread, Put Bear Spread, Butterfly Spread, Time (Calendar Spread) and Condor Spreads, have been discussed in a strategic way.

A **combination** is an option strategy in which the option trader takes a position in both calls and puts on the same underlying instruments. Various types of combination strategies are used in the option tradings. The popular combinations are Straddles, Strangles, Straps and Strips.

Thus, there are so many different option trading strategies available for traders each with different levels of profit and of risk. Each specific strategy is categorised as basic or complex. Basic option strategies are suitable for beginning traders while combination option strategies are best used once a trader has a fundamental understanding of option trading. So, it is important to educate oneself on different strategies so that a traders can make the best financial decisions possible.

SUGGESTIONS FOR FURTHER READINGS

1. Baird, Allen, Jon (1993), *"Position Risk Profiles"*, Chapter 4 in Option Market Making —Trading and Risk Analysis for the Financial and Commodity Option Markets, New York, Wiley.
2. McMillan, Lawrence G. (2002), *Options as a Strategic Investment* (4th Edn), New York, New York Institute of Finance.
3. Robert A. Strong, *Derivatives — An Introduction,* 3rd (Indian) Edition, 2006, Thomson Asia (P) Ltd.

EXERCISES

Quiz

1. State Whether the Following Statements are True or False.

(a) The profit of the option holder is equal to the loss of the option writer if the option is exercised.

(b) The directional option trading strategies are either bullish or bearish.

(c) Bullish Strategy in option trading is used when the option trader hopes that the price of the underlying stock will likely to move upward.

(d) The profit potential of a Long call is unlimited when the market moves upward, i.e., bullish trend.

(e) When the call holder does not exercise his option, then the maximum loss is limited to the premium paid-up front for the option.

(f) When the market moves downside, the short put trader will have unlimited potential gain.

(g) A spread is an option trading strategy whereby an option trader will take the position of Long and Short options simultaneously.

(h) In case of a Call Bull Spread, the option holder will have one long call with higher strike price and one short call option with a lower strike price.

(i) In case of a Put Bull Spread, the option trader will have one long put with a lower strike price and another short put option with a higher strike price.

(j) In case of a Long Synthetic, a trader buys one call option and sell one put option at two different strike prices when the market direction is bullish.

(k) A Back Spread is formed when the number of long options is more than the number of short options.

(l) In a covered call strategy, the trader owns the underlying asset and writes a call option.

(m) In case of a protective put, the trader owns the underlying asset and buys a put option.

(n) A Call Bear Spread is a combination of selling one call option with a lower strike price and buying one call option with a higher strike price.

(o) Put Bear Spread is a combination of selling one put option at a lower strike price and buying a put option at a higher strike price.

(p) The Short Synthetic results in either unlimited loss or unlimited profit.

(q) A Put Back Spread is used when the number of long (buy) positions is greater than the number of short (sell) positions.

(r) A Long Straddle comprises buying a call option and put option on the same strike price and expiry.

(s) A short straddle involves simultaneously selling a put and a call of the same underlying asset, strike price and expiration date.

(t) A strangle is very much similar to a straddle, but the two options have different strike prices and are normally OTM options.

(u) The components of Long Call Butterfly are long one ITM call, long one OTM call and short two OTM calls.

(v) The components of Short Call Butterfly are short one ITM call option, short one OTM call option and long two ATM call options.

(w) A Calender (Time) Spread is a spread trade involving the simultaneous purchase of options expiring at particular date and the sale of the same options expiring another date.

(x) It is best to implement a Time Spread when there is < 30 days to expiration is the front month.

(y) A calender spread can be formed by selling a call option with certain strike price and buying a longer-maturity option with the same strike price.

(z) A condor strategy of option trading involves four different strike prices.

Ans: (a) True, (b) True, (c) True, (d) True, (e) True, (f) False, (g) True, (h) False, (i) True, (j) False, (k) True, (l) True, (m) True, (n) True, (o) True, (p) True, (q) True, (s) True (r) True, (t) True, (u) True, (v) True, (w) True, (x) True, (y) True, (z) True.

2. Fill in the Blanks by Using the Words/Phrases Given in the Brackets

(a) A _____ trading strategy involves taking a position in two or more options of the same time, i.e., two or more calls or two or more puts.

(spread/covered call/protective put)

(b) A butterfly spread involves positions with _____ different strike prices.

(Three/Two/Four)

(c) _____ strategy involves buying a call and put with same strike price and expiration date. (Straddle/Strangle/Condor)

A. Short Type Questions

1. What do you mean by an option trading strategy?
2. What are the factors to be considered for constructing an option position?
3. What is bullish strategy for option trading?
4. What do you mean by bearish strategy for option trading?
5. What is a Long Call?
6. What is a Short Put?
7. What is Call Bull Spread?
8. What is Put Bull Spread?
9. What is Long Synthetic?
10. What is Call Back Spread?
11. What is a Covered Call?
12. What is Protective Put?
13. What do you mean by Short Call?
14. What is a Long Put?
15. What is Call Bear Spread?
16. What is Put Bear Spread?
17. What is Short Synthetic?
18. What is Put Back Spread?
19. What is Straddle?
20. Explain the concept of Long Straddle.
21. Explain the concept of Short Straddle.
22. What do you mean by "Strangle"?
23. What is long strangle?
24. What is short strangle?
25. What is Butterfly Spread?
26. What is Long Call Butterfly?
27. What is Short Call Butterfly?
28. Why a Time spread is known as horizontal spread?
29. What is condor spread?
30. What do you mean by Neutral strategy?

B. Long Type Questions

1. What are the various trading strategies involving options? Discuss.
2. What are the bullish strategies for option trading? Discuss.
3. Explain the following option trading strategies:
   (a) Covered Call
   (b) Protective Put
4. When the option trader expects that the price of the underlying stock will likely to move downwards, he decides to employ bearish strategies. What are these strategies? Briefly discuss.
5. Explain the following option trading strategies:
   (a) Call Bear Spread
   (b) Put Bear Spread
6. What is a straddle? How to construct a Long straddle and a Short sraddle? Explain.
7. Distinguish between a straddle and strangle.
8. What do you mean by Butterfly Spread? What are the various types of Butterfly Spread? Discuss.
9. Explain the followings:
   (a) Call Time (Calender) Spread
   (b) Put Time (Calender) Spread
10. Briefly discuss the charecteristics, components, risk and reward profile of the following neutral option trading strategies:
    (a) Long Condor
    (b) Short Condor
    (c) Short Butterfly
    (d) Long Butterfly

SWAPS

Learning Objectives

*After studying this chapter, you will be able to:

- Understand the basic concept of swap and its features
- Define the term swap
- Study the advantages and disadvantages of swaps
- Know the swap market and its present status
- Know different types of swaps
- Familiar with different valuation and pricing methods of swaps
- Know the various risks associated with swap contracts
- Aware the economic motives of the parties to enter into a swap contact

Chapter Outline

14.1 AN INTRODUCTION TO SWAPS

The word **'swap'** literally means an exchange. In the language of finance, swap is a derivative contract in which two counterparties exchange certain benefits. It is a customised contract in the form of Over The Counter (OTC) derivative. **Thus, swaps are non-standardised contracts that are traded over the counter (OTC).**

A swap contract is a type of derivative based on forward claims which can be understood from the following figure:

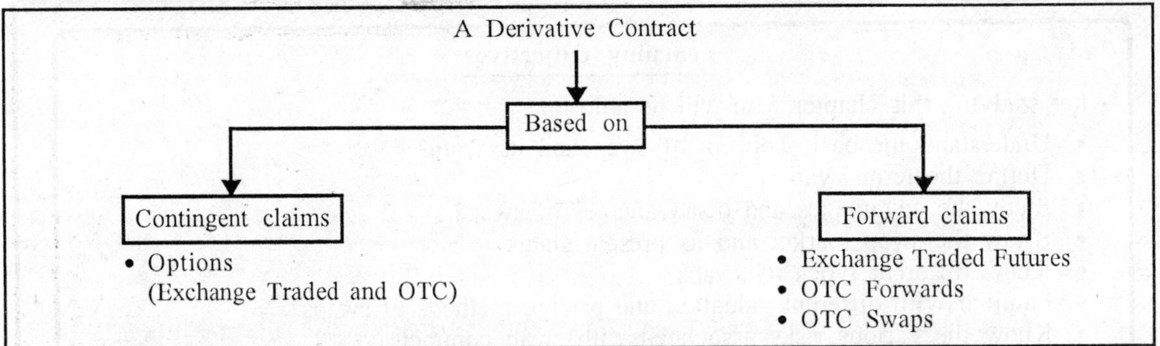

Fig. 14.1: A Swap is a Derivative Contract Based on Forward Claims

Further, a swap is a derivative whose value is derived from a specific underlying, may be financial or commodity. The following figure shows a conceptual relationship between a swap derivative and its corresponding underlying:

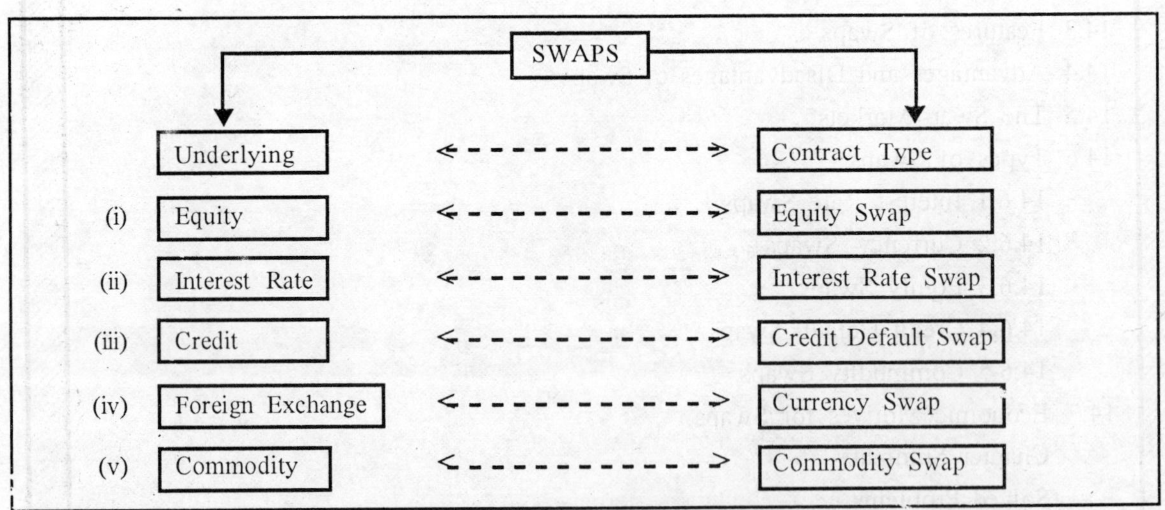

Fig. 14.2: A Conceptual Relationship between Underlyings and Contract Types of Swaps

From the above discussion, it is very clear that swap is a contract between two parties known as counterparties. The two counterparties agree to exchange one stream of cash flow against another stream. These streams are called the **legs** of the swap. The swap agreement specifies the following two elements:

(a) **Timing of Cash Flows:** The dates when the cash flows are to be made.

(b) **Methods of Calculation of Cash Flow Amount:** The swap agreement clearly specifies the way the cash flows are to be calculated.

Because swaps derivatives are OTC derivaties, there is always the risk of default of counterparty. So, corporations and financial institutions are the primary users of swaps and dominate the swap market globally.

14.2 DEFINITIONS OF SWAPS

The term swap or swap contract or swap derivative may be defined in the following lines:

(i) Swap means an exchange, something which is exchanged or offered in exchange, an exchange (of a sum of money) at different rates. – **The Chambers Dictionary**

(ii) A swap is a private agreement between two counterparties to exchange cash flows in the future according to a pre-arranged formula.

(iii) A swap is an agreement between two parties to exchange sequences of cash flows for a set period of time.

(iv) A swap is a contract between two parties to **exchange** cash flows in the future according to specific criteria or formula.

(v) A swap is an agreement between two companies or financial institutions to exchange cash flow in the future.

(vi) A swap is just what the name implies – two parties agree to swap something, generally obligations to make specified payment streams.

(vii) A swap is an agreement between two counterparties to exchange future obligations of cash flows.

(viii) A swap is a contract between two parties in which the parties: (a) promise to make payments to one another on scheduled dates in the future, and (b) use different criteria or formulas to determine their respective payments (cash flows).

14.3 FEATURES OF SWAPS

A swap is an agreement between two counterparties to exchange something (one "leg" of swap) for something else (the other "leg"). These "things" will generally be **cash flows** arising from different financial instruments, obligations or rights. Thus, a swap is an agreement between counterparties to exchange cash flows at pre-specified future times according to pre-specified conditions. The important features of a swap agreement are as follows:

1. **A Swap is a Series of Forward Agreement:** In a swap agreement, the two counterparties agree to exchange one stream of cash flows against another stream. Specifically, it defines the dates when the cash flows are to be paid and the way they are calculated. Basically, a swap is nothing but a combination of forwards. So, it has all the properties of a forward contract. Since it is traded over the counter (OTC), hence it is subject to credit default risk.

2. **Intermediary Facilitators:** A swap agreement requires the existence of two counterparties with opposite but matching needs. This has created a necessity for an intermediary to connect both the parties. Generally, the key role of intermediary is played by large international financial institutions or banks. These swap facilitators are having worldwide financial network in this innovative field by virtue of their special position in the financial market and their knowledge in the diverse needs of the customers. By arranging swaps, these intermediaries can earn income by way of charging commission to the parties.

3. **Double Coincidence of Counterparties Wants:** As stated earlier, a swap is a combination of forwards by two counterparties with opposite but matching needs. A swap contract is based on the three elements such as the financial market, the borrowers and the lenders. A brief discussion on three elements are as follows:

   I. ***The Financial Market:*** The financial market may be a long-term market or a short-term market.

   II. ***The Lenders:*** (i) In long-term market, i.e., bond market, lending is done at a fixed rate for a long duration. Therefore, the lenders do not have the opportunity to adjust the interest according to the situation prevailing in the market. So, the lenders are very much concerned expect a premium for the risk involved. This premium is high in the case of less creditworthy borrowers.

   (ii) In the short-term market, the lenders have the flexibility to adjust the floating interest rate (short-term rate) according to the conditions prevailing in the market as well as the current financial position of the borrower.

   III. ***The Borrowers:*** In the financial market, some borrowers enjoy comparative credit advantage in floating rate debts while others enjoy comparative advantage in fixed interest rate debt like bonds.

The short-term floating interest rate is cheaper to the borrower with low credit rating when compared with the fixed rate of interest. But, for borrowers with high credit rating, both the rates are cheaper. However, their advantage is comparatively higher in the case of fixed debt instruments.

The Result: A borrower with high credit rating will go for long-term funds while a borrower with low credit rating will opt for short-term funds at floating rates. In such a situation, if the borrower with low credit rating wants long-term funds at fixed rates, he has to swap the **floating rate of interest** with fixed rate of interest with counterparty, i.e., borrower with high credit rating. Thus, two borrowers must have opposite and matching needs.

The above feature of a plain vanilla interest rate swap is depicted as follows:

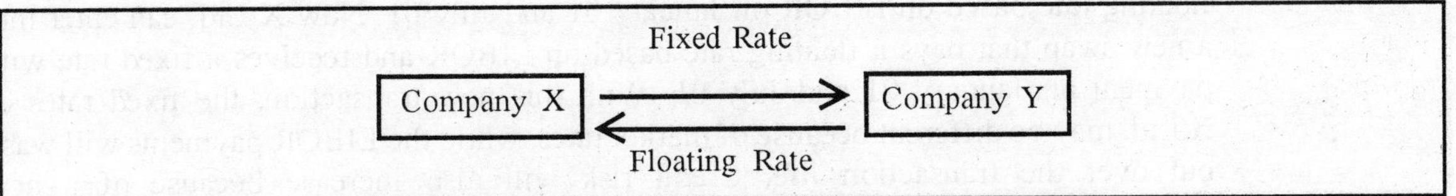

Fig. 14.3: Plain Vanilla Interest Rate Swap.

4. **Cash Flows and Settlement Procedure:** A swap is an agreement between two parties to exchange sequence of **cash flows** for a set period of time. Usually, at the time when the contract is initiated at least one of these series (sequences) of cash flow is determined by a random or uncertain variable such as an interest rate, foreign exchange rate, equity price or commodity price. Thus, when a swap contract is initiated, neither party exchanges any cash, a swap has zero value at the beginning.

   The cash flows are calculated over a **notional principal** amount, which is usually not exchanged between counterparties. On the other hand, a stream of fixed rate interest is exchanged for a floating rate of interest, and thus, there are streams of cash flows rather than single payment.

   Example: X Ltd. and Y Ltd. are the counterparties of an interest swap contract. X Ltd. agrees to pay a fixed rate interest to Y Ltd. and at the some time, X Ltd. agrees to receive a floating rate of interest from Y Ltd. Both these rates are calculated on a **notional principal** and there is a continuous exchange of interest during the period of agreement.

Points to Note:

(i) The notional principal is not exchanged between counterparties.

(ii) The notional principal is used only for calculating the size of cash flows to be exchanged.

(iii) Netting is permissible – parties make payments to each other on a settlement date. They may decide to just exchange the differences that is due to each other. This is called netting.

(iv) There is no such thing as single payment on the due date. Final payment is made on the termination date.

5. **Swaps are Generally Long-term Contracts:** Generally, **swaps** are in the nature of long-term agreement and they are like long-term forward contracts. It may be noted that **forwards** are arranged for short period only. Long period forward rate contracts are not preferred because they involve more risk of default, risk of interest rate fluctuations etc.

6. **Termination:** The easiest way to terminate the contract is to hold it to maturity. Since it is a contract between two companies, so, it cannot be terminated at one's instance. However, if one or both parties in a swap contract wish to terminate, the following methods may be adopted:

(i) Enter into a Separate and Offsetting Swap:

Example: X Ltd. has a swap contract with Y Ltd. to pay a fixed rate and receive floating rate based on LIBOR on January 01 and July 01. Now X Ltd. can enter into a new swap that pays a floating rate based on LIBOR and receives a fixed rate with payment on January 01 and July 01. With this new transaction, the fixed rates of X Ltd. may be different because of market rates, while the LIBOR payments will wash out over the transaction life. Credit risk will also increase because of a new counterparty for the new swap.

(ii) Cash Settlement Based on Market Value:

Example: Let X Ltd. assumes a swap contract with a market value of ₹ 1,00,000. The contract could be terminated if the other party pays the market value of the contract to X Ltd. In other words, if the party holding the swap has a negative value, it can terminate his swap by paying its counterparty the market value of swap. This terminates the contract for both parties, but this is usually available only if it is stated before the contract is entered into or agreed upon by both the parties at a latter date.

(iii) Selling the Swap to a Third Party:

This usually requires permission from the other party. This is not commonly used in the marketplace.

(iv) Use a Swaption:

A swaption works like an option by giving the owner the right to enter into another swap at terms that are set in advance. By executing the swaption, the party can offset its current swap as explained in the first way to terminate the contract.

Thus, the features of a swap contract can be depicted is as follows:

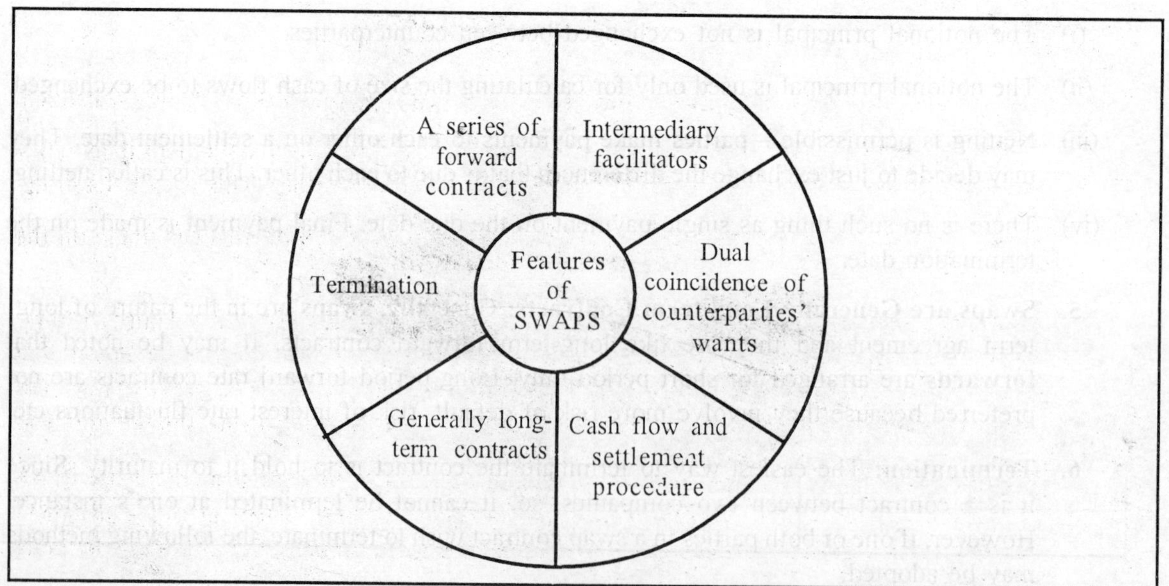

Fig. 14.4: Features of Swaps

14.4 ADVANTAGES AND DISADVANTAGES OF SWAPS

Swaps are contractual agreements between two parties in which each party agrees to exchange a stream of cash flows for a stipulated period of time based upon certain agreed parameters and the price fluctuations in the specified underlyings. The advantages and disadvantages of these swap contracts are mentioned below:

Advantages

(i) Highly flexible and can be customised to the parties.

(ii) Cost of transacting in the market is fairly low.

(iii) Private transaction between two parties.

Disadvantages

(i) It requires to find a counterparty with opposite and matching need and willing to accept the terms.

(ii) Swap market is an illiquid market. It requires the consent of counterparty to terminate.

(iii) It is highly unregulated. It suffers from unlimited potential credit risks.

14.5 THE SWAP MARKETS

Swaps are not exchange traded instruments. These are customised contracts that are traded in the over-the-counter (OTC) market. As few regulations are applicable to swap market, hence a swap contract provides high degree of privacy. Today, firms, financial institutions, banks and even government use swaps. Because, swaps occur on the OTC market. There is always the risk of a counterparty on the swap.

The first interest rate swap was transacted between IBM and the World Bank in 1981. However, despite their relative youth in comparison with other derivatives like futures and forwards, swaps have exploded popularity in 1987. According to the statistical reports of the International Swaps and Derivative Association (ISDA), the swap market has a total notional value of $ 865 billion. By mid-2006, this figure exceeded USD 415 trillion according to the Bank for International Settlement. The majority of this (USD 192.0 trillion) was due to interest rate swaps. These USD 292.0 was split by currency as follows:

National Outstanding as on 31.12.2006
(Interest Rate Swap in USD trillion)

Currency

Euro	US Dollar	Japanese Yen	Pound Sterling	Swiss Franc	Total
112.10	97.60	38.00	22.30	3.5	292.0

Indian Swap Market

At present, only swaps are the only types of rupee derivatives which can be traded in India. There are three main types of swap instruments having specific criteria. These are:

- Plain Vanilla Interest Rate Swaps
- Currency Swaps
- G-see linked swaps

These three categories of Indian swaps have been discussed as follows:

(i) Plain Vanilla Interest Rate Swaps

It is the most common type of swap instrument and actively traded in the Indian derivative market. This plain vanilla interest rate has the following three Reference/Benchmark rates in the Indian market.

(a) Overnight Index Swap (OIS) Rate

(b) MITOR (Mumbai Interbank Tomorrow Offered Rate)

(c) MIFOR (Mumbai Interbank Forward Offered Rate)

The Overnight Index Swaps (OIS) is most popular and liquid benchmark especially in the interbank market. It is known as MIBOR, i.e., Mumbai Interbank Offer Rate (MIBOR-015).

In India, there are many debt market securities available for the participants. There are number of debt service rates such as prime lending rate, treasury bill rate, 10-year bond rate, commercial paper rate, CD rate and repo rate etc. are also offered. But for other financial/derivative instruments, few key rates which are considered as benchmark against which other rates are set.

For example, LIBOR is considered as the benchmark rate globally. In India, the following rates are considered as benchmark.

1. MIBOR – Mumbai Interbank Offer Rate
2. The Reuters MIBOR – Mumbai Interbank Overnight Average
3. MIFOR – Mumbai Interbank Forward Offered Rate
4. MITOR – Mumbai Interbank Tomorrow Offered Rate

14.6 TYPES OF SWAPS

A swap is a derivative contract to exchange cash flows in the future. Its value is derived from the specific underlyings such as interest rate, foreign exchange, equity, credit amount and commodity etc. According to the nature of underlyings, there are five generic types of swaps. These are as follows:

1. Interest Rate Swaps (IRS)
2. Currency Swaps
3. Equity Swaps
4. Credit Default Swaps (CDS)
5. Commodity Swaps

A swap is a contractual deal which is used to hedge the risk. There are numerous risks which are associated with swap deals. These risks are market risk, interest risk, foreign currency exchange risk, default or credit risk, settlement risk and so on. Hence, many other types of swaps may be introduced to hedge the risks of the counterparties. But in this section, we will discuss only the five generic type of swaps as stated above.

14.6.1 Interest Rate Swap (IRS)

An Interest Rate Swap is an exchange of two sets of interest flows based on different interest rates in same currency, with no exchange of underlying notional principal. In other words, it is a contractual agreement between two counterparties under which each party agrees to make periodic payment of interest to the other for an agreed period of time based upon a notional principal amount. It is also known as **Coupon Swap**. Interest Rate swaps often exchange a fixed payment for a floating payment that is linked to an interest rate. These are very popular highly liquid instruments and used to hedge interest rate risks.

14.6.1.1 Features of Interest Rate Swaps

The important features of Interest Rate Swaps are stated as follows:

(i) Notional (Theoretical) Principal Amount: In a swap agreement, the interest (whether fixed or floating rate) is calculated on the notional or theoretical principal amount. The concept "Notional or Theoretical" principal signifies that there is no need to exchange the actual amount of principal between the counterparties. It is used only for the purpose of calculation of interest which will be periodically exchanged.

Thus, this notional principal is neither borrowed by one party, nor lent by the other party, but is used for calculating the size of cash flows to be exchanged.

(ii) Interest Rates: The most common type of interest rate swap is the exchange of fixed rate flows for floating rate flows. A ***fixed for floating*** interest swap is often referred to as a ***"plain vanilla swap"***.

Example:

Fixed rate payer	:	A
Fixed rate	:	5 per cent, semi-annual
Floating rate payer	:	B
Floating rate	:	3-month MIBOR (Mumbai Interbank Offer Rate)
Notional Amount	:	₹ 1,00,00,000
Maturity	:	5 years

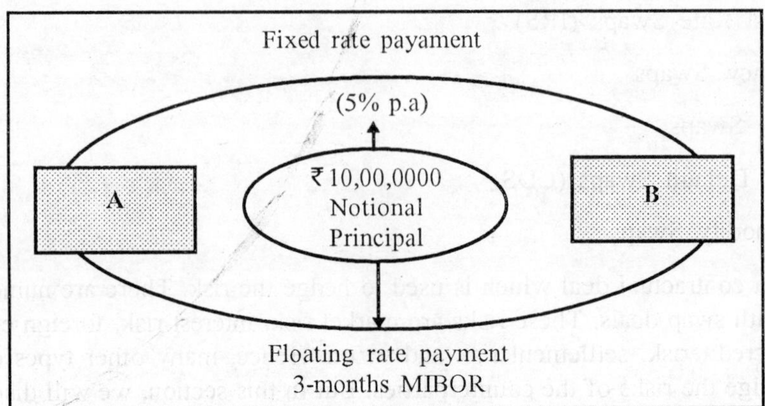

Fig. 14.5: Interest Rate Swap Structure

Cash flow from A to B

A, the fixed rate payer, agrees to pay 5.0% of ₹ 1,00,00,000 on a semi-annual basis to B for the next five years. Here, A will pay 2.5% of ₹ 1,00,00,000 (one crore) i.e., ₹ 2,50,000, twice a year.

Cash flow from B to A

B, the floating rate payer agrees to pay 3-month MIBOR (as a percentage of the notional amount) on a quarterly basis to A for the next 5 years.

Here, B will pay the 3-month MIBOR rate, divided by four and multiplied by the notional amount, four times per year.

Mathematically,

$$\text{B's floating rate cash outflow} = \frac{\text{MIBOR}}{4} \times ₹\ 1,00,00,000$$

Points to Note:

(a) The fixed rate is known as **the swap rate** while the floating rate is called **reference rate**. In the above example, the fixed rate, i.e., 5% p.a. is the swap rate.

(b) According to usual market convention, the counterparty paying the fixed rate is called the **"the payer"** (while receiving the floating rate) and the counterparty receiving the fixed rate is called the **"receiver"** (while paying the floating rate).

(c) There is no exchange of the principal amount, i.e., ₹ 1,00,00,000 and the interest rates are on a "notional" (i.e., theoretical) principal amount.

(d) The periodic floating rate is variable which is normally based on Interbank Rate plus basic points (bps). To determine the periodic floating rate, we have to use the market indexes like LIBOR or MIBOR.

LIBOR, i.e., London Interbank Offer Rate is the rate of interest offered by banks on deposits from other banks in Euro currency market. It may be noted that LIBOR is a **reference** rate for loans in international financial market.

MIBOR, i.e., Mumbai Interbank Offer Rate is the rate of interest offered by banks on deposits from other banks in Indian financial market. Ideally, the determination of the reference rate must be outside the control of the counterparties, otherwise a conflict of interest will arise. In practice, the periodic floating rate calculated as follows:

Periodic Floating Rate = Reference Rate + Base Point

While Reference Rate = LIBOR or MIBOR

Base point = Certain per cent per annum

One basic point = 0.01 per cent.

(e) At origin only the first floating rate is known and the subsequent floating rates are unknown.

(iii) Set of Dates of Swap Transactions: Each cash flow is based on a pre-set index, notional principal amount and set of dates of exchage.

Consider the following figures:

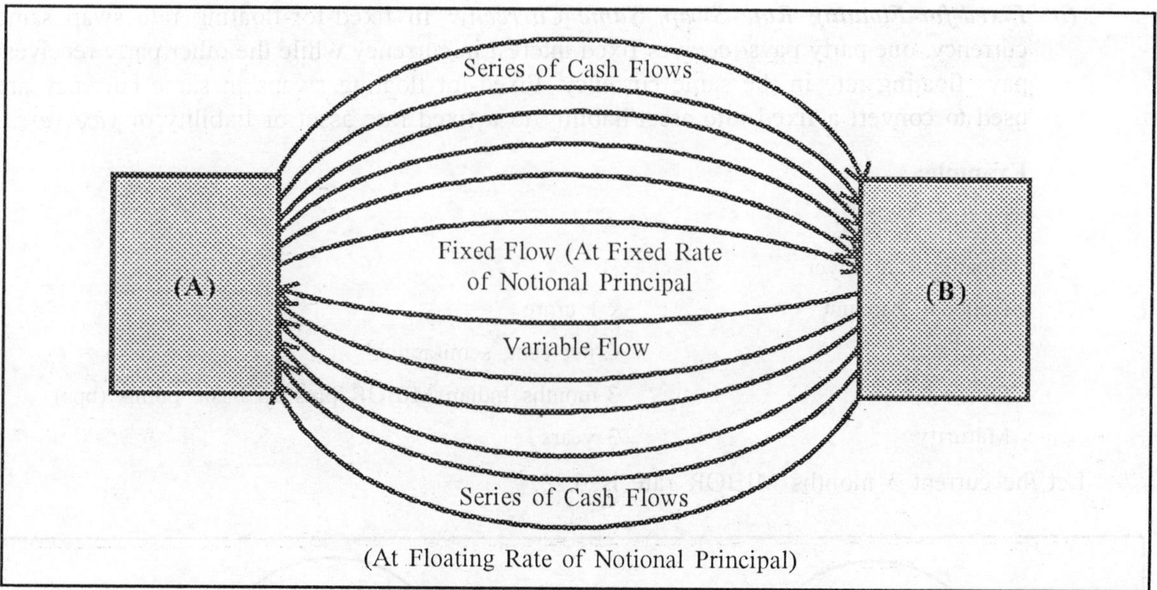

Fig. 14.6: Series of Cash Flows and the Corresponding Dates of a Swap Contract

For A, a series of interest payments which are to be calculated by using a fixed rate of interest on a notional principal amount. Similarly for B, a stream of interest payments to be calculated by using a floating rate of interest on such notional principal. The fixed rate interest payments are normally paid **semi-annually**. The date from which the first fixed and floating payments commence to due is known as effective date. The date on which the swap deal is agreed up by the parties is known as the **trade date**. Typically, the first floating rate payment is determined on the **trade date**.

14.6.1.2 Types of Interest Rate Swaps

Interest Rate Swaps are OTC derivatives and customised in nature. Hence, these can be structured to meet the specific needs of the counterparties. It has two legs. Based on how the interest under the two legs is determined, swaps are classified into various types. The most common type of Interest Rate Swaps are:

(i) Fixed-for-floating rate swap, same currency

(ii) Fixed-for-floating rate swap, different currencies

(iii) Floating-for-floating rate swap, same currency

(iv) Floating-for-floating rate swap, different currencies

(v) Fixed-for-fixed rate swap, different currencies

(vi) Other interest rate swaps.

These above stated swaps have been explained here.

(i) Fixed-for-Floating Rate Swap, Same Currecny: In fixed-for-floating rate swap same currency, one party pays/receives fixed interest in currency while the other party receives/pays floating rate in the same currency. Fixed-for-floating swaps in same currency are used to convert a fixed rate asset/liability to a fixed rate asset or liability or *vice versa.*

Example:

Fixed rate payer	:	A
Floating rate payer	:	B
Notional Amount	:	₹ 1 crore
Fixed rate	:	6 per cent, semi-annual
Floating rate	:	3-months Indian MIBOR plus 25 basic points (bps)
Maturity	:	3 years

Let the current 3 months MIBOR rate is 6.25.

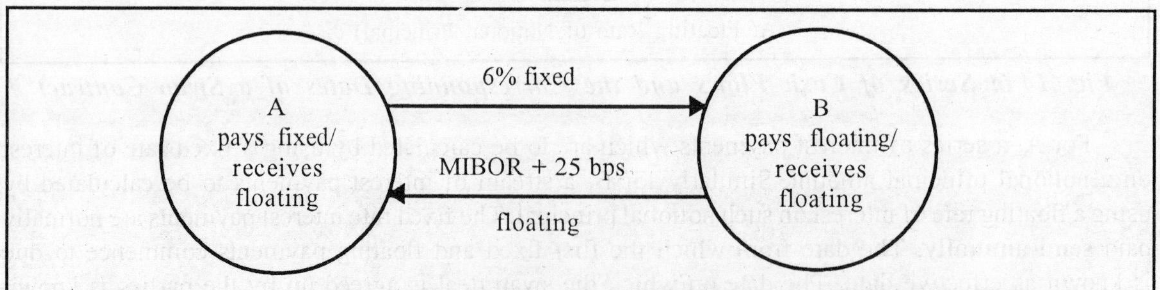

Fig. 14.7: Structure of Fixed-for-floating Swap

A will pay 3% of ₹ 1 crore for every six month, i.e., ₹ 3,30,000 for 3 years.

B will pay 3-month MIBOR (as a per cent of the Notional amount) on a quarterly basis to A for the next 3 years. In general, the floating rate is quoted on a money market yield basis.

The first interest payment of B will be calculated as follows:

$$\text{Notional Amount} \times \frac{\text{MIBOR} + \text{bps}}{100} \times \frac{1}{4}$$

$$\text{i.e., ₹ } 1{,}00{,}00{,}000 \times \frac{6.25 + .25}{100} \times \frac{1}{4} = \text{₹ } 1{,}62{,}500$$

Practical Difficulty: While we calculate interest payment for semi-annual basis or quarterly basis, the number of days of a particular semi-annual/quarter differs. For example

Semi-annual Number of Days

	January-June	July-December	Total Days
2011	181	184	365
2012	182	184	365

Number of Days in a Quarter

	January-March	April-June	July-September	October-December	Total Days
2011	90	91	92	92	365
2012	91	91	92	92	366

From the above tables, we find that there is no fixed number of days in case of semi-annuals as well as quarters. Thus, the number of days in the year is one of the issue in the swap contract. However to resolve this differentiation, the following principles would be followed:

(a) A 365 days year is assumed for fixed amount flow side.

(b) A 360 days year is assumed for floating amount flow side

(ii) ***Fixed-for-Floating Rate Swap, Different Currencies:*** In a Fixed-for-floating rate swap, different currencies, one party pays/receives fixed interest in a currency (say US Dollar) and receives/pays floating rate in another currency (say Japanese Yen).

Fixed-for-floating swaps in different currencies are used to convert a fixed rate asset/ liability in one currency to a floating rate asset/liability in a different currency, or *vice versa.*

(iii) ***Floating-for-Floating Rate Swap, Same Currency:*** In a floating-for-floating rate swap, same currency, one party pays/receives floating interest in a currency (say in Indian rupee ₹) to/from the counterparty and receives or pays floating interest rate in same currency from/to the counterparty on a notional amount for a tenure of certain years.

(iv) ***Floating-for-Floating Rate Swap, Different Currencies:*** In a floating-for-floating rate swap in different currencies, one party pays/receives floating interest rate in one currency (say ₹) to/from the counterparty and receives pays floating rate from/to the counterparty in another currency (say USD) on a notional principal amount at an initial exchange rate of foreign exchange for a tenure of certain years.

(v) ***Fixed-for-Fixed Rate Swap in Different Currencies:*** In a fixed-for-fixed rate swap in different currencies, one party pays/receives fixed interest in one currency and the counterparty receives pays the fixed interest in another currency.

(vi) ***Other Interest Rate Swaps:*** Interest swap is a customised and over-the-counter contract. So, it can be designed to meet the objective of a swap trader. However, we find the following other types of popular swaps in the market:

— Basis swap

— Zero coupon to floating swap

— Forward swap

— Swaption

— Amortising swap

— Leveraged swap

— Power swap

Basis Swap: In general, a swap is fixed to floating or floating to fixed. But in case of Basis Swap, it involves both the legs are based on floating rate indices. However, the benchmark (reference) rates for determining the two legs of payment are different. Where the traders in the contract are tied to assets or liabilities based on one reference rate and want to convert the same to another reference rate, then this BASIS SWAP is practiced. Thus, in this cases cash flows are determined by one floating reference rate are exchanged for cash flows determined by another floating reference rate.

14.6.2 Currency Swap

A currency swap is an over-the-counter derivative. It is closely related to interest rate swap. It involves the exchange of cash flows between counterparties which takes place in two different currencies. In case of **Interest Rate Swap**, the parties swap only interest. But in case of **currency swap**, the parties swap both interest and/or principal.

Definition

"A currency swap is an over-the-counter derivative. It is a foreign exchange agreement. It involves the exchange of principal and/or interest payment on a loan or an asset in one currency for principal and/or interest payment on an equivalent loan or an asset in another currency."

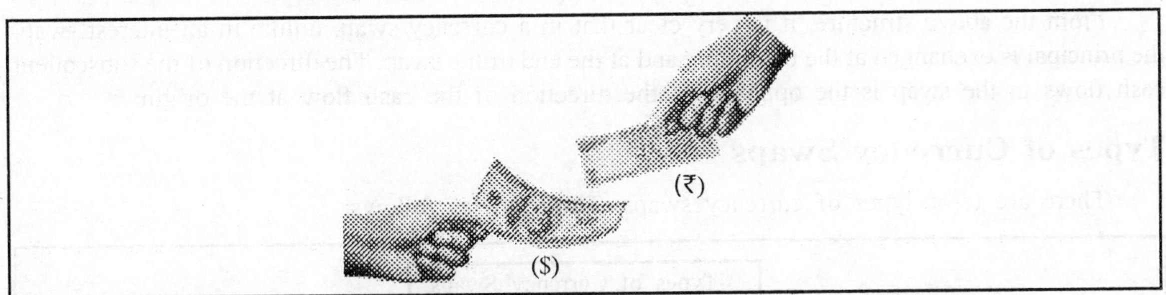

Fig. 14.8: Currency Swaps

14.6.2.1 Features of Currency Swaps

1. **A Currency Swap is a Foreign Exchange Agreement.** A Currency swap is an agreement between two parties to exchange the principal and/or interest of a loan in one currency for the same (principal and/or interest) in another currency.

2. **Currency Swaps are Over-the-counter Derivatives.** It is a contract between two parties to swap. The Banks, multinational corporations and institutional investors are the common parties in a swap contract.

3. **Exchange of Principal Amounts at the Beginning and at the End of the Swap Contract.** In a swap contract, the principal amounts must be specified in each of the two currencies. By using the prevailing exchange rate, the principal amounts must be calculated which are equivalent approximately. These principal amounts are usually exchanged at the beginning and at the end of the contract.

4. **Exchange of Interest during the Tenure of the Swap.**

14.6.2.2 Categories of Cash Flows in a Currency Swap

From the features of a currency swap, we observe that there are three categories of cash flows associated with a Currency Swap. These are as follows:

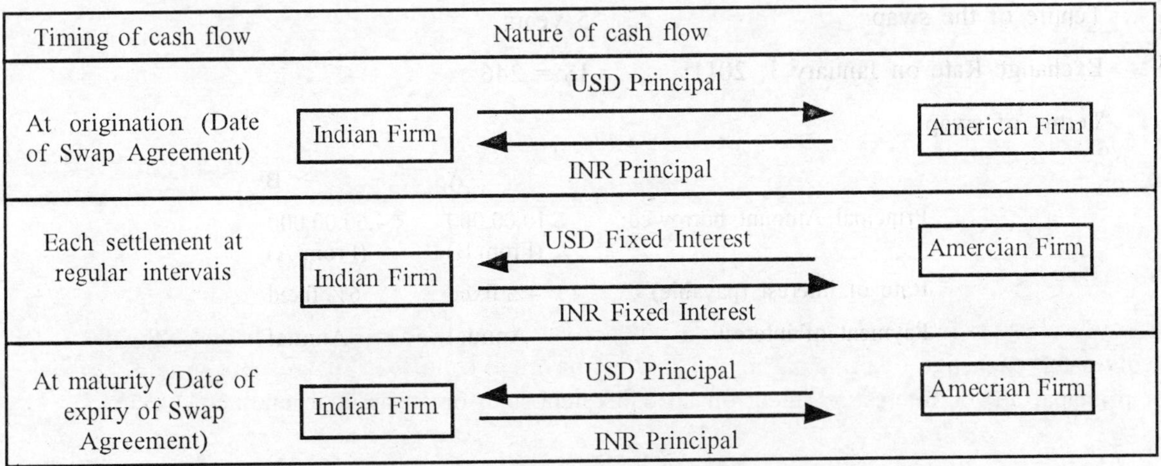

Fig. 14.9: Categories of Cash Flows in a Currency Swap

From the above structure, it is very clear that in a currency swap, unlike in an interest swap, the principal is exchanged at the beginning and at the end of the swap. The direction of the subsequent cash flows in the swap is the opposite of the direction of the cash flow at the origin.

Types of Currency Swaps

There are three types of currency swaps. These are as follows:

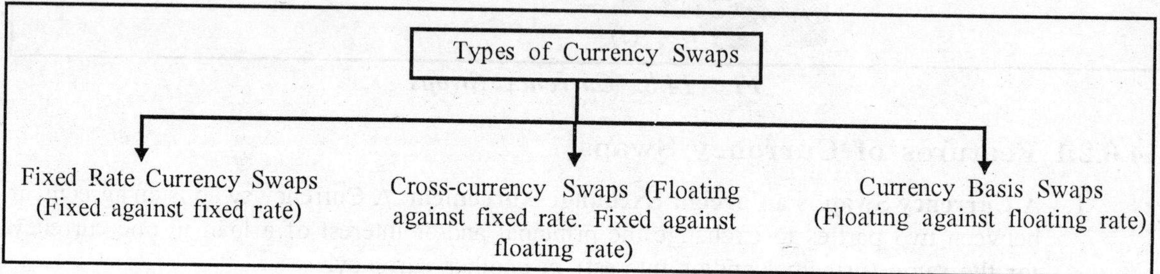

Fig. 14.10: Types of Currency Swaps

- **Fixed Rate Currency Swap:** In this currency swap agreement, the interest rates are fixed for both the parties.
- **Cross-currency Swaps:** In this case, the interest rate on one leg is based on a floating rate and the interest rate on other leg is based on the fixed rate.
- **Currency Basis Swap:** In this case, the interest rate on both legs are based on floating rates.

Example: A swap agreement is signed between two firms with the following details:

Parties to swap agreement:	(a) An Indian firm say (A)
	(b) An American firm say (B)
Date of origin:	January 1, 2012
Tenure of the swap:	5 years
Exchange Rate on January 1, 2011:	1$ = 246

Terms of swap:

	A	B
Principal Amount borrowed:	$ 10,00,000 (From B)	₹ 4,60,00,000 (From A)
Rate of interest (payable)	4% fixed	6% fixed
Payment of interest	Annual	Annual

The initial, intermediate and terminal cash flows will be computed as follows:

On January 1, 2012

A borrowed $ 10,00,000 from B. B paid $ 10,00,000 to A

B borrowed ₹ 4,60,00,000 from A. A paid ₹ 4,60,00,000 to B

Thus, the initial cash flow would be:

	A	B
Inflow	₹ 10,00,000	$ 4,60,00,000
Outflow	₹ 4,60,00,000	₹ 10,00,000

On January 1, 2013, 2014, 2015, 2016

A will pay annual interest of $ 40,000 to B and A will receive ₹ 27,60,000 from B as annual interest. Thus, the intermediate annual cash flow would be:

	A	B
Inflow	₹ 27, 60,000	$ 40000
Outflow	₹ 40000	₹ 27,60000

Terminal cash flows as on 1st January, 2017

	A	B
Inflow:	₹ 4,60,00,000	$ 10,00,000
	₹ 27,60,000	$ 40,000
Total	487,60,000	$ 10,40,000
Outflow:	$ 10,40,000 (USD)	₹ 4,87,60,000 (INR)

The above stated figures can be put in a swap structure as follows:

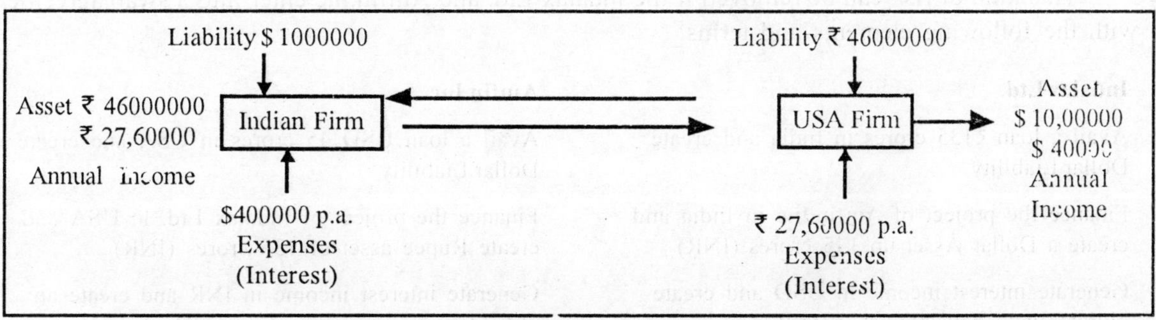

Fig. 14.11: Currency Swap – Structure

14.6.2.3 Uses of a Currency Swap

A currency swap involves a services of exchanges of cash flow. These cash flows are made in different currencies. These amounts of cash flows are determined on the basis of exchange rates. Swap transactions are useful in the following ways:

(a) Heading the exchange risk by way of converting a liability/asset in one currency into a liability/asset in another currency.

(b) Reduction of borrowing or financing cost (in case of foreign currency borrowing or financing) through currency swaps.

(a) Hedging Exchange Rate Risk by Currency Swap

Currency swaps can be used to hedge against exchange rate risks by converting liabilities or assets from one currency to another.

Let us consider an example to see how multinational investors can easily hedge foreign exchange risk through swap agreement.

Example: Indalax Ltd., an Indian company needs ₹ 135 crores to finance a project in USA. This company raises **funds in India in Indian** Rupees (INR) by availing a loan from a Bank. These funds of ₹ 135 crores are converted into USD ($) to acquire assets in USD ($). If the time of acquiring assets in USA, the exchange rate in 1$ = ₹ 45, then ₹ 135 crores will be equivalent to $3 crores. Further, the Indalax expects 10% return (fixed) in its investment which is equal to $30 lakhs US (equivalent to ₹ 13.5 crores).

Similarly, Amfin.Inc an American company wants to invest in US $3 crores in a project in India. This American firm also expects 12% return (fixed) on its investment.

If there will be an adverse movements of exchanges rates, then both firms will be at an risk. For example, if there is an appreciation of rupee, then it harms the profitability of an Indian company. Thus, in this situation, the Indian firm will face a risk while the American firm is a gainer. In case rupee depreciates, the US firm is at loss, while the Indian firm is a gainer. Thus, both the firms will likely to exposure of exchange rate risk.

This kind of risk can be removed if the Indalax Ltd. and Amfin.Inc enter into a swap agreement with the following elements and terms:

Indalax Ltd.	**Amfin.Inc**
Avail a loan ₹135 crores in India and create Dollar Liability	Avail a loan USD 45 crores in USA and create a Dollar Liability
Finance the project of Amfin.Inc in India and create a Dollar Asset up 145 crores (INR)	Finance the project of Indalax Ltd. in USA and create Rupee asset of 135 crores (INR)
Generate interest income in USD and create obligation to pay interest in INR	Generate interest income in INR and create an obligation to pay interest in USD

According to swap agreement, Amfin.Inc agrees to pay rupee generated income out of the Indian operations to the Indian firm in exchange for the Indalax Ltd. agreeing to pay dollar generated out of its USA operations. By such mutual swap agreement, the mismatch of cash inflows and outflows in two currencies for both Indalax Ltd. and Amfin.Inc can be eliminated.

Results:

(i) The Rupee Asset income flows to the Indian firm will meet the rupee obligation liability.

(ii) The Dollar Asset income flows to US firm will meet to its USD obligations.

Thus, through the swap agreement, both the firms will have assets and liabilities translated in the same currency and the risk of exchange rate will automatically be eliminated.

The structure of the above swap agreement is depicted in the Figure 14.12:

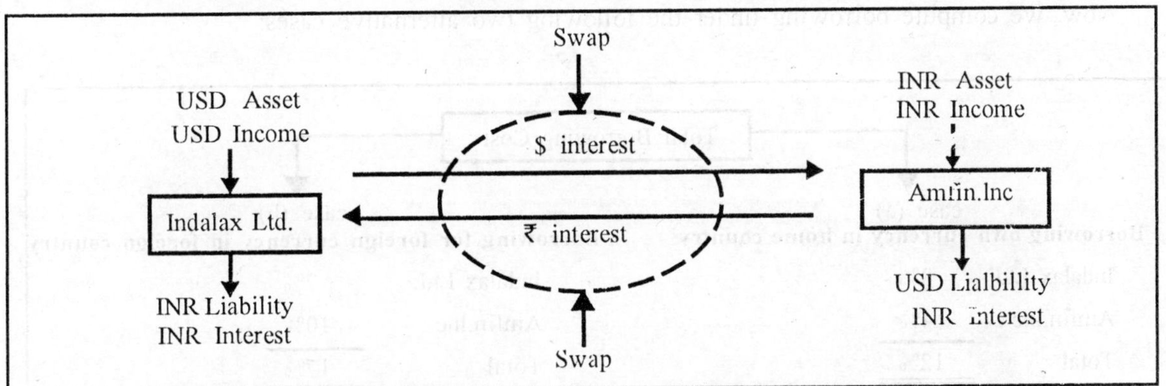

Fig 14.12: Converting Assets/Liabilities from One Currency to Another through Currency Swap

(b) Reduction of Borrowing Cost (in Case of Foreign Currency Borrowings) through Currency Swaps

Multinational firms need funds in different currencies. They follow the principle of comparative advantage. As different countries have their own economic policies as well as distinct and separate financial markets, the multinationals can avail maximum benefits through currency swap transactions.

Consider the following example:

Let Indalax Ltd., an Indian company and Amfin.Inc an American company, both are multinational firms. Both the multinational firms enjoy excellent and equivalent credit rating in their respective countries. They raised funds to meet their financial requirements from the financial market of their own countries. Now, they need to raise funds across the nations to meet their present financial requirements, and to capitalise on the interest rate differentials that may exists in various currencies.

Following is the cost of capital for Indalax Ltd. and Amfin.Inc in their respective currencies.

Financial Market

	In India (INR market)	In America ($ market)
Indalax Ltd.	8%	7%
Amfin.Inc	10%	7%
Advantage – Amfin	–2%	+3%
Advantage – Indalax Ltd.	+2%	–3%

From the above facts, it is very clear that the Indalax Ltd., being the Indian firm enjoys the fundings cost advantage over American firm in India. Similarly, the Amfin.Inc, being the American firm enjoys the funding cost advantage over Indian firm in America.

Now, we compute borrowing under the following two alternative cases:

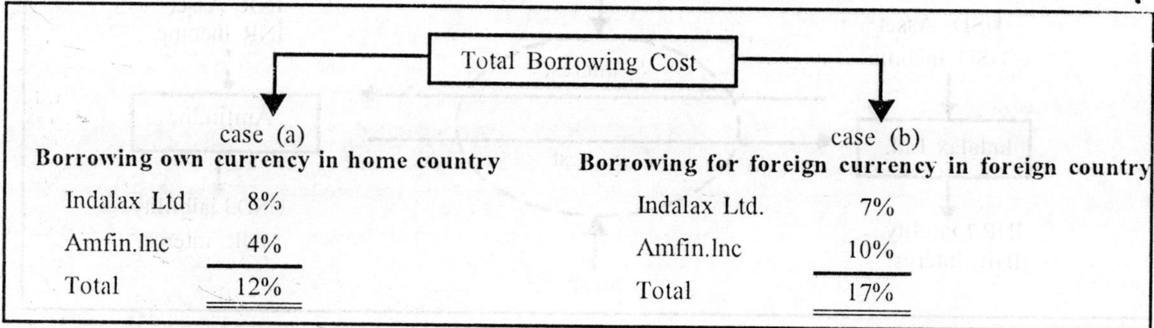

Fig. 14.13: Reduction of Borrowing Cost through Swap

The comparative advantage here is 17% – 12% = 5%. If the two companies borrow in the foreign currencies, the total cost of fund will be 17%, i.e., the Indalax Ltd. will borrow Dollar at 7% and the Amfin.Inc will borrow Rupee at 10%. However, if they borrow as per the comparative advantage theory and exchange each other's commitment, the total cost of funds can be reduced to 12% with the American firm borrowing dollar at 4% and Indian firm borrowing rupee at 8%. Both the firms can benefit by 5% in aggregate if they enter into a swap arrangement with the following conditions:

(a) Indalax Ltd. will borrow funds in rupees in the Indian market at 8%.

(b) Indalax Ltd. will lend the fund to Amfin.Inc at one per cent higher, i.e., 9%.

(c) The Amfin.Inc will raise funds in the American market in USD at 4%.

(d) Amfin.Inc will lend the same fund to the Indalax Ltd. at 5%.

(e) Exchange the interest rate periodically.

(f) Finally, exchange the principal upon redemption.

The cost of funds for the both parties of this currency swap is shown in the following diagram:

Cost of Funds for Two Firms

	Indian firm		**USA firm**	
1. Payment to investors	INR	8%	USD	4%
2. Payment to counterparty	USD	5%	INR	9%
3. Receipt from counterparty	INR	9%	USD	5%
Cost of borrowing (1 + 2 – 3)	USD	4%	INR	8%

INR Principal

₹ 8% Indalax Ltd. (Indian company) ₹ 9% $ 5% Amfin.Inc (American company) $ 4%

USD Principal

Fig. 14.14: Currency Swap: Conceptual Framework for Reducing Funding Cost

Through the swap arrangement, Indalax Ltd. (Indian firm) is now able to get Dollar funds at 4% as against 7% in the absence of swaps. Thus, it enjoys the reduction of 3% interest burden cost. Similarly, the US firm gains to raise rupee funds at 8% and benefit of 2%. The aggregate benefit is equal to the comparative advantage of 5% which may be shared by the two firms depending on the strengths and bargaining skills of the two parties involved.

14.6.3 Equity Swaps

Equity swaps are similar to interest rate swap contracts. There are two counterparties. They agree to exchange a set of future cash flows at set dates in future. The two cash flows are usually referred as "legs" of the swap. These are as follows:

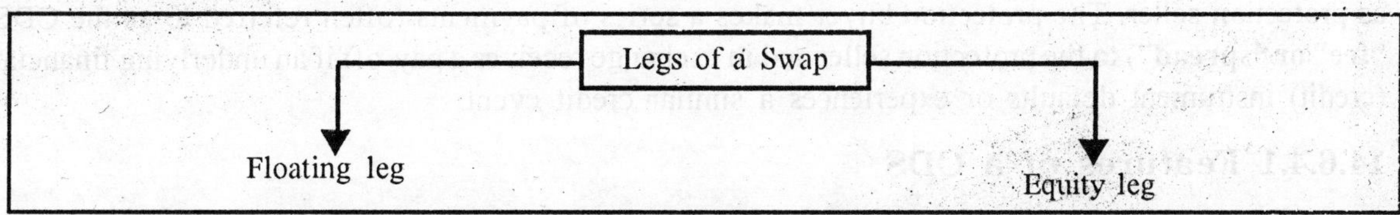

Fig. 14.15: Legs in an Equity Swap

(i) Floating Leg: The leg of an equity swap which is usally pegged to a floating rate such as MIBOR or LIBOR is known as "floating leg".

(ii) Equity Leg: This is the other leg of a swap which is based on the performance of either a share of a stock or a stock market index. It is commonly referred to as equity leg.

An Equity Swap is the exchange of two payment streams between two counterparties over an agreed period where the first party makes payments that are based on the returns on a stock or a stock index and the counterparty makes payments of either a fixed amount or a floating amount or payments based on the returns of a stock or a stock index.

14.6.3.1 Applications of Equity Swaps

1. Traders in the capital markets entered into swap contracts to avoid transaction costs and security transaction taxes etc. Most equity swaps today are conducted between large financing firms investment banks and capital lending institutions. They do not require to follow the rules of investment on equity stock when they entered into equity swaps.

2. An investor in a physical holding of shares loses his position on the shares once he sells his position. However, using an Equity swap, the investor can pass on the negative returns on equity position without loosing the possession of shares and hence the voting rights.

   Example:

   Mr. X holds 1000 shares of P Ltd. In near future, the market price of these stock will likely to fall and will give negative return. However, his holding gives him a strategic voting right in the Board of P Ltd. which he does not want to loose. Hence, he enters into an Equity Swap deal wherein he agrees to pay the counterparty Mr. Y the return on his shares against MIBOR plus 25bps on a notional amount. If Mr. X is proven right, he will get money from Mr. Y on account of his negative return on the stock as well as MIBOR + 25bps on the notional amount. By this strategy, he will mitigate the negative returns on the stock without loosing his voting rights.

3. An Equity deal facilitates an investor to receive the return on a stock which is listed in such a market where he cannot invest due to certain legal restrictions.

Thus, Equity Swaps, if effectively used, can make investment (on Equity) barriers vanish and help an investor create leverage similar to those seen in derivative products.

14.6.4 Credit Default Swaps

A "CREDIT DEFAULT SWAP" (CDS) is a credit derivative contract between two counterparties. The buyer of a CDS is known as protection buyer and seller of a CDS is known as protection seller. The protection buyer makes a series of payments (often referred to as the CDS **"fee" or "spread"**) to the protection seller and in exchange receives a pay-off if an underlying financial (credit) instrument defaults or experiences a similar credit event.

14.6.4.1 Features of a CDS

1. **Bilaterial Contract:** A credit default swap is a bilateral contract between the buyer and seller of protection.

Fig. 14.16: Counterparties in a CDS

2. **Reference Entity:** The CDS may refer to a specified loan or bond obligation of a corporation or government. Such corporation or government is known as **"Reference Entity" or "Reference Obligor"**

Note: The reference entry is not a party to the swap contract.

3. **Regular Premium Payments by the Protection Buyer:** The buyer of protection will make regular premium payments to the protection seller. If the associated credit instrument suffers no credit event, the protection buyer will continue the payment till the maturity of the contract.

   Example: Let Mr. X, an investor, buys a CDS from Mumbai Bank, where the reference entry is Indian Risky Corporation. The date of swap contract is 1st January, 2012. The contract period is 10 years. Mr. X has to pay quarterly premium to Mumbai Bank till 31st December, 2022.

4. **Termination of Contract on Default:** If the Reference Entity defaults on its debt, then the investor (the protection buyer) will cease paying premium and the protection seller will pay the buyer for the loss.

Points to Note:

(i) The CDS will be terminated on default.

(ii) The protection buyer will receive one-time payment on default or at maturity of CDS.

(iii) A default is referred to as a **"credit event"** and include such events as failure to pay, restricting and bankruptcy.

5. **Settlement:** In case the Reference Entity defaults, one of two kinds of settlement can occur:

   (i) ***Physical Settlement:*** The protection buyer delivers a defaulted asset to the protection seller for payment of the par value, which is known as physical settlement.

   (ii) ***Cash Settlement:*** The protection seller pays the protection buyer the difference between the par value and market price of the specified debt obligation, which is known as cash settlement.

6. **Risk:** In a Credit Default Swap, both the buyer and seller of credit protection are exposed to counterparty risks.

Schematic Structure of a CDS:

A. *CDS (NO DEFAULT)*

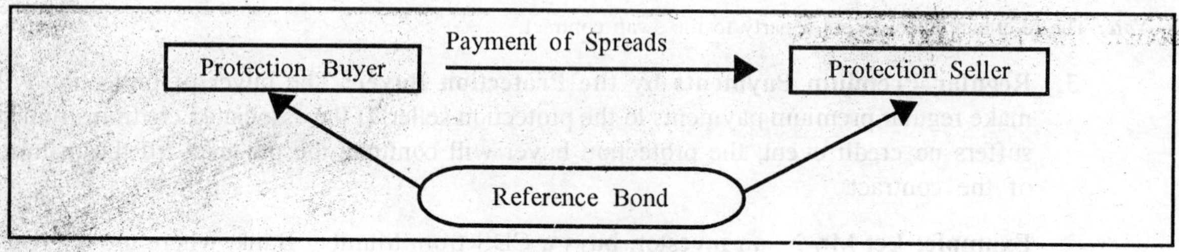

Fig. 14.17

B. *CDS (DEFAULT)*

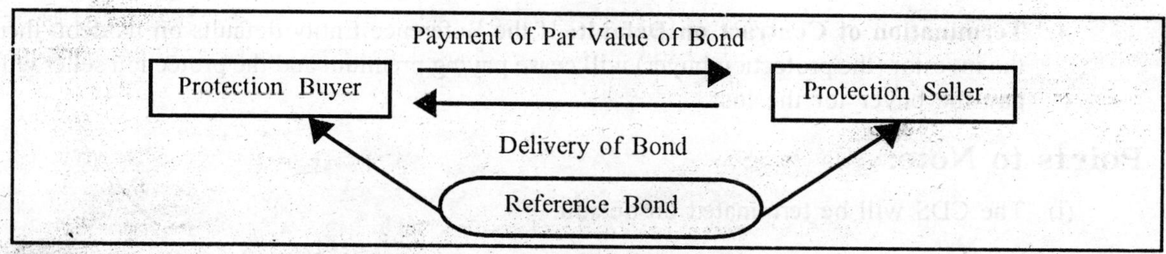

Fig. 14.18

14.6.5 Commodity Swaps

A commody swap is an agreement between two counterparties to exchange cash flows depending upon the price of a given commodity. Essentially, it is an agreement whereby a **floating price** is exchanged for a **fixed price**. One party will pay a fixed price for the given commodity (notional underlying), while the counterparty will pay floating price for the same commodity on the settlement date. Commodity swaps are used to lock-in the price of a commodity.

Basics of a Commodity Swap

1. It is equivalent to a series of forward contracts on a commodity.
2. Both the counterparties determine the Notional Principal in terms of the commodity. For example 5 kg gold. They also determine the fixed price of the commodity.
3. The Notional Principal is not exchanged.
4. In a commodity swap, the counterparties determine the settlement dates or the dates on which the commodity price is recorded. On these dates, only cash flows are exchanged by comparing the actual price of the commodity.

Example: M/s Karnatakgold, a gold mining firm wants to fix the price it will receive for the gold it will mine over the next 3 years. M/s Taniska Jewellers, a gold user firm wants to fix the price it will have to pay for the gold it needs for the next 3 years. Notional Principal in terms of gold is fixed 100 kg. The gold price is fixed ₹ 25,000/- 10 grams. The settlement is semi-annual, based on average price of gold during the past six months. The swap flows will be made as follows:

Time	Average gold price during past 6 months (per 10 grams)	M/s Karnatakgold pays (-) or receives
0.50 year	₹ 23000	(+) ₹ 2.00 crores
1.00 year	₹ 26000	(–) ₹ 1.00 crores
1.50 year	₹ 28000	(–) ₹ 3.00 crores
2.00 year	₹ 29000	(–) ₹ 4.00 crores
2.50 year	₹ 24000	(+) ₹ 1.00 crores
3.00 year	₹ 21000	(+) ₹ 4.00 crores

14.6.5.1 Types of Commodity Swaps

There are two types of commodity swaps. These are as follows:

(i) Fixed-for-floating swap

(ii) Commodity for interest swap

Fixed-for-floating commodity swap is just like the fixed-for-floating interest swap. Here, floating rate a specified commodity is based on commodity index.

Example:

GSCI – Goldman Sacks Commodity Index

CRBI – Commodities Research Board Index

These two indices place different weights on the various commodities so that they will be used according to swap participants' requirements.

Commodity-for-interest swap is similar to the equity swap in which a total return on the commodity in question is exchanged for some money market rates.

14.6.5.2 Additional Costs and Legal Issues

Commodity Swaps involve additional costs in addition to the potential price paid on the settlement date. The additional costs include brokerage and commission, risk analysis cost and other administrative costs. Further, legal ramifications of commodity swaps also affect the type of swap contracts. The factors like creditworthiness of counterparties, availability of security and termination rights of the parties are the prime considerations of a swap contract. Both the **additional costs and legal issues** can affect the party's ultimate choice of commodity swap type.

14.6.5.3 Hedging Price Risk through Commodity Swap

The type of commodity swap depends upon the investment strategy, status of the participant in the swap contract, i.e., whether a party is an **"end-user"** such as a consumer of the commodity or a **producer** or a **speculator** who attempts to make money from the price fluctuations.

End-users need to hedge the prices at which they can purchase these commodities. For example, an Airline wants to lock-in the price of the jet fuel it needs to purchase in order to satisfy the peak in seasonal demand for travel.

A producer needs to manage his risk of fluctuations in the prices for his goods produced. He is primarily concerned with fixing prices on contracts to sell his produce. For example, a gold producer wants to hedge his losses attributable to a fall in the price of gold for his current gold inventory.

A speculator who can either buy or sell commodity by participating in the global commodities market. Traditionally, he wants to hedge against inflation. If the general price level goes up, it is probably attributable to increase in input prices.

14.7 ECONOMIC MOTIVES FOR SWAPS

As stated in the earlier sections, there are many economic motivations for firms to enter into swap contracts. Some of the important motivations are mentioned below:

1. Swaps are used as hedging techniques to cover exchange rate risk through currency swaps or interest rate risk through interest rate swaps or credit default risk through credit swaps.
2. Swaps are used to change the complexion of asset or liability from one currency to another currency.
3. Currency Swaps are used by multinational firms to reduce the funding cost when they raise fund in foreign currency.
4. Commodity Swaps are highly motivational to the end-users, producers as well as the speculators. The end-users can be able to hedge the price risk for the commodities they use in their business operations. Producers can fix their expected income and able to hedge their losses in case of fall in the prices of commodities. Similarly, speculators of commodity swaps can hedge against inflation risk.
5. Finally, the economic rationale for Equity Swap is the reduce transaction cost, avoid security transaction tax and make the investment (on Equity) barriers vanish.

To sum up, the following figure depicts the various motivational factors underlying the swap contracts:

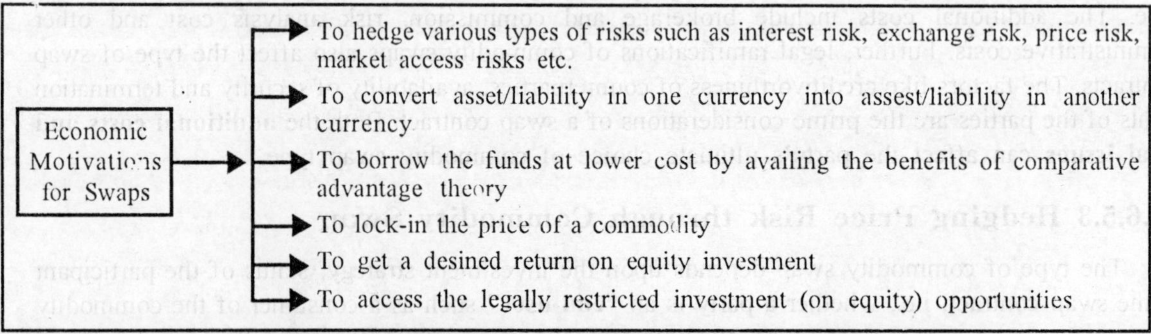

Fig. 14.19: Economic Motivations for Swaps

14.8 CHAPTER SUMMARY

A swap is a private agreement between two or more counterparties to exchange (swap) sets of cash flows over a period in the future. Specifically, the two counterparties agree to exchange one stream of flows againts another stream streams are called the legs of the swap. Essentially, a swap has an opening leg (the initial exchange), the intermediate legs (subsequent cash flows) and finally a closing leg (the final exchange). For example:

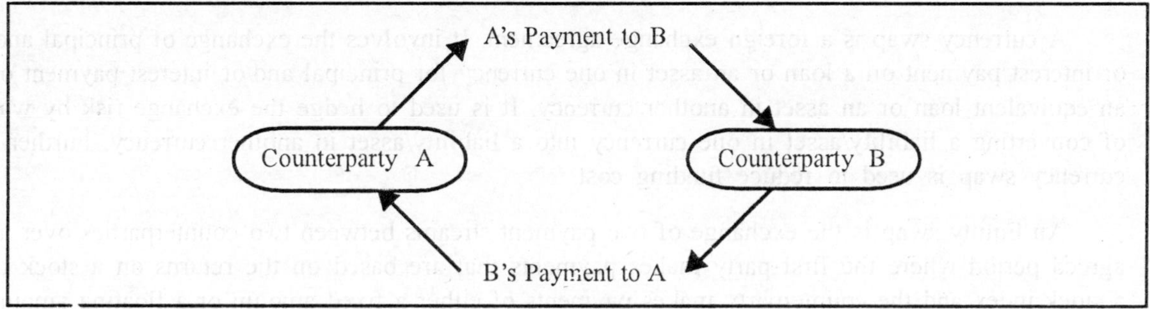

Fig. 14.20

The common features of financial swaps are:

- A swap is a series of forward agreements.
- Intermediary facilitators, i.e., banks and financial institutions.
- Double coincidence of counterparties' wants.
- Underlying notional principal: There is an underlying notional principal (specified as an amount of a commodity swap, specified as a stock portfolio in an equity swap).
- Cash flows and settlement procedure – One party pays fixed while the other party pays floating or both party pay at floating rates.
- There is a fixed tenure contract particularly long periods.

The major types of financial swaps are interest rate swaps, currency swaps, equity swaps, credit swaps and commodity swaps. Interest Rate Swaps (IRS) are the most heavily traded swap product.

Interest Rate Swaps (IRS) arise when the cash flows are interest payments. In case of a Plain Vanilla Interest Swap, interest payments based on a fixed rate are exchanged for interest payments based on floating rate. Interest is calculated on an amount called **Notional Principal** (or just Notional) of the swap. The Notional Principal is not exchanged. For example:

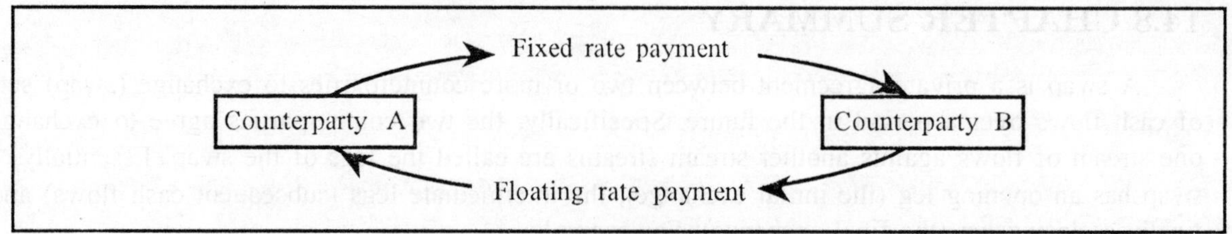

Fig. 14.21

A currency swap is a foreign exchange agreement. It involves the exchange of principal and/or interest payment on a loan or an asset in one currency for principal and/or interest payment on an equivalent loan or an asset in another currency. It is used to hedge the exchange risk by way of converting a liability/asset in one currency into a liability/asset in another currency. Further a currency swap is used to reduce funding cost.

An Equity swap is the exchange of two payment streams between two counterparties over an agreed period where the first party makes payments that are based on the returns on a stock or a stock index and the counterparty makes payments of either a fixed amount or a floating amount or payment based on the return of a stock or a stock index.

A Credit Default Swap (CDS) is a credit derivative contract between a protection buyer and protection seller. The protection buyer (the investor) makes a series of payments to the protection seller and in exchange receives a pay-off if an underlying financial (credit) instrument defaults or experiences a similar risk. The CDS may refer to a specified loan or bond obligation of a corporation or government.

A commodity swap is an agreement between two counterparties to exchange cash flows depending upon the price of a given commodity, i.e., oil or gold. One party will pay a fixed price for the given commodity (notional underlying), while the counterparty will pay floating price for the same commodity on the settlement date.

Swaps are attractive mechanisms to hedge various types of risks such as interest rate risks, price risks, market access risks, exchange risks and fluctuation risks; to convert asset/liability in one currency into asset/liability in another currency; to borrow the funds at lower cost; to lock in the price of a commodity; to generate a desired return on equity investment and to access the legally restricted investment (on equity) opportunities.

4.8 SOLVED PROBLEMS

1. M/s Sunfin Ltd., Mumbai raised funds ₹ 100 crores by issuing bonds @ 14% p.a. on 1st January 2011. These bonds will be redeemed after 5 years. In December 2011, the interest rate was reduced to 13%. This interest rate will further decline as the economy is moving in positive direction.

You have been appointed as Director Finance of this company. The Chairman-cum-Managing Director is worried about the high borrowing cost, i.e., 14% and requested to find a better solution of this financial problem.

The CMD of Sunfin Ltd. has given a proposal to M/s Yes Bank for entering into an Interest Rate Swap with the following terms and conditions:

- Yes Bank will pay 13% fixed and receive MIBOR as floating rate on the notional principal of ₹ 100 crores.

In December 2011, the present MIBOR is 13.2%.

Would it be advisable to go for swap contract at 13% fixed rate offered by M/s Yes Ltd.? Advise to your CMD.

Solution:

M/s Sunfin Ltd. is currently paying 14% p.a. to the bond holders. It is a fixed liability irrespective of the current interest rates in the market.

If M/s Sunfin Ltd. will enter into a swap agreement with M/s Yes Bank, then the fixed liability will be converted into floating liability.

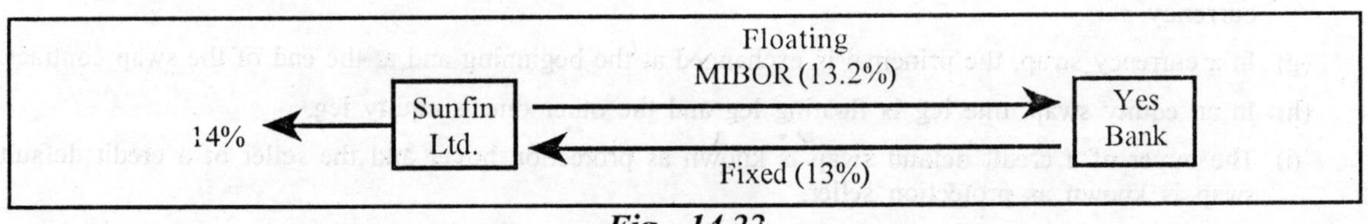

Fig. 14.22

After the swap contract, the net financial burden would be as follows:

Interest payment to Bond holders	14%
Payment to Yes Bank	MIBOR
Received from the Yes Bank	(-)13%
Cost of funds for Sunfin Ltd.	MIBOR +1%

At present, the current rate of MIBOR is 13.2. So, the cost of funds for Sunfin Ltd. would be 13.2% + 1% = 14.1%.

But, the economy of the nation is improving. If the interest rate will future decline in 2012, 2013, 2014, 2015 and 2016, M/s Sunfine Ltd. will be gainer.

So, it recommend this proposal and advise my CMD to enter into this swap contract.

SUGGESTIONS FOR FURTHER READINGS

1. Sharpe, W.F. and Alexander. G.J., *Investment*, Pentice-Hall, 2000.
2. Marshall, J.F. and Kapnae, K.R., *Understanding Swap Finance*, Cincinnati, OH, South Western, 1990.
3. Website of International Swap and Derivative Association (www.isda.ong).
4. Srivastava R, Mishara A., *Financial Management*, Oxford Higher Education, 2008.
5. Mc Laughlin, Robert, L. (2003), *Derivatives Markets,* Boston: Addison-Wesley.

EXERCISES

Quiz

A. State Whether the Following Statements are Ture or False.

(a) A swap is a contract between two parties to exchange cash flows in future according to specified criteria or formula.

(b) A swap is a series of forward contract.

(c) MIBOR/MIFOR/OIC are the benchmark rates for Plain Vanilla Interest Swaps in India.

(d) In a swap agreement, the interest (whether fixed or floating rate) is calculated on the notional or theoretical principal amount.

(e) In an Interest Rate Swap, the fixed rate is known as the swap rate and the floating rate is called as reference rate.

(f) A currency swap involves the exchange of principal and/or interest payment on a loan or an asset in one currency for principal and/or interest payment on an equivalent loan or an asset in another currency.

(g) In a currency swap, the principal is exchanged at the beginning and at the end of the swap contract.

(h) In an equity swap, one leg is floating leg and the other one is equity leg.

(i) The buyer of a credit default swap is known as protection buyer and the seller of a credit default swap is known as protection seller.

(j) The Credit Default Swap may refer to a specified loan or bond obligation to a specified loan or bond obligation of a corporation or government. Such corporation or government is known as Reference Equity or Reference Obligor.

(k) The reference entity of a credit default swap is not a party to the swap contract.

(l) The protection buyer of a credit default swap will receive one-time payment from the protection seller on default.

(m) The protection buyer makes a series of payments to the protection seller under a Credit Default Swap agreement. Such payment is known as CDS fee or spread.

(n) In a commodity swap, both the counterparties determine the Notional Principal in terms of commodity.

(o) GSCI stands stands for Goldman Sachs Commodity Index.

(p) CRBI stands for Commodities Research Board Index.

(q) ISDA stands for International Swaps and Derivative Association.

(r) MIBOR stands for Mumbai Interbank Offer Rate.

(s) As swap is an OTC derivative so it is associated with counterparty risk.

(t) A swaption is an option on a swap.

(u) In a currency swap, the three basic sequential steps are exchange of principal at origination, ongoing exchange of interest and re-exchange of principal amounts on maturity.

(v) A cap is a financial contract which gives the right to the owner but not obligation to borrow a pre-set amount of money at a pre-set interest rate with a pre-set maturity date.

(w) A floor is a financial contract which gives the owner the right but not obligation to lend a pre-set amount of money at a present interest rate with a pre-set maturity date.

(x) In a Plain Vanilla Interest Rate Swap, one leg is fixed interest rate and the other is a floating interest rate. But in a BASIS SWAP, both legs are based on floating rate indices.

(y) LIBOR is a benchmark rate in international finance which is established by the British Bankers' Association and represents the average of rates quoted by about 16 multinational banks.

(z) An equity swap facilitates an investor to receive the return on a stock which is listed in such a market where he cannot invest due to certain legal barrier.

Ans: (a) True, (b) True, (c) True, (d) True, (e) True, (f) True, (g) True, (h) True, (i) True, (j) True, (k) True, (l) True, (m) True, (n) True, (o) True, (p) True, (q) True, (r) True, (s) True, (t) True, (u) True, (v) True, (w) True, (x) True, (y) True, (z) True.

B. Short Type Questions

1. What is a swap?
2. Define the term "swap" is the language of financial derivative?.
3. Why swaps are designed as long-term contracts?
4. What is a swaption?
5. What are the three popular types of swap instruments used in the Indian swap market?
6. What do you mean by Interest Rate Swap?
7. What is basis interest swap?
8. What is a currency swap?
9. What are the three categories of cash flows in a currency swap?
10 What do you mean by cross-currency swap?
11. What is Equity swap?
12. What is a Credit Default Swap?
13. What do you mean by "Reference Entity" in a Credit Default Swap?
14. What is a commodity swap?

C. Long Type Questions

1. Define the concept "swap". Briefly discuss the features of swap contracts.
2. Write short notes on the following:

   (a) Indian swap market

   (b) Types of swaps
3. What is an Interest Rate Swap? Discuss the features of an Interest Rate Swap.
4. Discuss various types of Interest Rate Swaps with suitable examples.
5. What is a Currency Swap?. What are the features? Discus.
6. What is a currency swap? Briefly discuss three types of currency swaps.
7. What are the uses of Currency Swaps? Explain with examples.

8. What is an Equity Swap? What are the two legs of an Equity Swaps? Briefly discuss the applications of Equity Swaps in the derivative market.
9. What is a Credit Default Swap? What are the features of a credit default swap? Discuss.
10. Briefly discuss the basis and types of commodity swaps.
11. Swaps are useful to end-users, producers as well as the speculators of commodities. Briefly discuss the motives underlying such commodity swaps.
12. Briefly discuss the important economic motives for swap derivatives.

PRACTICAL PROBLEMS

1. M/S Mumbai Venture Capital Ltd. raised ₹ 100 crores through issue of 12% Bonds on 1st January, 2012. These bonds will be matured after 10 years. In March 2012, the interest rate was declined to 11% due to the better economy in India. It is expected that there will be further decline in future.

   This company is currently facing the financial burden due to higher funding cost, i.e., 12%. To hedge this risk, now the company decides to have a swap agreement with New Bombay Bank. Thue terms of the swap agreement are as follows:

   — New Bombay Bank will pay 10% fixed and receive MIBOR as floating rate on the notional principal of ₹ 100 crores for next 10 years.

   — At present (in March 2012), the MIBOR is 10.5.

   — Would it be advisable to go for swap contract at 10% fixed rate offered by. New Bombay Bank Ltd.? Advise.

GLOSSARY OF DERIVATIVE CONCEPTS

A

American Style Option: An option that can be exercised at any time during its life.

Arbitrage: The act of taking advantages in price between markets. It is a process of buying an asset in the cheaper market and simultaneously selling it at higher price in another market.

Arbitrageur: Arbitrage is defined as "simultaneous purchase and sale of equivalent assets at prices which guarantee a fixed profit at the time of the transaction. So, an Arbitrageur is a person who actively seeks arbitrage situations, and by exploiting them helps keep the marketplace efficient.

Asian Option: It is an average rate option. An Asian option is exercised against average price over period.

Ask Price: Ask price is the lowest price at which the trader expresses his willingness to sell a security.

At-the-Money Option: An option in which the Exercise Price equals the current market price of the underlying asset.

B

Backwardation: It is a situation in the future market, where the price of an underlying asset of a futures contract for future delivery is lower than the spot price (i.e., futures price is less than the cash price), or where a short dated futures contract at a higher price than the longer dated contract, or where a distance future delivery price is lower than a nearer future delivery.

Backwards Induction (Process): It is a step in the Binomial Option Pricing Model. Stock prices are calculated by Forward Induction (Process) procedure where option prices are calculated by backward induction (process) at each step in the Binomial Tree. Thus, it is a procedure for working from the end to its origination in order to value an option.

Barrier Option: An option contract for which the maturity, strike price and underlying assets are specified at origination in addition to barrier price.

Basis: The difference between the spot price and the futures price of a commodity.

Basis Point (bp): Change (increase or decrease) in interest rate is made by basis points. It is one hundredth of one percent (= 0.01 percent).

Basis Risk: The term "risk means" variation. The basis risk arises because the changes in futures prices and spot prices are not equal. In other words, the basis risk is the result of uncertainty about the basis at a future time.

Bearish: The tendency of moving down. In capital market when we predict that the price of a particular stock will decline, it is a bearish tendency.

Bermurdan Option: An option which can be exercised on specified dates during the life of the option.

Beta: It is a measure (method) which is used to determine the systematic risk of an asset.

Bid-ask Spread: The amount by which the ask price exceeds the bid price.

Binomial Model: It is an option pricing model. Mr. Cox, Mr. Ross and Mr. Rubinstein developed this model in 1979. This model assumes that the price of the stock at every point of time may have only two possible states, i.e., move up or move down. Initially, a tree of stock prices is drawn to show the possible stock prices at every point of time in a forward form (left to right). Finally, the option price is calculated by using backward induction method.

Binomial Tree: A tree that represents all the possible paths that stock price can take during the life of the option.

Black-Scholes Option Pricing Model (BSOPM): It is a mathematical model (an equation form) for option valuation. This model incorporates several variables like S_o (current price of stock), X (strike price), T (Time to expiration), (Volatility of the stock price), r (Risk-free interest rate) and D (Expected dividend) etc. This model attempts to determine the theoretical price of an option.

Bullish: The belief that the price of an asset will increase.

Bull Spread: An option spread that becomes profitable when the price of the underlying asset rises. For example, A long position in a call with strike price X_1 combined with a short position in a call with strike price X_2, where $X_2 > X_1$.

Butterfly Spread: A spread involving three option positions. For example, one long call with a strike price X_1, another long call with a strike price X_3 and one short call with a strike price X_2 where $X_3 > X_2 > X_1$ and $X_2 + 1/2(X_1 + X_3)$. Thus, a trader takes short and long positions in calls and puts simultaneously with different strike prices.

Buying Hedge: It implies that a hedger goes a long to protect some economic interest.

C

Call Option: The option that gives the holder the right (without obligation) to buy the underlying asset by a certain date for a certain price.

Capital Asset Pricing Model (CAPM): A model that states the relationship between risk and expected return and that is used in the pricing of risky securities. CAPM describes that the expected return of a security or a portfolio equals the rate on a risk-free security plus a risk premium. The model is:

$$E(R_i) = R_f + \beta_i \; E(R_m - R_f)$$

where $E(R_i)$ = Expected return on the capital asset, R_f = Risk-free rate of interest, β_i (the beta) is the sensitivity of the expected return, i.e., beta of the security, R_m is the expected market return.

Cash Settlement: It is a conditional term is the futures contract settlement. It is a procedure for settling a futures contract in cash rather than by delivering the underlying asset.

COD: Cash on Delivery

Clearing House: A clearing house is a financial institution that provides clearing and settlement services for financial and commodity derivatives and securities transactions.

Collar: Collar is an option strategy that limits the range of possible positive or negative returns on an underlying to a specific range.

Combination: In finance, a combination is an option trading strategy that involves taking a position in both calls and puts on the same underlying. Examples of combinations are Collar, Fence, Iron Butterfly, Iron Condor, Straddle, Strangle, Strap and Strip.

Commodity Swap: A swap in which exchanged cash flows are dependedent on the price of an underlying commodity. A commodity swap is usually used to hedge against the price of a commodity.

Consumption Asset: Consumption assets is an asset that is typically held for consumption. Some examples are : oil, copper, cattle, rubber and sugar,

Condor: A less risky type of strangle that involves four different strike prices.

Contago: It is a situation where futures contract price is above the cash price (expected futures spot price).

Contag· Market: The futures market in which the futures contract price exceeds cash price.

Continuous Compounding: When interest is compounded daily, it is called continuous compounding. In case of continuous compounding, the Futures value and present value will be calculated by using the following formula:

$FV = Pe^{rT}$ or $P = FV\, e^{-rT}$

Where, FV = Future Value, P = Present Value, r = Rate of interest p.a and T = Time (no. of years)

Counterparty: The opposite side in a financial derivative contract.

Counterparty Risk: The chance of loss due to default by the other party to a derivative contract.

Coupon Rate: The specified interest rate that determines the Rupee amount of interest a bond pays.

Covered Call: A call option where the call writer owns the underlying asset.

Credit Risk: When a borrower will be unable to repay the principal and interest as agreed. It is also known as default risk.

Credit spread: An option spread strategy where the premium received on the option written (sold) is higher than the premium paid on the option bought.

Currency Swap: A swap where the interest and principal in one currency are exchanged for interest and principal in another currency.

D

Day Count: A Convention for quoting interest rates.

Day Trade: A trade that is entered into and closed out on the same day.

Delta (Δ): The rate of change of the price of a derivative with the price of the underlying asset. Option delta is the sensitivity of an option's theoretical price to changes in the value of the underlying asset.

Derivative: It is a financial instrument. It's value is derived from or depends on the value of another asset.

Diagonal Spread: An option strategy established by simultaneously entering into a long and short position in two options of the same type (two call options or two put options) but with different strike prices and expiration dates.

Dynamic Hedging: A dynamic hedge is one that needs to be adjusted as the price (and some times other characteristics) of the portfolio or security it is hedging changes.

E

Equity Swap: A Swap in which at least one party's payments are based on the rate of return on an equity index such as the S&P 500. The other party's payments can be based on the fixed rate, a non-equity variable rate or even a different equity index.

European Style of Option: An option that can be exercised only at the end of its life, i.e., on maturity date or at the expiry date of option.

Exchange Traded Contract: It is a standardised derivative contract (e.g., futures and options) which is transacted on an organised future exchange.

Exercise Price (Strike Price): It is the price at which the underlying transaction will occur upon exercise. It is the price at which the call's (put's) buyer can buy (or sell) the underlying asset.

Expiration Date: The expiration date, or expiry, which is the last date the option can be exercised. It is the last date of an option's life.

Exotic Derivatives: Exotic as opposed to Varilla refers to the fact that the pay-off is not standard, as is the case for a regular call option.

Exotic Option: An option like contract with unusual terms, i.e., a non-standardised option.

F

Financial Asset: An asset (resources) for which there is a corresponding liability (source).

Financial Engineering: Financial Engineering is a multidisciplinary field relating to the creation of new financial instruments and strategies, typically exotic options and specialised interest rate derivatives. The field applies engineering methodologies to problems in finance and employs financial theory and applied mathematics as well as computation and the practice of programming.

Floor: A portfolio of put options, with successive expiration dates, on an interest rate.

Floor Broker: A member of an Exchange who executes the orders for other members. He charges for such duty which is known as broker's fees.

Floating Rate: In a swap contract, one counterparty may pay an interest rate which is variable. This variable or floating rate changes periodically as some benchmark rate changes.

Foreign Currency Swap: An agreement to make a currency exchange between two foreign parties. The agreement consists of swaping principal and interest payments on a loan made one currency for principal and interest payments on a loan equal value of another currency.

Forward Contract: It is a bilateral agreement between two parties to trade in future. One party agrees to buy or sell an asset for a pre-determined delivery price at a certain future time.

Forward Market Commission:

Forward Rate Agreement: Forward Rate Agreement (FRA) is a contract by which the counterparties lock-in a forward interest rate. On the date of settlement, the rate specified in FRA is compared with the agreed upon benchmark/reference rate. The differential amount is settled by exchanging cash.

Futures: A futures is a forward contract traded on an organised exchange. It is a legal, transferable standardised contract.

Futures Option: It is a special type of option. It gives the holder of a call the right to assume a long position in a futures contract, while the holder of a futures put has the right to go short a futures contract. Thus, it is an option on futures contract.

G

Gamma: Gamma is an option greek. It measures the rate of change of delta. It is the sensitivity of delta to changes in the stock price. It is positive for all long options and negative for all short options.

Greeks: Through mathematical formulas, certain numbers are generated to estimate various types of risks associated with options derivatives. These numbers are collectively known as "Greeks". These numbers are the hedge parameters and represented by the Greek letters like Δ (Delta), θ (Theta), γ (Gamma), ν (Vega) and ρ (Rho) etc.

H

Hedge: Hedge means protect oneself from loss. Loss is the result of risk. To hedge means to reduce or eliminate risk associated with price of on asset in the market.

Hedger: Hedgers face risk associated with the price of an asset. The want to eliminate or reduce some type of economic risk by using derivatives like futures and options.

Hedge Ratio: A ratio comprising the value of a position protected via a hedge with size of the entire position itself. Mathematically, it is expressed as:

$$HR = \frac{\text{Futures Positions}}{\text{Cash Market Positions}}$$

Historical Volatility: Volatility is a measure of the variability in the asset's rate of return. It is estimated by using a standard deviation (σ). Historical Volatility is calculated from the historical stock prices. The historical stock prices may be daily or weekly stock prices. It is calculated before the computation of option price by Black-Scholes formula.

Horizontal Spread: An option strategy of simultaneous long and short position, in which the options are chosen simultaneously from the financial listings. It is also known as time spread or calender spread.

I

Implied Volatility: Volatility implied from a option price (determined by using the Black-Scholes formula) is called implied volatility. In other words, when the volatility of the stock implies the current option price we consider it as implied volatility. Basically implied volatility helps in determining the fair option price, while historical volatility helps in determining the theoretical value of an option.

Index Futures: When the underlying asset of a futures contract is a stock index, it is called Index futures. For example, stock index on Nifty.

Interest Rate Swap: An exchange of a fixed rate of interest on a notional principal for a floating rate of interest on the same notional principal.

In the-Money Option: In-the-money option, the holder should have positive intrinsic value on exercise. When spot price of the underlying asset on exercise date exceeds the strike price, then the call option is said to be In-the-money. Contrary to this, when spot price of the underlying asset on exercise date is less than the strike price, then the put option is said to be in-the-money.

Intrinsic Value: The intrinsic value of an option that can be realised it the option is exercised. Therefore, only in-the-money (ITM) options have intrinsic value. The intrinsic value of an option is the difference between the exercise price and current spot price of the underlying asset.

Investment Asset: An asset held primarily for investment purpose such as gold, financial securities like stocks, shares, bonds etc. For the purpose of valuation of forward contract (where the underlying is the investment asset), all the investment assets are classified into three categories, i.e., investment assets generate no income, investment assets generate a known cash income and investment assets generate a known dividend.

L

LIBOR: London Inter Bank Offer Rate. It is the rate which is offered by banks on Eurocurrency deposits. This rate is used by one bank to borrow from another bank.

Limit Order: A limit order in a futures contract is like a market order with one exception that the price takes highest priority. A limit order may be limit buy order or limit sell order.

Limit Buy Order: A customer will use a limit buy order if he desires to buy the futures contract, but he wants to pay no more than a specified price.

Limit Sell Order: A customer will use a limit sell order if he desires to sell futures contract, but wants to receive at least some specified price, i.e., the limit price.

Lognormal Distribution: A lognormal distribution is a probability distribution of a random variable whose logarithm is normally distributed.

Long Hedge: A situation where an investor has to take a long position in futures contracts in order to hedge against future price volatility.

Long Position: The buying of a security such as a stock, commodity or currency with the expectation that the price of the asset will rise in future. In context of options, the buying of an option contract is an example of long position.

Long Straddle: The long straddle is simply the simultaneous purchase of a long call and a long put on the same underlying security with both options having the same expiration and same strike price.

Long Strangle: It is the simultaneous purchase of long call and long put on the same underlying security with both options having the same expiration but where the put strike price is less than a call strike price.

M

Maintenance Margin: The buyers as well as the sellers in futures contracts have to maintain minimum balance in their Margin Account. When the balance in a trader's margin account falls below the maintenance margin level, a trader receives a margin call from the exchange/clearing house and deposit the required money immediately.

Margin Call: It is known as maintenance call. A broker demands on the investor to deposit additional margin to bring the level of margin account upto maintenance level.

Margin: A margin is collateral that the holder of a financial instrument has to deposit to cover some or all credit risks of their counterparty (most often their broker or an exchange).

Mark to Market (MTM): It is a measure of the fair value of accounts that can change over time such as assets and liabilities. In simple language, it is a practice of revaluing the assets and liabilities to reflect the current values.

Maturity Date: It is the last date of the derivative contrat, i.e., date of expiry.

N

Naked Call: A naked call occunrs when a speculator writes (sells) a call option on a security without ownership of that security. It is one of the riskiest options strategies because it carries unlimited risk as opposed to a naked put where the maximum loss occurs if the stock falls to zero. A naked call is the opposite of a covered call.

Normal Backwardation: It is situation in a futures contract where the futures price is below the expected futures spot price. It is the opposite of contago.

Normal Distribution: It is a standard bell-shaped distribution of statistics. The bell-shaped curve is symmetric and mean is equal to mode and median, i.e., X = Mode = Median.

Notional Principal: In a swap contract, notional principal is used to calculate payments of interest. The principal is "notional" because it is neither paid nor received.

O

Open Interest: The total number of options and/or futures contracts that are not closed on a particular day. In other words, the term "Open Interest" represents the number of buy market orders before the stock market opens.

Option: An option is a financial derivative or contract. It offers the buyer the right but not obligation, to buy (call) or sell (put) a security or other financial asset at an agreed upon price (the strike price) during a certain period of time or on a specific date (exercise date).

Out-of-the-money Option: A call option is said to be out-of-the-money where the asset price is less than the strike price. Similarly, a put option is said to be out-of-the-money when the asset price is more than the strike price.

Over-the-Counter Market: In the OTC market, trading occurs via a network of middlemen, called dealers, who carry inventories of securities to facilitate the buy and sell orders of inventors. It is a decentralised market of securities not listed on an exchange where market participants trade over the telephone, facsimile or electronic network instead of a physical trading floor. There is no central exchange or meeting place for this market. Thus, non-standard products are traded in the so-called over-the-counter derivatives markets.

P

Pay-off: The amount realised by the trader or option holder at the end of the derivative contract.

Plain Vanilla: Any standard derivative contract containing usual terms and conditions.

Premium (or Option Premium): The price of an option.

Protective Put: A put option conbined with a long position in the underlying asset.

Put-Call Parity: Put-call parity is a financial relationship between the price of a put option and a call option on the same underlying instrument with identical strike price and expiry.

Put Option: An option which conveys the right to sell something is called a put. A put option gives the holder the right to sell an asset at a specified price on or before a certain date, i.e., over a given time period.

Put Spread: It is an option trading strategy. It is created by using put option.

R

Rho: It is an option greek. It is the rate of change of the price of an option derivative with the interest rate. In other words it is the sensitivity of the value of an option to small changes in interest rates.

Risk-free Rate (r): The rate of interest that is earned without assuming any kind of risks.

Risk-neutral Valuation: The valuation of any asset or derivative without the influence of any kind of risk.

Risk: The probability of negative result due to adverse or unfavourable market situation.

S

Settlement Price: A futures contract can be settled by physical delivery and payment of cash. It can also be settled by cash. Payment without physical delivery on any day before the delivery date.

Short Call: When a call option is written.

Short Put: When a put option is written.

Spread: The difference between the bid and ask prices of a security.

Stock Index: An Index which is determined by taking the prices of selected stocks which are capable of representing the whole market or a specified sector, or a segment of market. It helps in computing and monitoring the value of a portfolio of stocks.

Stop Limit Order: It is a combination of a stop order and a limit order. In a stop limit order, two prices are specified. The second part of the order specifies a limit price. It is used in similar way as a regular stock order but the exception of the transaction is restricted to the limit price or better.

Stop Order: A stop order is an order to buy or sell an existing futures position at the market but only after the specific stop price has been reached.

Straddle: It is an option trading strategy. In this strategy, the trader takes a long position in a call and a put with same strike price.

Strangle: It is an option trading strategy. In this case, the trader takes a long position in a call and a put with different strike prices.

Strap: It is an option trading strategy. In this strategy, the trader takes a long position in two call options and one put option with the same strike price.

Strike Price: It is the exercise price of an option. At this price, the asset will be purchased or sold if option is exercised.

Swap: A swap is an exchange of cash flows based on the terms and conditions as agreed upon by the contracting parties.

Swaption: A swaption is an option on swap. It gives the holder the right without any obligation to do so. Thus A swaption is an option granting its owner the right but not obligation to enter into an underlying swap.

Synthetic Option: A synthetic option is a synthetic position that is constructed without actually buying or selling the option. Synthetic long call, synthetic short call, synthetic long put and synthetic short put are four possible synthetic option positions.

Systematic Risk: It is the market risk or undiversifiable risk. The systematic risk is inherent to the entire market or entire market segment.

T

Theta: Theta is a measure of the rate of decline of option's time value resulting from the passage of time (time decay). It provides an estimate of the rupee amount that an option price will lose each day due to the passage of time and there is no move in either the stock price or volatility.

Time Decay: The ratio of the change in an option's price to the decrease in time to expiration. Since options are wasting assets their value decline over time. As an option approaches its expiry date without being in-the-money, its time value declines because the probability of that option being profitable (in-the-money) is reduced.

U

Underlying: A derivative is a financial instrument whose price is based (derived) from an economic variable (Asset). The underlying asset is the financial instrument (e.g., stock, commodity, stock index currency) on which a derivative's price is based.

Unsystematic Risk: Company or industry specific risk that is inherent in each investment. The amount of unsystematic risk can be reduced through appropriate diversification. It is also known as diversifiable risk or specific risk or residual risk.

V

Variation margin, also known as mark-to-market margin, is additional amount of cash that a trader requires to deposit in his futures trading account after his futures position has taken sufficient losses to bring it below the maintenance margin. Futures traders are typically required to provide variation margin through "Margin Calls".

Value of Risk (VaR): A technique used to estimate the probability of portfolio losses based on the statistical analysis of historical price trends and volatility.

Volatility Smile: The volatility smile is a long observed pattern in which at-the-money option tend to have lower implied volatilities than in-the-money or out-of-the-money options.

Vega: The sensitivity of a derivative product's value (option value) to changes in implied volatility, all other factors remaining as such.

W

Warrant: A warrant is a security that entitles the holder to buy the underlying stock of the issuing company at a fixed exercise price until the expiry date.

Writer: The seller of an option is known as writer.

Y

Yield: The term yield describes the amount in cash that returns to the owners of a security. It is the income return on investment.

Z

Zero Coupon Bond: Zero coupon bonds are bonds that do not pay interest during the life of the bonds. Instead, investors buy zero coupon bonds at a deep discount from buy their face value, which is the amount a bond will be worth when it matures or comes due. Thus, a debt security that doesn't pay interest (a coupon) but is traded at a deep discount, rendering profit at maturity when the bond is redeemed for its full face value.